REVELATION [EXPOUNDED]

or

Eternal Mysteries Simplified

●

This complete exposition of Revelation and the prophetical parts of Daniel is sane, scriptural, and free from sensational and foolish speculation concerning prophetical events. Literally thousands of questions of vital importance concerning near future and eternal events are fully answered with Scripture.

●

Over Six Thousand Scripture References Confirming
the Truths Expounded Herein

●

A Book for the Classroom and the Home

Written by
REV. FINIS JENNINGS DAKE
Dake Bible Sales, Inc. P. O. Box 1050   Lawrenceville, Georgia 30046

PREFACE

The original manuscript of *Revelation Expounded* was written in 1926 when the author was only twenty-four years of age. At that time and in the years that followed there was much foolish and sensational speculation among prophetical teachers. This book was written to counteract this sensationalism and to set forth the true teachings of the Bible concerning prophetical subjects.

Regardless of world changes, the rise and fall of many governments, and the coming and going of men hailed as the Antichrist, the essential truths presented in *Revelation Expounded* did not have to be altered for the later editions. This in itself verifies the fact that the book is safe, sane, and scriptural in its entire contents.

The author works on the chief fundamental principle of Bible interpretation—THAT OF TAKING THE BIBLE LITERALLY WHEREIN IT IS AT ALL POSSIBLE. When the language of a passage cannot possibly be literal, then it is clear from the passage itself, as well as from other Scriptures, that it is figurative. It must be remembered, however, that all figurative language conveys literal truth.

As a young man the author was taught many things that were contrary to the plain Scriptures themselves when taken literally. He had to make a decision either to believe that God was intelligent enough to express Himself in human language as men do, and that He did do so, or, that God gave His revelation in terms different from those used by men so as to deliberately confuse them regarding the true meaning of His revelation. This latter idea the author could not conceive of God, so he had to settle upon the fact that God meant what He said and said what He meant, and that the Bible is clear in itself when taken in the plain literal sense that the same language would be taken if found in another book.

The author also saw that he could not believe all Bible teachers on every point, for they differed so widely, so he decided to follow a new course of taking the Bible to be God's own Word and Revelation to men, not interpreting it but letting the Bible be its own interpreter. He found that when all passages on a subject were gathered together and harmonized that the Scripture was clear in itself without any further interpretation. Having decided on his course, he made a covenant with God that he would never teach anything that he could not give two or three plain Scriptures to prove.

In trying to find Scriptures to prove what he had been taught, many times he found just the opposite to be truth. To maintain any degree of honesty with God and His Word, he had to make a decision to teach what the Bible taught in preference to what men were teaching. He found that much of present-day prophetical teaching was unscriptural as we shall see in the exposition to follow.

The first edition of the book has had a wide circulation and many letters of commendation have been received from prominent ministers of many denominations who have hailed the book as "a scriptural exposition," "a Bible study book of real merit," "a book of more than usual interest . . . a wealth of material that is well classified," "an unusual book . . . brings out some very remarkable and helpful interpretations." Some have written, "It bears the marks of most diligent research and real scholarship," "backed by a profusion of Scripture texts," "the best book ever published on prophecy," etc. One review reads, "If one should read it with the idea that his preconceived theories are not to be overturned it would make very uncomfortable reading, for he says many things, and proves them by a startling array of proof. The book gives evidence of an amazing amount of highly intelligent work done."

This second edition of *Revelation Expounded* is sent out with a prayer that it will be a blessing to all who desire to know the truth of events that are to happen from 1948 into eternity.

The author claims no special revelation concerning the many new truths that he has discovered in over 75,000 hours of diligent study of the whole Word of God—truths that any common reader can see for himself are written in plain English in his own Bible. To enable the reader to see for himself what the Bible says, over six thousand references are given—at least two or three to prove each point. Let the Scriptures themselves be the final word of authority on any question. If the reader has intelligence enough to understand what is written, he has intelligence enough to believe what is written and that is all that is necessary.

—*Finis Jennings Dake.*

Table of Contents

sealed. The great tribulation saints—who they are and when they are saved and martyred.

will do. How long he will continue. The mark of the beast—why it cannot be given today and why it is not 666.

Egypt, Assyria, Babylon, Medo-Persia, Greece, Rome, and Revised Rome made up of the ten kingdoms inside the old Roman Empire in the latter days.

the natural subjects of the kingdom and ruled by outward laws. Universal peace and prosperity and a universal religion with salvation offered to all as now.
Changes in the animal kingdom, the planets, and general living conditions. Millennium to end with the last
rebellion of Satan and man on earth.

100 PER CENT CORRECT PREDICTIONS OF THINGS TO COME

Over One Hundred Great Future Prophetic Wonders from 1948 into Eternity

This book answers hundreds of questions on prophecy and brings out scores of new truths never before taught in the prophetical world—truths that we predict will completely revolutionize modern prophetical teaching. This book guarantees to prove from plain English Scriptures the following truths:

That there will be at least three more European wars before the second coming of Christ and the Battle of Armageddon.

That the automobile, airplane, atom bomb, or no single modern invention is once mentioned in Scripture.

That the Roman Empire will never be revived.

That a revival of kings as rulers of the old Roman Empire territory will take the place of the present forms of governments therein.

That the Antichrist cannot be any man now prominent in world affairs.

That he cannot come from the Vatican, Italy, Germany, Russia, or any place in Europe, Africa, the Americas, Australia, the Islands of the Seas, or from heaven or hell.

That he cannot come until AFTER the formation of ten kingdoms inside the old Roman Empire and the rapture of the Church.

That he will never bring universal peace and prosperity.

That he will not rule over America or be a world-wide dictator.

That Russia will not fulfill prophecies that students say she will.

That Russia will be conquered by the Antichrist.

That the mark of the beast will never be in America and it is not 666.

That the tribulation is not to be world-wide.

That the Church is never called the bride of Christ, nor is it spoken of as a woman, a lady, a virgin, or referred to by feminine pronouns.

That the Holy Spirit will never be taken from the world.

That the fig tree of Matt. 24 does not represent the Jews.

That "two in the field, one taken and another left" does not refer to the rapture.

That the ten virgins do not represent any class of Christians today.

That the sun-clothed woman and the manchild do not represent Christians today.

That Antichrist has never lived on the earth before.

That the beast of the abyss is not the human Antichrist.

That the world will never come to an end.

That there will be eternal generations of natural people on earth.

That God changes His headquarters from heaven to earth.

That man will have his original dominion restored to him as before the fall, and both natural and resurrected man will rule the sun, moon, stars, and all planets in infinite space in all eternity.

That the earth will be made perfect the third and last time and righteousness will prevail eternally on the eternal earth.

Don't miss reading these and scores of other truths! Your Bible will be a new book to you!

Chapter One

ESSENTIAL FACTS ON INTERPRETATION

There are certain facts and principles of interpretation that must be clearly apprehended before an individual can arrive at a complete and correct understanding of the Revelation, so marvelous and replete with meaning to one who is spiritually minded, 1 Cor. 2:14; 2 Tim. 3:16, 17.

I. Pertinent Questions and Importance of the Book.

Without the book of Revelation the canon of Scripture would be incomplete. Will sin continue? Will sorrow, pain, and death go on? Where are we in God's plan? Will the Holy Spirit be taken out of the world at the rapture? When will the church be raptured in connection with the tribulation? What are the qualifications for the rapture? Is Christ coming to the earth? What are we to expect on earth before His coming? In what order are the events of the last days to come? Where is Christ to reign during the Millennium? Is He to reign after that? Who are to reign with Him? What of Daniel's Seventieth Week and the tribulation? Who is Antichrist? Where does he come from? When is he revealed? Will he reign over America? What about church unions? Are Rome and Greece to be revived? When will Armageddon be fought and by whom? Will natural life on the earth be perpetual? Will the world come to an end? Are saints to spend eternity in heaven? Will the present earth and heaven cease to exist? Is the heavenly Jerusalem literal? Are all the saved to be glorified? What will be the conditions of the New Heaven and New Earth? These and other indispensable questions are nowhere fully answered apart from the Revelation which we will consider in this exposition.

II. Schools of Interpreters.

1. **The Preterist School** claims that the Revelation was fulfilled in the struggles of the Jews and early Christians and in the conquests of Greece and Rome.

2. **The Historical School** insists that the prophecies herein are being progressively fulfilled and that the greater part has been fulfilled since Christ.

3. **The Spiritual School** believes that the Revelation depicts the spiritual conflict between Christ and Satan, between good and evil.

4. **The Futurist School** believes that the Revelation is yet future; that is, that the first three chapters describe the present Church Age and that the remainder of the prophecy will be fulfilled after the rapture of the Church. This is the most logical and Scriptural method of interpretation of the book as it holds to the literal meaning of the language of Scripture with due consideration to grammatical construction.

III. Literalness of the Book.

11

The book is admittedly both literal and symbolic. It is to be taken as literal whenever possible. In other words, when a statement is made it should be taken to mean just what is written unless such interpretation should be highly improbable and against all the dictates of rhetoric and spiritually enlightened reason, or against Scriptures elsewhere on the same subject. If the passage does not admit a literal interpretation, then, of course, we must look elsewhere for an explanation. This method of interpretation is the only safe one as is clear from the fact that the book is a "Revelation" in itself. To treat it as a mystery or to spiritualize it is to deny what it professes to be. Every scene and every truth in the book is clearly understood in the book itself. The reader must first find out what the book itself says concerning its own truths and revelations before going to other parts of the Bible for additional light upon the subject in question. Pre-Revelation prophecy will throw much light upon these simple revelations and help in a more detailed study of almost every truth in the book. This Revelation is in perfect harmony with all preceding prophecies and is the logical and harmonious completion of them. Correct translation will also throw much light upon certain parts of the Revelation and help in arriving at the exact meaning of the words and phrases used in the book.

IV. Symbols of Revelation and Their Interpretation.

1. **Definition.** A symbol (from the Greek words **sun** meaning "together" and **ballo** meaning "to throw") is an object, animate or inanimate, standing for or representing something moral, intellectual, or real, as the wolf to symbolize selfish greed; lamb, meekness; dove, peace; sceptre, power; etc.

2. **The Interpretation of Symbols.** In the treatment of symbols, as in parables, types, and other forms of Scripture teaching, the method of procedure should be to collate a sufficient number and variety of examples and then mark carefully the principles set forth in the exposition of those which are explained. A study of the symbols that have been explained reveals the following:

(1) **The names of symbols are to be understood literally.**

(2) **Symbols always denote something essentially different from themselves.**

(3) **The resemblance, more or less minute, is traceable between the symbol and the thing symbolized;** e.g., the wine and bread in the Lord's Supper are symbols of the body and blood of Christ. Symbols are not the exact representation of that which they are intended to represent. Rather, they are suggestive signs; e. g., the seven candlesticks are symbols of the seven churches of Asia (1:20). Symbols are timeless and may represent something past, present, or future. They are never used

for the purpose of abolishing the thing symbolized, or to make the truth conveyed less real than if expressed in literal language. They merely give variety of expression and beauty to the thing expressed; e.g., the word "dove" is used as a symbol of peace. Shall we say there is no peace just because of such symbolism, or shall we make the bill, feet, wings, etc., of the dove symbolize different aspects of peace? So with the symbols of Revelation, the symbol and the thing symbolized must be clearly distinguished, and each dealt with separately, and only the part of the symbol conveying the truth be emphasized. Symbols are always clear in Scripture as well as the thing symbolized. The very language and statements of the subject make the basis of distinguishing the symbol and the thing symbolized and convey the intended truth, which is always clear in the passage itself or in parallel passages on the same subject. Therefore, no confusion need arise.

3. **The Symbols of Revelation.** These are composed of numbers, colors, animate and inanimate forms, as follows:

(1) **Numbers of Revelation used with symbols.**

A. "Four winds" (7:1-3). Other numbers of "four" are not symbolical (4:6-8; 7:1; 9:13-15; 20:8).

B. "Seven golden candlesticks" (1:12, 13, 20); "seven stars" (1:16, 20); "seven lamps of fire," "seven horns," "seven eyes" (1:4; 4:5; 5:6); "seven heads" (12:3; 13:1; 17:8-11); "seven crowns" (12:3); "seven mountains" (17:8-11). Other numbers of "seven" are not symbolical (1:4; 5:1; 8:2; 10:3; 11:13; 15:1-8; 16:1; 17:1, 10; 21:9).

C. "Ten horns" (12:3; 13:1; 17:12-17); "ten crowns" (13:1; 17:12). Other numbers of "ten" are not symbolical (2:10; 5:11; 17:12).

D. "Twelve stars" (12:1). Other numbers of "twelve" are not symbolical (7:5-8; 21:12, 14, 16, 21; 22:2).

(2) **Colors of Revelation used in symbols.**

A. White (3:18; 19:8).

B. Red (6:4; 12:3).

C. Purple (17:4; 18:12, 16).

D. Black (6:5).

E. Pale green (6:8).

These colors in all other passages are literal, not symbolical, because they are used in literal language.

(3) **Animate forms in Revelation as symbols.**

A. The Lamb (See point 6, (2), chapter seven).

B. The beast of chapters 11, 13, 14, 16, 17, 19 and 20.

C. A married woman (12:1-17).

D. The dragon (12:2-12; 13:2; 16:13; 20:1-10).

E. The lamb-like beast (13:11-18; 16:13; 19:20).

F. The great whore (17:1-18).

G. The white horse rider (6:1, 2).

H. The red horse rider (6:3, 4).

   I.   The black horse rider (6:5, 6).

   J.   The pale and red horse riders (6:7, 8).

   K.   The manchild (12:5).

   (4) Inanimate things in Revelation as symbols besides those in point (1) above.

   A.   Odors (5:8; 8:2-5).

   B.   The two olive trees and candlesticks (11:3-13).

   C.   The rod of iron (2:26; 12:5; 19:15).

   D.   The harvest and vintage (14:14-20; 19:11-21).

   E.   Many waters (12:15; 17:1, 15).

   F.   Fine linen (19:8).

   G.   The sword (2:12, 16; 19:15, 21).

Apart from these thirty-five symbols, the whole of the book is literal, so understand everything in the plain literal sense as we do other books. Even the symbols convey literal truths and it is these truths we must get and not stumble over the symbols that convey the truths.

V. The Key to the Interpretation.

"Write the things which thou hast seen, and the things which are, and the things which shall be hereafter" (1:19).

   1.   **Part I.** "**The things which thou hast seen**"; i.e., Christ in the midst of the seven candlesticks (1:12-18, 20), as seen by John before he began to write.

   2.   **Part II.** "**The things which are**"; i.e., the things concerning the churches then existent and those which should exist throughout the Church Age to the rapture. This division takes in only Rev. 2-3.

   3.   **Part III.** "**The things which shall be hereafter**"; i.e., the things which shall come to pass after the rapture of the Church. This division includes all of Rev. 4-22. One has only to believe this threefold natural division as given by Christ to understand the book fully, especially as to the time of the fulfillment of the things of each division. The moment these divisions are forgotten and the reader begins to derange them and insert certain things into the one or the other that are not a part of the division, he will become confused as to the divine order of these "things" which are so clearly given in consecutive order, and will miss the true intent of the "things" written herein. That we refrain from confusing these "things" is absolutely imperative if a true understanding of them is to be gained.

VI. The Division of the Book by Classes, 1 Cor. 10:32.

   1.   Rev. 1-3 deals primarily with the Church on earth.

   2.   Rev. 4-5 pictures the Church and the Old Testament saints with God in heaven after the rapture, represented by the twenty-four elders.

   3.   Rev. 6-19 deals primarily with Israel under the last oppression by the Gentiles in fulfillment to the prophecy of Daniel's Seventieth Week after the rapture of the Church.

   4.   Rev. 20-22 relates to all three classes, the Church, the Jews,

and the Gentiles. The earthly Jews will be the head of all earthly Gentiles and the Church with Christ will reign over both forever and ever.

VII. The Consecutive Order of Revelation.

The book is a succession of consecutive events from the beginning to the end and not an unsystematic and confused book. The events are to be taken in the order as God gave them and not according to our own finite ideas as to their occurrence. It is almost universally recognized that Rev. 1-5 and Rev. 19-22 form a consecutive story. Therefore, we may logically conclude in view of this fact, and since the book begins with things in John's day and ends with things in the New Earth, that the events intervening between the beginning and the end are also consecutive events. If the events of Revelation are not to be taken consecutively, upon what grounds do we attempt to fix another standard of arrangement, and where can we obtain any other authorized and authentic standard than that which is so plainly evident in the book itself? Why hopelessly confuse a plain prophecy given by the Lord concerning "things which must shortly come to pass" and change the order of events from that given by the Lord? Certainly He must have given events in their proper order so as not to confuse those to whom He was imparting the Revelation.

When we speak of consecutive order we necessarily omit the parenthetical passages, which occur as explanatory statements of things that transpire with the main order of events, and which are inserted in that capacity between the consecutive events. These are separate from the principal thought both as to reception and fulfillment, but are necessary to understand fully the principal thought.

These passages are clear in themselves as to the time of their fulfillment as we shall see in the exposition. They are inserted between Rev. 6-19, because these chapters are fulfilled in Daniel's Seventieth Week, as we shall later note. In Rev. 6-19 the principal order of events is the seven seals, seven trumpets, and seven vials, the contents of which occur in succession from the beginning to the end of the week. The consecutive order and the parenthetical passages can be distinguished in the outline of Revelation in point IX below. The parenthetical passages are placed in parentheses and are not necessarily in consecutive order. Some are and some are not.

VIII. How to Interpret Prophecy.

Thousands of preachers and teachers of the Bible constantly make the statement that prophecy is hard to understand. A colored preacher in Atlanta was recently asked if he ever preached on Revelation. He answered, "No, suh, I dodges that. I once preached on it but I didn't know what I was talking about." How true this is of many. It is true that it is hard to understand if one has to harmonize all the many foolish speculations and interpretations of men on the subject. But thank God it is not hard to understand if one will follow the few common-sense rules below:

1. **Give the same meaning to the words of prophecy that are given to words of history;** that is, give the same meaning to the words of the entire Bible that are given to the same words outside the Bible. The common theory that just because a word is found in prophecy, or because it is in the Bible, it automatically has a mystical meaning and cannot be understood in the literal sense is entirely wrong. For example, the word "year" is generally taken to mean a "day" and a "day" to mean a "year." On this basis the 2,300 days of Dan. 8:14 are taken to be 2,300 years; the 1,260 days of Rev. 11:3; 12:6 are taken to be 1,260 years; etc. Why would an intelligent God say "years" when He really meant "days" and say "days" when He really meant "years"? There is no sense to this play on human words. This is not what He meant. He knows what "days" and "years" mean as well as do men, but men, in order to prove prophetical and foolish date-setting of certain events, change days to years as they please.

On the same basis "the times of the Gentiles" are taken to be 2,520 years long by interpreting the "seven times" of Lev. 26:18 thus: a "time" means a year of 360 days and 360 days means 360 years and seven times 360 years is 2,520 years. The peculiar thing with this interpretation is that the phrase "seven times" is used four times in Lev. 26:18, 21, 24, 28 and each so-called 2,520 years were to be additional to the preceding one and all four periods were to be before God would scatter the Jews among the nations. This would make 10,080 years from Israel's breaking the law in the time of Moses to 70 A.D. when they were scattered among the nations, but it was not fulfilled that way. "The times of the Gentiles" did not begin with Babylon about 606 B.C. but they began with the Egyptian bondage over 1,000 years before Nebuchadnezzar's time, as we shall see in chapter thirty-six. So all the prophetical date-setting based upon this false theory is unscriptural.

Just because God told Israel to wander in the wilderness forty years according to the number of days they sent spies into Canaan is no ground for making "days" to be "years" and "years" to be "days." In that case days were literal days and years were literal years, and so it will always be among men. If we are to understand the phrase "seven times" in the Bible to be 2,520 years then let us believe that Jacob bowed down before Esau 2,520 years (Gen. 33:3); that Israel sprinkled blood every atonement day for 2,520 years (Lev. 4:6, 17; 8:11); that every time a leper was cleansed it took 2,520 years for the process (Lev. 14:7, 16, 27, 51); that Israel marched around Jericho 2,520 years (Josh. 6:4, 15); that Elijah's servant looked for rain 2,520 years (1 Kings

18:43); and that the resurrected boy sneezed 2,520 years (2 Kings 4:35).

The prophetical sensationalist may object to this reasoning because these "seven times" in these verses are found in history and not in prophecy as in Lev. 26, but let us use the same reasoning in prophecy. We would have to believe that Naaman was to dip himself in Jordan 2,520 years, for the prophecy was that if he would do this he would be made clean (it may be that anyone would be clean if he dipped that long in a river, 2 Kings 5:10, 14); that Nebuchadnezzar ate grass with the beasts of the field for 2,520 years (Dan. 4:16, 23, 25, 32); that the seven years covenant between Antichrist and Israel will be for 2,520 years (Dan. 9:27), and that the two witnesses are to prophesy, Jerusalem is to be given back to the Gentiles, the woman flees into the wilderness, the manchild is caught up and is in heaven, the Devil is cast out of heaven to be on earth, and the beast is to reign over the ten kingdoms of Revised Rome and give men a mark or kill them for 1,260 years ending with the second coming of Christ (Rev. 11:1-3; 12:5, 6, 14; 13:5, 16-18).

2. Do not change the literal to a spiritual or symbolic meaning.

One modern writer in his book of lectures on Revelation is a fair example of the modern trend of changing words and statements from the literal meaning to any meaning that suits one's fancy. He interprets the word "earthquake" of **the sixth seal** (Rev. 6:12-17) to be the breaking up of society instead of a literal earthquake; the sun darkened to be a type of Christ rejected and God dethroned; the moon turned to blood to be the destruction of derived authority; the stars falling to be the downfall and apostasy of religious leaders in the ecclesiastical heavens (whatever they are); and the heavens departing as a scroll to be that all organized Christianity will be destroyed.

He says concerning the trumpet judgments, that they are not literal. The grass of **the first trumpet** (Rev. 8:7) means the common people and the trees mean the dignity of man, so instead of the grass and one third of the trees being literally burned, as is plainly stated, all common men and only one third of the dignity of man will be burned.

Instead of a third of the sea being turned to blood, one third of the creatures dying, and one third of the ships being destroyed in **the second trumpet** (Rev. 8:8, 9), the burning mountain causing this, he says, it means spiritual Babylon cast into the sea of nations and destroyed by the people.

Instead of the drinking waters being made bitter by a star falling from heaven causing the death of many men as in **the third trumpet** (Rev. 8:10, 11), he says, the star falling from heaven means the pope of Rome or some religious dignitary. But how could the pope fall from heaven into the waters and poison them? How will he ever get to heaven to fall from heaven in the tribulation? How could he poison the drinking waters if he did fall in them? He surely must not be that poisonous.

The third of the sun, moon, and stars being made dark as in **the fourth trumpet** (Rev. 8:12), he says, means spiritual darkness instead of the literal darkening of part of the earth.

This writer explains **the fifth trumpet** (Rev. 9:1-12) thus: **The star that falls from heaven** with the key to the abyss is the pope or the apostate religious leader of the third trumpet. (This would make the pope fall from heaven two times, once under the third trumpet and once again under the fifth trumpet.) **The key** is the system that opens the abyss. **The smoke of the pit** is the blotting out of the true light in man's spiritual sky by demon powers when false religions are dominant after the Holy Spirit is taken out of the world. **The locusts** are not literal but they symbolize these false religions spreading like locusts. **The torment** of the stings of these creatures is the torment that these religions will bring. **The faces of men** that these creatures have means intelligence and reason (but since they are not real creatures how are they to exercise these faculties?). **Their hair like women** means an unholy life and **the iron breastplates** mean that the conscience is destroyed. **The grass and the trees** are not symbolical as they are in the first trumpet. **The five months** these creatures torment men are not literal and it is not known what they mean, thus nothing is literal if we believe this method of interpretation.

The sixth trumpet (Rev. 9:13-21), he says, is not literal, but the 200,000,000 creatures refer to Asiatic hordes that overran Europe and Palestine through many centuries.

He says **the two witnesses** are not two men, but are symbolical of the witnessing Jewish remnant. **The manchild** is Christ; **the woman** is Israel; **the sun** the glory of the New Testament; **the moon** the glory of the Old Testament; **the twelve stars** the twelve tribes; **the 1,260 days** of Rev. 12:6 mean the first part of Daniel's Seventieth Week when the woman flees, or Israel is scattered among the nations; the "times" of Rev. 12:14 refer to the last half of the Week; and **the water** the dragon casts out of his mouth is evil teaching but Israel will escape these teachings and be the only testimony for God.

He says the beast of Rev. 13 is the Revived Roman Empire; the seven heads are seven hills on which the city of Rome is built; and the head wounded to death is imperial Rome Revived, but how could one of these literal hills be imperial Rome to be revived if it is part of the ground on which Rome is built? (See chapters twenty and thirty-six for proof that this is all wrong.)

He says **the seven vials** (Rev. 16:2-21) are not literal except the fourth and fifth ones, but who is he to decide for us that these are the only judgments of the seals, trumpets, and vials that are literal? He explains the sores of **the first vial** as a spiritual plague; **the second and third vials** are the drying up of the source of life (whatever that means) and not the sea and rivers literally turned to blood as it reads. **The sixth vial** is the destruction of the Turkish Empire instead of the literal drying up of the river Euphrates, but why not give this river the same meaning elsewhere in Scripture and see how ridiculous it would be, as in Gen. 2:14; 15:18; Jer. 13:4-7; 46:2-10; 51:63; Rev. 9:14? He says that **the "earthquake" of the seventh vial** that destroys the city Babylon and many cities of the nations is not literal. It means the destruction of every religious institution and civilization as we now know it today.

This method of interpretation of Revelation really should be called "How Not to Interpret Prophecy" for it does away with the literal meaning of God's own revelation and substitutes man's theories instead. If these ideas are really what God wanted revealed as going to happen, could not God have made this clear when He gave the Revelation instead of giving us what He did reveal? Would He have to wait until now to finally get to us what He was really intending to convey?

3. Do not seek to find hidden meanings to the words of Scripture, or add to Scripture. Be satisfied with what God has seen fit to reveal and never read between the lines or add to Scripture in order to understand it. For example, men of recent years have chosen about thirty-five men in past history and some that are still alive and have transliterated their names into Greek to see if their names equal "666" and to see if they could possibly be the Antichrist. Every name that equals this number men conclude that that man must be the Antichrist referred to in Rev. 13:18. Forget it! This is all foolish speculation and proves nothing concerning the mark or the name of the Antichrist, as we shall see.

Others find the United States in prophecy by taking the letters U.S.A. out of the name Jer-USA-lem. If this is the only way we can find the United States in prophecy, it would be best to leave her out. The fact is that the United States is not once mentioned in prophecy anywhere. Isa. 18 refers to the inhabitants of the Sudan "which is beyond the rivers of Ethiopia" and not to the United States. The white horse rider of Rev. 6, or the false prophet of Rev. 13:11-18; 19:20; 20:10, does not refer to the United States, as we shall see in chapters ten and twenty-two.

Still others find the mark of the beast in the fasces on the American dime, in keeping Sunday as the sabbath, in union cards, in social security numbers, in rationing, and many other things that are ridiculous. These and many other senseless theories are constantly preached to the ignorant masses who take them up and scatter such ideas world-wide while truth is getting on its boots. The more foolish and sensational a man is and the more he finds so-called hidden meanings to Scriptures the more intelligent he is heralded by men that should know better. And the Devil stands back and laughs at such foolish speculation and changing of God's Word, for he knows such silly interpretations disgust intelligent men and cause many to discard prophecy and be skeptical about any real truth when they do hear it.

4. Believe that prophecy can be understood just as it is without any changes or additions and that it is simply a record of things yet to happen sometime after its utterance. Prophecy should be understood as literally as history. After all, history is simply a record of what has happened and prophecy is a record of what is going to happen. Both kinds of records are in the same everyday human language and both are to be understood on the same basis. God expects us to understand both as they are written and He will judge us for not using our common intelligence to understand both as they are plainly written.

5. Forget the idea that prophecy must be fulfilled before it can be understood. If prophecy must be fulfilled before it can be understood, then it has failed in its purpose of revealing to man beforehand what is to happen. Many authors apologize for their uncertainty concerning the things they write about and declare we cannot hope to fully understand prophecies until their final fulfillment. Such men had better not write at all than to be uncertain about what they are writing. If one has a definite "thus saith the Lord" for what he says he does not need to apologize.

What we mean to emphasize by this point is that all true prophecy is clear in itself as to what is to happen and it is as clear before it happens as it is after it is fulfilled. Take the subject of modern inventions as being a fulfillment of prophecy. Men never dreamed of an automobile and never interpreted Nahum 2:3, 4 in connection with one until they were invented. Men never dreamed of airplanes, radios, locomotives, or any single invention and never interpreted any Scripture as definitely predicting them until after they were invented. After we got them, prophetical students soon found them in prophecy. A little over three years ago Bible students never dreamed of atom bombs but immediately after they were dropped not only did Japan wake up but prophetical sensationalists arose from their long slumber and ignorance and found it in prophecy. In such a short time nearly everyone in Christendom (if sensationalists are believed) knows that it is a fulfillment of several prophecies and they also know now just how several others are going to be fulfilled. The world is coming to an end and many other things are now going to happen by the atom bomb, so these men say.

The sooner we all have our speculative, prophetical, sensational appendix removed the better off all of us will be and the sooner the good name of prophecy will be restored, and men will again respect true prophecy as stated by God. The fact is that no single invention is mentioned in particular in the Bible. The so-called automobile in Nahum 2:3, 4 refers to horse-drawn chariots of the king of Nineveh and those of Nebuchadnezzar in

actual combat in the streets of Nineveh over the possession of
the Assyrian Empire, as is clear in Nahum 2:1-4, 13; 3:1-3, where
we have mention of "the whip . . . rattling of the wheels, and of
the prancing horses" and "the horsemen." The so-called loco-
motive of Job 41 is "king over all the children of pride," according
to the last verse. The phrase "as birds flying" in Isa. 31:5
does not refer to the airplane but to the second coming of Christ
as proved in the passage itself. It states that "as birds flying"
God will come down to fight for Israel and in that time every
man shall cast away his idols forever, and we all know that
this did not happen in 1917 when General Allenby took Jerusalem
from the Turks. It will be fulfilled when the armies of heaven
come with Jesus "as birds flying" as in Zech. 14:1-5; 2 Thess.
1:7-10; Jude 14; Rev. 19:11-21; etc. And so it goes with any
single invention that men have found in prophecy. The context
proves that the subject of the passage is not some modern invention. Dan. 12:4 is the only verse in all the Bible that covers
inventions of today. One can use this verse and preach on
these things and not be so sensational and foolish in using
passages that do not refer to inventions.

6. **Do not interpret God's own interpretation of any symbol
or prophecy or change God's meaning from that which is plainly
and obviously clear.** God always interprets His own symbols as
plainly seen in Dan. 2:38-44; 7:17, 23-26; 8:20-23; 9:20-27;
11:2-45; 12:1-13; Rev. 1:20; 12:9; 13:18; 17:8-18; etc. Plain literal
prophecy needs no interpretation as it is simply history written
beforehand. If God uses a word or a figure of speech or any
other form of human expression in a different way than that
which is commonly understood, we have a right to expect Him
to make due explanation. Otherwise take it as it is commonly
used and understood. When there is no explanation of a symbol
or a figure of speech, etc., it is to be taken for granted that it is
clear in itself, as well as it is clear from its usage elsewhere
in Scripture, especially when it is harmonized with all other
Scriptures on the same subject.

7. **Give only one meaning to a passage and that the plain
literal meaning unless it is made clear that a double meaning
should be understood.** There are two laws in prophecy that
should be understood in order to understand certain prophecies.

(1) **The law of double reference.** In some passages two distinct persons are referred to, the visible person addressed and
the invisible person who is using the visible one as a tool. In
Gen. 3:14, 15 the serpent (the tool of the invisible Satan) is
addressed, but it also refers to Satan who was to meet defeat
by the seed of the woman. In Isa. 14:4-27 and Ezek. 28:11-19
the kings of Babylon and Tyre are the ones addressed, but in
these passages Satan is also referred to as falling "from heaven,"
of invading heaven to be like the most High (Isa. 14:12-14),
and of being perfect in beauty and perfect in his ways from

his creation until he sinned (Ezek. 28:12-17). In Matt. 16:23 Peter is addressed but also Satan is referred to as using Peter as a tool to keep Christ from going to the cross.

The way to distinguish between the visible and invisible persons in such passages is to take those statements that could not refer to a visible person as referring to the invisible person. No king of Babylon or Tyre could ever have the statements of Isa. 14:12-14 and Ezek. 28:12-17 refer to him, for no one of them was ever cast out of heaven, was created, was an angel or cherub, etc. Peter could not be Satan so when Jesus said "Get thee behind me, Satan," He could only refer to Satan, but the remainder of the verse could apply to Peter as well as to Satan.

(2) **The law of prophetic perspective.** This law is the describing of future events as if they were continuous and successive events, but the fact is that there may be thousands of years between the events. For example, in Isa. 61:1-3, as recorded in Luke 4:17-20, Christ stopped in the prophecy at the words "the acceptable year of the Lord." He closed the book and said, "This day is this Scripture fulfilled in your ears." Had He continued to read the prophecy, "and the day of vengeance of our God," and would have said this was fulfilled that day His statement would have been untrue, for "the day of vengeance" has not yet come. There has been already about two thousand years since "the acceptable year of the Lord." The day of vengeance has not yet come, and will not come until the tribulation of the future. Both events are in one verse in the prophecy and have only a comma between them, which would indicate that both events being given together would follow each other in succession, but they did not.

In other words, the prophets see things in the same vision as one would look at a distant range of mountain peaks where the valleys between them are not seen. One must learn to take each separate event in prophecy and collect together all that is said about it in all the Bible and see when it will be fulfilled in connection with the other events. This is rightly dividing the word of truth, 2 Tim. 2:15.

8. The key to the interpretation of many prophecies is to regard the prophet primarily as a preacher of righteousness. A prophet was not only a **foreteller** but a **forthteller.** He was a speaker for God to rebuke, to instruct, and to correct people in his day, as well as to foretell future events. He had powers of **insight** and **foresight** and he was more than a foreteller of future events. He was caused to see conditions about him and the purposes of God in these things. The present was only a moment in the divine plan which was working toward the end of establishing the kingdom of God again on earth and ridding the earth of all rebellion. Hence, the prophet was a teacher, a social reformer, and a statesman, as well as a herald of the future kingdom. Many of his utterances were really sermons preached as the occasion demanded. This is especially true of

Isaiah, Jeremiah, Ezekiel, and the Minor Prophets, although in their books are many prophecies of the future. Daniel and John were mainly prophets of **foretelling** future events, although in their books there is the element of **forthtelling** as seen in Dan. 2, 4, 5, 6; etc., and Rev. 2, 3.

9. One main thing to keep in mind in all prophecy is the history of the writer and his times and the circumstances under which he wrote. One must understand the exact position of the writer as to the age in which he lived and the purpose of his predictions and the people to whom he wrote and the subject of his message. With a knowledge of the historical background, the manners and customs of the age and of people to whom he wrote, the peculiar idioms and human expressions of his times, and the purpose he had in view, there cannot possibly be any misunderstanding of one thing about which any one of them writes.

IX. Outline of the Book of Revelation.

Introductory Remarks (1:1-11, 19).
   1. The Introduction (1:1-3).
   2. The Salutation (1:4, 5a).
   3. The Exaltation (1:5b, 6).
   4. The Chief Theme (1:7).
   5. The Eternity of the Son of God (1:8).
   6. The Prophet—John (1:9-11).
   7. The Key to the Interpretation (1:19).

I. **"The things which thou hast seen"** (1:12-18, 20).
   1. The Vision of Christ (1:12-18).
   2. The Symbols of the Vision Interpreted (1:20).

II. **"The things which are"** (2:1-3:22).
   1. Ephesus (2:1-7).
   2. Smyrna (2:8-11).
   3. Pergamos (2:12-17).
   4. Thyatira (2:18-29).
   5. Sardis (3:1-6).
   6. Philadelphia (3:7-13).
   7. Laodicea (3:14-22).

III. **"The things which shall be hereafter"** (4:1-22:5).
   1. **The Heavenly Tabernacle:** the raptured saints with God (4:1-5:14).
      (1) The Heavenly Door (4:1).
      (2) The Heavenly Throne (4:2, 3, 5).
      (3) The Heavenly Elders (4:4).
      (4) The Heavenly Sea of Glass (4:6a).
      (5) The Heavenly Living Creatures (4:6b-8).
      (6) The Heavenly Worship because of Creation (4:9-11).
      (7) The Heavenly Book (5:1-4).
      (8) The Heavenly Lamb (5:5-7).
      (9) The Heavenly Worship because of Worthiness to the Lamb (5:8-14).

2. **Daniel's Seventieth Week** (6:1-19:21).
 (1) The First Six Seals (6:1-17).
  (Parenthetical, 7:1-17).
 (2) The Seventh Seal and Six Trumpets (8:1-9:21).
  (Parenthetical, 8:2-6, 13; 10:1-11:13).
 (3) The Seventh Trumpet (11:14-13:18).
  (Parenthetical, 14:1-20).
 (4) The First Six Vials (15:1-16:12).
  (Parenthetical, 15:2-4; 16:13-16).
 (5) The Seventh Vial (16:17-18:24).
  (Parenthetical, 17:1-18).
 (6) The Marriage of the Lamb, the Second Advent and Armageddon (19:1-21).
  (Parenthetical, 19:1-10).

3. **The Thousand Years and After** (20:1-15).
 (1) The Expulsion of Satan from the Earth (20:1-3).
 (2) The Millennial Reign of Christ and His Saints (20:4-6).
 (3) Satan's Post-Millennial Career and Doom (20:7-10).
 (4) The Final Judgment (20:11-15).

4. **The Eternal Perfect State—the Ages of the Ages (21:1-22:5).**
 (1) The New Heaven (21:1).
 (2) The New Earth (21:1).
 (3) The New Jerusalem (21:2, 9-21).
 (4) The New Peoples (21:3).
 (5) The New Conditions (21:4-8).
 (6) The New Temple (21:22).
 (7) The New Light (21:23-27).
 (8) The New Paradise (22:1-5).

The Conclusion (22:6-21).
 1. The Confirmation of Revelation (22:6, 7).
 2. The Mistake in the Object of Worship (22:8, 9).
 3. The Last Instructions (22:10-19).
 4. The Last Promise and Last Prayer (22:20, 21).

Chapter Two

INTRODUCTORY REMARKS, Rev. 1:1-11

In these remarks we will consider the Introduction, the Salutation, the Exaltation, the Chief Theme, the Eternity of the Son of God, and the Prophet—John.

I. The Introduction, Rev. 1:1-3.

"The Revelation of Jesus Christ, which God gave unto him, to shew unto his servants things which must shortly come to pass: and he sent and signified it by his angel unto his servant John: Who bare record of the word of God, and of the testimony of Jesus Christ, and of all things that he saw. Blessed is he that readeth and they that hear the words of this prophecy, and keep those things which are written therein; for the time is at hand," Rev. 1:1-3.

1. The Title of Revelation.

Men call the book "The Revelation of St. John the Divine"; God entitles it, "The Revelation of Jesus Christ." The significance of the word "Revelation" must be understood. The words "Revelation" and "Apocalypse" are synonymous and are derived from the Greek word **apokalupsis,** meaning "to unveil, reveal, or uncover." It is used in Luke 2:32; Rom. 2:5; 8:19; 16:25; 1 Cor. 1:7; 14:6, 26; 2 Cor. 12:1, 7; Gal. 1:12; 2:2; Eph. 1:17; 3:3; 2 Thess. 1:7; 1 Pet. 1:7, 13. It means "to lift up a curtain" so as to clearly show what had been covered. There is no more excuse for different interpretations of this book than there is for interpretations of the unveiling of other things.

2. The Origin of Revelation.

The Revelation had its origin in the mind of God. The things contained therein were in His mind from eternity, but were not given to Christ until after He was exalted as the head of the Church. "God gave unto him" this Revelation. This statement expresses the often reiterated doctrine that Christ laid aside all His divine powers and attributes in taking the form of man and was not omniscient in "the days of his flesh," but grew in wisdom and understanding and in favor with God and man, Luke 2:40, 52. Both prophets and apostles taught that Christ was limited as man and could not do one single miracle without the anointing of the Holy Spirit, Isa. 11:1-7; 42:1-7; 50:4-7; 61:1, 2; Acts 10:38; Phil. 2:5-8; Heb. 2:5-18; 4:14-16; 5:7-9.

Jesus, Himself taught that it was only through the Father and the indwelling Spirit that He did all of His supernatural works, Matt. 12:18-32; Luke 3:21, 22; 4:1, 14-21; John 5:19, 20, 27, 30; 6:38; 7:16, 28; 8:26-29; 12:49; 14:10; etc. There were certain things that Christ did not know during His earthly life, Mark 6:5, 6; 13:32; John 5:19, 30; 8:28, 29, 49; 14:10; etc. With these facts in mind, one can understand how the Revelation contained truths that the Son did not know until the Father revealed them to Him. Hence it became His Revelation after having received it of the Father through the Holy Spirit, John 17:2-8; Eph. 1:20, 21; Phil. 2:5-11; Matt. 28:18.

3. The Subject of the Revelation.

God's title of the book does not suggest that Christ, His offices and powers are the subject any more than the man-made title suggests that John and his ministry are the subject matter. It is not the unveiling of Christ in His person, offices and glory in any greater measure than what has already been unveiled in the rest of the Bible. It is simply a revelation of "things which must shortly come to pass" (1:1). Christ is only one of the many persons in the activities of the book. There are many "things" in the book which do not directly concern Christ. The "things" shortly to come to pass do not primarily concern the revelation of "persons" but new "things" concerning "persons" who are, with but few exceptions, clearly revealed in the writings of the former apostles and prophets. It is the logical completion of many former prophecies and their fulfillment and the answer to scores of mysteries in the Old Testament, which could never be answered apart from this book. The tribulation and the Seventieth Week of Daniel are previously mentioned, but here they are unfolded in detail; the destiny of the raptured saints is stated before, but here it is unfolded in detail; the final conversion and restoration of Israel have been foretold, but here is explained the method God will use in bringing them to complete repentance, thus fulfilling His covenants made with their fathers. These and many other truths are enlarged upon and a detailed account is given as to the fulfillment of many previous prophecies. Then too, there are the revelations of "things" never before stated, which shall be made clear in the exposition.

4. The Object of Revelation.

The purpose of the Revelation is "to show (point out to His servants) things which must shortly (with speed) come to pass" (1:1; 22:6). Everything in the book should be perfectly clear to "His servants" whether they are to anyone else or not. About seventeen times the word "things" is used emphasizing the object of the book. "The secret things belong unto the Lord our God, but those **things which are revealed** belong unto us and our children for ever," Deut. 29:29; 1 Cor. 2:14; 2 Tim. 3:16, 17.

The book is its own interpreter, for the subject matter is sufficient for its own explanation. Somewhere in the book one will find an explanation for every scene in the book. First, let us find out what the book itself says concerning its own revelations before going into other parts of the Bible for further explanation of the truths contained therein. The truths in Revelation can be generally understood from its own subject matter, although the details are often more fully elaborated in other Scriptures. Many truths which have been cloaked in mystery during the past ages, even to the prophets of old, are now clearly revealed to us through this book. John saw certain things prophetically and understood the meaning of his writings while other prophets did not understand many of their prophecies (22:10; 1 Pet. 1:10-12).

5. The Transmission of Revelation.

The Revelation was transmitted from God to men in this manner: God gave it to Christ; Christ gave it to His angel; the angel gave it to John; and John gave it to "his servants." It was given largely in symbolic language, as is stated in Rev. 1:1. "He sent and **signified** it by his angel unto his servant John." There are more signs and symbols in this book than in any other book of the Bible. No one can understand the book of Revelation fully who does not understand the interpretation of symbols.

The word "angel" in this verse does not refer to one of the angels of God, but to a man, for, when John fell down to worship him, the angel said, "See thou do it not: for I am thy fellowservant, and of thy brethren the prophets, and of them that keep the sayings of this book" (19:10; 22:8, 9). He could be any one of the old prophets who had died before John's reception of Revelation, for Christ had "led captivity captive" and all righteous souls were then in heaven awaiting the resurrection of the body. God used Moses on the mount to speak of the sufferings of Christ (Matt. 17:1-9). Moses could not have had a resurrected body at this time for Christ had not become the "firstfruits" of the resurrection. If God could use Moses in his "soulish body" (1 Cor. 15:44) and if the "souls" could be seen in heaven and hell without their resurrected bodies (Rev. 6:9-11; Luke 16:22-24), certainly He could use any one of the departed prophets who were residing in heaven without their resurrected bodies. Or the angel could be one of the "many" saints whose bodies arose after the resurrection of Christ and who perhaps went to heaven bodily, when Christ took all righteous souls from the underworld of departed spirits with Him, Eph. 4:7-11. How many of these angels in Revelation are redeemed men is not certain, but we know that some of them are, as we shall see.

6. The Authorship of Revelation.

John, the beloved disciple and apostle of Jesus, was the author of Revelation, not in the sense that he was the originator of its contents, but the chronicler of them (1:1, 4, 9, 11, 19; 2:1, 8, 12, 18; 3:1, 7, 14; 22:8-10). The pronoun "I" is used over seventy times in the book. This is quite a contrast to the Gospel of John, which does not use this pronoun. The early church Fathers unite in ascribing the authorship to the Apostle John. The date of writing, by almost unanimous consent of the early church writers, is ascribed to the close of the reign of the Emperor Domitian, about 96 A.D., at the time of the second persecution of Christians by the Roman Emperors. It was originally sent to the pastors of the seven churches (1:11, 20; 2:1, 8, 12, 18; 3:1, 7, 14).

7. The Threefold Authenticity of Revelation.

1. **"Of the word of God."** This has reference to the same sense in which the term is used in both Testaments, 1 Sam. 3:7; 1 Chron. 17:3; Jer. 1:4; Heb. 4:12.

2. **"Of the testimony of Jesus Christ, which is the spirit of prophecy"** (1:9; 6:9; 19:10; 2 Tim. 1:8). This testimony is both concerning Him and from Him.

3. **"Of all things that he saw."** This relates to John as the receiver of the Revelation from God to man (1:1). It was John who bore record of the Word of God, the testimony of Jesus Christ, and all things that he saw. The next to the last verse of John's Gospel (21:24) can well be quoted here as proving the authenticity of this book as well as his Gospel. "This is the disciple which testifieth of these things, and wrote these things: and we know that his testimony is true." The authenticity of Revelation then is based upon the testimony of God the Father, Jesus Christ the Son, and John who was moved upon by the Holy Spirit (1:10; 4:2; 17:3; 19:10; 21:9, 10) to record "all things that he saw" from the Father and the Son. The force of the word "saw" (Greek **eidon**) implies not only the mere act of looking, but the actual perception of the object. It is used forty-five times in the book.

8. The Nature of Revelation.

The Revelation is not history, proverb, riddle, mystery, psalmody, allegory, type, fable, enigma, or parable, but plain prophecy given in literal, symbolical, and dramatized form. With the exception of parts of chapters 1 and 22, the book is a prophetic message from beginning to the end, as is proved by the following:

(1)   The "blessing" promised in 1:3 makes it clear that all the book is a prophecy.

(2)   "The Object of Revelation" mentioned previously proves it to be a prophecy.

(3)   The term "word of God" mentioned previously shows a direct prophetic communication.

(4)   The term "testimony of Jesus," which is "the spirit of prophecy" (19:10), proves it to be all prophecy, for it is "the word of God" and "the testimony of Jesus Christ" which compose "all things that he saw."

(5)   The expressions "this prophecy" (1:3), "the sayings of the prophecy of this book" and "the things which must shortly be done" (22:6-10) prove all to be a prophecy.

(6)   The messages to the seven churches prove that the book is prophetical for they apply to individuals throughout this age. If this were not true there would be no meaning in the promises therein to anyone who overcomes. Neither would there be a meaning to Rev. 1:3; 22:7-10, 16-19.

(7)   "The time is at hand" (1:3; 22:10) clearly indicates that fulfillment begins and continues throughout this age to the time of the New Earth.

(8)   The book has 404 verses in twenty-two chapters. Fifty-four verses are history and 350 verses are prophecy. Ten of these

350 verses have been fulfilled, but the rest remain to be fulfilled.

9. The Beatitudes of Revelation.

The blessings of Revelation are seven in number and are based upon certain requirements of God as follows:

(1) The first (1:3) is for all and is based upon the individual's use of this "prophecy" in a threefold way: first, it is to be read; secondly, it is to be heard (attended to, Matt. 13:11-16); thirdly, it is to be kept (made a rule of faith and practice, Jas. 1:22-25; Rev. 3:10; 22:7, 9). See the use of the word "hear" in 1:3; 2:7, 11, 17, 29; 3:6, 13, 20, 22; 9:20; 13:9.

(2) The second is based upon faithfulness in death under Antichrist, Rev. 14:13. Cf. Rev. 6:9-11; 7:9-17; 13:16, 17; 15:2; 20:4-6.

(3) The third is based upon watchfulness in view of the second advent, Rev. 16:15. Cf. Matt. 25:1-13.

(4) The fourth is based upon preparedness to be called to the marriage of the Lamb, Rev. 19:9.

(5) The fifth is based upon righteousness in this life, Rev. 20:6; John 5:28, 29. Cf. 1 John 1:7-9; Rev. 19:8.

(6) The sixth is based upon keeping the sayings of this prophecy, Rev. 22:7. Cf. Rev. 1:3; 3:10; 22:7-9.

(7) The seventh is based upon doing the commandments of God (22:14); that is, the New Testament commandments, John 14:15, 21; 15:10; Acts 1:2.

II. The Salutation.

"John to the seven churches which are in Asia: Grace be unto you, and peace, from him which is, and which was, and which is to come; and from the seven Spirits which are before his throne; and from Jesus Christ, who is the faithful witness, and the first begotten of the dead, and the prince of the kings of the earth," Rev. 1:4, 5a.

The book is addressed to the seven churches in Asia, which shows a personal relationship between the writer and these churches. Cf. the personal salutation from other writers in 1 Cor. 1:1-3; Gal. 1:1-3; Eph. 1:1, 2; 1 Pet. 1:1-3; etc. This is the only one of John's five books that mentions his name. It seems clear from 1:4, 9-11 that John had been ministering to these churches prior to this revelation. The book is addressed to the seven churches, yet it is applicable to all peoples of the present time, 2 Tim. 3:15-17. In these verses we have the origin of Revelation enlarged upon as from the Triune God.

1. **"From him which is, and which was, and which is to come."** This refers to God the Father who is spirit, infinite, eternal, unchangeable in His being, wisdom, power, holiness, justice, goodness and truth, in whom all things have their source, support, and end. God is seen throughout the book sitting on the throne and as the center of all actions of the book in their process of reception and fulfillment.

2. **"From the seven Spirits which are before his throne."** Some interpreters have chosen seven titles of the Holy Spirit to

be these seven Spirits. The names generally chosen are the Spirit of God, the Spirit of His Son, the Spirit of Love, the Spirit of Holiness, the Spirit of Wisdom, the Spirit of Grace, and the Spirit of Glory. The objection to this interpretation is that there are many other titles from which to choose and one might choose any seven of the many and be as nearly right as another. Who is to decide which seven of the many titles are referred to? The word "seven" in this connection denotes spiritual perfection and completeness, and represents the fulness of the Spirit in the life and ministry of Christ. (See 4:5; 5:6 and points 1, 2 above).

3. **"From Jesus Christ"** who is represented in a threefold way:

(1) **As "The faithful witness,"** Greek **martus,** used twenty-eight times in the New Testament of God, Christ, apostles and other witnesses (1:5; 3:14; 11:3; Acts 22:15; 26:16; Rom. 1:9; Heb. 12:1; 1 Pet. 5:1; etc.) This refers to His ministry on earth in teaching, preaching, and healing as the prophet and witness of God in the last days, Deut. 18:15-19; Isa. 55:4; Matt. 4:23; 8:17; Heb. 1:1-3; 3:1.

(2) **As "the first begotten of the dead."** Cf. Rom. 8:29; Col. 1:15-18; 1 Cor. 15:20-23; Heb. 1:6. This proves that Enoch, Moses, Elijah or anyone else did not have resurrected and glorified bodies before Christ.

(3) **As "the prince of the kings of the earth."** The word "prince" means ruler as in John 12:31; Dan. 10:13-20. Cf. 19:16; Ps. 2:6-12; 89:27, 37.

III. The Exaltation.

"Unto him that loved us, and washed us from our sins in his own blood, and hath made us kings and priests unto God and his Father; to him be glory and dominion for ever and ever. Amen," Rev. 1:5b, 6.

Here John sets forth a marvelous incentive for the ascription of all glory and dominion to God. These verses refer to three unspeakable benefits which are principal and essential subjects of the Bible:

1. **He "loved us."** This is the central theme of the Bible, to which whole chapters are devoted, John 3:16; Rom. 5:8, 9; 1 Cor. 13; 1 John 3, 4; etc.

2. **He "washed (loosed) us from our sins in his own blood."** This has been the uppermost thought in the mind of God since the fall of man, Matt. 26:28; Rom. 3:25; 5:8-11; 2 Cor. 5:19-21; Heb. 8-10; 1 John 1:7; etc.

3. **He "made us."** This refers to the work of re-creation, through the love of Christ and the washing in His own blood, (1 Cor. 15:10; 2 Cor. 5:17; Rom. 8:1-13). Men in the natural state of sin are estranged from God, and morally unworthy of, and unable to accept God's blessings (Rom. 1:18-3:30; 5:12-21; 7:5-25; Eph. 2:1-3) so must be made new through the atonement of Christ. When that is done they become co-heirs with Christ, hence kings and priests; and with Him shall own all things and administer the affairs of the universe, Rom. 8:14-25; Heb. 1:1-3; 2:5-8; Ps. 8:3-6; Dan. 7:18-27; Isa. 9:6, 7; 1 Cor. 4:8; 6:2; 2 Tim.

2:12; Rev. 5:9, 10; 20:4-6; etc.

IV. The Chief Theme of Revelation.

"Behold he cometh with clouds; and every eye shall see him, and they also which pierced him: and all kindreds of the earth shall wail because of him. Even so, Amen," Rev. 1:7.

The second coming of Christ is the chief theme of the book. The important events that occur in and between the seals, trumpets, and vials, are in the plan of God, preparatory to Christ's coming. It is announced at the beginning (1:7), in the middle (11:15-18), and at the end of the prophecy (22:20). His second coming is referred to many times in the book and is vividly described in Rev. 19:11-21. The word for "see" in 1:7 is not the ordinary word meaning merely to look upon, but one meaning to gaze or to stare at with wide open eyes, as at something remarkable, something absolutely horrifying to the beholder, producing fear, hatred or reverence, as the case may be. (See chapter thirty-seven for a study of this subject.)

V. The Eternity of the Son of God.

"I am Alpha and Omega, the beginning and the ending, saith the Lord, which is, and which was, and which is to come, the Almighty," Rev. 1:8.

In this verse Jesus claims equality with the Father in eternity, state of being, power, and Lordship, as stated of the Father in Rev. 1:4; 4:8; 11:17; 15:3; 16:7, 14; 19:6, 15; 21:22; 2 Cor. 6:18. In these passages the Greek **Pantokrator**, which is a title of God as Creator, in expressing His relationship to all the creation and His power over all His works, is used and is always translated "Almighty" except in Rev. 19:6 where it is "Omnipotent." Christ is also the Creator of all things, Rev. 3:14; Eph. 3:9; Col. 1:15; Heb. 1:1-3. The words "Alpha and Omega" are used in Rev. 1:8, 11; 21:6; 22:13 and always with the expression "the first and the last" or "the beginning and the ending." These last expressions are used in Rev. 1:8, 11, 17; 2:8; 21:6; 22:13 and always of the Son, except in Rev. 21:6 where they refer to the Father. They express both eternity and authority. Cf. Ps. 90:2; Mic. 5:2.

VI. The Prophet—John.

"I John, who also am your brother, and companion in tribulation, and in the kingdom and patience of Jesus Christ, was in the isle that is called Patmos, for the word of God and for the testimony of Jesus Christ. I was in the Spirit on the Lord's day, and heard behind me a great voice, as of a trumpet, saying, I am Alpha and Omega, the first and the last: and What thou seest, write in a book, and send it unto the seven churches which are in Asia; unto Ephesus, and unto Smyrna, and unto Pergamos, and unto Thyatira, and unto Sardis, and unto Philadelphia, and unto Laodicea," Rev. 1:9-11.

Here we have a brief history of John in his relation to the seven churches of Asia. Cf. 1:1, 2, 4-6. See also under "The Salutation" for John's relation to these churches. This passage is clear in itself so we shall merely mention the facts that the churches were undergoing persecution by the Roman Emperors; that John was just a fellow-partaker in this tribulation and was banished to Patmos, a small rocky isle off the western coast of Asia Minor, about thirty miles southwest of Ephesus; that he was banished there for the Word of God; and that while there, he was quickened by the Spirit and saw these revelations of things which would "shortly come to pass," Rev. 1:10; 4:2; 17:3; 21:10.

The phrase "Lord's day" means the first day of the week, the day of the Lord's resurrection, Matt. 28:1; John 20:19; Acts 20:7; 1 Cor. 16:2. This was the day set apart by Christians for worship as is clear in these passages. There is no ground for believing that this Lord's day refers to the future "day of the Lord" or the Millennium, or that John was not simply in a state of spiritual exaltation on the first day of the week. **That he was transported in Spirit into the future day of the Lord and saw things that are to take place then seems unscriptural because:**

1. This is a misapprehension of the day of the Lord, which is never called the Lord's day in any passage. The expression "Lord's day" came to be used at the time of John for the day set apart to worship the Lord. Until recent years it was supposed that the modifying word, Lord's, was a purely Christian word, but discoveries have proved that it was in common use in the Roman Empire before Christ. It signified "imperial" or "belonging to the lord (the Emperor)" and so its adoption by Christians as the name of a day in the sense of "belonging to the Lord" was very natural. There is every reason to believe that the Church used the word in protest against Caesar-worship and used this phrase "the Lord's day" in contrast to the phrase "the Augustean day," which denoted a day especially dedicated in the honor of Caesar-worship. The words, "the Lord's day" occur only here in the Bible, but in post-apostolic literature there are many references to "the Lord's day" and always they are associated with Sunday, the day of the Lord's resurrection, the one kept by Christians. See our book, "God's Plan for Man," Lesson Thirty-Two.

2. The phrase "the day of the Lord" is found in Isa. 2:12; 13:6-13; 34:8; Joel 1:15; 2:1-31; 3:1-21; Amos 5:18; Zeph. 1:8-18; Zech. 14:1-21; Mal. 3-4; 1 Thess. 5:1-11; 2 Pet. 3:3-10; 2 Thess. 2:1-12; Rev. 16:14 and always refers to the Millennium which begins with the second advent and ends at the last rebellion of Satan, Rev. 20:7-10. After that it will be "the day of God" when the Father will be all and all. 1 Cor. 15:24-28; 2 Pet. 3:10-13. This nullifies the theory that John saw things that will take place in the day of the Lord, for all of Rev. 1:1-20:3 and 20:11-22:21 are fulfilled before and after that.

3. There is no need for perverting the plainly implied meaning, and project John forward in time about two thousand years from his day. If he could have been transported in Spirit into the day of the Lord that he might see things which take place in that day, could he not see things in vision on the Isle of Patmos that were to take place in the future? Isaiah and others saw events that were to take place in the future and no claim is made that they were transported in Spirit into the time when

those events were to be fulfilled. They saw and received things in the Spirit in the same way that John did on Patmos, Ezek. 1:1, 28; 2:1, 2; 3:12-14, 24; 8:3; Dan. 7:1-16; 8:16-19; 9:20-23; 10:5-12; etc.

The voice that spoke to John is called "a great voice." Note the many other "great" things in the book: 1:10; 6:4, 12, 15, 17; 7:9, 14; 8:8, 10; 9:2; 11:8, 11, 12, 13, 15, 17, 18, 19; 12:1, 3, 9, 12; 13:2, 5, 13, 16; 14:2, 8, 19; 15:1; 16:1, 9, 12, 14, 17, 18, 19, 21; 17:1, 6, 18; 18:1, 2, 10, 16, 17, 18, 19, 21, 23; 19:1, 2, 5, 6, 17, 18; 20:1, 11, 12; 21:3, 10, 12.

The Key to the Book of Revelation

1. PART I: "Write THE THINGS WHICH THOU HAST SEEN," that is, the vision of Christ of Rev. 1, which he saw before he was told to write the three divisions of the book, Rev. 1:19; 4:1.

2. PART II: "Write THE THINGS WHICH ARE," that is, the things concerning the churches, which John wrote about in Rev. 2-3, Rev. 1:19; 4:1. This is the only part of the entire book of Revelation that is now being fulfilled. When the Church is raptured before the beginning of the fulfillment of any detail of Rev. 4-22, naturally the messages to the churches will cease to apply to the Church. The Church age will be finished and the things which must be fulfilled after the churches will begin to be fulfilled.

3. PART III: "Write THE THINGS WHICH SHALL BE HEREAFTER," that is, the things which must be after the churches. To confirm this threefold division stated in Rev. 1:19, after John had written "THE THINGS WHICH ARE" concerning the churches in chapters 2-3, he was told to "come up hither (to heaven), and I will show the THINGS WHICH MUST BE HEREAFTER," that is, after the churches, Rev. 4:1. This means that every single detail shown to John in Rev. 4-22 must be fulfilled after the Church age — after the rapture of the Church.

The literal translation of Rev. 4:1 reads, "THINGS WHICH MUST BE AFTER THESE THINGS," meaning that the "THINGS" of Rev. 4-22 must be fulfilled after the "THINGS" of the churches and not at the same time.

The secret of a clear, scriptural understanding of all these things is to keep the things in each division of the book to which they belong instead of bringing one thing from one division into another. To do this would result in unity of truth whereas the mixing of historical events with these prophetical events would be foolishness indeed, as we shall see, beginning with the next chapter.

Chapter Three

THE VISION OF CHRIST, Rev. 1:12-18, 20

"And I turned to see the voice that spake with me. And being turned, I saw seven golden candlesticks; and in the midst of the seven candlesticks one like unto the Son of man, clothed with a garment down to the foot, and girt about the paps with a golden girdle. His head and his hairs were white like wool, as white as snow; and his eyes were as a flame of fire; and his feet like unto fine brass, as if they burned in a furnace; and his voice as the sound of many waters. And he had in his right hand seven stars: and out of his mouth went a sharp twoedged sword: and his countenance was as the sun shineth in his strength. And when I saw him, I fell at his feet as dead. And he laid his right hand upon me, saying unto me, Fear not: I am the first and the last: I am he that liveth, and was dead: and behold, I am alive for evermore, Amen; and have the keys of hell and of death," Rev. 1:12-18.

The person of this vision is Christ, the Son of Man. This title "Son of Man" is used eighty-eight times with reference to Christ and always with the definite article. It is used in the Old Testament, 111 times in the singular (one hundred times of Ezekiel), and thirty-nine times in the plural and nearly always without the definite article. When used of Christ it denotes the "last Adam" with reference to His taking the place of the first Adam over the works of God's hands, Ps. 8:4-8; 1 Cor. 15:24-28; Heb. 2:5-9.

The position of Christ here is "in the midst" of the seven churches, and in fact, of all the churches, for He is the head of the Church, Eph. 1:20-23; 2:19-22; 5:21-32. His ministry now in heaven is as our High Priest, Rom. 8:34; Heb. 4:14-16; 5:1-10; 6:20-10:39; 12:1-3, 18-24.

The Eight Characteristics of Christ.

1. His **body** was "clothed with a garment down to the foot, and girt about the paps with a golden girdle." There is no need for speculation in determining whether Christ is a judge, a king or a priest. To determine that is not the purpose of the vision. Other prophets have had similar visions at the beginning of the reception of their revelations and we do not attempt to find out the particular office of the person seen. Cannot Christ be described having on clothing that is ordinary to Him in His glorified state without our finding hidden meanings in the very details of the description? The only symbolism in the vision is that of the candlesticks, stars, and a sword. The remainder is merely a description of what John saw—the glorified Christ who was imparting to him these things. Cf. Isa. 6; Ezek. 1; 10; Dan. 10:5-10.

2. "His **head** and his **hairs** were white like wool, as white as snow." Cf. Ezek. 1:7; Dan. 7:9-14; 10:5-10.

3. "His **eyes** were as a flame of fire." Cf. Heb. 4:12, 13.

4. "His **feet** were like unto fine brass, as if they burned in a furnace." Cf. Dan. 10:6.

5. "His **voice** was as the sound of many waters." The following passages exemplify this characteristic of God: Rev. 1:10; 8:5; 10: 3, 4; 11:15; 14:2; 16:17, 18; 19:6; Jer. 25:30; Ps. 29; Ezek. 1:24; 43:2; Heb. 12:26.

6. "He had in his **right hand** seven stars." Cf. Exod. 15:6; Ps. 17:7; 20:6; Isa. 21:10-13; 48:13. Here Christ is pictured as upholding the ministry of the Church, Acts 20:26-30; Rom. 12:5-8; 1 Cor. 12:27-30; Eph. 2:19-22; 4:7-16.

7. "Out of his **mouth** went a sharp two-edged sword," which is a symbol of the destructive power of the Word of God, Rev. 2:12, 16; 19:15, 21; Eph. 6:17; 2 Thess. 2:8; Heb. 4:12. Cf. Ps. 55:21; 57:4; 59:7; Isa. 11:4; 49:2.

8. "His **countenance** was as the sun shineth in his strength." Cf. Heb. 12:28; 1 Tim. 6:16; Dan. 10:6.

The Effect of the Vision upon John.

This vision of Christ was something new to John. He had seen Him and walked with Him in the days of His flesh, but there was no such fear then as this vision produced. John no doubt felt uncomfortable in the awe-inspiring presence of the Son of God. He was actually overcome and fell at the feet of Christ as one dead. He did not lie long in this state, however, for Christ laid His hand upon him and said, "Fear not." The effect of the vision upon John was the same as that upon others who have got a glimpse of the glory of God, Isa. 6:1-8; Ezek. 1:28; 2:3; Dan. 8:27; 10:5-10, 17, 18; Acts 9:3-8. Cf. the attitude of heavenly creatures toward God, Rev. 4:6-11; 5:8-14; 7:9-17; 11:15-18; 14:1-5; 15:2-4; 19:1-10.

The phrase "Fear not" is used eighty times in the Bible and generally of God in quieting the fear of man because of His presence. No true Christian has a right to fear. John's attitude here was contrary to what he taught (1 John 4:18), which shows that he was not yet made complete in love. This which he had was real fear and not a reverence, for Christ certainly would not tell John not to reverence God.

The Symbols of the Vision Interpreted.

"The mystery of the seven stars which thou sawest in my right hand, and the seven golden candlesticks. The seven stars are the angels of the seven churches: and the seven candlesticks which thou sawest are the seven churches," Rev. 1:20.

The word "angel" means messenger and has reference to the pastors of the seven churches. It is used of men in Rev. 1:1, 20; 2:1, 8, 12, 18; 3:1, 7, 14; 15:1, 6, 8; 16:1-17; 17:1; 21:9, 17; 22:8-10; Jude 13. Literal stars are luminaries in the heavens to give light on the earth. In this respect they are fitting symbols of men who are to "shine as luminaries in the world," Phil. 2:15. These candlesticks are not those of the earthly or heavenly tabernacles, but are symbols of the churches in a twofold aspect: first, to manifest Christ within; secondly, to hold forth the Word of Life in this darkened world, Phil. 2:16. The word candlestick means lampstands or portable lamps, and is used seven times in the book, Rev. 1:12, 13, 20; 2:1, 5. See also Rev. 18:23; 22:5.

PART II.

"THE THINGS WHICH ARE," Rev. 2:1-3:22.

Chapter Four

THE SEVEN CHURCHES, Rev. 2:1-3:22

The messages to the seven churches are given immediately after the vision of Christ in the midst of the churches. Chapters 2 and 3 contain only "the things which are"; i.e., the things concerning the Church on earth and to its rapture.

The Threefold Application of the Letters.

1. **A local application** to the churches in John's day. These seven epistles, as a whole, portray actual conditions in seven local churches in Asia. This is clear from the messages themselves as well as from Rev. 1:4, 11, 20.

2. **A prophetical application** to the churches throughout this dispensation to the rapture, revealing the spiritual conditions of local churches and individuals in the churches. This point is clear from the fact that the book is a "prophecy." Then too, these letters are as applicable to the saved all through this age as are the other New Testament epistles and other Scriptures, 2 Tim. 3:16, 17.

They reveal the will of God in this age concerning the saved to the rapture. It seems clear that "the things which are" could not be contemporaneous with "the things which shall be hereafter," Rev. 1:19; 4:1. The one must be finished before the other begins. These letters do not permit solely a local application any more than other epistles which are addressed to local churches or peoples or individuals as the case may be, 2 Tim. 3:16, 17. All the book is addressed to the seven churches, and if it were confined to them, and had no part yet to be fulfilled, it would lose its peculiar character as a "prophecy" of "things shortly to come to pass" and be purely historical. Furthermore, the Lord does not speak to all the churches of Asia in John's time, but picks out seven of the many churches because local conditions in them are characteristic of the course of this age and they are concrete examples to local churches throughout this dispensation. Again, if the letters were confined to these seven churches there would be no "mystery" (1:20) and no need for a universal call to individuals to hear and to overcome throughout this age.

3. **An individual application,** so that the individual may be warned by the failure revealed therein, and, profiting by the warning, may find encouragement from the promises to the **overcomer.**

The dispensational application of these church letters; i.e., that they portray seven church periods or phases of church history is really based upon human theory alone. There can be no Scripture produced to prove this theory in any one aspect. Similarity to certain phases of church history proves nothing.

One can even find similarities between the history of the Church and Israel and there is no end to similarities that could be found in history between almost any two things one chooses to compare. Anything that is based upon human theory is not dependable and is misleading and unscriptural. If there was such an application of these letters there would have been two or three passages to support each letter and its application to some definite period in history.

Much confusion and many false teachings are based upon this method of interpretation. Some teachings are as follows: that we are in the Philadelphian or Laodicean periods; that the rapture of the Church takes place in either one of these two periods; that the Church Age ends with Philadelphia; that Laodicea deals with things after the rapture; that the Ephesian period ended with the apostles; and many other theories are unscriptural. We still have the conditions of Ephesus, etc., in local churches today. These conditions existed in John's day and they will continue to exist as long as the Church is on earth, so seeing there are Scriptures to prove a local, prophetical, and individual application, and anything said about a dispensational application must rest upon human theory and cause numberless differences as to interpretation, it would be best to forget this application entirely.

With the seven letters to the seven churches in Asia (Rev. 2:1-3:22), we end all in the book which concerns the churches on earth. From Rev. 4:1 on, the Revelation concerns things which will happen after the rapture of the Church.

Points of Similarity in the Letters.

1. In nearly every message there is a reference to some one or more of the eight characteristics of Christ listed in chapter three.

2. The headings of all letters addressed to the various pastors, correspond.

3. Christ commends each church, except the last, for its "works" and other virtuous characteristics.

4. Christ rebukes every church except the second and sixth.

5. The first, third, fifth, and seventh churches are commanded to repent while the second, fourth, and sixth are not. The second and sixth have nothing of which to repent, having been purged by persecution. The fourth has sufficient evil of which to repent, but has become reprobate and past redemption.

6. A warning of judgment is given to every one except the second and sixth ones.

7. Every church, except the second and sixth, is more corrupt than its predecessor; the last is the most corrupt of all, without one single virtue to commend it. There are about ten points of commendation in favor of the first church and the same number of condemnation against the last church.

8. There is a promise to the overcomer in each letter.

9. The same admonition is given to each church, "He that

hath an ear let him hear what the Spirit saith unto the churches."

10.   In each letter John is told to "write." This shows that he is being directed by Christ. When each letter is made complete the next begins. This makes evident the consecutive order of the "things" of the book. When the last letter is completed John is told to write "the things which shall be hereafter." Thus we have a new order of "things" after the churches, which do not concern the Church on earth, for it is in heaven during the fulfillment of Rev. 4:1; 19:10 and it will come back to earth with Christ at the second advent as pictured in Rev. 19:11-21.

We shall not attempt to discuss each application, nor go into all the details of the letters. The applications, of course, are clear in themselves as applying to any one in any local church throughout this dispensation where these same conditions exist. To overcome them and be rewarded is the message to the believer in any local church in this whole age. All these conditions have existed more or less in local churches since that time and will always exist, so the duty of each person who reads these letters is clear so that comment on them is not necessary. This will save space for discussion on more important truths in the book.

1.   The Church at Ephesus.

"Unto the angel of the church of Ephesus write: These things saith he that holdeth the seven stars in his right hand, who walketh in the midst of the seven golden candlesticks; I know thy works, and thy labour, and thy patience, and how thou canst not bear them which are evil: and thou hast tried them which say they are apostles, and are not, and hast found them liars: and hast borne, and hast patience, and for my name's sake hast laboured, and hast not fainted. Nevertheless I have somewhat against thee, because thou hast left thy first love. Remember therefore from whence thou art fallen, and repent, and do the first works: or else I will come unto thee quickly, and will remove thy candlestick out of his place, except thou repent. But this thou hast, that thou hatest the deeds of the Nicolaitanes which I also hate. He that hath an ear, let him hear what the Spirit saith unto the churches: To him that overcometh will I give to eat of the tree of life, which is in the midst of the paradise of God," Rev. 2:1-7.

This promise to the overcomer with 2:17; 19:9; Matt. 26:29; Luke 24:29, 30, 41-43; John 21:5-14 shows that saints will eat when in a glorified state.

2.   The Church at Smyrna.

"And unto the angel of the church in Smyrna write: These things saith the first and the last, which was dead, and is alive; I know thy works, and tribulation, and poverty, (but thou art rich) and I know the blasphemy of them which say they are Jews, and are not, but are the synagogue of Satan. Fear none of those things which thou shalt suffer: behold the devil shall cast some of you into prison, that ye may be tried; and ye shall have tribulation ten days: be thou faithful unto death, and I will give thee a crown of life. He that hath an ear, let him hear what the Spirit saith unto the churches. He that overcometh shall not be hurt of the second death," Rev. 2:8-11.

The overcomer is promised that he will not be hurt by the lake of fire, Rev. 14:9-11; 19:20; 20:13-15; 21:8.

3.   The Church at Pergamos.

"And to the angel of the church in Pergamos write: These things saith he which hath the sharp sword with two edges; I know thy works, and where thou dwellest, even where Satan's seat is: and thou holdest

fast my name, and hast not denied my faith, even in those days wherein Antipas was my faithful martyr, who was slain among you, where
Satan dwelleth.   But I have a few things against thee, because thou
hast there them that hold the doctrine of Balaam, who taught Balac to
cast a stumblingblock before the children of Israel, to eat things sacrificed unto idols, and to commit fornication. So hast thou also them
that hold the doctrine of the Nicolaitanes, which thing I hate. Repent;
or else I will come unto thee quickly, and will fight against them with
the sword of my mouth. He that hath an ear let him hear what the
Spirit saith unto the churches; To him that overcometh will I give to
eat of the hidden manna, and will give him a white stone, and in
the stone a new name written, which no man knoweth saving he that
receiveth it," Rev. 2:12-17.

Here the overcomer is promised the privilege of eating the hidden (concealed as in Matt. 13:44; John 12:36; 1 Tim. 5:25; Heb.
11:23; Rev. 6:15, 16) manna, which is real and will be eaten as
much as will be the tree of life. He will also be given a white
stone with a new name in it. The white stone was known to
the ancient as a "victory" stone. All these things are literal, and
not spiritual, for we are now blessed with "ALL spiritual blessings," Eph. 1:3. These are things given as rewards and not as
blessings. Cf. this manna with Exod. 16:14; Ps. 78:24, 25 and
the "new name written" with 3:12; Isa. 62:2; 65:15; Acts 15:17.

4. The Church at Thyatira.

"And unto the angel of the church in Thyatira write: These things
saith the Son of God, who hath his eyes like unto a flame of fire, and
his feet like fine brass; I know thy works, and charity, and service,
and faith, and thy patience, and thy works; and the last to be more
than the first.   Notwithstanding I have a few things against thee,
because thou sufferest that woman Jezebel, which calleth herself a
prophetess, to teach, and to seduce my servants to commit fornication,
and to eat things sacrificed unto idols. And I gave her space to repent of
her fornication; and she repented not. Behold, I will cast her into a bed,
and them that commit adultery with her into great tribulation, except
they repent of their deeds.   And I will kill her children with death;
and all the churches shall know that I am he which searcheth the reins
and hearts: and I will give unto every one of you according to your
works. But unto you I say, and unto the rest in Thyatira, as many as
have not this doctrine, and which have not known the depths of Satan,
as they speak; I will put upon you none other burden. But that which
ye have already hold fast till I come. And he that overcometh, and
keepeth my works unto the end, to him will I give power over the nations: And he shall rule them with a rod of iron; as the vessels of a
potter shall they be broken to shivers: even as I received of my Father.
And I will give him the morning star. He that hath an ear, let him
hear what the Spirit saith unto the churches," Rev. 2:18-29.

Here the overcomer is promised authority over the nations as
promised to Christ (Ps. 2; Rev. 19:15), the manchild (12:5), and
the tribulation saints (Rev. 20:4-6), and all saints of all ages,
(Ps. 149:6-9; Rev. 20:4-6, Dan. 7:18). He is also to have "the
morning star," Rev. 22:16.

5. The Church at Sardis.

"And unto the angel of the church in Sardis write: These things
saith he that hath the seven Spirits of God, and the seven stars; I know
thy works, that thou hast a name that thou livest, and art dead. Be
watchful, and strengthen the things which remain, that are ready to
die: for I have not found thy works perfect before God. Remember
therefore how thou hast received and heard, and hold fast, and repent.
If therefore thou shalt not watch, I will come on thee as a thief, and
thou shalt not know what hour I will come upon thee. Thou hast a few
names even in Sardis which have not defiled their garments; and they
shall walk with me in white; for they are worthy. He that overcometh,
the same shall be clothed in white raiment; and I will not blot out his
name out of the book of life, but I will confess his name before my
Father and before his angels. He that hath an ear, let him hear what
the Spirit saith unto the churches," Rev. 3:1-6.

Here the overcomer is promised that he will be clothed in white raiment, and have his name perpetually in the book of life and have it confessed before God and the angels.

6.   The Church at Philadelphia.

"And unto the angel of the church in Philadelphia write: These things saith he that is holy, he that is true, he that hath the key of David, he that openeth, and no man shutteth; and shutteth and no man openeth; I know thy works: behold, I have set before thee an open door, and no man can shut it: For thou hast a little strength, and hast kept my word, and hast not denied my name. Behold, I will make them of the synagogue of Satan, which say they are Jews, and are not, but do lie; behold, I will make them to come and worship before thy feet, and to know that I have loved thee. Because thou hast kept the word of my patience, I also will keep thee from the hour of temptation, which shall come upon all the world, to try them that dwell upon the earth. Behold, I come quickly: hold that fast which thou hast, that no man take thy crown. Him that overcometh will I make a pillar in the temple of my God, and he shall go no more out: and I will write upon him the name of my God, and the name of the city of my God, which is new Jerusalem, which cometh down out of heaven from my God; and I will write upon him my new name. He that hath an ear, let him hear what the Spirit saith unto the churches," Rev. 3:7-13.

Here the overcomer is promised that he will be made a pillar (authority as in Gal. 2:9. See also 1 Tim. 3:15; Rev. 10:1) in the temple of God and have the above names written on him. This is all literal as any other writing is literal. The Greek **grapho** occurs 186 times in the New Testament and means to grave or to write and is always used of visible writing. It is never used of spiritual engraving of God's laws in the inward parts. Cf. Rev. 13:16; 14:1, 11; 19:20; 20:4; 22:4; Isa. 62:2; 65:15.

7.   The Church at Laodicea.

"And unto the angel of the church of the Laodiceans write: These things saith the Amen, the faithful and true witness, the beginning of the creation of God; I know thy works, that thou art neither cold nor hot: I would thou wert cold or hot. So then because thou art lukewarm, and neither cold nor hot, I will spue thee out of my mouth. Because thou sayest, I am rich, and increased with goods, and have need of nothing; and knowest not that thou art wretched, and miserable, and poor, and blind, and naked: I counsel thee to buy of me gold tried in the fire that thou mayest be rich; and white raiment, that thou mayest be clothed, and that the shame of thy nakedness do not appear; and anoint thine eyes with eyesalve, that thou mayest see. As many as I love, I rebuke and chasten: be zealous therefore, and repent. Behold, I stand at the door, and knock: if any man hear my voice, and open the door, I will come in to him, and sup with him, and he with me. To him that overcometh will I grant to sit with me in my throne, even as I also overcame, and am set down with my Father in his throne. He that hath an ear, let him hear what the Spirit saith unto the churches," Rev. 3:14-22.

Here the overcomer is promised a throne. (See chapter forty-one, point (4).

Chapter Five

DANIEL'S SEVENTIETH WEEK AND THE TRIBULATION

The lack of space will not permit a detailed study of these subjects, but the following brief study will help the reader to understand them as they are connected with Revelation.

I. The Vision of the Seventy Weeks, Dan. 9:24-27.

The expression "seventy weeks" literally means "seventy sevens" of years. If days were meant it would be so expressed as in Dan. 10:3. Daniel's prayer, to which this vision was an answer, did not concern days, but years (9:2). Then too, we know from Scripture that the last Week (9:27) is divided into two parts of three and one-half years each, Dan. 7:25; 12:7; Rev. 11:2, 3; 12:5, 14; 13:5. The whole period of "seventy sevens" is 490 years which are "determined" or "marked off" apart from all other years and concern only "thy people (Israel) and thy holy city (Jerusalem)," for which Daniel was praying, Dan. 6:10; 9:1-23. **Six events are to take place during these 490 years relative to Israel and Jerusalem** for six purposes:

1. **"To finish the transgression,"** Hebrew **pasha,** meaning to revolt, rebel, or sin against lawful authority. It is often translated "transgression," Ps. 51:13; Isa. 43:27; etc. This transgression has reference to Israel in her rebellion against God. This prophecy foretells the culmination of that rebellion. The law was added because of transgression until the Seed should come, and it served as a schoolmaster to lead Israel to Christ, Gal. 3:17-25. Israel failed to receive the Messiah and was broken off in unbelief from God's favor as a nation. She will not be fully received back again until the second coming of Christ, who will turn ungodliness from Jacob and cause a nation to be born at once, Rom. 11:25-29; Isa. 66:7-10; Ezek. 36: 24-30.

2. **"To make an end of sins."** Israel's sins, if collected in the form of concrete matter, would fill the whole earth, for, from her beginning to the fulfillment of this prophecy at the return of Christ, she has been and will be in continued rebellion against God. This "end of sins" will not be made until after the tribulation, but from that time Israel will obey God forever, Ezek. 36: 24-30; 37: 24-27; Zech. 14:1-21.

3. **"To make reconciliation (atonement) for iniquity,"** Hebrew **avon,** meaning perverseness, to be crooked or wrung out of course, 1 Sam. 20:30; 2 Sam. 19:19; Job 33:27. Atonement was made on the cross for the whole world but Israel as a nation has not yet appropriated its benefits and will not until the return of Christ, Zech. 13:1-7; Rom. 11:25-27.

4. **"To bring in everlasting righteousness."** When the transgression has been finished, the end of sins made, and full benefits of the atonement will have been realized by Israel, then everlasting righteousness will be ushered in, Isa. 9:6, 7; 12:1-6; Dan. 7:13, 14, 18, 27; Matt. 25:31-46.

5. **"To seal up the vision and prophecy,"** i.e., make an end of them by fulfillment of prophecies concerning Israel and Jerusalem. The word "prophecy" should be translated "prophet" as elsewhere. It means that there will be no need of inspired men to rebuke Israel in an attempt to lead them into the way of righteousness "for all shall know the Lord from the least unto the greatest."

6. **"To anoint the most Holy."** This refers to the cleansing of the holy of holies, the temple and the city of Jerusalem from the abomination of desolation and the sacrilege of Gentiles and to the establishment and anointing of the Millennial temple.of Ezek. 40-43; Zech. 6:12, 13. The "most Holy" is never used of a person, nor would the Jews ever associate this term with their Messiah, who is distinguished from this term in this passage by the title "Messiah." This vision needs no explanation other than that of the angel. All that is needed is an understanding of the explanation, the association of it with other Scriptures on the same subject, and the finding out of the time of its fulfillment.

The 490 years are divided into three periods:

1. **The first period** consisted of seven sevens or forty-nine years during which time the Holy City, street, and wall were to be built "even in troublous times," Dan. 9:25. These 490 years began with "the commandment to restore and build Jerusalem unto the Messiah." There were three decrees for the restoration of the city. The first decree was given during the first year of the reign of Cyrus, King of Persia, Ezra 1:1-4; 3:8; Isa. 44:28; 45:1-4; 46:11. Cyrus reigned nine years, then Cambyses, his son, reigned seven years. In the reign of Cambyses the work on the temple and city ceased, Ezra 4:1-24. Darius I of profane history reigned thirty-five years. In the second year of his reign he reconfirmed the decree made by Cyrus and the work was started again. The temple was finished in the sixth year of his reign but the city was not then restored although fifty-seven years had passed since the first decree by Cyrus, Ezra 6:1-15. Xerxes reigned twenty-one years (Dan. 11:1-3) during which time the city was not yet completed. Artaxerxes reigned after Xerxes twenty years and then gave the third decree to Nehemiah to restore "Jerusalem unto the Messiah," Neh. 2:1-6:19; Dan. 9:25, 26. Nehemiah restored the walls in fifty-two days after he reached Jerusalem, but this was by no means the full restoration. That took place seven sevens or forty-nine years after the third decree, which was given about 452 B. C.

We believe that this third decree is the one mentioned in this vision as the starting point of the 490 years, because the first two would not fulfill the prophecy which required exactly forty-nine years for the full restoration of Jerusalem. There were fifty-seven years between the first commandment and the time when the temple was fully built. If it took this long to build the temple it certainly would take longer to build the city. There were ninety-two years from the first decree and seventy-two years from the second decree to the third decree and still the city was not fully restored. The fact that there were three decrees proves that the city was not fully restored until after the third decree. If the forty-nine years began with the first two, this prophecy would not have been fulfilled. Again, Neh. 4:1-23 records the only "troublous times" under any of these decrees, when the work continued despite opposition, and this was under the third. Ezra deals with the restoration of the temple and Nehemiah with the restoration of the city.

2. **The second period** consists of sixty-two sevens or 434 years. It began immediately after the first period of seven sevens or forty-nine years and continued without a break to the time when the Messiah was "cut off" or crucified, Dan. 9:26. This phrase "cut off" is from the Hebrew **karath,** meaning "to cut off in death," Gen. 9:11; Deut. 20:20; Jer. 11:19; Ps. 37:9. These forty-nine and 434 years make 483 years from the third decree to the crucifixion of the Messiah, or sixty-nine of the seventy sevens of years, leaving the last period of seven years concerning Israel and Jerusalem to be fulfilled after the crucifixion.

3. **The third period** will consist of one seven-year period better known as Daniel's Seventieth Week. The crucifixion of the Messiah ended the sixty-ninth Week and God ceased dealing with Israel as a nation. They were broken off in unbelief and their city destroyed as foretold in this same vision of Seventy Weeks (9:26) and by Jesus in Matt. 21:43; 23:37-39; 24:2; Luke 21:20-24. See also Acts 13:45-49; Rom. 11. This Seventieth Week will be fulfilled when Israel, partially gathered, will exist as a nation in possession of Jerusalem. That Jerusalem will be in their possession again is proved from the fact that it will again be given to the Gentiles in the middle of the Week, Rev. 11:1, 2. Not one of the six above events have been fulfilled. They must be in the future. The Seventieth Week will be the last seven years of this dispensation and will parallel the seven years covenant between Antichrist and Israel, Dan. 9:27. It is to be the time when all the events of Rev. 6:1-19:21 will be fulfilled, and when the whole tribulation will run its course. What was to happen during this Week was not revealed to Daniel in detail, but was revealed to John. This Week of years will begin after the rapture of the Church, end at the second advent, and fulfill all the above six things concerning Israel. Between the sixty-ninth and Seventieth Weeks, during the time of Israel's rejection, the present Church Age comes in. It is fulfilled before the Seventieth Week, which is primarily in connection with Israel as were the first sixty-nine weeks.

II. The Tribulation, Rev. 6:1-19:21.

1. The Time and Length of the Tribulation.

The tribulation will begin to affect Israel before the Seventieth

Week begins; how long before is not certain, but when Antichrist rises at the beginning of the Week, Israel will be undergoing persecution by the whore and the ten kings of Revised Rome who are dominated by the whore until the middle of the Week. Antichrist will come out of one of these ten kingdoms and make a seven years covenant with Israel assuring them protection in their continued establishment as a nation, Dan. 9:27. The Jews will not accept the whore when she again sways the nations of the old world and begins to murder all heretics as she has done in the past. Because they will not, there will be a widespread persecution of the Jews and "they shall be hated of all nations" during the time of "the beginning of sorrows" when Antichrist will be endeavoring to conquer all these nations, Matt. 24:4-12. Antichrist will need Jewish moral and financial support to help him rise over these nations, so he will make an alliance with them for seven years. The time of the tribulation then is during the whole of Daniel's Seventieth Week, Dan. 9:27. It will end at the second advent, Matt. 24:29-31.

2.   The Divisions of the Tribulation.

(1)   **The first division** takes in the first three and one-half years of the Seventieth Week and is termed "the lesser tribulation" for it is not as great in severity as the last three and one-half years, because of the protection of Israel by the Antichrist during that time. Israel's persecution then will be from a source entirely different from that of the last division. In these years she will be persecuted by the whore and the ten kings as stated above. This part takes in the fulfillment of Rev. 6:1-9:21. The judgments of the sixth seal and first six trumpets come in this period thus proving tribulation during this time.

(2)   **The last division** takes in the last three and one-half years of the Week and is termed "the great tribulation" because it will be more severe in persecution upon Israel than the first three and one-half years. Antichrist, who will protect Israel the first three and one-half years, will break his covenant with her in the middle of the Week, become her most bitter enemy, and try to destroy her, which calls for the judgments of the seven vials of the last three and one-half years. This part of the tribulation includes the fulfillment of Rev. 10:1-19:21. Jesus, Daniel, Jeremiah, and many others speak of this time of Israel's trouble as being worse than any that has ever been on earth or ever will be, Dan. 12:1; Jer. 30:4-11; Matt. 24:21, 22; Rev. 11:1, 2; 12:14-17; 13:5-7; etc.

3.   The Purpose of the Tribulation.

(1)   To purify Israel and bring them back to a place where God can fulfill the everlasting covenants made with their fathers, Isa. 2:6; 3:26; 16:1-5; 24:1-23; 26:20, 21; Ezek. 20:33, 34; 22:17-22; Rom. 11:25-29.

(2)   To purify Israel of all rebels, Ezek. 20:33, 34; 22:17-22; Zech. 13:8, 9; Mal. 3: 3, 4.

(3)   To plead with and bring Israel into the bond of the new covenant, Ezek. 20:33, 34; 36:24-28; Jer. 30:3-11; Zech. 12:10-13:9; Mal. 4:3, 4.

(4)   To judge Israel and punish them for their rejection of the Messiah and make them willing to accept Him when He comes the second time, Ezek. 20:33, 34; Zech. 12:10-13:9; 14:1-15; Matt. 24:15-31.

(5)   To judge the nations for their persecution of Israel, Isa. 63:1-5; Joel 3; Rev. 6:1-19:21.

(6)   To bring Israel to complete repentance, Zech. 12:10-13:9; Rom. 11:26-29; Matt. 23:39.

(7)   Fulfill the things of Dan. 9:24-27; Rev. 6:1-19:21; Matt. 24:15, 29; etc.

(8)   To cause Israel to flee into the wilderness of Edom and Moab and to be so persecuted by the nations that Israel will have to turn to God for help, Isa. 16:1-5; Ezek. 20:33-35; Dan. 11:40-12:7; Hos. 2:14-17; Matt. 24:15-31; Rev. 12.

4. The Character of the Tribulation.

The character of the tribulation can easily be understood in view of God's wrath being poured out upon mankind for their wickedness and corruption which will exceed the days of Noah and Lot, Gen. 6; Matt. 24:37-39; Luke 17:22-37; 2 Tim. 3:1-12. Men will be rejecters of truth until God will turn them over to the "strong delusion" of the Antichrist who will cause them to believe a lie and be damned, 2 Thess. 2:8-12; 2 Pet. 3:1-9. Even after God pours out His judgments upon men they will still defy Him, Rev. 9:20, 21; 16:2-11; 17:1-18; 18:1-24. Words cannot describe the utter rebellion and wickedness of men during this period of final struggle between God and the devil over possession of the earth, Rev. 11:15; 12:7-12; 19:11-21; 20:1-3.

5. Will the Tribulation Be World-wide?

The old theory that the tribulation will be world-wide is not stated in one Scripture. On the contrary, the Bible is clear that the Antichrist will not reign over the whole world, but only over the ten kingdoms that are to be formed inside the old Roman Empire (See chapters twenty-one and thirty-five). Most of the judgments of the trumpets and vials are stated as being only upon a third or fourth part of the earth (Rev. 8:7-12), and upon "the men which had the mark of the beast" and "upon the seat (throne) of the beast: and his kingdom" (Rev. 16:2, 10, 12). Nothing is said, however, as to the limitation of the extent of the demon locusts or of the extent of the Devil's wrath when he is cast out, Rev. 9:1-11; 12:7-12. The sixth trumpet kills only a third part of men, Rev. 9:12-21.

When we speak of the tribulation we mean the troubles God's people will have to undergo, especially the Jewish people, as Daniel's Seventieth Week concerns only Israel and their city Jerusalem.   The last half of the Week will be "the time of Jacob's trouble" and these troubles primarily concern Israel.

Chapter Six

THE RAPTURE OF THE CHURCH

The rapture of the Church is also called "the coming of the Lord" but never the second coming of Christ. At this coming He does not appear visibly to the earth but in the air to catch up, or rapture the dead and living saints who rise together to meet the Lord in the air. There are many ideas about these two comings, which have made it difficult to distinguish one from the other. There are so many Scriptures misapplied to the one or the other that it is no wonder that many have found themselves involved in a labyrinth of difficulties, from which they are unable to extricate themselves. This coming is purely a New Testament doctrine and was first revealed to Paul as a special revelation (1 Cor. 15:51-58) while the second coming of Christ is not only a New Testament doctrine, but one of the chief themes of the Old Testament. The Old Testament prophets never saw the New Testament Church, much less the rapture of the Church.

These two comings cannot be mixed and still be clear. The Scriptures that apply to one do not apply to the other. Not one of the passages under the second advent in chapter thirty-nine refers to the rapture, and not one of those below refers to the second coming as can be seen upon examination of them. There is not one passage in the Bible that refers to both events as if they were one. They are two distinct comings separated by several years and not two phases or stages of one coming. The rapture takes place several years before the literal advent of Christ to the earth. When Christ meets the saints in the air He takes them back to heaven with Him and presents them to the Father where they remain while the tribulation is running its course on earth. The saints are in heaven before God, and not in the air, from the time of the rapture to their coming again with Christ to reign as kings and priests. This seems clear from the facts that the saints are judged, are given their rewards and partake of the marriage supper in heaven and not in the air. Christ departs from heaven at His coming to earth and not from the air, Rev. 19:11-21; 2 Thess. 1:7-10. The rapture must first take place before Christ can come back to earth with His saints. At the rapture, the Lord is coming from heaven as far as the air or earthly heavens and the saints are to be "caught up to meet Him in the air." At this event the Lord is not to be raptured, but the saints. At the second coming the saints are not to be raptured, neither is Christ, but both will come back to the earth together. The rapture takes place before the tribulation, while the second advent takes place after the tribulation. The rapture may occur any moment. The second advent cannot occur until all the signs in chapter thirty-nine come to pass and certain prophecies are fulfilled.

We have separated these two comings, as they should be

separated, for the sake of clearness and because they are always distinct in Scripture. This subject has no part in the chief theme of Revelation, but it forms an integral part of the book. The following points will help the reader to distinguish the rapture from the second coming and give a scriptural understanding of this New Testament revelation.

I. The Fact and Manner of the Rapture.

We need not be ignorant concerning this subject when it is fully and clearly revealed in many passages of the New Testament. The **fact** and **manner** of the rapture are clearly revealed in the following Scriptures: Luke 21:34-36; John 14:1-3; 1 Cor. 15:23, 51-58; 2 Cor. 5:1-8; Eph. 5:27; Phil. 3:11, 20, 21; 1 Thess. 2:19; 3:13; 4:13-17; 5:9, 23; 2 Thess. 2:1, 7, 8; Col. 3:4; Jas. 5:7, 8; 1 John 2:28; 3:2; 1 Pet. 5:4. Not one of these passages refers to the second advent. We shall not use any verse in Matt. 24 and 25 in this connection for there is not one in those chapters which refers to the rapture as will be seen in chapter eight. We shall deal only with those passages which refer to the rapture and which can be consistently explained only in this connection. **There are two Greek words used in most of the passages on the rapture as follows:**

1. **Parousia** means "personal coming or appearance" and is used of both the rapture and the revelation of Christ. At the rapture, Christ appears personally in the air to meet the saints, while at the second advent He appears personally to mankind on earth with His saints. This word is generally translated "coming" hence the rapture and the revelation are both called "the coming of the Lord" but they are two different comings, and for two different purposes. The word is used in this connection in 1 Cor. 15:20-23; 1 Thess. 2:19; 3:13; 4:15; 5:23; 2 Thess. 2:1; Jas. 5:7, 8; 1 Jno. 2:28. All these passages are clear as referring to the rapture but 1 Thess. 3:13; 5:23; 2 Thess. 2:1 are sometimes used in connection with the second advent. 1 Thess. 3:13; 5:23 refer to the time when the Father pronounces the saints "blameless" before His throne in heaven after Christ has first met the saints in the air and has taken them to heaven and presented them "before God."

"The coming of our Lord Jesus Christ with all his saints" in these passages refers then to the time of His coming back to heaven with the saints at the time of the rapture, and not to the time when He comes to the earth with the saints at the second advent. We are made "blameless" to be preserved forever in that state at the time of the rapture, and not at the time of the revelation, 1 John 3:1-3; Phil. 3:21; 1 Thess. 3:13; 5:23; Col. 3:4. The last reference (2 Thess. 2:1) refers to the rapture also, as is proved from the Greek **esposunagoge**, which means a complete collection or gathering of all the dead **in Christ** and all the living **in Christ,** from all parts of the earth, and out of all denominations and dispensations to meet Christ in the air. We are gathered "unto him" at the rapture and not at the revelation, Luke 21:34-36; John 14:1-5; 1 Cor. 15:51-58; 2 Cor. 5:1-8; 1 Thess. 4:13-18; 2 Thess. 2:6-8.

This event is called in Phil. 3:11 as "the resurrection of the dead," or literally, "the out-resurrection," that is, the resurrection from out among the dead. The term "resurrection of the dead" is frequently used in the New Testament and includes the resurrection of the just and unjust, John 5:29; Acts 24:15. The "out-resurrection" is used only in the above passage and implies the resurrection of some, the former of these two classes, the others being left behind, Rev. 20:1-7. These dead "rise first"; then the living who are saved will be "caught up together with them in the clouds, to meet the Lord in the air," 1 Thess. 4:13-18. All the above passages as well as those below on the rapture can be easily harmonized by the student with these few thoughts on the subject.

2. **Phaneros,** which means "to shine, be apparent, manifest, or be seen," is used in 1 John 2:28; 3:2; 1 Pet. 5:4; Col. 3:4. The English translation is "appear" and means that Christ is to appear to the saints in the air at the rapture and will not appear to the world until His second coming.

The rapture will include Old Testament saints and the Church saints who are saved in the scope of redemption from Adam until the rapture, 1 Thess. 4:13-18; 2 Thess. 2:1 as explained above. We do not mean to say that the scope of redemption ends with the rapture, for it is eternal as we shall see in the last five chapters of this exposition.

The "trump of God" (1 Thess. 4:16) is not the same as the seventh trumpet of Rev. 11:15; 13:18. One is at the rapture of the Church and the Old Testament saints, while the other is at the rapture of the manchild; one is the trumpet of God, the other is the trumpet of the seventh trumpet angel; one is to herald one single event which takes place "in the twinkling of an eye" (1 Cor. 15:51-58), the other is to herald many events which are days in duration (Rev. 10:7); one is a trumpet of blessing, the other is a trumpet of "woe" (Rev. 8:13; 12:12); one is at or before the beginning of the Seventieth Week, the other is in the middle of the Week; one is before the saints, represented by the twenty-four elders, are caught up, the other is after the elders are already in heaven; one is before the seven seals and first six trumpets (Rev. 6:1-9:21), the other is after them. Thus we do not need to confuse this trumpet and rapture with the seventh trumpet and rapture of the manchild.

II. The Purpose of the Rapture.

The purpose of the rapture is to take all the saints out of the world before the tribulation comes and to resurrect the just who are dead, in order that they may have fulfilled in them, the purpose for which God has saved them. Jesus told the disciples that some would escape the terrible things that were to transpire on the earth in the last days. He said, "Pray that ye may be accounted worthy to escape **all** these things (of Matt. 24, 25; Luke 21:1-19, 25-28) that shall come to pass, and to stand before the Son of man," Luke 21:34-36. This passage is practically the same in essence as John 14:1-3.

These two passages are the only ones in the Gospels that are clear concerning the rapture. Jesus did not reveal this mystery. It was revealed by Paul many years later, 1 Cor. 15:51. The disciples did not have the slightest idea as to how they were to escape, unless they thought that Christ would deliver them from these things through His power. The "how" was not revealed or even mentioned before Paul explained how they were to escape. Now in the light of the mystery revealed we can see that the rapture is what Christ had in mind when He spoke of some being worthy to escape these things. The Thessalonians were taught that they could expect the living to be taken out of the world, but some were confused as to whether the dead believers would have a part in the rapture, so Paul explained in his first epistle that both the living and the dead would be caught up to meet Christ in the air, 1 Thess. 4:13-18. In this passage we have the purpose of the rapture expressed "so shall we ever be with the Lord." It is to enable the saints to escape the tribulation days and serve God in all eternity in whatsoever capacity He chooses.

This rapture is the first of a series of raptures that will take place during the first resurrection. Besides this rapture there will be the rapture of the manchild (7:1-3; 12:5; 14:1-5), the rapture of the great multitude of tribulation saints (6:9-11; 7:9-17; 15:2-4; 20:4), and the rapture of the two witnesses (11:3-13). The teaching of more than one rapture is not only required and stated in the above passages, but necessary to make clear what Paul meant when he said, "every man in his own order," 1 Cor. 15:20-23. The Greek for "order" is **tagma** and occurs only here. It is used in the Septuagint of a body of soldiers and an army, Num. 2:2; 2 Sam. 23:13. It means a company or body of individuals. In order for every man to be raptured "in his own order" or company there must be different companies of redeemed people saved and raptured at different periods. (See point three, chapter nine for the four different redeemed companies).

The purpose of the rapture may be summed up thus:

1. To receive the saints to Himself, John 14:1-3; Eph. 5:27; 2 Thess 2:1.

2. To resurrect the dead "in Christ" from among the wicked dead, 1 Cor. 15:21-23, 51-58; 1 Thess. 4:13-17; Phil. 3:11, 20, 21; Rev. 20:4-6.

3. To take the saints to heaven where they will receive judgment for works done in the body; receive their rewards; and partake of the marriage supper, John 14:1-3; Col. 3:4; 1 Thess. 3:13; 2 Cor. 5:10; Rev. 19:1-11.

4. To change the bodies of saints to immortality, 1 Cor. 15:21-

23, 51-58; Phil. 3:20, 21.

5. To present the saints before God the Father, to be forever with Him, 1 Thess. 3:13; 4:13-17.

6. To make the saints "whole" in body, soul, and spirit, 1 Thess. 3:13; 5:23. The Greek word translated "unto" in 1 Thess. 5:23 should have been translated "at" to make the passage clear, as it is translated in 1 Thess. 2:19; 3:13.

7. To receive the fruit of the early and latter rain, Jas. 5:7.

8. To cause the saints to escape the tribulation and "all these things," and stand before the Son of man, Luke 21:34-36; 2 Thess. 2:7, 8; Rev. 4:1; 1 Thess. 5:9.

9. To remove the hinderer of lawlessness, 2 Thess. 2:1-8.

10. To permit the revelation of the Antichrist, 2 Thess. 2:1-8.

III. Qualifications for Partakers in the Rapture.

The **qualifications** for partakers in the rapture are also revealed in the above Scriptures. The one and only necessary requirement, whether dead or alive, is to be "in Christ," 1 Thess. 4:16, 17; 2 Cor. 5:17; 1 Cor. 15:23. This qualification is expressed in a ninefold way in Scriptures; one **must**

1. Be "Christ's," 1 Cor. 15:23; Gal. 5:24.
2. Be "in Christ," 1 Thess. 4:16, 17; 2 Cor. 5:17.
3. Be "blessed and holy," Rev. 20:4-6.
4. "Have done good," John 5:28, 29.
5. Be in "the way, the truth, and the life," John 14:1-6.
6. Be "worthy," Luke 21:34-36.
7. Be in "the church" or "body of Christ," Eph. 5:27; 1 Cor. 12:13. The body of Christ and the Church are the same, Eph. 1:22, 23; Col. 1:18, 24.
8. Purify "himself, even as he is pure," 1 John 3:2, 3; 2 Cor. 7:1; Gal. 5:16-24; Heb. 12:14.
9. Be without "spot or wrinkle . . . and without blemish," Eph. 5:27.

If one has met these scriptural qualifications, what could he do more? This implies that a person going up in the rapture is walking "in the light as he is in the light," 1 John 1:7; 2:6, 9-11; 3:8-10; 5:4, 18. Being "in Christ" means that one is a "new creature: old things are passed away; behold, all things are become new. And all things are of God, who hath reconciled us to himself by Jesus Christ," 2 Cor. 5:17, 18. Again, "They that are Christ's have crucified the flesh (of Gal. 5:19-21) with the affections and lusts," Gal. 5:24. What more qualification could God require? It will be noticed that these nine points on qualifications are quoted from Scriptures definitely dealing with the rapture of the Church. If there were other, or more definite and important qualifications, they would have been stated in the passages on the rapture in the place of these that are given. We conclude that it is not receiving other experiences, whatever they may be, or however scriptural they may be, that qualifies one to go up in the rapture, but it is the maintenance of a holy walk in "Christ" at the time of the rapture or at the time of death as the case may be.

Why should some be protected and others have to go through the tribulation and be martyred? This is easily answered when we consider that at the rapture every one in Christ is taken up and there are no real Christians left. Those who are martyred in the tribulation are those who have refused to walk in the light and live "in Christ" and are not ready to go at the time of the rapture, else they would go as well as all others in Christ. They are saved after the rapture, having realized by then their mistake of not heeding the many warnings to be ready at any time. They will become determined to be faithful even unto death, which will be their only prospect of having a part in the first resurrection. Those who are not martyred but are taken through the tribulation and are on earth at the second coming of Christ will be permitted to enter the Millennium as an earthly people, who will make part of the subjects of Christ's kingdom over whom the raptured saints will reign forever.

IV. The Time of the Rapture.

The time of the rapture, like the second advent, is not definitely stated as to the day or hour, but we do know that it will take place before the tribulation and the revelation of the Antichrist, as will be proved in chapter seven.

V. The Signs of the Rapture.

We may say, and be entirely scriptural, that there are no signs of the rapture as there are of the second advent. None of the signs and prophecies stated in chapter thirty-nine on the subject of the second coming ever refer to the rapture. There never was a sign required to come to pass nor a prophecy to be fulfilled before the rapture. The rapture could have taken place any time in the past since the apostles, and can take place any time now, or the future, without a sign or prophecy being fulfilled. If there are certain things to be fulfilled before the rapture then we must look for those things to be fulfilled first instead of looking for the rapture. It is possible that some of the above signs and prophecies may come to pass before the rapture, but that remains to be seen. We do know by certain indications, that some of them are now beginning to be fulfilled, thus showing us that the second coming is very near; and if this is near, the rapture is nearer, for the rapture is at least seven years before the revelation, as we shall later note.

VI. The Lord's Comings are Practical Doctrines.

These doctrines of the Lord's comings (the rapture and second advent) are two of the most practical and fruitful ones in Scripture. They are real incentives to holiness (1 John 3:1-3); profitable in exhorting to watchfulness and faithfulness (Matt. 24, 25; 1 John 2:28); patience (Jas. 5:7, 8); death to self (Col. 3:3-5); endurance (1 Pet. 1:7; 4:13); holy conversation and godliness (2

Pet. 3:11-13); soberness and righteousness (Tit. 2:11-13); consolation (1 Thess. 4:13-18); blamelessness (1 Cor. 1:4-8); pastoral diligence and purity (1 Pet. 5:1-4); sincerity (Phil. 1:9, 10); mildness (Phil. 4:5, 6); and hope (1 Cor. 15). The rapture will be to the saints the beginning of eternal and ever increasing joy and glory. The second coming will be to Israel and all righteous earthly nations the beginning of eternal and ever increasing blessing and favor.

Before considering many proofs that the rapture of the church takes place before the fulfillment of any event as revealed in Rev. 4-22, let us emphasize again the importance of the threfold division of the book of Revelation as stated by Jesus Christ, Himself.

If "THESE THINGS" of Rev. 4-22 must be "AFTER THESE THINGS" of Rev. 1-3 which concern the churches, then "THESE THINGS" must be AFTER the churches. Therefore any interpretation which mixes the"THINGS" of the churches with the "THINGS" which must be AFTER the churches is false and in direct contradiction to the Lord's statement and teaching of a threefold division of the Revelation in 1:19; 4:1.

Thus, it is erroneous for instance, to place the historical birth and ascension of Jesus Christ in the 12th chapter of Revelation, identifying Him as the manchild when the manchild and all that is related thereto are among the "THINGS" which must be after the churches. For the same reason it is wrong to say that any seal, trumpet, or vial of the book has been fulfilled, or that the 144,000 are Seventh Day Adventists, Jehovah's Witnesses, or some other religious group.

We must therefore always keep in mind that the fulfillment of all these "THINGS WHICH MUST BE HEREAFTER" including the "THINGS" concerning the two witnesses, the beasts, the mark of the beast, the great whore, and numerous other things will be AFTER the churches. And, any teaching which violates this fact in any degree will lead to a wrong understanding of the Revelation.

Chapter Seven

REASONS FOR THE RAPTURE OF THE CHURCH IN REV. 4:1

We believe that the Church and the Old Testament saints are to be raptured in fulfillment of the book in Rev. 4:1, that this is foreshadowed by the bodily ascension of John to heaven, and that those raptured are represented in heaven by the twenty-four elders throughout the remainder of Revelation. All the prophecies, especially of "the things which shall be hereafter" the Church Age, as in the third division, were to take place in the future from John's day, but were seen in vision and acted out before John and with him, as though they were already being fulfilled. We must clearly distinguish between the reception of the Revelation at the time of John and the actual fulfillment of the "things" therein from John's day to the New Heavens and the New Earth. In John's bodily ascension to heaven at this juncture of the **reception** of the Revelation we have a prophetical foreview of the rapture of the Church which is to take place at this juncture of the **fulfillment** of the Revelation. **We give as proof the following:**

1. There is a **marked change in God's attitude** toward humanity in general, from that of mercy (Rev. 1-3) to that of judgment, Rev. 6-19. Rev. 4-5 pictures the raptured Church and Old Testament saints with God in heaven before the tribulation. We know that from the inauguration of the Church until its rapture is a period of extended mercy and leniency without judgments from heaven, but from the rapture until and including the second advent of Christ, judgments are predominant. The seals and the first six trumpets (6:1-9:21) take place in the first three and one-half years of the Week, or the lesser tribulation. The sixth seal and the whole seven trumpets reveal terrible judgments on earth **from heaven** as do the seven vials during the last three and one-half years of the Week, or great tribulation. The infernal designs of Antichrist inspired by the dragon and the satanic prince out of the abyss (11:7; 17:8) constitute this latter tribulation which calls forth the vial judgments of God. The evil designs of the whore and the ten kings of Revised Rome, before the Antichrist gains control of the ten kings and destroys the whore (17:12-17), cause the former tribulation which calls forth the judgments of God in the sixth seal and seven trumpets. The judgments themselves in either part of the Week do not make the tribulation. They are sent because of the tribulation.

Scarcely anyone admits that the Church will undergo the tribulation. Some who believe that the Church is not caught up until the middle of the Week make the mistake of placing the seals and trumpets in the last three and one-half years, in order to correspond with their conviction that the Church is not here during their fulfillment.

It is true that the Church will not undergo these judgments, but to place them in the last three and one-half years or take them out of their proper setting, in order to prove that the Church escapes them, is out of harmony with the plain consecutive order of the Revelation. It is a fact that the Church will not undergo these judgments, but it is also a fact that these judgments happen in the order in which they are given from the beginning to the middle of the Week when the seventh trumpet blows and the manchild is caught up. These things prove that the Church will be raptured in Rev. 4:1 before the beginning of the Week and not in Rev. 12:5, as the manchild, in the middle of the Week. If this is true then the manchild is not a symbol of the Church. It seems somewhat inconsistent to take these events out of their proper place in the first three and one-half years and put them in the last three and one-half years of the Week when that is not the order in which they are given.

It is generally admitted that the events of chapters 11:15-13: 18 will take place in the middle of the Week, and it is also admitted that the seventh trumpet will blow in the middle of the Week. If this is understandable then why is not the fact that the seven seals and the first six trumpets take place before the seventh trumpet in the middle of the Week, understandable also? Did not God give them in logical order as He said He was going to do? (1:1, 19; 4:1). If the seven seals and the first six trumpets are to take place after the seventh trumpet, and the seventh trumpet is to be fulfilled in the middle of the Week then the seventh trumpet will not be the seventh trumpet at all, but will become the first. The fact that the seals and the trumpets reveal terrible conditions on the earth and judgments of God from heaven on men during the first three and one-half years, proves that there is tribulation during that time. If the Church does not go through these things or any part of the tribulation then she must be raptured before they start at the beginning of the Week in Rev. 4:1. We conclude, therefore, that Rev. 4-5 pictures the raptured saints with God, represented by the elders and that Rev. 6-19 pictures the whole of Daniel's Seventieth Week.

2. If the **natural divisions of the book** are to be taken as clearly stated in Rev. 1:19; 4:1 there can be no alternative, but that the rapture takes place in Rev. 4:1. Why then should we place the rapture in chapter 12? If the expression "the things which must be hereafter," i. e., after the churches, is literal and applies to Rev. 4:1 where it is given, then it cannot apply to the middle of the Week in Rev. 12:5. If the third division of the book is from the middle of the Week on, why is it given in the beginning of the Week?

3. Never are **the words "church" or "churches"** mentioned in the book after Rev. 3:22 except in the conclusion after the revelation of the "things which must be after the churches," Rev. 22:6-21. If the Church were to be on earth during the Week, it surely would have been mentioned in some connection. The words are used nineteen times in Rev. 1-3. Why the con-

tinued use in these chapters and not once afterwards if the Church is to be still on the earth?

4. **The enthroned elders** are representative of the raptured saints and they are always seen in heaven after Rev. 4:1, as is seen in chapter nine, point 3.

5. There can be **no Scripture** produced to show that the Church is on earth during any part of the Week.

6. An individual is recognized and identified by his features and characteristics. A body of individuals is also identified by its peculiarities. So in this case, **if the Church is to be seen on earth during the fulfillment of Rev. 4-19 we must see her earmarks. But such are not to be found. On the other hand, evidence of Israel is seen everywhere in the book after Rev. 4:1,** a fact more striking, since Israel is not mentioned at all in Rev. 1-3. This shows that the two different institutions are dealt with in different parts of the book; first, the Church to the time of its rapture, Rev. 1-3; secondly, Israel after the rapture of the Church to the second coming of Christ, Rev. 6-19. The book is written in Greek but its thoughts and idioms are Hebrew. This links it with the Old Testament and shows that its great purpose is to declare God's final dealings with the Jews. **The Hebrew character of the book after Rev. 3 is seen as follows:**

(1) In Matthew, the Hebrew Gospel, there are about ninety-two quotations from, and references to the Old Testament. In the epistle to the Hebrews there are 102. In the Revelation there are about 285. This emphatically gives the book a close relationship to the Old Testament and Israel.

(2) The word "Lamb" is used of Christ twenty-seven times after chapters 1-3, but not once in this section relating to the churches. It is never used in the Pauline Epistles to the churches. Outside of Revelation it is used only in John 1:29, 36; Acts 8:32; 1 Peter 1:19 and always in connection with the Messiah of Israel, and as the antitype of all the Jewish sacrifices.

(3) "The Lion of the tribe of Judah" and "the Root of David" (5:5) show the same Jewish connection as the Lamb above.

(4) The 144,000 of Rev. 7:1-8; 14:1-5 are Jewish.

(5) The events of the seals, trumpets, and vials will be a partial repetition of the plagues upon Egypt and for the same purpose, that of judging the nations for their treatment of Israel. They are to be the fulfillment of scores of prophecies concerning Israel and her enemies in the latter days. No prophecies of such plagues were ever stated to fall upon mankind for their treatment of the Church or Gentile Christians. (See point 1 on preceding page.)

(6) The tribulation will primarily concern Israel, and, as it will last throughout Rev. 6-19, Israel is the one dealt with in these chapters. (See chapter five, point II.)

(7) Daniel's Seventieth Week will include the fulfillment of everything in Rev. 6-19, after the rapture of the Church. The

Seventieth Week will concern Israel as did the first sixty-nine Weeks. The Church Age, as is generally admitted, comes in between the sixty-ninth and seventieth Weeks and not between the sixty-ninth and the last half of the Seventieth Week. It seems preposterous to believe that the Church Age is parenthetical and due to come in **between** the sixty-ninth and seventieth Weeks and at the same time believe that the Church will be raptured in the middle of the Seventieth Week. Both cannot be true. Can it not be seen that God pursues the same policy in the Seventieth Week, that of dealing with the Jews as He did in the first sixty-nine Weeks, since all seventy of the Weeks were determined upon Israel? Is it not clear also that this excludes the Church from being the woman or manchild? (See chapter five.)

(8) The "great multitude" of Rev. 7:9-17; 15:2-4 and the 144,000 of Rev. 7:1-8; 14:1-5 are the only companies of redeemed seen on earth during the whole of Rev. 6-19. It is clear that they are not the Church, and, since the Church is not seen except as represented by the elders in heaven, it is sure to be raptured before the fulfillment of these chapters.

(9) The ministry of the angel around the altar (8:2-5) and "the horns of the altar" (used twenty-six times in the Old Testament and not in any church epistle) are familiar only to Israel.

(10) "The mystery of God" (10:7), promised by the old prophets, is Jewish, for the things concerning "the days of the seventh trumpet" reveal only things concerning Israel as seen in chapters 11-13. Such a mystery to the Church was never spoken of, for the prophets did not see the Church.

(11) The temple, altar, temple worship, court of the temple, Holy City, olive trees, ark of the covenant, etc., of chapter 11, are all Jewish, as seen in chapter fourteen.

(12) When "The kingdoms of this world" (11:15) become the possession of God and Christ, the fulfillment of Jewish prophecies of national restoration will be made. All prophecies reveal the kingdom as being Jewish with its capital at Jerusalem. (See chapter forty-one.)

(13) The woman and the manchild are Jewish, as will be proved in chapters sixteen through eighteen.

(14) The dragon and beast (chapters 12, 13, 17) are not fitting symbols in connection with the Church, since she has not existed, as has Israel, throughout the length of the seven world empires represented by the seven heads. Such symbols have always been in connection with Israel, as we shall see in chapters sixteen through thirty-five.

(15) Michael (12:7) always stands for Israel (Dan. 10:13-21; 12:1-9) and is never mentioned in connection with the Church.

(16) The remnant (12:17) is Jewish. The Church or any part of the Church is never spoken of as a remnant, as in the case with Israel, as seen in chapter 19, point III.

(17) Literal Babylon (chapter 18) is spoken of as having a latter-day relationship with Israel, but it is never mentioned relative to the Church. (See chapter thirty-seven.)

(18) The Battle of Armageddon and the second advent (14:14-20; 19:11-21) are not for the deliverance of the Church but of Israel, as seen in chapter thirty-nine.

(19) The Millennium, the New Earth and many other things of Rev. 20-22 too numerous and detailed to mention here, will be fulfilled in accordance with scores of Jewish prophecies in the Old Testament. Other people are not to be excluded, but Israel is to be the head of all peoples forever. We believe, therefore, that the Church is raptured in Rev. 4:1 before all these things concerning Israel come to pass.

7. There is **no other place in Revelation for the rapture** of the Church and the Old Testament saints than in Rev. 4:1. The manchild is the only company of saints raptured from the beginning to the middle of the Week, and that company is not the Church, as we shall see. The only other company of saints which is to be caught up during the Week is that of the great multitude which will be martyred during the Week. That could never be the Church. Therefore, the Church is either caught up in Rev. 4:1 or is never seen in the Revelation as to its rapture. If it were to be caught up during the Week surely it would have been mentioned in some connection in chapters 6-19 which deal with this Week.

8. **In Luke 21:34-36 we have the promise of Jesus** that some will be "accounted worthy to escape **all** these things (pictured in Matt. 24:4-26; Luke 21:5-19) that shall come to pass, and to stand before the Son of man." Who can be these worthy ones referred to, if not the living saints who are on earth just before these things are about to come to pass? The 144,000 Jews and the great multitude cannot be the ones referred to, for they are saved and raptured after the rapture of the Church, as proved later. If the living believers who are on earth just before these things transpire are to go through them and undergo the judgments of the Seventieth Week this is a false hope.

9. **In 2 Thess. 2:6-8 we have conclusive proof** that the Church will be raptured preceding the Week and before the revelation of the Antichrist at the beginning of the Week. "And now **ye know what withholdeth** that he might be revealed **in his time . . .** only he who now letteth (hindereth, Isa. 43:13; Rom. 1:13), will let (hinder) until he be **taken out of the way.** And **then** shall that wicked be revealed" and not before.

What besides governments, the Church, and the Holy Spirit is hindering the powers of darkness from having full sway, thus preventing the revelation of the Antichrist? There is nothing, so this hindrance must be one of these. Governments will be more in evidence during the coming strict reign of Antichrist than now, yet it will not hinder the revelation of Antichrist. The

Spirit will not be withdrawn during the tribulation and after the rapture as is shown in Joel 2:28-32; Acts 2:17-21; Zech. 12:10; John 14:16; Rev. 7:9-17; etc. (Note the tribulation setting and context of these passages.) Rev. 7:9-17 proves that multitudes will be saved during the tribulation, and we maintain that no man ever has been or will be saved except through the ministry of the Holy Spirit. John 3:5-8; 16:7-11; Rom. 8:9; Eph. 2:18; 1 Cor. 6:11; Tit. 3:5; etc. Acts 2:16-21 proves an outpouring of the Spirit during the tribulation. Since governments and the Holy Spirit remain here during the tribulation, it follows by the logic of elimination that the Church is the hindrance referred to. That hindrance will be withdrawn for the simple reason that the Church, including every person born of the Spirit, is raptured. Then the Antichrist will be revealed.

The tribulation on earth will not affect the Spirit, so why should He go and leave the saints here who will be in desperate need of Him? How could they withstand these things and how could others be saved? After the rapture of all true believers, the Spirit who remains will save multitudes but He will not hinder the powers of darkness from carrying out their purpose in the fulfillment of prophecy. The pronoun "he" in this passage can refer to the Church as well as the Spirit, for the Church is spoken of as a "man" in Eph. 2:15; 4:13. The Church can be called a "man" because it is the body of Christ, who is a man, 1 Cor. 12:12, 13, 27; Eph. 1:20-23; 2:14-22; 4:12-16; Col. 1:18-24; etc. Therefore, in view of the fact that the Holy Spirit is not taken out of the world, that the Church is called a "man" and can be referred to in the masculine gender, and since it has been proved that the Church will be raptured or taken out of the world, we conclude that "he who hindereth" and "is taken out of the way" is the Church and not the Holy Spirit.

It is clear from this passage that the Antichrist cannot possibly be revealed until after the Church is taken out of the way. Now comes the question of whether the Antichrist will be revealed at the beginning or at the middle of the Week. If it can be proved that he will be revealed at the beginning instead of the middle of the Week, then it can also be proved that the Church is raptured before the beginning and not in the middle of the Week as the manchild. **The following points prove that he is revealed at the beginning of the Week:**

(1) In Dan. 9:27 we have one indisputable argument that he is revealed at the beginning of the Week, for he makes a covenant for **seven** years with Israel and not for three and one-half years. The breaking of the covenant in the middle of the Week is not a revelation of him on the scene of action, but an unfolding of what he is to do in the middle of the Week, three and one-half years after his revelation. This passage gives the only scriptural marks by which we may know who the Antichrist is and when he is revealed.

(2)   The white horse rider of Rev. 6:1, 2; the "little horn" of Dan. 7:8-11, 20-26; 8:23-25; and the wilful "king" of Dan. 11:35-45 are identical and show the rise of the Antichrist out of the ten kingdoms of Revised Rome at the beginning of the Week and before the seals and trumpets of the first three and one-half years of the Week. He will conquer three of these ten kings and gain the others in the middle of the Week when he is seen under the seventh trumpet coming out of the sea with the ten kings under his control, Rev. 13:1-8.   Since the Church escapes the seals, trumpets, and vials and is taken before the revelation of the Antichrist, and as he is revealed at the beginning of the Week, the Church must be raptured before the beginning of the Week.

10.   If the Church is raptured in the middle of the Week there is a definite time set for the rapture and we need to quit looking for the rapture at any time and look for the events which mark the appearance of the Seventieth Week. If the Church goes through the terrible events of the seals and trumpets, then the promise of Jesus that the true believer shall "escape all these things" is contradicted and Paul's teaching that the Church is caught up before the revelation of the Antichrist is also contradicted, for Antichrist is here three and one-half years before the middle of the Week.   But once we understand that **the Church can be raptured any day and that there is no definite time set for** that event, then we can conscientiously teach others that they should be ready for the rapture at any and all times.

11.   **In 1 Thess. 5:1-11 we have another definite promise** assuring us that saints will escape the wrath which precedes the day of the Lord. "God hath not appointed us to wrath, but to obtain salvation (deliverance from this wrath) by our Lord Jesus Christ, who died for us, that, whether we wake or sleep, we should live together with him."   The second advent marks the beginning of the day of the Lord.

This wrath is revealed in Matt. 24, 25; Luke 21; Rev. 6:1-19:21 and is to be fulfilled during the Seventieth Week. If the saints escape this wrath the Church must be raptured before the Week or in Rev. 4:1.

12.   The **final reasons** for the rapture in Rev. 4:1 and before the Week are found in the following exposition of Matt. 24, 25.

Chapter Eight

EXPOSITION OF MATTHEW 24 AND 25

The following study will throw much light on the second advent, correct many errors concerning the rapture, and help in a better understanding of the end of the age and the fulfillment of Rev. 6-19 during the Seventieth Week. These chapters are among the most simple as to interpretation, and yet, unaccountably, are two of the most misunderstood and hopelessly mixed of any in the Bible. They picture a series of events that are in consecutive order as given. The occasion of this discourse was when the disciples showed Christ the beauties of the temple. Jesus then said, "There shall not be left one stone upon another that shall not be thrown down." **This brought forth three questions as follows:**

I. "Tell us when shall these things be?"

This question refers to the above statement of Jesus concerning the destruction of Jerusalem which was fulfilled in 70 A.D. by the Romans, Dan. 9:26; Luke 21:20-24. This question and answer are clear so we shall confine our remarks to the last two questions which are fully answered in Matt. 24, 25; Mark 13; Luke 21.

II. "What shall be the sign of thy coming?"

This question does not concern the rapture, but the second coming of Christ to earth with the saints. The disciples knew nothing of the rapture for that was reserved for Paul to reveal (1 Cor. 15:51-58) as we have seen in chapter six. They had often heard of the second coming, Matt. 18:1; 19:29; etc. This is further proved by Luke 21:29-33. This question is fully answered in Matt. 24:4-26, 37-39; Mark 13:5-23; Luke 21:8-19. These passages give the signs of Christ's coming that have to do with the answer to this question.

Signs of the Second Coming of Christ.

1. False Messiahs before the middle of the Week, or setting up of the abomination of desolation, Matt. 24:4, 5, 15; Mark 13:5, 6; Luke 21:8; Dan. 9:27.

2. Wars and rumors of wars, Matt. 24:6; Mark 13:7; Luke 21:9.

3. Nations against nations, Matt. 24:7; Mark 13:8; Luke 21:10.

4. Famines, pestilences and earthquakes, Matt. 24:7; Mark 13:8; Luke 21:11.

5. Persecution of the Jews by all nations, Matt. 24:9; Mark 13:9-11; Luke 21:12.

6. Many offences and betrayals, Matt. 24:10; Mark 13:12, 13; Luke 21:16.

7. False prophets before the middle of the Week, Matt. 24:11, 15; Dan. 9:27.

8. Iniquity abounding and love waxing cold, Matt. 24:12.

9. The gospel of the kingdom to be preached again as a witness to all nations, Matt. 24:13, 14.

10. The abomination of desolation set up, Matt. 24:15; Dan. 9:27; 12:7-11; Rev. 13:1-18; 14:9-11; 20:4-6.

11. Flight of Israel into the wilderness, Matt. 24:16-20; Mark 13:14-18; Isa. 16:1-5; Ezek. 20:33-35; Hos. 2:14-16; Psa. 60:8-10.

12. The great tribulation days, Matt. 24:21, 22; Mark 13:19, 20.

13. False Messiahs after the middle of the Week, Matt. 24:23-26; Mark 13:21, 22.

14. False prophets after the middle of the Week, Matt. 24:23-26; Mark 13:22.

15. Conditions of the days of Noah repeated, Matt. 24:37-39.

16. Fearful sights and distress on earth, Luke 21:11.

17. Great signs in the heavens, Luke 21:11; Acts 2:16-21.

All these signs and those of chapter thirty-nine, point 5, as well as many others, must take place before the second coming of Christ which the disciples had in mind. This proves that the coming asked about by the disciples was not the rapture, but the second advent. Therefore, we must understand Matt. 24 and 25 in view of the second coming and not the rapture. The first nine signs will be fulfilled down to the middle of the Week when the abomination of desolation will be set up, as stated in Matt. 24:15. The first four signs were given and then Jesus said, "All these are the beginning of sorrows." The word "sorrows" means "birth pangs" and refers to the agonies of Israel under the ten kings and the whore in the first three and one-half years of the Week. The "birth pangs" must continue until Israel comes to birth at the end of the Week. This means, then, that, from the first sign to the last, there is to be an increase of these sorrows. They are to last throughout the whole Week. Perhaps they will begin sometime before the Week, for Israel seems to be persecuted when Antichrist makes the covenant with her to protect her for seven years, Dan. 9:27. There are three questions that naturally rise at this juncture, in view of this method of exposition:

1. How do we know that Israel is the one primarily dealt with in these chapters instead of the Church or Christians? The reasons are:

(1) Jesus is speaking to the Jews and is answering a question which is purely Jewish, for it concerns their Messiah and His coming to deliver them from the oppression of the Gentiles, Matt. 25:34; Luke 21:12; 22:29; Acts 1:6.

(2) The deceptions by false Messiahs primarily concern Israel.

(3) The fifth sign of persecutions by all nations can be harmonized only with what is prophesied of Israel. This sign is connected to the time of the "birth pangs" of Israel by the connecting word "then," thus showing the time of its fulfillment to be the same as the time of sorrows.

(4) The sixth, seventh, eighth, and ninth signs are also connected to these days of "birth pangs" by connecting words, thus showing that all the first nine signs will be fulfilled between

the times of these sorrows and the end of the Week, Matt. 24:4-14.

(5)   The time of the fulfillment of all these things is during one generation at the end of this age, for those who suffer these things are blessed only upon the condition that they endure to the end of the age, Matt. 24:13.   How could some endure to the end of the age if they were not living at that time?   How could these things be endured by people at the end of the age, if these things were to be endured at any time throughout the age and not particularly at the end of it?   Who besides the Jews are to be dealt with in any such way at the end of the age?   The tribulation saints will be martyred, but they cannot be the reference here.   The Church saints will have been caught away so they cannot be the reference.   Christ is answering a Jewish question concerning the Jews and not concerning Gentile martyrs or Church saints.

(6)   "The gospel of the kingdom" is Jewish and is the good news that the kingdom of heaven is at hand, because of the nearness of the King of the Jews.   This gospel will be preached during the tribulation as "a witness to all nations"; and **then** shall the end come.

(7)   The abomination of desolation proves a Jewish connection, Matt. 24:15; Dan. 9:24-27.

(8)   The fleeing of the Jews in Judea proves a Jewish connection, Matt. 24:16-20; Isa. 16:1-5; Ezek. 20:23; Hos. 2:14; Psa. 60:8-10; Rev. 12:6-17; Dan. 11:41-45.

(9)   The "sabbath day" which would limit the flight of Jews from the Antichrist to a mile proves a Jewish connection, Matt. 24:20-22; Jer. 30:1-7; Dan. 12:1.

(10)   The great tribulation primarily concerns Israel, Matt. 24:21, 22; Jer. 30:1-7; Dan: 12:1.

(11)   The "elect" in 24:21-26 are Jews as proved in Matt. 24:31; Isa. 11:11.

(12)   The coming of Christ, referred to in the question, is to deliver Israel and fulfill all the prophecies of their restoration, Joel 3; Zech. 14:1-21; Rom. 11:24-29.

(13)   The judgment of the nations is based upon how they have treated the Jews or "brethren," Matt. 25:31-46.

(14)   In none of these passages could we insert the Church, for it is raptured before "all these things," Luke 21:34-36.   This passage is given as a promise of Jesus to believers after He has fully answered these questions, and therefore, has nothing to do with the answer to the questions.   It shows that some will escape all the things mentioned in the answers to these questions. Even if we believe that the Church is to be raptured in the middle of the Week, we could not insert the Church in Matt. 24:15-25:46, for the middle of the Week is mentioned in Matt. 24:15 and everything after that verse concerns things which happen after the middle of the Week.   This is proved by con-

necting words as "then," "for then," etc., used throughout these chapters after Matt. 24:15.

2. **Are these things fulfilled in one particular generation?** That they are fulfilled in one and the last generation in this age is clear from the following:

(1) "The days of Noah" refer to one generation only, Matt. 24:37-39; Gen. 7:1.

(2) That one generation only is referred to in these chapters is stated in Matt. 24:34, and clearly taught in the parable of the fig tree as we shall see below.

(3) Jesus plainly promised that some would escape "all these things" and such could not be true if they were being fulfilled throughout this age.

(4) Some will "endure to the end" and such could not be unless those who endure were not living at the end of the age.

(5) The abomination of desolation will be set up in the middle of the Week, or three and one-half years before the end of the age so the first nine signs immediately preceding this can easily be fulfilled in the same generation, Matt. 24:15.

3. **If these things are to be fulfilled during the last generation of this age what signs are there that are being fulfilled today to show us that we are near the second advent and can look for the rapture at any time?** The above signs are concerning a definite period just before the end of the age and after the rapture of the Church, as has been proved. If the Church is to escape "all these things" above, then all of them must be fulfilled after the rapture of the Church. There are sufficient indications in other passages to prove that the second advent is near and that we are in the last days. (See chapter thirty-nine, point 5, (4), (5), (9), and (12).

The answer to the question of the signs of Christ's coming to earth may be summed up thus: In Matt. 24:4-14 we have things that take place before the abomination. These and the things of Matt. 24:15-26 that take place after the abomination will continue to the end of the age when Christ will come as pictured in Matt. 24:27-31. At this coming the answer to the third question will be realized.

III. "And of the end of the age?"

This end of the age is the same "end" mentioned in Matt. 24:13, 14. It was a very familiar subject to the disciples, as also was His coming, for He had often spoken to them of both. See "the end of the age" and the second coming in Matt. 13:37-42, 49, 50; 22:13; 24:3; 25:31-46. This third question is fully answered in Matt. 24:27-25:46; Mark 13:24-37; Luke 21:24-33.

The Parable of the Fig Tree, Matt. 24:32, 33.

This parable is so commonly interpreted as applying to the Jewish nation and its restoration that people in general believe that this is the true meaning of the parable. A close study will reveal that this is not the thought at all. The restoration of Israel was not inquired of by the disciples, and therefore, could not be the subject illustrated by the parable. This is just a simple illustration of the proximity of Christ's coming which is the same subject as in Matt. 24:4-31. "Now learn a parable (illustration) of the fig tree (Luke adds, and all the trees, 21:29); when his branch is yet tender and putteth forth leaves **ye know** (What?) **that summer is nigh:** So likewise ye, when ye shall see **all these things** (all the above signs of Christ's coming) know that **it** (the second advent) is near, even at the doors." What could be more clear? We do not have to use this as the basis for the doctrine of the restoration of Israel. There are many plain passages which teach that. It is permissible to use this parable as an illustration of this truth or any other we may desire to illustrate with it, but never should we insist that it represents the Jews when there is no clue to indicate that. That all of Matt. 24:4-26 is fulfilled in one generation and that all the signs appear during a short period is further evident from the parable, for no tree puts forth leaves throughout the season.

This Generation—Which?

In Matt. 24:34 we have definitely stated that the particular generation seeing "all these things" shall not pass away "till (10:23; 16:28; 23:39) all these things be fulfilled." This phrase "be fulfilled" refers to the first sign as well as to the last. The phrase "this generation" is used sixteen times in the New Testament (11:16; 12:42; 23:36; 24:34; Luke 17:25; etc.) and has reference to one particular generation as is clear in each passage where it is used. It never has reference to a race of people, for all peoples are eternal as is proved in chapter forty-four. See also Matt. 12:39-45; 16:4; 17:17; Acts 2:40; etc., which speak of a particular generation that rejected the Messiah.

Prophetical Date-Setting—Foolish.

In Matt. 24:35 we have the infallibility of these truths stated. In Matt. 24:36 it is stated that no man will know the day nor the hour of the second advent. This is also expressed in Matt. 24:42, 44 and is the thought illustrated by the parables in Matt. 24:36-51; 25:1-30. In Matt. 24:37-39 we have an exhortation to watchfulness by a comparison of the days of Noah with those of the time when Christ shall come to earth. The coming of Christ, like the flood, will bring destruction and judgment to the world. The rapture will not bring destruction. It deals purely with the deliverance of saints. This further proves that the second advent is the coming which is dealt with in these chapters and not the rapture of the Church.

Rapture or Destruction—Which?

In Matt. 24:40-42 we have three verses which are the most misunderstood in the Bible by some because they interpret the passage as referring to the rapture instead of events at the time of the second coming of Christ. It is clear from the context that the rapture is not referred to. Again, we repeat, the rapture is not involved in the questions of the disciples. These verses are connected to the "coming of the Son of man" or the second advent by the word "then." "Then (at the second coming of Christ to earth with His saints) shall two be in the field; the one shall be taken, and the other left . . . Watch therefore; for ye know not what hour your Lord doth come."

Why should we take these verses out of their proper setting which is at the coming of Christ to earth **with** the saints, and make them refer to the coming of Christ in the air **for** the saints? We do not have to use this passage to prove that there will be a rapture. There are other proofs as suggested in chapters six through eight. So why base a doctrine upon a passage that does not concern the subject? If, then, these verses refer to the literal coming of Christ, what do they mean? Where are these persons taken? These questions are fully answered in the following passages which show that the gathering of these persons refers to the gathering of the nations, both men and women, to the Battle of Armageddon.

In Luke 17:34-37 we have a parallel passage to these verses which further proves that they refer to the coming of Christ to the earth, and not the rapture. The verses in Luke are the conclusion of a discourse (17:34-37) concerning "the day when the Son of man is revealed" when two shall be here, and two there, "the one shall be taken and the other left." This was a new teaching to the disciples, and they asked, "Where, Lord?" that is, where are they to be taken? The answer was, "Wheresoever the body is, thither will the eagles be gathered together." This answer in Matt. 24:28 is "For wheresoever the carcase is, there will the eagles be gathered together." Both Matthew and Luke connect the fulfillment to the coming of Christ to the earth and not the rapture.

The Greek for "carcase" is **ptoma,** meaning "a body fallen in death, a dead carcase." The Greek for "body" is **soma,** meaning a corpse. Both Matthew and Luke use the same Greek word **aetoi** for eagles meaning the natural eagles and birds of the heavens. Thus if these passages were dealing with the rapture we would have Christ pictured as a dead carcase or corpse and the saints pictured as living beings caught up to the carcase. This is beyond our conception. Neither Christ nor saints are pictured under such figures in the Bible. These verses refer to the Battle of Armageddon, when the angel will stand in the sun crying for the fowls of heaven to be gathered to eat the carcases of all men who have been slain by Christ and His armies, and who have previously been gathered to the battle— one from here and one from there, Rev. 19:11-21; Ezek. 39:17-21. This picture of eagles being gathered to the slain on the battle-field was a familiar one to the disciples. It is clearly described in Job 39:27-30.

This mobilization of the hosts to Armageddon where they will meet death and make the supper for the fowls and beasts is pictured in Joel 3:1-21; Zech. 14:1-21; Rev. 16:13-16; 19:11-21; etc. After this battle the carcases of the hosts will lie all over the mountains of Palestine (Ezek. 38:16; 39:2-5, 17-21) making the great feast as described in the above passages. "For wheresoever the carcase is (on the battlefield) there will the eagles be gathered together." This destruction is illustrated with and compared to the destruction at the time of the flood. Even as the flood came and "**took them all away** (destroyed them, Luke 17:27); so shall also the coming of the Son of man" bring "sudden destruction" upon His enemies, Matt. 24:39; 1 Thess. 5:1-11; 2 Thess. 1:7-10; Jude 14 and 15. Just as eight souls were not "taken" or destroyed by the flood so many will be spared from being taken away (destroyed) at the Battle of Armageddon. The "left" ones will replenish the earth in the Millennium like the "left" ones at the flood replenished the earth at that time, Zech. 14:16; Matt. 25:31-46. The coming of Christ to earth is pictured in Matt. 24:27-31 as being at the end of this age, while Matt. 24:32-25:46 may be considered as supplementary, in that it gives details of things which will take place at His coming, and sounds forth warnings of watchfulness and faithfulness in view of His coming. The passage in question (24:40-42) is in this supplementary portion and records the simple fact of the mobilization of mankind to Armageddon to fight against Christ. So, instead of teaching a gathering of the godly from the ungodly at the rapture, these verses picture a gathering from the nations of ungodly men and women, who will take their supposedly triumphant, but disastrous stand against Christ at His coming with the saints. At the rapture you want to be the "taken" one, but at the second advent you want to be the "left" one.

In Matt. 24:43-51 we have two more parables, that of the goodman of the house and that of the slothful servant. Thus we have three parables in Matt. 24. The parable of the fig-tree illustrates the nearness of Christ's coming, the parable of the goodman of the house, preparedness; and the parable of the slothful servant, faithfulness in view of His coming.

The Parable of the Ten Virgins, Matt. 25:1-13.

From the statements above on Matt. 24 and 25 it can be seen that the events occur one after the other in logical order and that they are connected by the use of such words as "then," "for then," etc. The parable of the ten virgins is a continuation of the answer to the third question asked by the disciples, and is connected to the subject of the "coming of the Son of man" or the second coming of Christ to earth by another connecting word "then." Such connecting words certainly were inspired as much as all other words and perhaps were given to counteract the danger of our getting these events confused with other things of similar nature. The point illustrated by this parable then, is relative to the second advent and not the rapture.

In taking it to refer to the second advent, as the connecting word proves and as a study of both chapters reveal, the parable has a different setting than that which is commonly understood. "Then (When? At the time of Christ's literal advent to earth, as all of chapter 24 makes clear) shall **the kingdom of heaven be likened** unto ten virgins." The whole truth illustrated by the parable is watchfulness as in Matt. 25:13. "Watch therefore, for ye know neither the day nor the hour wherein the Son of man cometh." Since this is the truth Jesus is illustrating by this oriental wedding ceremony, then there is no other one definitely outlined by Him here. Why, then, should we base various doctrines upon this illustration?

A parable is merely a simple illustration of some moral or spiritual truth, and the details are not to be stressed unduly. They are necessary for the completion of the story used as the illustration of a truth, but there is no need for giving to them mystical and hidden meanings. So many unwise and unscriptural doctrines are founded upon this parable that it is advisable to notice from this example the inconsistency of basing any doctrine upon the details of any parable in total disregard of literal passages which deal with the doctrine in question.

It is almost universally believed that the oil in the parable of the ten virgins, symbolizes the Holy Spirit and that the virgins symbolize different classes of Christians or people in Christendom. Some insist that the wise are those who have received the baptism of the Holy Spirit and that the foolish are those who have not. Thus, it is implied that both the foolish and wise have salvation (lamps), but only the wise have the Holy Spirit (oil). Others go further to insist that only those who have the baptism of the Spirit will be caught up in the rapture and that Christians in general who have not had that experience, will be left here to go through the tribulation. Still others say that anyone is not saved without the baptism of the Spirit, for only those who are baptized in the Spirit are in the body of Christ, as supposedly suggested in 1 Cor. 12:12, 13. (For this theory see chapter seventeen, point IV.)

Many preach these things as an incentive for seeking the experience of the baptism of the Spirit, but regardless of the ultimate aim of such a message, it may be stated here that in the light of other plain Scriptures these doctrines are erroneous. This type of teaching seems to be disastrous from two viewpoints: first, it arbitrarily condemns many earnest-hearted and devout Christians who have not yet received light on the subject as taught by this school, and suggests that others who have had light are not living clean lives because they have not yet received the baptism of the Spirit; secondly, it automatically sets up a standard of cleansing, other than the blood-washed way, and ultimately advances qualifications for the rapture and entrance into the body of Christ which are not taught in plain passages of Scripture on the subject.

These interpretations break down at every point when considered in the light of the details of the parable as well as in the light of other plain Scriptures. The lamps cannot symbolize salvation, profession or anything of that nature as is proved by the usage of the word in Exod. 27:20; 1 Sam. 3:3; 2 Sam. 22:29; Ps. 119: 105; Prov. 13:9; 20:20; Rev. 4:5; 8:10; etc. In these passages the word "lamp" is used to symbolize the Word of God and the completeness of the Holy Spirit, but never salvation or the body of man. The word "oil" has no more reference to the Spirit here than in Gen. 28:18; Prov. 5:3; Jer. 41:8; Hos. 12:1; Mic. 6:7; Luke 7:46; 16:6; etc. For the Biblical usage of the word "foolish" see Matt. 7:24-29; Luke 12:16-22.

How could people, saved and filled with the Spirit, be in such lethargy as are these ten virgins, both foolish and wise? The Lord says to such, "I will spue thee out of my mouth," Rev. 3:16; Rom. 13:11; 1 Cor. 15:34; Eph. 5:14. Let it be noticed further, that at the time of the rapture people will have no time to rise and trim their lamps (salvation) as did these virgins, for the rapture is to take place "in the twinkling of an eye," 1 Cor. 15:51-58. If anyone after the rapture becomes sufficiently worthy to receive the baptism of the Spirit (oil) would Christ be likely to say to him, "I know you not" as was said to the five foolish virgins who finally came back with oil? Thus, it is evident that an attempt at a detailed meaning of this simple illustration is out of harmony with the doctrines of the Bible. Let us bear in mind that any attempt of basing doctrines upon the details of parables should be avoided inasmuch as the truth illustrated by a parable is clearly stated in the parable itself.

In **Bible Lands** by Henry J. Van Lennep, pages 548-52 will be found a description of an oriental wedding ceremony, which is parallel to the one used by Christ to illustrate the necessity of watchfulness in view of His second coming. It might be worth while to mention here that in oriental weddings, the bride was always attended by a number of virgins. In the illustration of Matt. 25 the ten virgins were, beyond doubt, not the bride, but the attendants of the bride. Just as these virgins should have been ready to carry out their part of the wedding ceremony, so Jesus warns the people in the kingdom of heaven after the rapture to be ready for His coming to earth, if they expect to be rewarded, Matt. 13:40-43; 24:42-51; 25:14-46. Who the bride and groom, or the virgins were, is not stated but they were people who lived in the days of Christ and which He used to illustrate "watchfulness" in view of His second advent, and this is all the lesson we should take from the story of this ancient wedding.

In Matt. 25:14-30 we have the last parable in these chapters which shows the judgment of the people in the kingdom of heaven for the quality of service rendered. It refers to the same time as the above parable. Following this fifth and last parable we have the judgment of the nations, showing how Christ is to judge the people of the kingdom of heaven (as mentioned in the above parables), 25:31-46. Notice the result of judgment in all the above passages.

Thus the two questions concerning signs of His coming and what will take place at the end of the age when He comes, are fully answered so as to prove that the Church will be raptured before "all these things." That means, as has been previously stated, that the rapture takes place in Rev. 4:1.

We shall now begin a study of the last division of the book, "THE THINGS WHICH MUST BE HEREAFTER," that is, after the churches, Rev. 4-22. We leave the Church age, for not one thing is said of the Church in the remaining part of the book until the Revelation is completed and some parting words of admonition are given to the Church, Rev. 22:6-21. The Church will have been raptured and will be in heaven during the fulfillment of all of Rev. 4:1-19:10, coming back as part of the armies of heaven of Rev. 19:11-21 who will be returning to the earth to reign for ever, Rev. 20:1-22:5.

In this last division of the book we have scenes in heaven and events on earth during the final seven years of this age — Daniel's Seventieth Week — happenings between the rapture of the Church and the second coming of Jesus Christ back to the earth with the Church to reign for ever, Rev. 6:1-22:5.

Not one detail of Rev. 4:1-19:21 that concerns any event on earth has been fulfilled as yet, but all will be fulfilled after the rapture and before and at the second coming of Christ. Rev. 20 reveals a thousand years' reign of Christ on the earth to put all enemies under His feet and bring an end to rebellion, Rev. 20:1-10; Eph. 1:10; 1 Cor. 15:24-28. Rev. 21:1-22:5 reveals the eternal reign of God, Christ, and the saints on earth after all rebellion has been put down.

If one will take all these events as being literal and in consecutive order as to fulfillment, there will be no mystery about the book of Revelation, and it will not be hard to understand. We warn you, however, that if you do not keep in mind that every detail of Rev. 4-22 is to be fulfilled AFTER the churches — after the rapture of the church — you will immediately become confused regarding the fulfillment of "THESE THINGS WHICH MUST BE HEREAFTER" the churches.

Part III.
"THE THINGS WHICH SHALL BE HEREAFTER,"
Rev. 4:1-22:5.

Chapter Nine
THE HEAVENLY TABERNACLE, Rev. 4:1-5:14

In these chapters we have almost a complete picture of the heavenly tabernacle after which the earthly tabernacle was patterned, Heb. 8:1-5; 9:1-10, 22-24; 10:1. See and compare the illustrations of the earthly and heavenly tabernacles on the chart. **The following nine points sum up the truths herein.**

1. The Heavenly Door.

"After this I looked, and, behold, a door was opened in heaven: and the first voice which I heard was as it were of a trumpet talking with me; which said, Come up hither, and I will shew thee things which must be hereafter," Rev. 4:1.

The first two words, "after this," are from the Greek phrase **meta touta** which means "after these things." It occurs in the following passages in the book and is translated thus: 1:19, "hereafter"; 4:1 (twice), "after this" and "hereafter"; 7:1, "after these things"; 7:9, "after this"; 18:1, "after these things"; 19:1, "after these things"; and 20:3, "after that." **Meta** with the accusative case always means "after" in connection with time as is clear in these passages and also in many others outside of this book; e.g., Matt. 17:1; 26:32; John 13:7. Rev. 4:1 literally means "after these things (the things which concern the churches) I looked . . . and the first voice . . . said, Come up hither, and I will shew thee things which **must be** after these things," that is, after the churches.

This emphasizes the third and last natural division of the book which includes "things" which "must be" after the rapture of the Church. These three divisions do not overlap, nor are they concurrent. One division is completely finished before the other begins. "After this," that is, after seeing Christ in the midst of the candlesticks and His foreview of the history of Christendom until the rapture of the Church, John looked and saw a door already opened in heaven. He saw the door to the heavenly tabernacle, which was the pattern for the door to the earthly tabernacle, Heb. 8:5; 9:23, 24.

It is not unreasonable to believe that this door is literal as plainly pictured here and in Rev. 11:19; 14:15-18; 15:5-8; 16:1, 17. There is no such thing as a spiritual door. The word "heaven" is used fifty-two times in Revelation and always is singular except in Rev. 12:12. There is no indication that heaven is spiritual and if it is literal then the door must also be literal.

The same silver-toned voice as of a trumpet that spoke to John in the first division (1:10) spoke to him here and said, "Come up hither, and I will shew thee things which **must be hereafter.**" John doubtless was caught up to heaven **bodily** as were Enoch (Gen. 5:21-24; Heb. 11:5), Elijah (2 Kings 2), and probably Paul (2 Cor. 12:1-10). The term "Come up hither" is used only once more in the book and then it is of the bodily ascension of the two witnesses to heaven, Rev. 11:12.

2. The Heavenly Throne.

"And immediately I was in the Spirit: and, behold, a throne was set in heaven, and one sat on the throne. And he that sat was to look upon like a jasper and a sardine stone: and there was a rainbow around about the throne, in sight like unto an emerald ... And out of the throne proceeded lightnings and thunderings and voices: and there were seven lamps of fire burning before the throne, which are the seven Spirits of God," Rev. 4:2, 3,5.

The first thing John saw in heaven was the throne of God, the Father, who was to look upon "like a jasper and a sardine stone." The jasper stone according to Pliny is semi-transparent. In Rev. 21:11 the light of the New Jerusalem is said to appear "like unto a stone most precious, even like a jasper stone, clear as crystal." The sardine stone is one of red color. John saw a rainbow circling the throne which was green in color like an emerald. Cf. 10:1; Gen. 9:13; Ezek. 1:28. This throne is the center of all the activity of the book. It is the one seen throughout the book down to 21:22-22:5 where it is associated with the throne of the Lamb. It is literal as much as the door is literal. The same things that prove one is literal will prove that the other is also literal. Some cannot conceive of God sitting on a real throne, but there is no such thing as a spiritual throne. We have no ground at all for making these scenes symbolical or unreal, and not as they were actually seen by John. Our misconception of things cannot disprove their existence.

If saints without their bodies can be clothed and exist in spirit form and be confined to a literal place and if spirits can be confined to literal places as tartarus (2 Pet. 2:4; Jude 6, 7), hades (Luke 16:19-31; Rev. 20:11-15), the altar in heaven (Rev. 6:9-11), the abyss (Rev. 9:1-21; 20:1-3), etc., it seems also reasonable and certainly comprehensible that God as Spirit could sit on a literal throne as He is seen doing many times, Isa. 6:1; John 5:37; Acts 7:55; etc. If God could create literal thrones, heavens, planets, etc., it seems He should be able to sit on or in any of them He desires. The revelation of God in this book disproves the idea that men will never see the Father face to face. John saw Him several times in these visions and it is expressly stated that men shall "see his face" in the New Earth, Rev. 21:3; 22:4.

The word "throne" is used 173 times in both Testaments and generally always of a literal throne. It is used over forty times in Revelation and always of a literal throne as is clear in the passages themselves. The plain statements concerning the throne in this book prove it to be more than mere sovereignty or power; e.g., Rev. 3:21; 22:1-5. In Rev. 4:5 lightnings, thunderings, and voices proceed from the throne and seven "lamps of fire" burn before the throne, which symbolize the Holy Spirit. (See "The Salutation," chapter two.)

3. The Heavenly Elders.

"And round about the throne were four and twenty seats (thrones): and upon the seats I saw four and twenty elders sitting, clothed in white raiment; and they had on their heads crowns of gold," Rev. 4:4.

There are twenty-four elders who occupy twenty-four literal

thrones, and not ordinary seats, as translated in this verse. The same Greek word is translated "throne" in Rev. 4:2 and "seats" in Rev. 4:4. This may be due to the fact that the translators thought God's throne was not the same in substance as these twenty-four thrones. If one of these twenty-five thrones is literal all must be. The position of these elders is "around" the throne of God. Cf. Dan. 7:9-10.

The question as to whom the elders are is very important and must be understood in order to make clear some of the Revelation. We advance the following points to prove that they are redeemed men and representatives of the raptured and glorified saints.

(1) They are crowned with crowns of gold and sit on thrones. God, Christ, and men are the only beings in Scripture who are seen sitting on thrones or are promised thrones in heaven before God. Christ is the only one seen in this book wearing a crown (14:14; 19:12) besides these elders (4:4, 10). Angels are never seen either on thrones, or wearing crowns. They are not promised such in the book. Men are promised both, not only in this book but elsewhere, if they overcome, Rev. 2:10; 3:21; 20:4; Matt. 19: 28; 1 Cor. 9:25-27; 2 Tim. 4:8. Since the third division concerns "things" yet future, after the rapture, it would seem that these elders are raptured before this time in the fulfillment of these "things" and are seen in heaven enjoying the rewards promised to saints who overcome. Angels are mentioned only two times in the whole Bible in connection with thrones, Isa. 14:13; Col. 1:15.

(2) "White raiment" in Revelation is never used of angels, but always of Christ and His saints, Rev. 3:5, 18; 6:11; 7:9, 13; 15:6; 19:8, 14.

(3) Angels are seen many times in the book, but they are always distinguished from men and their identity is always clear. Because these elders are not clearly revealed as being angels the natural understanding of them would be that they are men.

(4) References to the earth and to nations are in their speeches which seem to connect them with the earth and man, Rev. 4:9-11; 5:8-10; 7:13, 14; 11:16-19.

(5) They are distinguished from angels as much as the four living creatures are, so they must be men, Rev. 5:11-14.

(6) The word "elder" is never applied to angels or any other being except man. In the majority of the 152 places in the Old Testament where the word is used it means the representative head of a family, city, tribe, or nation, so, no doubt, here these twenty-four elders serve as representatives of redeemed saints. The Greek **presbuteros** translated "elders" here is used sixty-six times in the New Testament, twelve times in this book, and always it means older, senior, or presbyter as applied to men. Angels do not grow older or become seniors as do men, hence these elders must be men.

(7) One unanswerable argument to the effect that they are redeemed men is found in Rev. 22:8, 9 where it is clear that the

angel that shows John the Revelation (1:1) was not a common angel, but one of the prophets, perhaps one of the Old Testament prophets, who, as one of the elders, talked with John and showed him several things in the book, Rev. 5:5-7; 7:13-15. So if this particular elder, the angel of Rev. 1:1; 22:8, 9 is a man, the others must be. (See also chapter twenty-four, point I.)

(8) That they are themselves redeemed men is the most natural and logical understanding of them for this view harmonizes with all other passages concerning the elders as will be proved as we proceed.

If they are redeemed men, representative of the raptured and glorified saints, who are carrying out a part of the fulfillment of these things after they have been raptured, of **what company or companies are they representatives?** Before this question can be fully answered we must clearly distinguish between the different companies of redeemed. **There are four different companies of redeemed saved at different periods from Adam to the end of the first resurrection:**

(1) **The Old Testament saints.** John the Baptist completed this company, Matt. 11:1-12; John 3:29. Jesus and John both recognized it as being separate from the Church saints. (See also Acts 7:38; Heb. 11:1-4; 12:1.)

(2) **The Church saints.** Such passages as Matt. 16:18; 1 Cor. 12:27, 28; Eph. 1:20-23; 2:14-22; 4:12-16; 5:21-32; Col. 1:18, 24 prove that the Church of the New Testament did not begin before Christ's ministry on earth, for He is the head and founder of it.

(3) **The 144,000 Jews** are identified as a separate company from any others in Rev. 7:1-8; 14:1-5, for which see chapters eleven and eighteen.

(4) **The great multitude of tribulation saints** are proved to be a company distinct from the above three in Rev. 7:9-17; 14:13; 15:2-4; 20:4, for which see chapter eleven.

The twenty-four elders must be one of these four companies. That they are not of the last two companies is proved in Rev. 7:11-14; 14:1-5 where the elders are seen as being separate from either of them. Nor could they be of the manchild, who is one of these four companies, for they are seen in heaven when the seventh trumpet blows which includes the rapture of the manchild, Rev. 11:15-13:18. Therefore, the company to which they belong is raptured at or before the beginning and not in the middle of the Week. It is clear from the above passages that the 144,000 and the great multitude are not raptured at the beginning of the Week for the 144,000 are not sealed until after the sixth seal. They are protected through the trumpet judgments down to the middle of the Week. The great multitude is martyred during the Week. Therefore, it stands to reason that the elders are of either or both the first two companies—the Church and the Old Testament saints. Could it be that the Old Testament saints are raptured at the beginning of the Week and that the Church is the manchild raptured in the middle of the Week? This would have to be the case if the Church were the manchild, and the 144,000 and the great multitude were also raptured during the Week. But such cannot be reconciled with the passages concerning the rapture of the Church and the Old Testament saints which picture them as the first companies to be raptured.

If this is true, then the Church and the Old Testament saints are not the manchild, and the elders must be identified as being of the Church and the Old Testament saints who are caught up before the Week. This view harmonizes with all the Revelation and all other Scriptures as we shall see.

But why twenty-four elders? This is not difficult when we consider the twelve tribes of Israel and the twelve apostles of the Lamb, which are both spoken of in the description of the New Jerusalem, 21:10-14. The elders are just twenty-four individuals out of the raptured saints who are caught up before the Week and are seen on twenty-four thrones before God and in the activities of the fulfillment of the last division of the book during the Seventieth Week. The whole priesthood at the time of David was represented or headed by twenty-four individuals according to God's commandment, 1 Chron. 24:1-9. These twenty-four elders are no doubt exalted permanently on the twenty-four thrones to serve in the highest official capacity in God's Kingdom. It is possible that they will be the head of all the redeemed in the sense that the twenty-four individuals of old were the heads of the whole priesthood.

The idea that those in the New Testament Church will have the highest position before God in eternity and that they will be exalted above any individual of the Old Testament is contradicted by the fact that David, Abraham, Isaac, Jacob, etc., are to be exalted higher than the majority of those in the Church, Jer. 30:9; Ezek. 34:24; 37:24, 25; Dan. 7:18; Hos. 3:5; Matt. 8:11; Gal. 3:7, 9; Rom. 4:1, 12-16; Heb. 11; etc. Not even everyone in the Church will be exalted to the same position. The above passages speak of Abraham, "our father," and picture many coming to sit down with Abraham, Isaac, and Jacob rather than suggesting that they sit down with others who are exalted higher than they. David will reign over all Israel while the twelve apostles will have only one tribe each (Luke 22:30), hence David will be exalted higher than the apostles. All saints will have their own part in the eternal plan of God and that part will be determined by their present life, character, conduct, yieldedness, deeds, work for God, conformity to Him, etc. (See chapter seventeen, point I, 2.)

Some believe that they are angelic spirits who vacate these thrones for saints, but this is contrary to God's purpose, plan, and character. God is not redeeming men to take positions held faithfully and loyally from all past ages by the angels. The angels will continue in their present capacity as servants of God. We have no such doctrine of promotions mentioned in the Bible. **The twenty-four elders are seen in the book:**

(1) Sitting on thrones, wearing crowns, and white raiment (4:4; 19:7, 8).

(2) Worshipping with audible voices (4:9-11; 5:8-10).

(3) Casting their crowns before the throne (4:10).

(4) Falling down before the throne (4:10; 5:8, 14; 11:16; 19:4).

(5) Singing and playing harps of gold (5:8-10).

(6) Officiating in a priestly capacity (5:8).

(7) Explaining certain mysteries to John (5:5; 7:13, 14).

They are associated with God, the Lamb, living creatures, angels, and other redeemed peoples so must be different from any of them (5:6, 11; 14:3; 19:4).

4. The Heavenly Sea of Glass.

"And before the throne there was a sea of glass like unto crystal," Rev. 4:6a.

This sea of glass does not represent the seas on earth, but is another actual part of the heavenly tabernacle which looks "like unto crystal." Its position is **before** the throne. It is unoccupied here but in Rev. 15:2-4 it is occupied by the great multitude. It reminds us of the "molten sea" made by Solomon for the temple to replace the laver in the earthly tabernacle, 1 Kings 7:23-26; 2 Chron. 4:2-15. This sea of glass must be vast in its dimensions in order to accommodate a "multitude that no man could number," Rev. 7:9-17; 15:2-4.

5. The Heavenly Living Creatures.

"And in the midst of the throne, and round about the throne, were four beasts full of eyes before and behind. And the first beast was like a lion, and the second beast like a calf, and the third beast had a face as a man, and the fourth beast was like a flying eagle. And the four beasts had each of them six wings about him; and they were full of eyes within: and they rest not day and night, saying, Holy, holy, holy, Lord God Almighty, which was, and is, and is to come," Rev. 4:6b-8.

The Greek zoa translated "beasts" should be "living creatures" as in the R. V. and margin of many Bibles. It is not the same Greek word **therion** translated "beast" in chapters 13, 14, 15, 16, 17, 19, 20, which means a wild beast. These zoa are to be distinguished from the redeemed (4:9-11); the seraphim (Isa. 6:1-8); the cherubim (Ezek. 1:4-28; 10:1-22); the angels (5:11, 12); and other beings in the Spirit World. An examination of these passages will reveal the differences. There is only one passage (5:8-10) where it would seem from the English translation that the living creatures were redeemed, but this is not the case as we shall see in its exposition.

Some have tried to make these zoa four representations of birds, beasts, and man because they have the faces of these creatures. If this be true then the beasts of the field have more representatives than man or the fowls, and creeping things and fishes have no representatives. God's covenant was with Noah and "every living creature" and not only with the beasts, fowls, and man. It was an everlasting covenant and this could not be if any one of those involved were not everlasting. Therefore, this representation is incomplete and this theory without scriptural warrent. Can we not take them just as four living creatures like similar creatures mentioned in Isaiah and Ezekiel, created for the purpose of calling attention to God's glory and holiness? They cry, "Holy, holy, holy, Lord God Almighty, which was, and is and is to come." The word "holy" is the first of seventeen heavenly utterances in the book (4:8, 11; 5:9, 10, 12, 13, 14; 7:10, 12; 11:15, 17; 12:10-12; 14:13; 15:3; 19:1-3, 4, 5, 6, 7. Cf. God as Almighty here with the Son as Almighty in Rev. 1:8. **The zoa are seen in the book:**

(1)   Calling attention to the holiness of God, (4:4-8).

(2)   Falling down before the Lamb (5:8-10).

(3)   Singing and playing on harps of gold (5:8-10).

(4)   Officiating in a priestly capacity (5:8-10).

(5)   Calling for the horsemen of the first four seals to "Come" (6:1-8).

(6)   Giving the seven vials to the seven angels (15:7).

They are associated with God, the Lamb, elders, angels and all classes of redeemed and always are separate from them, so must be different from all of them (5:6, 11, 14; 7:11; 14:3; 19:4).

6. The Heavenly Worship Because of Creation.

"And when those beasts give glory and honour and thanks to him that sat on the throne, who liveth for ever and ever, the four and twenty elders fall down before him that sat on the throne, and worship him that liveth for ever and ever, and cast their crowns before the throne, saying, Thou are worthy, O Lord, to receive glory and honour and power: for thou hast created all things, and for thy pleasure they are and were created," Rev. 4:9-11.

Here we have worship from the living creatures and the elders because of God's creation and the purpose of it. The living creatures are first seen giving glory to God who sits on the throne, who liveth "to the ages of ages." After this the elders cast their crowns before the throne and fall prostrate in worship to God. The purpose of creation is given here as being for God's pleasure and for His will and desire.

7. The Heavenly Book.

"And I saw in the right hand of him that sat on the throne a book written within and on the backside, sealed with seven seals. And I saw a strong angel proclaiming with a loud voice, Who is worthy to open the book, and to loose the seals thereof? And no man in heaven, nor in earth, neither under the earth, was able to open the book, neither to look thereon. And I wept much, because no man was found worthy to open and to read the book, neither to look thereon," Rev. 5:1-4.

This book was in the hand of God ready to be given to the worthy one if he could be found. It was "written within" and sealed on the "backside" with seven seals. This means that it was a sealed book and was to be opened only by a worthy one. The Greek for "sealed" is used only here and in Job 9:7; 37:7 in the Septuagint. "A strong angel" proclaimed with a loud voice, "Who is worthy to open the book and to loose the seals thereof?" This is the first real angel in the Revelation. The living creatures are angelic beings but different from ordinary angels. There are about twenty-six unidentified angels in the activities of the Revelation besides the fifteen angels who are identified as men, Christ (8:2-6; 10:1-11:3), Lucifer (12:1-9), Michael (12:7-10), and the innumerable angels around the throne (3:5; 5:11; 7:11). This angel was a "mighty angel" as to strength, which is very significant, for if he was not able to prevail with his strength to open the book who could expect to do so? But "no man in heaven, nor in earth, neither under the earth" was able to open the book, either to look thereon. This fact had an overwhelming effect on John and he "wept much." What a time of suspense and anxiety for him! Would the plan break now? Would there not be found someone to open the book or would it remain a mystery forever?

In this passage we have the first of nine questions asked in the book. The other questions are found in Rev. 6:10, 17; 7:13; 13:4; 15:4; 17:7.

The angel proclaimed with a "loud voice," which phrase is found thirteen times in the book, Rev. 5:2, 12; 6:10; 7:2, 10; 8:13; 10:3; 12:10; 14:7, 9, 15, 18; 19:17.

8. The Heavenly Lamb.

"And one of the elders saith unto me, Weep not: behold, the Lion of the tribe of Juda, the Root of David, hath prevailed to open the book, and to loose the seven seals thereof. And I beheld, and, lo, in the midst of the throne and of the four beasts, and in the midst of the elders stood a Lamb as it had been slain, having seven horns and seven eyes, which are the seven Spirits of God sent forth into all the earth. And he came and took the book out of the right hand of him that sat upon the throne," Rev. 5:5-7.

The words of the elder and the appearance of a "Lamb as it had been slain," instantly relieved John's agonizing suspense as well as that of all beings of heaven, for, when the Lamb had taken the book, worship to Him began with the living creatures and elders and reached throughout all creation. Christ is called here "the Lion of the tribe of Juda" as the fulfillment to agelong prophecies, Gen. 49:9, 10; Num. 24:17-19; Mic. 5: 1, 2. He is also called "the Root of David" according to many prophecies, 2 Sam. 7:8-17; Ps. 89:35-37; Isa. 9 : 6 -7; 11:1-9; Jer. 23:5, 6. The word "prevailed" is from the same Greek word translated "overcometh" in the messages to the churches of chapters 2 and 3. The Greek word **arnion** translated "Lamb" means a "little" Lamb, John 21: 15. The seven horns and seven eyes symbolize the complete anointing of the Holy Spirit upon Christ in His redemptive work, for which see chapter two, points I, 2 and II, 2.

The book is not one of redemption, for the expressions "hath prevailed," "a Lamb as it had been slain," "Thou wast slain" and "worthy is the Lamb that was slain" (5:6, 9, 12), prove that redemption has already been accomplished and nothing more needs to be done along this line. All that is necessary now is to appropriate the benefits of redemption. **The thought is** that the Lamb, because He has already overcome and finished His redemptive work, is now worthy to take the book of future "things shortly to come to pass," and loose the seals and reveal what is "written within."

This book contains part of the Revelation that God gave unto Him after His exaltation. The contents of the seals are revealed in Rev. 6:1-8:1 and the things "written within" are revealed in the latter part of Revelation as we shall see in chapter thirteen.

This proves the book to be one of judgments and not redemption. Everything in the Revelation, including the book and its contents, "must be hereafter" the churches, much more after Christ has finished redemption, John 17:1-5; 19:30; Eph. 1:19-23; Phil. 2:5-11. The contents of the book are "things" which shall transpire after the rapture and during the Week, for in the fulfillment of the Revelation, the Lamb does not begin to loose the seals and open the book until Rev. 6:1, which is after the Church Age. These facts also prove that **the book is not a book of title deeds to the earth,** for we find no such doctrine in Scripture. God needs no titles to something He has created for His glory.

9.   The Heavenly Worship Because of Worthiness to the Lamb.

"And when he had taken the book, the four beasts and four and twenty elders fell down before the Lamb, having every one of them harps, and golden vials full of odours, which are the prayers of the saints. And they sung a new song, saying, Thou art worthy to take the book, and to open the seals thereof; for thou wast slain, and hast redeemed us to God by thy blood out of every kindred, and tongue, and people, and nation; And hast made us unto our God kings and priests: and we shall reign on the earth. And I beheld, and I heard the voice of many angels round about the throne and the beasts and the elders: and the number of them was ten thousand times ten thousand, and thousands of thousands; Saying with a loud voice, Worthy is the Lamb that was slain to receive power, and riches, and wisdom, and strength, and honour, and glory, and blessing. And every creature which is in heaven, and on the earth, and under the earth, and such as are in the sea, and all that are in them, heard I saying, Blessing, and honour, and glory, and power, be unto him that sitteth upon the throne and unto the Lamb for ever and ever. And the four beasts said, Amen. And the four and twenty elders fell down and worshipped him that liveth for ever and ever," Rev. 5:8-14.

These verses picture universal worship to God and to the Lamb because of the worthiness of the Lamb to open the book. In the future fulfillment when the Lamb takes the book, the living creatures and elders will fall down before the Lamb with harps, and bowls full of odors, and offer up the prayers of the saints. Then they will sing a new song ascribing worthiness to the Lamb because of the accomplished redemption.

The substance of the song according to most Greek texts is, "Worthy art thou to take the book, and to open its seals; because thou was slain, and didst purchase to God by thy blood, out of every tribe and tongue and people and nation, and didst make them (saints whose prayers are being offered) to our God, kings and priests; and **they** shall reign over the   earth." This is no doubt the correct rendering and the original thought as is recognized by such New Testament Greek authors as Lachmann 1842-50, Tischendorf 1865-72, Alford 1862-71, and Wordsworth 1870 A. D. All omit the first **"us"** of the A. V. and Griesbach 1805, Tregalles 1857-72, Lachmann, Tichendorf, Alford and Wordsworth all omit the second "us" in their Greek Testaments, and instead, have **"them."** Then all agree and omit the **"we"** of Rev. 5:10 and add instead **"they"** the antecedent of which is the "saints" of 5:8 whose prayers are being offered up by the **zoa and** elders.

This is the only translation that harmonizes with the rest of the passages of the **zoa** and elders which teach that **the elders are**

redeemed, while the zoa are not. Both the **zoa** and elders offer up the prayers of the saints and ascribe worthiness to the Lamb as do other creatures in Rev. 5:11-14. The purpose of the song which the **zoa** and elders sing is not to show that either were redeemed, but to give glory to the victorious Lamb, for angels and others sing the same song (5:11-14) and we know they are not redeemed.

That worthiness to God and the Lamb is the theme of the various songs of these chapters seems clear not only from Rev. 5:8-14, but also from 4:6-11; 5:1-6. In Rev. 5:8-14 we have different ascriptions to God and the Lamb. Other ascriptions in the book are found in Rev. 1:5, 6, 17; 7:9-12; 11:15-18; 14:2, 3; 15:2-4; 19:1-7.

We now come to "THE THINGS" of the Revelation that will be fulfilled mainly on earth during the last seven years of this age — Daniel's Seventieth Week, Rev. 6:1-19:21.

The seven seals, the two companies of redeemed, and the first six trumpets will transpire during the first half of the Week, Rev. 6:1-9:21. An angel will then come down from heaven to make certain announcements of what will happen when the seventh trumpet blows in the middle of the week, Rev. 10. In this middle of the Week two witnesses will appear on earth, and the events of the sun-clothed woman, the manchild, war in heaven, casting out of Satan, and the two beasts will be fulfilled (Rev. 11:1-13:18), as well as the destruction of the great whore, Rev. 17.

During the last half of the Week all the events of Rev. 14-15, the seven vials, the total destruction of literal Babylon, the marriage supper of the Lamb, and the second advent of Christ will take place, Rev. 16:1-19:21.

When we take the events in a literal sense instead of making everything symbolic and mystical, and when we take them as consecutive in order as they are revealed (unless it is stated otherwise), there is no confusion as to what will happen and when it will happen. The time element is then clear. It is only when we take historical events, or things of the Church age that are to happen before the rapture, and mix them with future events that will happen after the churches, that we can become confused.

Chapter Ten

THE FIRST SIX SEALS, Rev. 6:1-17

The seven seals and the first six trumpets take place in succession in the first three and one-half years of the tribulation Week or from the beginning to the middle of the Week. The seventh trumpet takes place in the middle of the Week. For reasons why these seals and trumpets are not to be intermixed with the vials of the last part of the Week, or after chapter 12, see points V and VII of chapter one, and points 1, 2, 6, and 9 of chapter seven. The order of events in the book is plain and we have no authority to change it. If the middle of the Week were to take place before the seals and trumpets, it would have been described before them instead of after them, as is the case.

1. The First Seal: The Rise of Antichrist.

"And I saw when the Lamb opened one of the seals, and I heard, as it were the noise of thunder, one of the four beasts saying, Come and see. And I saw, and behold a white horse: and he that sat on him had a bow; and a crown was given unto him: and he went forth conquering, and to conquer," Rev. 6:1, 2.

The word "Come" in Rev. 6:1, 3, 5 and 7 is used to command the riders in the seals to come forth. The words "and see" are omitted in the original texts. The phrase "Come and see" can have no reference to John for he was already there looking at every scene. The rider cannot be Christ for He is the one opening the seals. He will not be the contents of them and open them also, for the little book of Rev. 5 contains "things" never before revealed and which no man but Christ is able to open and reveal.

This white horse is not to be confused with the ones in Rev. 19:11-21, for this one is symbolical, while those in Rev. 19 are literal. Because they are white in both passages is no proof that they are symbolical of Christ or righteousness any more than the white horses in Zech. 1:8; 6:3-6 are symbolical of Christ. Christ is symbolized by a Lamb in this book and not as a rider on a white horse. There is no Scripture corroborating the fact that Christ will go forth at the beginning of the Week "conquering and to conquer."

Nor could this be a symbol of a great revival of the Word of God according to Hab. 3:8, 9 for that passage which is in the past tense is a prayer of the prophet calling to remembrance the past dealings of God with Israel when He led them out of Egypt. In the New Testament the Word of God is symbolized by a mirror, meat, laver, light, bread, seed, and sword, but never by a bow. No definite period of national revival is symbolized in the Bible. **The following reasons are advanced as proof that the white horse rider symbolizes the future rise of the Antichrist at the beginning of the Week:**

(1) It is clear that the symbol is one of an individual, for he has a bow and is given a crown and he goes forth "conquering and to conquer." This is in fulfillment of Dan. 7:8, 24-26; 8:8-10,

20-25; 11:35-45 as to the rise of the Antichrist among the ten kings of Revised Rome. Through conquests he will become supreme over them by the middle of the Week. The giver of the crown is not mentioned here, but it merely symbolizes the rise of the Antichrist to power as king among the ten kings, through the operation of satanic powers, 2 Thess. 2:8-12; Rev. 13:1-4; Dan. 8:25; 11:36-39.

(2) It seems clear that this rider will cause the wars, famines, pestilences, death and hell of the following three seals. These blights always follow an ambitious conqueror. Antichrist is pictured as such in Dan. 7, 8, and 11.

(3) Antichrist is the only one prophesied to go forth "conquering and to conquer" at the beginning of the Week. He is not to come necessarily on a white steed, but he is to come as the false Messiah of Israel, Matt. 24:4, 5; John 5:43; Dan. 9:27. If this is not a symbol of Antichrist, then, this is one portion of Revelation that is obscure. But realizing that this passage is in perfect harmony with the above prophecies of Antichrist in his rise to power over the ten kings of Revised Rome, this part of Revelation becomes as clear as the rest of the book.

(4) If this is not Antichrist, then we do not find him mentioned in the book before the middle of the Week. Were that the case we would have two individuals going forth "conquering and to conquer" at the beginning of the Week—one clearly pictured in Daniel, and one here. The sphere of conquest of the one in Daniel is defined, the other is not. One can be identified, the other cannot. Both are successful in conquest, and prominent enough to receive mention by God, but only the one is explained in detail as to his rise, power, length of reign, end, etc. But considering this rider as the Antichrist, these discrepancies vanish.

2. The Second Seal: War.

"And when he had opened the second seal, I heard the second beast say, Come and see. And there went out another horse that was red: and power was given to him that sat thereon to take peace from the earth, and that they should kill one another: and there was given unto him a great sword," Rev. 6:3, 4.

The red horse rider is pictured as having a great sword with which to take peace from the earth and cause murder and wars and bloodshed among men. There can be no question as to what is symbolized here. War will be the natural result of the Antichrist's going forth "conquering and to conquer," Dan. 7:24; 11: 40-45; Matt. 24:6, 7. The "sword" is a general symbol of war, bloodshed, and national, civil and class conflicts of all kinds. We are not to expect peace until "the Prince of Peace" comes to reign over the world, Isa. 2:2-4; 9:6, 7.

3. The Third Seal: Famine.

"And when he had opened the third seal, I heard the third beast say, Come and see. And I beheld, and lo a black horse; and he that sat on him had a pair of balances in his hand. And I heard a voice in the midst of the four beasts say, A measure of wheat for a penny, and three measures of barley for a penny; and see thou hurt not the oil and the wine," Rev. 6:5, 6.

The black horse rider had a pair of balances in his hand for the purpose of measuring food. This is a symbol of famine. Bread by measure and weight signifies scarcity of food, Ezek. 4:10-17. The penny referred to was a day's wage (Matt. 20:1-16) and a measure (nearly a quart) of corn was a slave's daily ration, an amount usually purchasable for one-eighth of a penny. Ordinarily, one could buy eight measures of wheat or twenty-four measures of barley for a penny, but then only one measure of wheat or three measures of barley can be bought for a penny. This will make food eight times higher than usual. Let an ambitious conqueror rise and peace is taken from the earth. Then famine is the natural result, because of the lack of men to till the soil and harvest the crops. The olive and grape need no cultivation; hence their ruthless destruction by the invaders is forbidden in the statement "hurt not the oil or the wine." This picture is the same as Matt. 24:6, 7, which will be fulfilled in the first part of the Week during the wars of the Antichrist.

4. The Fourth Seal: Death and Hell

"And when he had opened the fourth seal, I heard the voice of the fourth beast say, Come and see. And I looked, and behold a pale horse: and his name that sat on him was Death, and Hell followed with him. And power was given unto them over the fourth part of the earth, to kill with sword, and with hunger, and with death, and with the beasts of the earth," Rev. 6:7, 8.

Here Death and Hell are personified. These two riders are named because they are not recognizable by man, as are the first three. The word "Death" has reference to a great pestilence that shall be sent on earth after the rise of the Antichrist, and after wars and famines have taken their toll of human life. It is referred to in Matt. 24:6, 7. The Greek **choloros** translated "pale" means green and is so translated in Rev. 8:7; 9:4; Mark 6:39. The color of the fifth horse is not given but perhaps it was red, for the name of the rider is Hell. The rampage of Death and Hell over the fourth part of the earth (ground) will be the natural result of the riders of the first three seals. The sword and hunger refer to the second and third seals which are followed by Death and Hell. Bodies of men killed by the riders of these first four seals will be eaten by the beasts of the earth. Cf. Ezek. 14:21.

5. The Fifth Seal: the Lesser Tribulation Martyrs.

"And when he had opened the fifth seal, I saw under the altar the souls of them that were slain for the word of God, and for the testimony which they held; and they cried with a loud voice, saying, How long, O Lord, holy and true, dost thou not judge and avenge our blood on them that dwell on the earth? And white robes were given unto every one of them; and it was said unto them, that they should rest yet for a little season, until their fellowservants also and their brethren, that should be killed as they were, should be fulfilled," Rev. 6:9-11.

Here John saw the souls of many martyrs under the "golden altar" of Rev. 8:3-5; 9:13; 14:18; 16:7. **These are to be people who have been saved after the rapture** of the Church and the Old Testament saints in Rev. 4:1 and martyred from that time to the fifth seal. It is clear here that **they will all be martyrs** and not a mixture of martyrs and souls who have died natural deaths, for they all will cry out for vengeance on their enemies on the earth. This cry is characteristic of the tribulation, not of the present day of grace and mercy. The martyrs will be killed by the whore and the ten kings during this period. They will have been slain "for the Word of God, and for the testimony which they held." (See the tribulation, chapter five, point II; chapter eight; and chapter twenty-nine, point IV.)

This passage answers the question of whether the tribulation saints will rise individually or collectively in a company. These martyrs are told to rest yet for "a little season, **until** their fellowservants also and their brethren, that should be killed **as they were** should be fulfilled" and the implication is that all the martyrs of the whole tribulation period of seven years or more will rise together as a company of saints as seen in Rev. 7:9-17; 15:2-4; 20:4. (See point II in chapter six.) These martyrs then are to wait until all who are to be slain during these years are killed, when they will be raptured together in one body at the end of the Week. This passage is contradictory to the theory of soul-sleep, for these souls are without their bodies after their martyrdom, awaiting the time of the resurrection of their bodies, and all this time they are fully conscious, can speak, see, remember, feel, and do all things that a conscious being can do. They desire judgment upon their murderers which shows that they will have been recently slain and their slayers still alive. Cf. Luke 16:19-31. They are called "lesser tribulation" martyrs, for they are slain during the first part or lesser tribulation of the first three and one-half years of Daniel's Seventieth Week.

6. The Sixth Seal: The Wrath of God.

"And I beheld when he had opened the sixth seal, and, lo, there was a great earthquake; and the sun became black as sackcloth of hair, and the moon became as blood; And the stars of heaven fell unto the earth, even as a fig tree casteth her untimely figs, when she is shaken of a mighty wind. And the heaven departed as a scroll when it is rolled together; and every mountain and island were moved out of their places. And the kings of the earth, and the great men, and the rich men, and the chief captains, and the mighty men, and every bondman, and every free man, hid themselves in the dens and in the rocks of the mountains; And said to the mountains and rocks, Fall on us, and hide us from the face of him that sitteth on the throne, and from the wrath of the Lamb: For the great day of his wrath is come; and who shall be able to stand?" Rev. 6:12-17.

Here under the sixth seal we have revealed for the first time the wrath of God. No wrath of God is contained in the first five seals for they reveal things that are only the natural results of the rise of a conqueror and the persecution of God's people. But here because of these terrible persecutions upon the people who will not conform to the Roman system of religion, God begins to reveal His great wrath and judgment upon those persecutors. This outpouring of God's wrath will produce great physical changes in the earth and heavens and distress among men. **There are seven main events to transpire under this seal.**

(1) **"A great earthquake."** Jesus spoke of earthquakes being in different places which would indicate His return to the earth, Matt. 24:7. There are several earthquakes mentioned in Bible his-

tory, Amos. 1:1; Zech. 14:5; Matt. 27:51; 28:2; Acts 16:26. There have been hundreds since then. **There are to be four great earthquakes during Daniel's Seventieth Week which are defined in this book.**

A. This one during the sixth seal which will take place prior to the sealing of the 144,000, the seventh seal, the trumpets, and vials, Rev. 6:12.

B. The one that will take place after the loosing of the seventh seal and before the blowing of the first trumpet, Rev. 8:5.

C. The one that will occur under the seventh trumpet in the middle of the Week, Rev. 11:19. Thus we have three earthquakes from the sixth seal to the seventh trumpet or during the first three and one-half years and the middle of the Week.

D. The one that will occur at the time of the ascension of the two witnesses at the close of the last three and one-half years of the Week, Rev. 11:13; 16:17-21; Zech. 14:4-8.

(2) **"The sun became black as sackcloth of hair."** There are three times in Bible history that this has taken place, Gen. 1:2; Exod. 10:21-23; Matt. 27:45. There was a dark day, May 19, 1880, in New England, when the stars shone and the chickens went to roost, but that was nothing compared to the darkness of this picture. **There are five times that the sun or part of it will be darkened during the tribulation Week.**

A. This one during the sixth seal in the early part of the Week, Rev. 6:12.

B. During the fourth trumpet one-third of the sun will be darkened, Rev. 8:12.

C. During the fifth trumpet the sun will be darkened by smoke from the pit, Rev. 9:2.

D. During the fifth vial, in the last of the Week, the sun will be darkened again, Rev. 16:10.

E. "Immediately after the tribulation" it will be darkened, Matt. 24:29; Isa. 13:10; 24:23; Ezek. 32:7; Joel 2:31; 3:15. All these passages speak of the same event at the same time, called "the day of the Lord."

(3) **"The moon became as blood." There will be five times in which the moon will become affected,** corresponding to the darkening of the sun above.

(4) **"The stars of heaven fell unto the earth." There will also be five times in which the stars will become affected,** as in the passages above on the sun and moon, but only two times are they spoken of as falling to the earth: first, during the sixth seal; secondly, at the coming of Christ after the tribulation, Matt. 24:29-31. There will be several years between the two events. These falling stars will not be the planets, all of which are many times larger than our earth, but meteors, which are not stars in the strictest sense of the word, but small bodies drawn

into our atmosphere and rendered luminous for a few moments by the friction of their rush through it. Meteors are not mere distempers of the air as was once believed, but bodies of a planetary nature, traveling round the sun in orbits as defined as that of the earth itself and in this sense they are called stars. They are small bodies of iron ranging in size from small particles of dust to thirty tons. Ordinarily, meteors are too small to be seen, but when they enter the earth's atmosphere, as thousands do daily, they become visible through being made hot from the friction of the air. The small ones burn up when far above the earth and are the familiar shooting stars that are seen in the sky by night. The larger ones reach the earth as meteorites, many of which can be seen in museums. A shower of meteors fell November 14, 1866, but that had nothing to do with the fulfillment of this prophecy. Cf. Isa. 34:4.

(5) **"The heaven departed as a scroll."** This does not mean that the heaven passes out of existence any more than the same expression does in Rev. 20:11; 21:1, for it is seen many times after this, Rev. 8:1, 10, 13; 9:1; etc. Cf. Acts 15:39.

(6) **"Every mountain and island were moved out of their places."** This does not mean that they pass away, for they are seen again several years later undergoing a like process of change, Rev. 16:20. It merely seemed to John that they were moved entirely out of their place because of the great shaking of the earth by the earthquake in this seal. They are not removed for men cry for them to fall upon them, Rev. 6:16.

(7) **"The great day of his wrath is come."** When the heaven departs as a scroll the thrones of God and of the Lamb are to be seen by men on the earth, and they will cry in terror to be killed, for they will realize that it is time for God to judge them for their sins. There are seven classes of men mentioned here and all will realize that God's wrath is at hand. This "great day of his wrath" is not the same as that in Rom. 2:5, 14, 15 which refers to the final judgment, Rev. 20:11-15. This wrath begins under the sixth seal in the first three and one-half years and continues through the trumpet and vial judgments to the end of the Week. What do the trumpet and vial judgments reveal but God's wrath? This wrath has reference to a period of time in which many judgments take place as is clear from 6:17; 11:18; 15:1, 7; 16:1, 19; etc. Because physical signs accompany the sixth seal and the second advent this does not prove that these two events are the same, or will take place at the same time. Between the sixth seal and the second advent all of Rev. 7:1-19:10 takes place, including all of the parenthetical passages. We have no authority to dislocate this seal from its proper place and make it the same as the seventh vial at the second advent for it is the sixth of twenty-one consecutive events, seven seals, seven trumpets, and seven vials.

The word "mighty" is used in this passage two times. See also its use in Rev. 10:1; 16:18; 18:10, 21; 19:6, 18.

Chapter Eleven

(Parenthetical, Rev. 7:1-17)

THE TWO COMPANIES OF REDEEMED

Rev. 7 is the first parenthetical passage of the book. It is inserted between the sixth and seventh seals and contains explanatory matter about things which will transpire after the sixth seal through the rest of the Week, and which are not contained in the seals, trumpets, and vials. It is recognized that this passage is parenthetical, for instead of the natural order of events with the seventh seal following the sixth immediately, this explanation of two companies of redeemed is given, which breaks the thought of the seals and explains certain things that will transpire in and between the main order of events.

I. The Sealing of the 144,000 Jews.

"And after these things I saw four angels standing on the four corners of the earth, holding the four winds of the earth, that the wind should not blow on the earth, nor on the sea, nor on any tree. And I saw another angel ascending from the east, having the seal of the living God: and he cried with a loud voice to the four angels, to whom it was given to hurt the earth and the sea, saying, Hurt not the earth, neither the sea, nor the trees, till we have sealed the servants of our God in their foreheads. And I heard the number of them which were sealed: and there were sealed an hundred and forty and four thousand of all the tribes of the children of Israel. Of the tribe of J u d a h were sealed twelve thousand. Of the tribe of Reuben were sealed twelve thousand. Of the tribe of Gad were sealed twelve thousand. Of the tribe of Aser were sealed twelve thousand. Of the tribe of Nepthalim were sealed twelve thousand. Of the tribe of Manasses were sealed twelve thousand. Of the tribe of Simeon were sealed twelve thousand. Of the tribe of Levi were sealed twelve thousand. Of the tribe of Issachar were sealed twelve thousand. Of the tribe of Zabulon were sealed twelve thousand. Of the tribe of Joseph were sealed twelve thousand. Of the tribe of Benjamin were sealed twelve thousand," Rev. 7:1-8.

The four angels of Rev. 7:1 are to be good angels for "another" angel is to speak to them of "our" God, the living God.

They will be the first four of the seven trumpet angels to whom will be given power to hurt the earth and the sea and the trees. A comparison of the judgments which these angels hold, together with the judgments the first four trumpet angels hold (8:7-12), proves that they are the same, else we have two sets of the same judgments. The time set for the one is revealed while the time for the other is not. The expression "four corners of the earth" (7:1; Isa. 11:12) means "four directions of the earth" (Matt. 24:31; Rev. 20:8). The winds here refer to the judgments of God which the trumpet angels hold and which will be poured out immediately after the seventh seal. Cf. Dan. 7:2; 8:8; 11:14; Zech. 2:6; 6:5.

Just as God reserved seven thousand men who would not worship Baal in Elijah's time so God will have 144,000 Jews who will not bow to the infernal designs of the whore in the first part of the Week during the rise of the Antichrist over the ten kings. Such a definite number from twelve of the thirteen tribes of Israel affords no difficulty, for the selection depends upon God's decree and sovereignty as well as on their yieldedness. They will all be Jews, as is clear, in that twelve thousand will be sealed from each of the tribes except one. They will have nothing to do with the Church for no tribeship is ever mentioned in connection with Jews saved in the Church. It is clear that they will all be sealed with the same seal after the rapture of the Church and before the trumpet judgments. Jews who are saved at the time of the rapture of all the dead and living saints "in Christ" will be raptured also, but these will still be here during the seals and trumpets, proving they were not saved when the rapture took place.

They are to be sealed for the express purpose of being kept through the trumpet judgments during the first part of the Week, for the angel that does the sealing cries to the first four trumpet angels saying, "Hurt not the earth, neither the sea, nor the trees, till we have sealed the servants of our God in their foreheads." Special direction is given to the fifth trumpet not to hurt the 144,000 (9:4), which applies also to the sixth trumpet. They will be caught up to heaven in the seventh trumpet, for, immediately after it blows, they are seen in heaven before the throne, Rev. 14:1-5. This angel, then, seals the 144,000 before the trumpets begin. The trumpets will begin immediately after the seals and continue to the middle of the Week. Therefore, it must be that the 144,000 are sealed about the middle of the first three and one-half years of the Week and between the sixth seal and first trumpet. **This seal will not be the seal of the believer by the Holy Spirit** (Eph. 1:13, 14; 4:30), **or the keeping of some sabbath, or any spiritual blessing, but a literal mark as an object of sight because:**

1. There is nothing to the contrary in the passage.
2. The locusts out of the abyss will be able to see it, Rev. 9:4.
3. The seal of the Abrahamic Covenant was literal, Rom. 4:11.
4. The sign of the passover was literal, Exod. 12:13.
5. The mark of the beast will be literal, 13:16-18; 14:9; 20:4.
6. It could not be salvation or any spiritual mark for the 144,000 were already the servants (bondmen) of God.
7. It is expressly stated that they will be sealed in the "foreheads," Rev. 7:3; 14:1. Spiritual blessings are never received in the forehead. What this seal or mark is, is clearly given as being God's name "written" in their foreheads, Rev. 14:1.
8. The promise is given to the overcomer that there will be written upon him **certain names which will be literal,** Rev. 3:12; 22:4. Cf. Rev. 9:4; 13:16-18; 14:9; 20:4.

The Antichrist, angered perhaps by the sealing of these servants of God in their foreheads, will try to destroy the 144,000 in the middle of the Week and will begin to seal his servants in their right hands or foreheads. The escape of the 144,000 from the plagues of the trumpets will be another cause to enrage men against them and when persecution comes to them they will be caught up to heaven. This "seal of the living God" will protect these Jews from the trumpet plagues until their rapture in the middle of the Week.

No Jew now knows for certain his own tribe, but the divine sealers know. In the names of these tribes, Dan and Ephraim are omitted, Levi and Joseph taking their places. To explain the omission of the former, many have used Lev. 24:10-16; Judg. 18:2-31; 1 Kings 12:26-33; Hos. 4:17 where they are spoken of as having sinned with idols, for which they were cut off according to Deut. 29:18-21. Such an explanation of their omission is neither Scriptural nor logical. Which one of the other tribes did not sin with idols during whole centuries?

If we can condemn and cut off Dan and Ephraim on this ground, then, to be fair we must also cut off all the other tribes for the same sin, 1 Kings 14:23; 18:21, 22; Isa. 2:8-20; 10:11; etc. This omission is not hard to understand when we consider that there were two sons of Joseph, making thirteen tribes in Israel (Josh. 14:4; Num. 17:1-5), and that the sealed ones will be selected from only twelve of the thirteen tribes, as stated. This really will omit only the tribe of Dan, for one of the sons of Joseph is given instead of Ephraim as has been the case many times in the Old Testament where Joseph's name is substituted for either Manasseh or Ephraim, Num. 1:10. Joseph is substituted for Ephraim in several passages speaking of the last days, Ezek. 37:16-19; 47:13. The tribe of Levi was never one of the twelve tribes making National Israel. It was the priestly tribe which lived off the tithe of the other twelve, Num. 1:47-54; 18:21-24.

In passages speaking of the restored Jerusalem and the New Jerusalem, Levi and Joseph are mentioned, never Ephraim or Manasseh, for they were not of the original twelve sons of Jacob, Ezek. 48:30-35; Rev. 21:12. In the eternal allotment of land for the twelve tribes neither Joseph nor Levi is mentioned but the two sons of Joseph are, Ezek. 48:1-29.

These facts seem to indicate that the reason Dan is not mentioned in the 144,000 is that there are none of that tribe saved as servants of God during this time. Since God will make these 144,000 an heavenly people, He is not obligated to save any particular one of the twelve tribes of National Israel, but can seal whom He desires and who will yield to Him of all the thirteen tribes. If none of the tribe of Dan will get saved in the first part of the Week, then such a simple fact as revealed should not be hard to believe. Acceptance of this fact solves all problems, so why complicate simple revealed facts?

II. The Great Tribulation Saints.

"After this I beheld, and, lo, a great multitude, which no man could number, of all nations, and kindreds, and people, and tongues, stood before the throne, and before the Lamb, clothed with white robes, and palms in their hands; and cried with a loud voice, saying, Salvation to our God which sitteth upon the throne, and unto the Lamb. And all the angels stood around the throne and about the elders and the four beasts, and fell before the throne on their faces and worshipped God, Saying, Amen: Blessing, and glory, and wisdom, and thanksgiving, and honour, and power, and might, be unto our God for ever and ever. Amen. And one of the elders answered, saying unto me, What are these which are arrayed in white robes? and whence came they? And I said unto him, Sir, Thou knowest, And he said to me, These are they which came out of great tribulation, and have washed their robes, and made them white in the blood of the Lamb. Therefore are they before the throne of God, and serve him day and night in his temple: and he that sitteth on the throne shall dwell among them. They shall hunger no more, neither thirst any more; neither shall the sun light on them, nor any heat. For the Lamb which is in the midst of the throne shall feed them, and shall lead them unto living fountains of waters; and God shall wipe away all tears from their eyes," Rev. 7:9-17.

The phrase "After this" shows that this company will be entirely different from the above, for the same expression in Rev. 7:1 shows the 144,000 to be a subject different from the seals among which it is inserted. These verses portray the second and last company of redeemed saints seen in the book, after the picture of the Church and the Old Testament saints with God in heaven, represented by the elders throughout chapters 4-19. These are all martyrs while the above are a living company only. These are martyred throughout the Week and raptured at the end of it while the above company is protected through the trumpets and caught up to God and His throne in the middle of the Week. This company is not to escape the tribulation as do the living saints in the Church, because they were not saved and ready to escape the tribulation with the Church.

We have seen under the fifth seal that the "souls under the altar" will be slain from the rapture to the fifth seal. They were told to rest yet for a "little season until their fellowservants also and their brethren, that should be killed as they were, should be fulfilled." This clearly implies that they are to join all other martyrs of the tribulation and that they will make one company.

This company is pictured with "white robes" which, in this book, clothe only Christ and redeemed humanity. These martyrs have also "palms in their hands" which is always a sign of rejoicing and victory. They are seen as distinct from the elders, living creatures, angels and all other beings. They come out of "the great tribulation," or literally, "the tribulation the great," which refers to the future tribulation. They will receive salvation in the same sense we do today and will be martyrs for the Word of God and the testimony of Christ as well as their own testimony as was stated of the martyrs of the fifth seal, Rev. 6:9-11. They will all be saved after the rapture, for if they would be "in Christ" at the time of the rapture they wil' be raptured also. The majority of them will be slain by Antichrist, Rev. 13:7, 15-18; 15:2-4; 20:4.

The rewards for being faithful unto death during the tribulation are: to be before the throne of God; serve God continually in His temple; have God among them; never hunger or thirst; never have the sun or heat (16:9) light on them any more; have the Lamb feed (tend, or shepherd) them and lead them unto living fountains of waters of life; have God wipe away all tears; rest from their labors and be commended for their work; have harps of God and sing upon the sea of glass; and reign with Christ forever, Rev. 7:14-17; 14:13; 15:2-4; 20:4.

Chapter Twelve

THE SEVENTH SEAL, AND THE FIRST SIX TRUMPETS,
Rev. 8:1-9:21

7. The Seventh Seal: Silence in Heaven.

"And when he opened the seventh seal, there was silence in heaven about the space of half an hour," Rev. 8:1.

In this verse the seven seals are resumed after the break between the sixth and seventh seals caused by the parenthetical passage on the two companies of redeemed, Rev. 7:1-17. This seal is a unique conclusion of the terrible things of the first six seals and is a fitting interlude between them and the terrible events of the seven trumpets. This "silence in heaven" needs no fanciful interpretation for it is just as literal as the contents of the other seals and as language can express. We certainly can conceive a half hour of silence on the planet heaven. This is clear from the verb "was" which means "came to be" and shows that when the seventh seal is opened, and all the contents of the first six seals are completed, there will be silence "in heaven" and not elsewhere.

The Seven Trumpet Angels and the Priestly Angel.
(Parenthetical, Rev. 8:2-6)

"And I saw the seven angels which stood before God; and to them were given seven trumpets. And another angel came and stood at the altar, having a golden censer; and there was given unto him much incense, that he should offer it with the prayers of all saints upon the golden altar which was before the throne. And the smoke of the incense, which came with the prayers of the saints, ascended up before God out of the angel's hand. And the angel took the censer, and filled it with fire of the altar, and cast it into the earth: and there were voices, and thunderings, and lightnings, and an earthquake. And the seven angels which had the seven trumpets prepared themselves to sound," Rev. 8:2-6.

This passage must also be considered parenthetical because it is an insertion of explanatory matter pertaining to the scene of preparation for the sounding of the seven trumpets after the seventh seal is finished. The time of its fulfillment is just as is given here, before the seven trumpets begin.

The seven angels here seem to be special ones who stand continually before God. To them are given seven trumpets. By whom they are given is not revealed. Perhaps it is one of the living creatures. Cf. 15:7. An apocryphal book called Enoch (chapter 20) gives the names of six archangels: Uriel, Raphael, Raguel, Michael, Sarakiel and Gabriel and in chapter 54 gives another, named Phanuel. In another apocryphal book, Tobiah, 12:15, Raphael is mentioned as being one of the seven angels who present prayers of saints before God. Whether these things be true or not we do know that those seen by John are trusted angels; whether of an official or higher order than common angels is not known. None of these trumpets they receive will have anything to do with the rapture as proved in chapter six, neither have they to do with anything in the Old Testament. They are seven trumpets which will be blown by seven angels in the order as given and after the seven seals and before the seven vials. When each is blown, certain judgments and events will transpire on earth. They are to be blown successively, and each after the preceding one has been completed. The first will be blown soon after the seventh seal and the last in the middle of the Week. Thus we have the seven seals and seven trumpets as fourteen consecutive events from the beginning to the middle of the Week.

Following the vision of the seven angels and their reception of the seven trumpets "another" angel came to the golden altar to minister as clearly stated in the above quotation, which, with Heb. 4:14-16; 6:20-7:28; 13:15, seems to indicate that this angel is Christ in His present ministry as our High Priest. The "censer" is always mentioned in connection with the High Priest, Lev. 16:12; Heb. 9:4. See the results of intruding into this office, Lev. 10:1; Num. 16:1-19; 2 Chron. 26:19; Ezek. 8:11. This angel offers up prayers of the saints as do the living creatures and elders in Rev. 5:8-10 which shows that those who offer prayers of saints are not necessarily redeemed.

After this ministry of Christ at the altar, the seven angels prepare to sound. They take their turn in blowing their trumpets which further shows that they are not contemporaneous with the seals or contained in them.

There is no ground for believing that the seven trumpets are contained in the seventh seal and that the seven vials are contained in the seventh trumpet. If so, where? On the contrary, in the vision the seven seals were finished before John saw the seven trumpets, and they in turn were finished before he saw the seven vials. The same will be true in their fulfillment. These plain facts will also exclude the idea that any of the seals or trumpets last throughout the fulfillment of the others. If such were true John would have seen them as taking place that way instead of the way he did. If we can insert the seven trumpets into the seventh seal and the seven vials into the seventh trumpet then all are the contents of the seventh seal. Then what would be the object of having the trumpets and vials if they are not different from the mere contents of one of the seals? Why not make the rest of Revelation also come out of one of the seals? If we have authority for the other we have for this. If these events are not to be understood as given, then the book ceases to be a revelation of "things shortly to come to pass" and becomes a mysterious record of events to be dealt with just as one fancies. The interpreters that hold the above ideas state that the first five or six seals are different and follow each other, so we argue that, if this be true, and even understandable to them, why then should not all the seals, trumpets, and vials be in the order as given, as twenty-one separate events?

Now as to the literalness of the events of the trumpets, they are to be just as real as the description can make them, and as literal as the contents of the seals will be. Why should we spiritualize and explain away plain literal events? They are just as literal as the judgments predicted and fulfilled in the past history of Israel and show what will happen again, Exod. 34:10; Deut. 28:10, 59; 30:1-10; Isa. 11:15, 16; Mic. 7:13-15; Jer. 23:7, 8. The plagues of Egypt were literal, why not these? The same trying conditions will be upon Israel in the tribulation as those were in Egypt, so why not believe that the future judgments will be as literal as those upon Egypt?

1. The First Trumpet: Hail, Fire, and Blood.

"The first angel sounded, and there followed hail and fire mingled with blood, and they were cast upon the earth: and the third part of trees was burnt up, and all green grass was burnt up," Rev. 8:7.

This is similar to the seventh Egyptian plague, and will be just as literal, Exod. 9:22-26. The only difference here is the addition of blood and the exception of animate life. This plague will affect only vegetation of one-third of the earth while in Egypt it affected vegetation, men, and beasts. The trees are literal here as in Rev. 7:1, 3; 9:4, and will be burned up as in Rev. 17:16; 18:8. During this plague agricultural progress will be impossible. There has been a modern instance of this plague. It is said that in 1921, in Cheh Shae, Yunnan, China, fire and hail mingled with blood fell all over the countryside.

2. The Second Trumpet: A Burning Mountain.

"And the second angel sounded, and as it were a great mountain burning with fire was cast into the sea: and the third part of the sea became blood; and the third part of the creatures which were in the sea, and had life, died; and the third part of the ships were destroyed," Rev. 8:8, 9.

This mountain is evidently a large meteor ablaze with fire which falls into the sea. To John, it looked "as it were" a mountain. The sea mentioned here is perhaps the Mediterranean as the events of the seals and the plagues of the trumpets and vials will be especially poured out upon the then known world—the Roman Empire—bordering upon that sea. Only one-third of the sea will become blood, and one-third of the living creatures in the sea and on the sea in ships will be destroyed. Business on the sea will be crippled and men will begin to realize these judgments are of God. This will be the same in nature as the first Egyptian plague, Exod. 9:14-21; Psa. 78:44; 105:29.

3. The Third Trumpet: The Star Wormwood.

"And the third angel sounded, and there fell a great star from heaven, burning as it were a lamp, and it fell upon the third part of the rivers, and upon the fountains of waters; And the name of the star is called Wormwood: and the third part of the waters became wormwood; and many men died of the waters, because they were made bitter," Rev. 8:10, 11.

This judgment falls in the form of a star from heaven burning "as it were a lamp." This is no doubt another meteor whose gaseous vapors will be absorbed by one-third of the waters of the rivers and fountains. They will become bitter as wormwood, and cause many men to die. Wormwood is a perennial herb, very bitter, and is used in the manufacture of absinthe. It was also formerly used as a vermifuge. This event is quite in contrast to the bitter waters made sweet and healthy by God in Exod. 15:26, 27. See Jer. 9:13-15; 23:15; Lam. 3:15.

4. The Fourth Trumpet: The Sun, Moon, and Stars Affected.

"And the fourth angel sounded, and the third part of the sun was smitten, and the third part of the moon, and the third part of the stars; so as the third part of them was darkened, and the day shone not for a third part of it, and the night likewise," Rev. 8:12.

This verse is plain as to what will happen under the fourth trumpet. These events are similar to what happened under the sixth seal and what will happen under the fifth vial further over. The length of time this darkness lasts is not known but it cannot be long, for in the very next trumpet, the sun is darkened again by the smoke from the abyss. This is further proof that the seals, trumpets, and vials are a succession of events, each of which is completed before the other begins. This judgment corresponds to the ninth Egyptian plague of darkness which lasted for three days—such darkness that could be felt, Exod. 10:21-23.

This condition of the planets is not the same as foretold by the Lord in Matt. 24:29; Mark 13:24; Luke 21:25, which refer to the coming of the Lord "immediately after the tribulation" and at least three and one-half years after the fourth trumpet. It is very possible that the planets can be affected at different times and in different ways during this period just as much as they can be affected once. (See under the sixth seal.)

Thus we see that the first four trumpet judgments have to do with plagues affecting vegetation, seas, rivers, and planets, as indicated in the message to the first four trumpet angels in Rev. 7:1-3. The last three affect not the material, but moral creation.

The Announcement.
(Parenthetical, Rev. 8:13)

"And I beheld, and heard an angel flying through the midst of heaven, saying with a loud voice, Woe, woe, woe, to the inhabiters of the earth by reason of the other voices of the trumpet of the three angels, which are yet to sound!" Rev. 8:13.

This verse is parenthetical in that it is an insertion of explanatory matter concerning the announcement of the three woes under the fifth, sixth, and seventh trumpets which hold such terrors that an angel will fly in the midst of heaven announcing three woes because "of the three angels, which are yet to sound!"

The three woes of the last three trumpets are:

1. The plague of demon locusts out of the abyss, 9:1-12.
2. The plague of demon horsemen out of the abyss, 9:13-21.
3. The casting out of Satan to earth, 11:14-13:18.

5. The Fifth Trumpet: The First Woe.

"And the fifth angel sounded, and I saw a star fall from heaven unto the earth: and to him was given the key of the bottomless pit. And he opened the bottomless pit; and there arose a smoke out of the pit, as the smoke of a great furnace; and the sun and the air were darkened by reason of the smoke of the pit. And there came out of the smoke locusts upon the earth: and unto them was given power, as the scorpions of the earth have power. And it was commanded them that they should not hurt the grass of the earth, neither any green thing, neither any tree; but only those men which have not the seal of God in their foreheads. And to them it was given that they should not kill them, but that they should be tormented five months: and their torment was as the torment of a scorpion, when he striketh a man. And in those days shall men seek death, and shall not find it; and shall desire to die, and death shall flee from them. And the shapes of the locusts were like unto horses prepared unto battle; and on their heads were as it were crowns like gold, and their faces were as the faces of men. And they had hair as the hair of women, and their teeth were as the teeth of lions. And they had breast-plates, as it were breastplates of iron; and the sound of their wings was as the sound of chariots of many horses running to battle. And they had tails like unto scorpions, and there were stings in their tails: and their power was to hurt men five months. And they had a king over them, which is the angel of the bottomless pit, whose name in the Hebrew tongue is Abaddon, but in the Greek tongue hath his name Apollyon. One woe is past; and, behold, there come two woes more hereafter," Rev. 9:1-12.

The "star" that will fall to the earth from heaven is not a literal star, but an intelligent being, as is clear from the fact that personal pronouns and personal acts are ascribed to it, Rev. 9:1, 2. Only an intelligent being can be given a key and a command to open the door of the pit. Satan's angels are referred to as stars, Rev. 12:4-9. It is clear that the angel fell from heaven right there before John in vision and that indicates that he will actually fall from heaven, in the tribulation period, the very moment the fifth trumpet sounds.

This angel is, no doubt, the same one that binds Satan at the beginning of the Millennium in Rev. 20:1-3. Christ has the keys of the underworld, Matt. 8:29; Luke 8:31; Rev. 1:18; 20:11-15. It seems unreasonable that He would trust Satan or one of the fallen angels with the key which holds captive millions of Satan's own subjects, lest he would take advantage of this trust and loose all the demons of the pit in order to swell the ranks of Satan in his last stand against God before he is bound. God could not trust a fallen being with this key, seeing that they betrayed His confidence when they fell. God always gives responsibility to those whom He can trust. A fallen angel would not cast Satan, his own ruler, into the pit, nor would God require such of Satan's own subjects when He has many good angels whom He can trust, and who would be glad for such an opportunity.

Further, this angel is not the "angel of the bottomless pit" of Rev. 9:11 for if he is a trusted angel of God, as is evident, he cannot be a king of demons. It seems clear that "the angel of the bottomless pit, whose name in the Hebrew tongue is Abaddon, but in the Greek tongue hath his name Apollyon," is a fallen angel who is bound in the abyss with the demon locusts and who will come out of the pit with them as their leader in this terrible woe. In the description of locusts out of the pit the literal reading is, "they have over them a king, an angel of (out of) the abyss."

In some Greek texts the definite article is before the word "angel" with a footnote that it should be omitted and should read "an angel of the abyss" which makes it clear that he is simply one of the fallen angels who are bound in the abyss. This one is loosed with the demon locusts. His name is given as **Abaddon** and **Apollyon** which means "destruction" and "destroyer." These names are never used of Satan in the Bible, hence he cannot be Satan as some teach.

The word Abaddon is translated "destruction" in **Job 26:6**; 28:22; 31:12; Psa. 88:11; Prov. 15:11; 27:20, and it is clear in the passages themselves that Satan is not meant. Compare also Isa. 16:4; Jer. 4:7; 6:26; Dan. 8:24, 25; 9:26; 11:44 where the destroyer has no reference to Satan. This "destroyer" then is not Satan, Antichrist, etc., but an angel bound at the present time in the abyss. He will be loosed when the angel of Rev. 9:1 comes from heaven and opens the pit for the purpose of loosing him and his demon locusts to torment men, as stated here.

When the abyss is opened, smoke will come out of it "as the smoke of a great furnace" which will darken the sun and the air. It can be seen that since the darkening of one-third of the sun, moon, and stars under the fourth trumpet they have become normal again. Out of the smoke came forth demon locusts upon earth and to them was given power as the scorpions of the earth have power. The smoke indicates that the abyss is a place of fire but it is not to be confused with hades, tartarus, or the lake of fire mentioned elsewhere in Scripture. The Greek **akris,** translated "locusts" here is always translated such, Rev. 9:3, 7; Matt. 3:4; Mark 1:6. Ordinary locusts were the principal meat of John the Baptist. They are classed as "clean" food by the law and have been eaten for centuries, Lev. 11:22; Eccl. 12:5.

These are not ordinary locusts because:

(1) They will eat no vegetable productions. Cf. the eighth Egyptian plague of locusts which destroyed every green thing, Exod. 10:3-20.

(2) They have a king. Ordinary locusts have not, Prov. 30:27.

(3) The description proves them to be different.

(4) They are not stifled by the smoke, or burned by the fire of the pit, as ordinary locusts would be.

(5) They arise from the infernal regions. Ordinary locusts do not.

(6) They are indestructible and are not mortal, else men would not fear them.

They are literal because:

(1) The language proves them to be.

(2) God has always sent literal plagues and woes.

(3) The grass, herbs, and trees which they are commanded not to hurt are literal. They must be literal or such a command is unnecessary.

(4) Smoke, fire, etc., are literal, so they must be.

(5) They are intelligent, for they receive commands not to hurt those men who have the seal of God in their foreheads, Rev. 9:4. All other men they "torment" in the same literal and

physical way as natural scorpions do, Rev. 9:5. The sting of a scorpion is exceedingly painful for several hours, but it is seldom fatal. Cf. Deut. 8:15; 2 Chron. 10:11-14; Luke 10:19.

(6) They are objects of sight, for men will flee from them and will seek death in preference to contact with them.

(7) Their description proves they are literal. They are winged creatures like war horses with crowns of gold, faces of men, hair of women, teeth of lions, breastplates of iron, and stinging tails of scorpions. They will be innumerable and make a thunderous noise as only literal creatures can do.

Thus we see that the first woe will be a literal plague of demon creatures whose outward appearance is like that of a locust. The length of this plague is five months, the same length of time the flood prevailed (Gen. 7:24) and the same length of time natural locusts appear, from May to September.

"One woe is past; and, behold, there come two woes more hereafter," Rev. 9:12.

6. The Sixth Trumpet: The Second Woe.

"And the sixth angel sounded, and I heard a voice from the four horns of the golden altar which is before God, Saying to the sixth angel which had the trumpet, Loose the four angels which are bound in the great river Euphrates. And the four angels were loosed, which were prepared for an hour, and a day, and a month, and a year, for to slay the third part of men. And the number of the army of the horsemen were two hundred thousand thousand: And I heard the number of them. And thus I saw the horses in the vision, and them that sat on them, having breastplates of fire, and of jacinth, and brimstone: and the heads of the horses were as the heads of lions; and out of their mouths issued fire and smoke and brimstone. By these three was the third part of men killed, by the fire, and by the smoke, and by the brimstone which issued out of their mouths. For their power is in their mouth, and in their tails: for their tails were like unto serpents, and had heads, and with them they do hurt. And the rest of the men which were not killed by these plagues yet repented not of the works of their hands, that they should not worship devils, and idols of gold, and silver, and brass, and stone, and of wood: which neither can see, nor hear, nor walk: Neither repented they of their murders, nor of their sorceries, nor of their fornication, nor of their thefts," Rev. 9:13-21.

The voice here may be the voice of an angel of heaven to whom it is given to cry this command to the sixth trumpet angel: "loose the four angels which are bound in the great river Euphrates." Such unidentified voices are common to this book, 5:2; 7:2; 8:13; 14:7, 8, 9, 15; 18:2, 4. Besides these, which are voices of angels, there are many others spoken of in the book without reference to the nature of the one who speaks, Rev. 6:6; 10:4, 8; 11:12; 12:10; 14:13; 16:1, 17; 18:4; 19:5; 21:3. Still other voices are those of Christ, etc., as is clear in the passages themselves, Rev. 1:10-15; 3:20; 4:1; 5:11, 12; 6:7, 10; 7:10; 10:3 with 11:3; 14:2-5; 19:1-6. Blood upon the horns of the altar in the earthly tabernacle spoke of mercy to those who had sinned in ignorance (Lev. 4), but here mercy has been changed to judgment because of wilful ignorance and rejection of Christ and the truth.

The four angels bound in the Euphrates are fallen ones because good angels are never bound. They are the leaders of the 200-000,000 demon horsemen who will be loosed out of the abyss after the plague of the demon locusts is finished. Each of these four angels will command 50,000,000 of these infernal cavalry. They will go in the four directions "to slay the third part of men." Euphrates is connected with the judgment in the tribulation as is clear from this woe. It is also mentioned in "the day of the Lord," at Armageddon, Rev. 16:13-16; Jer. 46:4-10. The literal reading of Rev. 9:15 is, "And were loosed the four angels who had been prepared for the hour, and day, and month, and year, that they might kill the third part of men." This refers to a fixed point of time, not a period or length of duration. These demon cavalry will slay men at a given time as the first-born were slain in Egypt on the night of the passover. At least one-third of the Roman Empire will be affected by this plague if not one-third of the whole earth. Approximately 98,000,000 men will be slain by these horsemen if the territory is limited to the boundaries of the Old Roman Empire. But, if it takes in the other countries outside of Rome which are now controlled by the twenty-six present states of Rome, the figure will be about 296,000,000 people. The fact that the plague starts in the vicinity of the Euphrates shows that it may be limited to the countries surrounding that river. (See chapter five, point II, 5.)

The points above under the demon locusts which prove that they are real, literal, indestructible demon creatures also prove that these horsemen are of the same nature, from the same place, and for the same purpose of bringing woe upon the moral creation. However, the horsemen will kill men while the locusts will merely torment them. The general appearance of these demons will be that of horses having heads like lions. Out of their mouths will issue fire, smoke, and brimstone which will be the three causes of the death of men in this plague. They also have tails like serpents with heads on the end of them "and with them they do hurt." They have riders on them who have breastplates of fire, jacinth, and brimstone. This second woe will really be three plagues in one. "These three" and "these plagues" of Rev. 9:18, 20 refer to the fire, smoke, and brimstone. The rest of the men who are not killed by these three plagues will not repent to give God glory, or to give up their demon and idol worship and vile sins, on account of which the plagues are sent. These verses (20, 21) picture the awful moral conditions of the whole tribulation.

The theories that these horsemen were 200,000,000 of various armies that overran Europe during past centuries or that they are to be 200,000,000 men under Antichrist at Armageddon, are out of harmony with the plain description given above. No human horsemen ever were or ever will be like these creatures as is evident if we take the passage literally. There is no other way to understand the passage except in the literal sense, so take it as being fulfilled under the sixth trumpet as stated here.

Chapter Thirteen
(Parenthetical, Rev. 10:1-11:13)

THE MIGHTY ANGEL, Rev. 10:1-11

"And I saw another mighty angel come down from heaven, clothed with a cloud: and a rainbow was upon his head, and his face was as it were the sun, and his feet as pillars of fire: And he had in his hand a little book open: and he set his right foot upon the sea, and his left foot on the earth, And cried with a loud voice, as when a lion roareth: and when he had cried, seven thunders uttered their voices. And when the seven thunders had uttered their voices, I was about to write: and I heard a voice from heaven saying unto me, Seal up those things which the seven thunders uttered, and write them not. And the angel which I saw stand upon the sea and upon the earth lifted up his hand to heaven, And sware by him that liveth for ever and ever, who created heaven, and the things that therein are, and the earth, and the things that therein are, and the sea, and things which are therein, that there should be time no longer: But in the days of the voice of the seventh angel, when he shall begin to sound, the mystery of God should be finished, as he hath declared to his servants the prophets. And the voice which I heard from heaven spake unto me again, and said, Go and take the little book which is open in the hand of the angel which standeth upon the sea and upon the earth. And I went unto the angel, and said unto him, Give me the little book. And he said unto me, Take it, and eat it up; and it shall make thy belly bitter, but it shall be in thy mouth sweet as honey. And I took the little book out of the angel's hand, and ate it up; and it was in my mouth sweet as honey; and as soon as I had eaten it, my belly was bitter. And he said unto me, Thou must prophesy again before many peoples, and nations, and tongues, and kings," Rev. 10:1-11.

This passage (10:1-11:13) is the fourth parenthetical passage in the book and explains certain things which are not the contents of the trumpets or vials, but which are fulfilled in conjunction with them as is clear from the passage itself. Chapter 10:1-11 is a vision of the "mighty angel," chapter 11:1, 2 of the temple and Holy City, and 11:3-13 of the two witnesses. This fourth parenthetical passage breaks the main vision of the trumpets and is inserted between the sixth and seventh trumpets just as the first parenthetical passage is inserted between the sixth and seventh seals. This alone is proof that it is parenthetical. As to the fulfillment of the events of this passage that is clear, chapter 10:1-11, like the first part (7:1-8) of the first parenthetical passage, will be fulfilled in the order in which it is given. The last part of this parenthetical passage (11:1-13) concerning the two witnesses, will be fulfilled from the middle of the Week onward like the last part of the first parenthetical passage (7:9-17), as is clear from both passages. Thus, the parenthetical passages are inserted in their proper places and will be fulfilled in the order as given, except for a few passages, which are always clear as to the time of fulfillment. It is only natural to understand that they are to be fulfilled in the order of events in which they are inserted unless it is stated otherwise.

This mighty angel is, no doubt, Christ, who will come down from heaven with the little book open having taken it from the right hand of God in Rev. 5 and having opened the seven seals in Rev. 6:1-8:1. He is now ready to reveal the contents of the things "written within." The word "another" shows that this angel is not one of the trumpet angels, as is supposed by some. Not only the description of the angel proves him to be Christ, but in 11:3 He speaks of the two witnesses as being **"my** two witnesses." Such could not be written of a common angel. About 150 times in the Bible God is mentioned in connection with clouds. In Rev. 10:1; 14:14-16 it is the Son of Man who is mentioned with clouds. Never in the Bible are common angels mentioned with clouds. The "rainbow" is never used in the Bible apart from God so this angel here must be the Son of God. Other details of the appearance of this angel correspond with the vision of Christ in Rev. 1:12-16. A common angel is never described as to his head, face, feet or other parts of his being, but God is described thus several times. This angel cries "as when a lion roareth" which connects him with "the Lion of the tribe of Juda," Rev. 5:5. Such passages as Isa. 31:4,5; Jer. 25:29-36; Hos. 11:10,11; Joel 3:16; Amos 3:8 speak of the Lord roaring in wrath as a lion in the day of the Lord. Then too, Christ is the only person with the same authority exhibited by this angel.

The "little book" which He holds in His hand is the same book sealed with seven seals in Rev. 5. It is not a book of redemption or title deeds to the earth as some believe, but **a book of judgment, as seems clear from the following:**

1. The language of Rev. 5 and 10 does not indicate a difference.

2. The book of Rev. 5 was not an empty book sealed on the "backside" with seven seals but "written within." The writing "within" and the seals on the "backside" are two different things, but it seems they contain the same nature of events. At least, there is no explanation to the contrary. The opening of the seals will not exhaust the contents of the book "written within" for a close study of Rev. 5-8 shows that the seals contain a description of seven events which will be revealed by the opening of the seals before the things "written within" can be revealed. If the things "written within" are to be identical with the contents of the seals then why are they spoken of as "written within" a book and sealed on the backside with seven seals thus making a distinction between the seals and the book itself?

3. The "little book" of Rev. 10 will be open when the angel comes down from heaven. It is evident that this opening will have taken place by this "mighty angel" before He comes down to earth. There is also to be a note of triumph in the actions of the angel, for He will set His right foot upon the sea, and His left foot on the earth, and cry with a loud voice, as in triumph, and raise His hand to heaven and swear by Him that liveth for ever and ever ... that there should be time (delay) no longer. Why these actions of triumph, "as when a lion roareth," on the part of this "mighty angel?" Because "the Lion of the tribe of Juda, the Root of David, hath prevailed **to open** the book, and **to loose** the seven seals thereof," Rev. 5:5.

4. Between Rev. 5 and 10 "the Lamb" (this mighty angel) has proved His worthiness **"to open** the book and **to loose** the seven seals thereof." Having loosed the seven seals He then will stand

with the book open. The loosing of the seven seals is recorded in Rev. 6:1-8:1 and if this "little book open" in Rev. 10 is not the same book of Rev. 5 with the seals broken then where else in the Revelation are the things "written within" mentioned? If the book of Rev. 10 is not the same as that of Rev. 5, then we have one more mystery and Revelation ceases to be a revelation of the things it mentions. But once we see that the books of both chapters are the same and that they will be opened to reveal the things "written within" there remains no mystery or confusion over the books of Rev. 5 and 10.

5. If the book in Rev. 5 is so important that "no man in heaven, nor in earth, neither under the earth, was able to open the book, neither to look thereon" surely Christ would not reveal the events contained in the seals, and let the things "written within" go unrevealed or unmentioned in the Revelation, and thus leave us mystified concerning what was "written within." The things written within are certainly important enough to be revealed also. If the things of the seals will be terrible events on earth and momentous events in heaven, it is reasonable that the things "written within" will be also of the same nature. Therefore, they must necessarily be revealed or else the Revelation is not a complete revelation of "things shortly to come to pass." All these difficulties are easily eliminated by recognizing that the books in both chapters are the same.

6. The effect upon John when he was told to "eat the little book" (a Hebraism for the reception of knowledge) is sufficient proof that the little book contained terrible events to transpire on earth in connection with mankind. The effect upon John was the same as that upon Ezekiel and Jeremiah and further proves that the little book contained part of God's revelation of His judgments upon mankind. Cf. Ezek. 2:3-3:14; Jer. 15:16; 20:7-9; Ps. 119:103. The truth set forth in all these passages is that the reception of messages from God through the Holy Spirit is always sweet to the taste, but bitter when the contents are noted and given out to the people, especially when they concern bitter woes pronounced upon the prophet's own people, Israel. Such is the case with Rev. 6-19 which is concerning Israel and fulfilled in the Seventieth Week of Daniel.

7. Verse 11 is the key to the contents of this little book. This verse does not teach that John will be one of the two witnesses as the words "again" and "before" are sometimes taken to mean. The word "before" should be translated "of" or "concerning." Literally translated this verse reads, "Thou must prophesy again (yet, further) as to (or concerning) peoples and nations and tongues and kings many." This is exactly what John did in the rest of the Revelation, even more so than in the first part. We recognize then, that the things "written within" are "concerning many peoples and nations and tongues and kings." Immediately after John ate the "little book" the angel said, "Thou must

prophesy again," which proves that the little book contained matter connected with John's work as a prophet. Therefore, it could not have been a book of redemption or title deeds to the earth. Why would John be prophesying of redemption when that was already accomplished? Why would he be prophesying of title deeds to the earth when no such things were ever mentioned in Scripture? The scenes in this chapter will actually take place between the sixth and seventh trumpets, about the middle of the Week. These scenes do not signify Christ's formal possession of the earth for the vision is not symbolic with the exception of John's reception of the contents of the little book. The scene of the angel shows that the seals which bind the book have been completed at this time, that the things "written within" are now ready to be fulfilled, and that the completion of "the mystery of God" under the seventh trumpet will be no longer delayed.

Rev. 10 is not Christ's Formal Possession of the Earth.

1. He does not actually take possession of the earth until three and one-half years later when He comes for that purpose, Dan. 7:13, 14, 18; Rev. 19:11-21; Zech. 14:1-21.

2. This scene is associated with the expressions "delay should be no longer" and "the kingdoms of this world are become the kingdoms of our Lord, and of his Christ," Rev. 10:6; 11:15. But neither of these statements refers to God's possession of the earth in the middle of the Week. This seems clear from the fact that if God did take possession of the earth at this time, formally or otherwise, the Devil and Antichrist could not be here for three and one-half years more. What would be the use of such formal possession, especially if it is connected with "delay should be no longer" and such possession is really delayed three and one-half years more?

3. Christ's presence on earth during the sixth and seventh trumpets can be understood apart from the idea that He takes possession of the earth at this time. He is to do just what this angel did before John, and it seems clear in this passage that it was not a possession of the earth, but that which had to do with the completion of the mystery of God which is explained next.

The expression "delay should be no longer" (10:6) has no reference to Christ's possession of the earth at this time, but refers to the immediate fulfillment of "the mystery of God" of the next verse, which reads, according to the literal translation, "But in the days of the voice of the seventh angel, when he is about to sound the trumpet, also **should be completed** the mystery of God, **as he did announce** the glad tidings to his bondmen, the prophets." The seventh angel sounds in the middle of the Week, 11:15. It is "days" in duration and includes all of Rev. 11:14-13:18 as we shall see in chapter fifteen.

Now to determine which of these events is the mystery that is to be finished we must keep in mind the following facts:

1. It is to be finished during the days of the seventh trumpet.

The word "finished," from the Greek **teleo,** is used in 11:7; 15:1, 8; 17:17; 20:3, 5, 7 and means that which has reached its end.

2. It is indeed glad tidings.

3. It has been proclaimed by the prophets since the world began (Luke 1:70; Acts 3:21; 2 Pet. 1:21).

4. It has been delayed throughout all the ages, but now "delay should be no longer" in completing it.

The Mystery of God Is the Casting Out of Satan.

1. It is the only event mentioned in the days of the seventh trumpet that really meets the required four facts above. This can readily be seen by noticing the events of the seventh trumpet one by one to see if any of them meet the above four facts. None will do so except the casting out of Satan. Some of them are glad tidings but not one besides this has been **delayed** by God since the world began as He has declared to all His prophets.

2. The casting out of Satan will be finished under the seventh trumpet as is clear from Rev. 12:7-12.

3. The casting out of Satan is indeed glad tidings to all heavens, and, although it is a temporary woe to the inhabitants of the earth, it will be a permanent blessing after the woe, for that is the only way God's eternal plan can be fully realized, Rev. 12: 10-12.

4. The casting out of Satan has been proclaimed by the prophets from the earliest times, beginning in Gen. 3:15 and ending in Rev. 12:7-12. It is one of the themes of the Bible and has been referred to directly many times by the prophets, Isa. 24:21; 25:7; 27:1; etc.

5. It is the only event that has been delayed throughout all centuries. The woman, manchild, beasts, etc., have not been delayed for they have not existed throughout all centuries.

6. The triumphant attitude of the angel shows that an enemy is involved in the long delayed mystery of God. Such an attitude is not fitting for any other event of the seventh trumpet. The very nature of the case indicates such a final and delayed victory.

7. The fact that the three woes were to be under the fifth, sixth, and seventh trumpets shows that the casting out of Satan is the reference, Rev. 12:12.

8. This view harmonizes perfectly with the announcement that the kingdoms of this world are to become God's, as we shall see in chapter fifteen.

When the angel set His feet on the earth and sea and cried with a loud voice seven thunders uttered their voices; i.e., there were seven clear and distinct utterances from heaven. John was about to write what was uttered, when he was told not to do so. What was uttered has not been revealed and all speculation is valueless. They were perhaps of a personal nature to John. The voice was perhaps that of God's, Ps. 29; John 12:29.

(Parenthetical, Rev. 10:1-11:13)

THE TEMPLE OF GOD AND THE TWO WITNESSES,

Rev. 11:1-13

This parenthetical passage (10:1-11:13) continues with the measuring of the temple of God and the revelation of the two witnesses, who will be on earth the last three and one-half years of Daniel's Seventieth Week.

I. The Temple of God.

"And there was given me a reed like unto a rod: and the angel stood, saying, Rise, and measure the temple of God, and the altar, and them that worship therein. But the court which is without the temple leave out, and measure it not; for it is given unto the Gentiles: and the holy city shall they tread under foot forty and two months," Rev. 11:1, 2.

The reed here is also referred to in Rev. 21:15, 16. It was about twelve and one-half feet long and like a rod or sceptre, as elsewhere in Rev. 2:27; 12:5; 19:15. This scene indicates measuring for destruction, not for building. Such passages as 2 Sam. 7:14; Ps. 2:9; 89:32; Isa. 11:4; Lam. 2:8; Ezek. 20:37; 1 Cor. 4:21; etc., with the above passages, bring out the thought of a rod of chastening.

This temple is not Herod's temple for that one was destroyed some twenty-five years before this vision at the destruction of Jerusalem, 70 A.D. Again, this temple cannot be the Millennial temple as described in Ezek. 40-48, because that will not be built until Christ comes to earth, Zech. 6:12, 13. The temple here is the one to be rebuilt by the Jews before Daniel's Seventieth Week. It will be destroyed at the end of the tribulation, either by the earthquake under the seventh vial (16:18, 19), or by the armies of Antichrist at the taking of Jerusalem, Zech. 14:1-5. Both Testaments are clear that there is to be such a temple where sacrifices will be offered for at least three and one-half years. Then it will be made desolate for three and one-half years and will be polluted by the Antichrist and the Gentiles, Dan. 9:27; 12:7-12; Matt. 24:15; 2 Thess. 2:2-4.

It is noticeable that the temple, altar, and worshippers of the temple are all that were measured, showing that everything about the Jewish part of the temple and the worship of the Jews will pass under the rod of judgment and desolation for the purpose of breaking the spirit of Israel. The court of the Gentiles was not measured to be trodden down of the Gentiles, for it was already in their possession, and was considered by the Jews as being polluted and fit only for Gentiles. This court is to be cast out in the sense that there will be no more worship there by the Gentiles, who will have worshipped there before entering into the temple itself to worship Antichrist and his image. Not only will the temple be given to the Gentiles to trod underfoot, but the city itself will be in their possession for forty-two literal months. The word "Gentiles" is from the Greek **ethnos** which occurs twenty-three times in the book and is translated "nations," except here.

This treading down of Jerusalem by the Gentiles for forty-two months proves that the times of the Gentiles will not end until the return of Christ at the end of the forty-two months. According to this, these times did not end in 1914, 1917, 1924, 1927, 1936, 1942 or any other year in the past. Neither can they end in 1954 for the ten kingdoms of the Revised Roman Empire must first be formed, after which will come the Antichrist and the seven years of tribulation. If the seven years were to begin this year (1948) it would be at least 1955 before the times of the Gentiles could end. How many years before the ten kingdoms are formed and before Antichrist is revealed is not certain so it is clear that the so-called 2,520 years of the length of the times of the Gentiles based upon the seven times punishment of Israel in Lev. 26 is a false theory. Certainly this plain passage concerning the times of the Gentiles continuing through the forty-two months is sufficient apart from the many other Scriptures and arguments. The phrases "forty and two months," "a thousand two hundred and three score days," and "a time, times, and half a time," all refer to a definite period of time, the last three and one-half years of Daniel's Seventieth Week when Antichrist reigns supreme. Rev. 11:2. 3: 12:6. 14; 13:5; Dan. 7:25; 12:7. (See our book "God's Plan for Man," Les. 15 and 16 and chapter thirty-six for a study of "the times of the Gentiles.")

II. The Two Witnesses.

"And I will give power unto my two witnesses, and they shall prophesy a thousand two hundred and threescore days, clothed in sackcloth. These are the two olive trees, and the two candlesticks standing before the God of the earth. And if any man will hurt them, fire proceedeth out of their mouth, and devoureth their enemies: and if any man will hurt them, he must in this manner be killed. These have power to shut heaven, that it rain not in the days of their prophecy: and have power over waters to turn them to blood, and to smite the earth with all plagues, as often as they will. And when they shall have finished their testimony, the beast that ascendeth out of the bottomless pit shall make war against them, and shall overcome them, and kill them. And their dead bodies shall lie in the street of the great city, which spiritually is called Sodom and Egypt, where also our Lord was crucified. And they of the people and kindreds and tongues and nations shall see their dead bodies three days and an half, and shall not suffer their dead bodies to be put in graves. And they that dwell upon the earth shall rejoice over them, and make merry, and shall send gifts one to another; because these two prophets tormented them that dwelt on the earth. And after three days and an half the spirit of life from God entered into them, and they stood upon their feet; and great fear fell upon them which saw them. And they heard a great voice from heaven saying unto them, Come up hither. And they ascended up to heaven in a cloud; and their enemies beheld them. And the same hour was there a great earthquake, and the tenth part of the city fell, and in the earthquake were slain of men seven thousand: and the remnant were affrighted, and gave glory to the God of heaven," Rev. 11:3-13.

First of all, let us determine just what this passage says about the two witnesses before we go to other Scriptures. Any theory of their identity must harmonize with these statements. They are two men and not two covenants, two dispensations, etc., as is clear from the plain description of them here and elsewhere. The truths given here are as follows:

1. They are "my (Christ's) two witnesses," Rev. 11:3.

2. They will be given power by Christ in the future, 11:3. This excludes the argument that they must be two men who have exercised this power in past history.

3. They will prophesy 1,260 days or during the same period of time that the Antichrist reigns supreme, the Holy City is trodden down of the Gentiles, and the woman flees into the wilderness for protection, Rev. 11:2, 3; 12:6, 14; 13:5. **That they will prophesy during the last three and one-half years, instead of the first three and one-half years, seems clear from the following:**

(1) All passages of forty-two months, 1,260 days, and three and one-half years, in both Daniel and Revelation, always refer to the last half of Daniel's Seventieth Week.

(2) The fact that the two witnesses are not mentioned until the middle of the Week or after the seals and the first six trumpets, proves that they do not prophesy during the fulfillment of these things in the first three and one-half years. If they were to prophesy during the first three and one-half years, the prophecy concerning them would surely be placed before the events of this period so that we should naturally understand that they were to prophesy during that time instead of during the last three and one-half years. Why should their ministry be revealed in connection with the middle of the Week if it is to end at that time?

(3) We naturally understand that the 1,260 days or forty-two months of Rev. 11:3 are the same as the forty-two months of Rev. 11:2, for both periods are in the same prophecy. There is no break between these verses as to two periods of time. Since the city is not trodden underfoot by the Gentiles until the last half of the Week, the two witnesses must prophesy during that time instead of the first half of the Week.

(4) The angel of Rev. 10 will come down from heaven after the sixth trumpet in the middle of the Week and just before the seventh. It is this angel who states, "I will give power to my two witnesses." This implies futurity from the time when the angel comes down. To place the fulfillment of Rev. 11:3-13 back during all the seals and trumpets is to take it out of the place given and intended of God.

(5) The main argument of those who teach that the two witnesses prophesy during the first three and one-half years is that the beast, when he comes out of the abyss in the middle of the Week will immediately destroy them. There is no statement that the beast comes out of the abyss in the middle of the Week and where can it be found that he destroys the witnesses immediately after he arises? Verse 7 does not teach that. It simply states that the beast which comes out of the abyss will destroy them at the end of their testimony, but as far as proving the above, it does not.

On the contrary, it is clear that the beast will come out of the abyss sometime before the Seventieth Week and cause the rise of the Antichrist out of the ten kingdoms, who, in turn will make the seven years covenant with Israel. (See chapters thirty to thirty-five.) This is further proved from the fact that the two witnesses will withstand Antichrist from the middle of the Week onward for the purpose of protecting the Israelites who do not flee into the wilderness. There will be no reason for protecting them during the first three and one-half years, for Antichrist will do that himself. Therefore, there will not be such a great need for the ministry of the two witnesses in the first three and one-half years. However, during the last three and one-half years the Antichrist will oppose Israel, hence the need for the protection of the two witnesses at that time. What will be the purpose of their prophecy and working of miracles unless Israel is to be persecuted during their ministry by Antichrist?

The fact that they cannot be killed by the beast until they have finished their testimony proves that the beast, when he comes out of the abyss, does not immediately destroy them, and further shows the antagonism between the beast and the two witnesses during the 1,260 days. God has no intention of withstanding the beast until he breaks his covenant with Israel and begins to destroy them. Therefore, the ministry of the witnesses would be without purpose during the first three and one-half years. Their ministry will be fitting only for the terrible days of the great tribulation caused by Antichrist in the last three and one-half years. God is retaining these two men in heaven for this particular purpose.

(6) If there were a statement to the effect that the two witnesses had prophesied three and one-half years previous to the time the passage was given to John then the position of it here would be clear, but there is no such statement. Unless it is clear in the parenthetical passage that it is not to be fulfilled in the place it is given, then we can rest assured that it is given in its proper order.

(7) Mal. 4:5, 6 proves that the time of their ministry is before the great and notable day of the Lord, which will begin at the coming of Christ. This, then, places their ministry during the last three and one-half years.

4. They are to be prophets for they will prophesy three and one-half years, Rev. 11:3. They may prophesy of the doom of Satan, the beasts out of the sea and earth, and of their followers and other future things, but the main thought is that they will preach to Israel and try to turn their hearts back to God and each other, in order to avert the judgment of God, Mal. 4:5, 6.

5. They will be clothed in sackcloth as a sign of mourning because of the judgments that are about to fall, Rev. 11:3. See 2 Sam. 3:31; 1 Kings 20:31, 32; Neh. 9:1; Esther 4:1; Ps. 30:11; 35:13; Jonah 3:5.

6. They "are the two olive trees and the two candlesticks standing (which stand) before the God of the earth," Rev. 11:4. This, with Zech. 4:3, 11-14, shows that two persons are repre-

sented. Whoever they are, they were standing before God by at least 500 B.C., when Zechariah prophesied and were still there when John prophesied about 96 A.D. This then would exclude the Apostle John from being one of the two witnesses as well as does the fact that he was the one who saw them there. The expression "God of the earth" shows that God is the rightful proprietor of the earth, Josh. 3:11, 13; Zech. 6:5.

7. They will be given power or authority and the liberty or right to exercise it at will, Rev. 11:5, 6. If any man desires to hurt them fire will come out of their mouths and devour their enemy. In whatever way their enemies may desire to hurt them they will be killed in like manner. The two witnesses will stop rain during their ministry, turn the waters to blood, and smite the earth with all plagues as often as they choose. This shows that both are to exercise the same power. These plagues and many others have been sent of God many times in history because of sin and idolatry, so it is no wonder that they will be sent again for these sins, Exod. 7:20-25; 15:26; Lev. 26; Deut. 11:14-17; 28:1-30:10; 1 Sam. 6:4; 2 Sam. 24:15.

8. When they finish their testimony they will be placed at the mercy of their enemies. The beast that will ascend out of the abyss will make war on them and will overcome them and kill them, Rev. 11:7. This is the first mention of the beast out of the abyss. The ascension of the beast out of the abyss will be dealt with in full in chapers thirty to thirty-five. The word "overcome" implies real conflict. It is the same word used of the overcomers in the Church epistles of Rev. 2, 3 and shows that the beast will finally gain greater power than that of the two witnesses because of the withdrawal of God's power when their ministry is finished. The struggle to conquer will have been waged continually for 1,260 days before the beast finally overcomes them.

The phrase "kill them" shows clearly that they will be two natural men who have never died but who will die at the hands of the beast. If these things be clear then it is equally as clear that they have both been translated in order to "stand before the God of the earth" and that they are still in natural bodies and will be sent back to the earth as mortals, else they can never be killed by the Antichrist. Nothing is more clear concerning the two witnesses than that they will die as every other man has died. This alone excludes the idea that they have resurrected or glorified bodies in heaven now, or while on earth during their ministry.

9. When they are slain by the beast their corpses are to lie in the streets of Jerusalem for three and one-half days. Men will not suffer them to be put into graves. They will gloat over their death and make merry because these two prophets which tormented them are dead. After three and one-half days the Spirit of life from God will enter into them and they will stand

upon their feet and ascend into heaven before their enemies. This will produce paralyzing fear upon their enemies and in the same hour a great earthquake will strike Jerusalem and seven thousand men will be slain and one-tenth of the city destroyed. The rest of men will give glory to God, 11:8-13. The seven thousand slain by the earthquake after the death of the two witnesses is quite a contrast to the seven thousand preserved in the days of Elijah, whom Jezebel desired to slay.

Here Jerusalem is called a "great city" indicating a large growth before that time. It will be rebuilt only to be destroyed again, Zech. 14:5; Rev. 16:19. It is also called here spiritually Sodom and Egypt where Christ was crucified. This thought is a very familiar one in connection with the Old Testament, Isa. 1:9,10; Ezek. 16:46, 53; 23:3, 8, 19, 27. These facts concerning the two witnesses in the Revelation simplify the question as to the identity. In fact, they do all but name them, and thus exclude all speculation on the subject.

The Identity of the Two Witnesses.

It is no doubt clear to the reader after due consideration of the above facts concerning the two witnesses that **there are only two men in the whole Bible that fit this plain Revelation.** They are Enoch and Elijah. That Elijah will be one of them seems too clear from Scripture. Elijah must come back in person to fulfil Mal. 3, 4. This first verse of Mal. 3 gives us a reference both to Elijah and John the Baptist, but beyond this verse John is not mentioned. John was never Elijah in person as some would take from the words of Christ in Matt. 11:14. John himself said that he was not Elijah, John 1:19-23. Both Christ and John were truthful. When John said that he was not Elijah he meant that he was not Elijah in person, for he could not have been the natural son of a Tishbite in the days of Ahab and also be the natural son of Zachariah and Elizabeth as in Luke 1. All Christ had in mind was that John was he who was to come in the "spirit and power of Elias" as in Luke 1:17. Mal. 3:2-6, 13-17; 4:1-6 have reference to the second advent of Christ because they speak of judgment and tribulation and the day of the Lord, and not of grace as in John's day. This seems to identify one of the two witnesses as being the Elijah of the Old Testament who was translated to be reserved before God unto the future day when God will have need of him again, to withstand Antichrist as he did Jezebel and Ahab of old.

Moses Could Not Be One of the Two Witnesses.

Moses would never fit the statements given above concerning the two witnesses. The arguments of this school are too general. It is believed that Moses and Elijah are the only two men who have exercised the powers of the two witnesses but this argument of past power is annulled by point 2 on page 105. Elisha had a double portion of Elijah's spirit and according to this argument, should be substituted for Elijah, for he had greater power than he had but that could not be. This school of interpreters attempts to separate the power of the two witnesses by assigning power over rain to Elijah and power over plagues to Moses, but this is contradicted by point 7 on page 107, which shows that they both have equal power. It further argues that the operations of Moses and Elijah identify them with the title "My two witnesses," and that witnessing was their vocation in that they witnessed on the mount of transfiguration (Matt. 17:3), at the tomb of Jesus (Luke 24:4-7), and at the ascension of Christ (Acts 1:11), always appearing in shining garments. Also, it is averred that Moses, being raised from the dead, typifies the resurrection saints and Elijah, translated, typifies the translated saints and that one was resurrected and the other translated for the express purpose of witnessing.

These arguments may appear sound to the superficial reader, but they are out of harmony with Scripture. This would seem to make Moses and Elijah the only two witnesses in the Bible but they are not, 1 Cor. 15:14, 15; Acts 1:8; 10:43; etc.

There is nothing in Scripture to intimate that the two who appeared at the tomb of Jesus and at his ascension were Moses and Elijah. Contrarily, it speaks of them as "two angels." There is no passage which proves that Moses' body was raised from the dead. Jude 9 shows that he was not raised from the dead, for God, after having rescued Moses' body from the Devil, who had the power of death (Heb. 2:14, 15) until Jesus conquered him, **buried** Moses in the land of Moab (Deut. 34:5-8). Surely if God intended to raise Moses from the dead, he would have translated him as he did Enoch and Elijah, or at least would have raised him before burying him. Then too, the fact that Moses and Elijah appeared with Christ on the mount in shining garments does not prove that every time beings with shining garments are seen that they are Moses and Elijah, nor does it prove that Moses was raised from the dead. Everyone in paradise is vested with shining raiment and no claim is made that they are all resurrected, so why assume that Moses was resurrected merely because he appeared in shining garments? Will not the souls under the altar in heaven be clothed with white raiment before they are resurrected? Rev. 6:9-11. The fact is, Moses could not possibly have been raised from the dead and have a glorified body on the mount for that was before Christ had become the "firstfruits" of "ALL that slept," 1 Cor. 15:20-23. The fact that the death of Christ was the subject on that day (Luke 9:31) seems to indicate that the reference to the appearance of Moses and Elijah was in connection with the law and prophets, which hailed Christ as the antitype of all the sacrificial types of the Old Testament.

Moses cannot have a glorified body now, as he would be sure to have if he were resurrected, and still be a mortal man as one of the two witnesses to come back to earth and die at the hands of Antichrist. A resurrected body can never be killed. "It is appointed unto men **once** to die but after this the judgment," Heb. 9:27. This appointed death has reference to that passed upon all men under the curse. It is true that a few have been raised from the dead temporarily, to show the glory and power of God, but no such person has ever seen corruption nor has he ever undergone his appointed death and lived again in this life to die the second time. Neither will Moses be once more in corruptible form during the tribulation after having died his appointed death and seen corruption. He could not have been resurrected and given a body before Christ's resurrection, hence, he was dead and his body in the grave nearly seventeen hundred years before this time, and if he was not one of the "many" (Matt. 27:52, 53) that rose from the dead after the resurrection of Christ, his body is still in the grave and will not be raised from the dead until the rapture of the dead and living in Christ, who will rise to meet Christ in the air. This excludes Moses as being one of the two witnesses, for he can never be killed by Antichrist as they will be.

There is also no Scripture to prove that either Moses or Elijah was resurrected or translated for the express purpose of witnessing in the future. If Elijah was translated for that purpose then it could also be argued that Enoch was translated for the same purpose and this same method of proof could also be carried out in the case of the raptured saints. Such a conclusion is inevitable when such proof is depended upon.

Enoch Will Be the Other Witness.

Since it seems unreasonable that Moses will be the other witness we advance Enoch as the obvious choice of God, although not with a definite "saith the Lord" as in the case of Elijah, Mal. 4:5, 6. It is clear, however, that Enoch and Elijah are the only two who have not tasted death, i. e., have not died their appointed death on earth. This, they must do as all others have done, Gen. 5:21-24; Heb. 11:5; 2 Kings 2. Both were prophets of judgment, Jude 14, 15; 1 Kings 17, 18. We know that Elijah was translated to heaven and is now one of the two olive trees and two candlesticks which stand before God. Is it not reasonable that Enoch, being the only other man translated that he should not see death during his lifetime on earth, and that for some definite purpose, is the other witness?

That both these men should come back and die their appointed death at the hands of Antichrist is not only not incredible but reasonable. Some argue that Enoch was translated that he should not see death "at all" but these words are not found in the passage in Heb. 11:5. What is said of Enoch in this verse could also be said of Elijah and yet we know that he is to come back and die according to Heb. 9:27. Enoch lived a natural life under the laws of degeneration and was subject to the law of death. He could not possibly escape it unless he were to live at the time of the rapture when the mystery of men being translated, without seeing death, will be fulfilled.

Paul showed the mystery of translation and entrance into an

eternal state without death, and if it was previously demonstrated by Enoch, then Paul revealed no mystery. If Paul, who wrote about the translation of Enoch, believed that Enoch was translated without the possibility of seeing death in the future, he no doubt would have used this as an example, as was his custom in illustrating his doctrine of translation without death.

Again, if Enoch was translated and given a glorified body which could not see death, he was given one over thirty-five hundred years before Christ received a glorified body. Then, in that event Christ was not the firstfruits of the eternal state among the sons of men and such He is stated to be, Rom. 5:12-21; 1 Cor. 15:20-23, 45-49. How could Enoch receive a glorified body "like unto His glorious body" (Phil. 3:21) before Christ had a body of that nature? If Enoch obtained a glorified body and God gave it to him before Christ and that through faith, then, others could have received theirs also by the same means. If that were the case there would have been no need for the conquest of death by Christ and His victory in resurrection and glorification, for God could have given such bodies without it. It is also clear from Heb. 1, 2 that Christ was the first to be exalted into an eternal state with a body of glory above the angels and every other creature. Since Enoch did not receive a glorified body before Christ, and since we have no record of such after Christ, he cannot permanently reside in heaven without dying, according to the above scriptures.

Enoch must come back and die. When will it be, if not in the tribulation? Elijah who has never died, must die. Enoch who also has never died, must die. If he is not the other witness, then mystery surrounds his death and destiny and his history is incomplete. God told Elijah that He was going to translate him for a special ministry in the future and he believed God and was translated by faith. Enoch was also translated by faith which shows that God told him that He was going to translate him. There must have been a purpose in the mind of God. It was not because he pleased God more than anyone else but it was "by faith" in taking God at His word. God had a purpose in translating Enoch, as well as Elijah, and what was it if not to supply the other witness? Elijah pleased God and was translated by faith. Enoch pleased God and was translated by faith. The cases are parallel and stand or fall together. These are the only two men who can possibly comply with the plain description of the two witnesses in every point.

Moreover, Enoch and Elijah as the two witnesses are supported by early tradition as is proved by the apocryphal writings which have come down to us. See the **Arabic History of Joseph the Carpenter, Gospel of Nicodemus** chapter 20, the apocryphal **Apocalypse of John,** page 95, etc.

Chapter Fifteen

7. THE SEVENTH TRUMPET: THE THIRD WOE,

Rev. 11:14-13:18.

"The second woe is past; and behold, the third woe cometh quickly. And the seventh angel sounded; and there were great voices in heaven, saying, The kingdoms of this world are become the kingdoms of our Lord, and of his Christ; and he shall reign for ever and ever. And the four and twenty elders, which sat before God on their seats, fell upon their faces, and worshipped God, Saying, We give thee thanks, O Lord God Almighty, which art, and wast, and art to come; because thou hast taken to thee thy great power, and hast reigned. And the nations were angry, and thy wrath is come, and the time of the dead, that they should be judged, and that thou shouldst give reward unto thy servants the prophets, and to the saints, and them that fear thy name, small and great; and shouldst destroy them which destroy the earth. And the temple of God was opened in heaven, and there was seen in his temple the ark of his testament: and there were lightnings, and voices, and thunderings, and an earthquake, and great hail," Rev. 11:14-19.

The first part of this passage announces the third woe, which is the last of the three woes announced by the angel in Rev. 8:13 that were to take place under the fifth, sixth and seventh trumpets. The third woe is not the earthquake of Rev. 11:13 which takes place when the two witnesses are caught up to heaven, but the casting out of Satan to the earth as under the seventh trumpet, Rev. 12:12. Neither is this earthquake the second woe for it takes place under the sixth trumpet as announced by the angel in Rev. 8:13. The two witnesses are not caught up under any of the trumpets, but at the end of the Week. Verse 13 ends the above parenthetical passage and verse 14 announces the third woe in the same way that the second woe was announced just before it began, Rev. 9:12.

The seventh trumpet is a period of time (10:7) and embraces the above statements, besides the vision of the woman, manchild, dragon, remnant, war in heaven, beasts, etc., of Rev. 11:14-13:18. It does not embrace any event beyond these chapters. When it sounds all the above statements are made by different creatures in anticipation of what is soon to take place. What happens under the seventh trumpet in the casting out of Satan, makes it possible for God to become supreme over the world. This does not indicate that God becomes absolute ruler over the world during the seventh trumpet, for God must first defeat the satanic powers in the heavenlies before He can carry out His purpose in the earth. This shows that the seventh trumpet need not last throughout the last three and one-half years as some teach, for God can cast out the usurper of the world, thus making it possible to take the world as His own, without actually taking possession of it. God becomes sovereign by this defeat of Satan, but it takes time for the results of this victory to be worked out on earth so that it is realized among men. This necessary delay of three and one-half years in actually taking possession of the earth in person, after the seventh trumpet, is caused for the completion of God's prophetic word in pouring out His wrath upon men for their persecution of Israel.

After the statement of God becoming sovereign over the kingdoms of this world, we have six sayings of the elders which are either fulfilled under the seventh trumpet or given in anticipation of the time each will be fulfilled, as the case may be. The first three statements are fulfilled at this time, but those relative to judging the dead, giving reward to saints and destroying the earth destroyers, will be fulfilled in their own time. They all have a definite time of fulfillment, but that time is not given here. We know that the dead will be judged at the final judgment after the Millennium, Rev. 20:11-15. The destruction of earth destroyers is both before and after the Millennium, 2 Thess. 1:7-10; Rev. 19:11-21; 20:7-10. The time to judge the saints, both earthly and heavenly, will be sometime during Daniel's Seventieth Week between the rapture and the second advent, for all saints will be rewarded by the time they reign during the Millennium, Rev. 20:4-6.

After the statements of the elders, John saw the temple of God in heaven opened where the ark of His testament was located. This temple is the same as discussed in chapters nine and twenty-four. The ark is not the one Moses made, but the heavenly pattern from which he made his. Cf. the thunderings, etc., of Rev. 11:19 with those of Rev. 8:5; 16:17-21.

The catching up of the manchild, the casting out of Satan from heaven, the flight of the woman into the wilderness, the persecution of the remnant, the rise of the beast out of the sea and the beast out of the earth, will all happen and will all be completed under the seventh trumpet. Just because the manchild is in heaven, the woman is in the wilderness, the devil is on earth, and the beasts of Rev. 13 continue for the last three and one-half years, that does not mean the seventh trumpet lasts that long.

The seventh trumpet is not the same as "the last trump" at the time of the rapture, as proved in chapter six, point I, 2. This trumpet blows in the middle of the Week at least three and one-half years after the rapture. That it does blow in the middle of the Week is clear from the fact that there is only a period of forty-two months (Rev. 11:2; 13:5), twelve hundred and sixty days (Rev. 11:3; 12:6), or three and one-half years (Rev. 12:14) from the blowing of the seventh trumpet to the end of the Week. If this be true, then it is only sensible to believe that the sixth trumpet blows before the seventh, the fifth before the sixth, the fourth before the fifth, the third before the fourth, the second before the third, and the first before the second, or that the first six trumpets blow in the first three and one-half years before the middle of the Week. Then, too, the whole seven seals all happen before the first trumpet, so we can scripturally conclude that the seven seals and first six trumpets are fulfilled before the seventh trumpet in the middle of the Week. The fifth trumpet is five months long, and naturally the others take time to be fulfilled, so we can also conclude that the seven seals and first six trumpets last the whole first three and one-half years of Daniel's Seventieth Week.

Chapter Sixteen

THE SUN-CLOTHED WOMAN, Rev. 12:1, 2, 5a, 6, 13-16

In these passages a complete revelation of the woman, as to her identification, motherhood, persecution, flight and protection, is given. These subjects in conjunction with other scriptures will now be taken up in their logical order.

I. The Identification of the Woman.

"And there appeared a great wonder in heaven; a woman clothed with the sun, and the moon under her feet, and upon her head a crown of twelve stars," Rev. 12:1.

The word "appeared" would be better translated "was seen," for the Greek word **horao** meaning to perceive with the eyes, is used of bodily sight, and with special reference to the object looked at. The word "wonder" is from the Greek **semeion**, which means a sign, and should be so translated in every passage where it is used. It has regard to the **significance** of the work wrought, whether in itself, or in the reason, object, design and teaching intended to be conveyed by it. It occurs thirty-one times in Matthew, Mark, and Luke and is rendered "miracle" only once, Luke 23:8. It occurs seventeen times in John and is quite wrongly translated "miracle" thirteen times and "sign" only four times. The word "wonder" should never be used for this word as the Greek word **teras** means "a wonder" and has regard to the effect produced on those who witness some mighty work. "There was seen a great sign in heaven" is the idea conveyed. **The symbol was seen in heaven by John but what is symbolized by the woman is in the earth as is proved by the following:**
1. The manchild will be caught up to heaven at its deliverance and such could not be true if the woman were in heaven, Rev. 12:5.
2. The woman will flee into the wilderness which is on earth, Rev. 12:6. (See point III on page 141.)
3. When the dragon is cast to the earth he will persecute the woman, Rev. 12:13.
4. The earth will help the woman and swallow the flood that is cast out of the dragon's mouth to devour her. This could not be said of her if she were in heaven, Rev. 12:15, 16.

The woman is a symbol and we must deal with her as a symbol and clearly differentiate between her and the thing she symbolizes. Here the reader should review the interpretation on symbols in chapter one. There is always, unless stated or clearly implied otherwise, only one central truth symbolized by a symbol and the details are not to be stressed. When details are given any attention at all they must harmonize with the main truth conveyed. This will eliminate all speculation on different parts of the symbol which are not stated or understood from other passages as having a separate meaning. **That the woman could not be** a symbol of the virgin Mary, the Church, or Christendom we shall see in the four theories on the manchild in the next chapter.

This woman symbolizes, we firmly believe, National Israel. By this term we mean all the Israelites who will be back in Palestine during the Seventieth Week and form the nation at that time, Joel 3; Zech. 9:10-16; 12:4-14; 13: 8, 9; 14:1-21; Matt. 24:15-26; Dan. 9:27. The Jews in all other lands will remain as they are today and will not be gathered back to their land until the second advent, Isa. 11:11, 12; Ezek. 37:1-28; Matt. 24:31. **Reasons why the woman symbolizes National Israel are:**

1. Israel is often mentioned in the Old Testament as a married woman, Isa. 54:1-6; Jer. 3:1-14. The whole book of Hosea is devoted to show the marriage of Israel and God, her backslidings in playing the whore and leaving God, and her future humiliation and brokenness in the wilderness and return to her husband, Hos. 2:14-23; Rom. 11; Acts 15:13-18. Israel here is symbolized by a married woman to show the actions of the nation during the middle of the Week and on to the coming of Christ. Israel is the only company of people in Scripture that is spoken of as a married woman. The great religious system of the last days is symbolized by a "whore" and not by a married woman, Rev. 17.

2. The Bible recognizes only three classes of people in the world today: the Church, the Jews, and the Gentiles, 1 Cor. 10:32. At the time this woman travails, in the middle of the Week, the Church will have been removed from the earth leaving only the last two classes, as proved in chapters six through eight. The woman certainly could not be the Gentile world or the Jews in the Gentile world. She must be the Jews who have left the nations and returned to their own land to await their Messiah, as we shall see.

3. If the sun, moon, and twelve stars mean anything they can only symbolize the same as was seen in the dream of Joseph in Gen. 37:9-11, namely, the twelve tribal heads and their parents. Here the whole twelve tribes are seen in national restoration, in the symbol of the woman.

4. Israel is the only one dealt with in Scripture that could fulfill the statements concerning the woman as is clear from the following studies. (See chapter seven, point 6, for nineteen reasons why Israel is being dealt with in Rev. 6-19 instead of the Church, which prove the woman to be Israel.)

II. The Travail of the Woman.

"And she being with child cried, travailing in birth, and pained to be delivered . . . and she brought forth a man child," Rev. 12:2, 5a.

The word "travailing" is from the Greek **odino** which is used here and in Gal. 4:19, 27; Matt. 24:8; Mark 13:8 and means to experience the pains of parturition, whether literally or figuratively. Here it is used in a figurative sense, for the woman is a symbol, and therefore, cannot travail literally. The Greek word for "pained" means tormented and is so translated in Rev. 9:5; 11:10; 14:10; 20:10. This helps us to understand that the travail and pain of Israel in the whole Seventieth Week is caused by the same sort of punishment she has always undergone under Gentile rule. (See chapter eight for the continued travail of Israel in both parts of the Week.)

The travails of Israel have been numerous in her past history as is clearly revealed in her bondages and deliverances, which began with Israel in Egypt and in the period of the judges and kings. They have continued, more or less, and will finally culminate in the worst period of travail she has ever known, Dan. 12:1; Matt. 24:15-26. Such passages as Exod. 18:8; Jer. 4:31; 6:24; 13:21; 22:22, 23; Mic. 4:9, 10 show some of the travails of Israel in the past. **There is to be a future continued travail of Israel in the tribulation Week with a twofold result:**

1. The deliverance of the manchild in the middle of the Week, Rev. 12:2-5; Jer. 30:6-9; Dan. 12:1; Isa. 66:7, 8. This will be the result of the terrible anguish and sorrow of Israel in the middle of the Week, because the Antichrist, with whom she has made a seven years covenant as a guarantee of her protection from the great whore and the ten kings of Revised Rome, will have broken this covenant and determined to completely destroy her. At this time of travail the manchild is to be delivered, because that company will not be deserving of the great tribulation, which will follow immediately.

Antichrist will be defeated in his purpose of destroying Israel at this time by the "tidings out of the north and east" (Dan. 11:44, 45); i. e., the northern and eastern European and Asiatic nations will league together against Antichrist to put a stop to his superhuman successes in his conquests. This will keep him occupied during the last three and one-half years of the Week, after he has gained the whole ten kingdoms, and thus cause him to let Israel alone for the time being or until he conquers his new enemies. Then, all nations which he has conquered in both parts of the Week, as well as other co-operative nations in the rest of the world (16:13-16), will be gathered against Israel to destroy them as he intended to do in the middle of the Week, then Christ suddenly comes to save Israel, Zech. 14.

The result of the travail of Israel at this time will be that God will undertake by catching up the manchild. After that He will supernaturally protect the woman in the wilderness and the remnant in Palestine by occuping the attention of the Antichrist through the threatenings of the northern and eastern nations as stated above.

2. The deliverance of the woman herself at the end of the Week when the Antichrist with many nations tries to destroy Israel, Isa. 66:7, 8; Mic. 5:3; Zech. 12:10-14:21; Joel 3:1-21. The result of this travail will be the conversion of Israel and the defeat of the Antichrist by the return of Christ to the earth with the saints and angels to exalt Israel and set up His own kingdom, Rom. 11:26, 27; Rev. 19:11-20:6; 2 Thess. 1:7-10.

III. The Persecution, Flight, and Protection of the Woman.

"And the woman fled into the wilderness, where she hath a place prepared of God, that they should feed her there a thousand two hundred and threescore days . . . And when the dragon saw that he was cast unto the earth, he persecuted the woman which brought forth the man child. And to the woman were given two wings of a great eagle, that she might fly into the wilderness, into her place, where she is nourished for a time, and times, and half a time, from the face of the serpent. And the serpent cast out of his mouth water as a flood after the woman, that he might cause her to be carried away of the flood. And the earth helped the woman, and the earth opened her mouth, and swallowed up the flood which the dragon cast out of his mouth," Rev. 12:6, 13-16.

The result of the war in heaven will be the casting out of Satan and his angels on earth. "When the dragon saw (actually realized) that he was cast unto the earth, he persecuted the woman, which brought forth the manchild." The dragon's first purpose will be to destroy the manchild "as soon as it was born," Rev. 12:4. Having failed in this because of the catching up of the manchild, he next will turn on the woman who brings forth the manchild and will bitterly persecute her by causing the Antichrist to break his covenant with Israel. The dragon will give his "power, throne and great authority" to the Antichrist (13:1, 2) and they together will make war on Israel. This persecution of Israel by the Antichrist is often referred to by the prophets, Isa. 10:20-27; 14:1-27; Jer. 30:3-9; Dan. 7:21-27; 8:23-25; 9:27; 11:40-45; Mic. 5:3-15, etc. The Jews will realize that the only way of escape is fleeing into some country that is not under the control of the Antichrist, Matt. 24:15-24; Dan. 11:40-45. This persecution will cause Israel to flee into the wilderness. She will be aided by God in her flight as symbolized by the "two wings of an eagle," which will be given her "that **she might fly** into the wilderness into **her place** where she is nourished for a time, and times, and half a time from the face of the serpent," Rev. 12:14. Cf. Exod 19:4; Deut. 32:11, 12.

The word "might" indicates that those in Israel who care to flee may do so, but not that all will flee into the wilderness from Judea, for a remnant will be left, Rev. 12:17. "Her purpose will be to flee "from the face of the serpent." There is to be such a place of security and she will know of it. Who but God could preserve a place for her and lead her to it under such conditions?

When the dragon learns that the woman is fleeing he will cast out of his mouth water "as a flood" to swallow the woman, but the earth will help her and open its mouth and swallow the flood, thus permitting the woman to escape the dragon. Now a symbolic dragon cannot cast out of his mouth a literal flood nor can a symbol be swallowed up by a literal flood. The dragon is symbolic of Satan, the woman of Israel, and the flood of the armies of the dragon and Antichrist, who will pursue after the fleeing Israelites to destroy them. The earth will open its mouth and swallow these armies as it did the company in Num. 16:29-35. Armies are often symbolized by floods, Jer. 46:7, 8; 47:2, 3; Dan. 9:26, 27; 11:21, 22, 26.

Besides the different symbols in this chapter, there are other things that are literal, such as the heaven, earth, nations, God and His throne, flight of the woman, wilderness, 1,260 days, war in heaven, Michael, Satan, angels, etc. The few symbols in the chapter symbolize literal persons and their actions. No symbol does away with realities. It pictures realities, enriches the language and thought of the Bible, and makes the meaning more beautiful in the light of other literal passages on the same subject.

There are many other prophecies in the Bible concerning the persecution, flight, and protection of the woman during the last three and one-half years of the Week which we shall now briefly consider.

1. **In Isaiah.** In Isa. 16:1-5 we have the first prophecy of importance concerning the flight of the woman. It names the very place to which she will flee. It is the rock hewn city of Sela, or Petra, as it was called by the Romans. It is in Mount Seir, near Mount Hor, in the land of Edom and Moab. This prophecy states that "as a wandering bird cast out of the nest, so the daughters of Moab shall be at the fords of Arnon" (which is a little stream at the north border of Moab) to welcome the Israelites as they flee into this wilderness city and country.

The next verses speak of Israel as being "outcasts" with the command for Moab to welcome, hide, and be a cover to them from the "face of the spoiler (Antichrist)" and "to betray" them not to Antichrist. Verse 5 shows that immediately after this the throne of David will be re-established. This, as well as the latter part of verse 4, relative to the end of the oppressor and the spoiler has never been fulfilled, and therefore, clearly shows a latter-day fulfillment to the whole passage.

The city, Petra, is located in Edom proper, but the prophet speaks of Moab as being the protector of Israel at that time. This country forms part of the great wilderness mentioned so often in Scripture where Israel wandered for forty years. Petra was a commercial center in the days of Solomon and was taken by Amaziah, king of Judah, 2 Kings 14:7; 2 Chron. 25:11, 12. It is mentioned several times as "the rock" because Sela means rock or stronghold, Judg. 1:36; Isa. 42:11; Jer. 48:28; 49:16; Obad. 3. In the first and last reference, the R. V. translates it "Sela." It is also called "Bozrah," Amos 1:12; Isa. 34:5, 6; 63:1-5; Jer. 48:24; 49:13, 22. The ancients gave it the name of "Bozrah of the Rock." In 105 A.D. the Romans conquered this country and called it Arabia-Petra. When the dominion of the Roman Empire waned, this territory fell back into the hands of the Arabians and was completely lost to the civilized world in the seventh century. It was rediscovered in 1812 by Burckhardt.

The city lies in a large valley and is reached only by one narrow passageway, so narrow, at places, that two people cannot ride abreast. The sides at the top of this passage are so close to each other as to shut out the light of the sun. The mountains that form the wall of the city on all sides are from two hundred to one thousand feet high. The sides of this canyon are lined with temples, houses and tombs, all hewn out of the rock with great skill and look as fresh as if they had been cut yesterday. An idea may be had concerning the scale by which the work was done from the size of the temple which furnishes an accommodation for three thousand people. Tradition says that Paul visited this city when he went into Arabia, Gal. 1:17.

The next passage in Isa. 26:20, 21 shows that this will be the place prepared of God to feed Israel for the 1,260 days. "Come my people (Israel) enter thou into thy chambers and shut thy doors about thee: hide thyself as it were for a moment (three and one-half years) until the indignation (great tribulation) be overpast." The setting of this passage is positively identified as being fulfilled in the last days for the next verse states, "The Lord cometh out of His place to punish the inhabitants of the earth for their iniquity."

In Isa. 63:1-5 we have a vivid picture of Christ coming to earth to destroy the nations at Armageddon, which answers the question asked here; i. e., "Who is this that cometh from Edom, with dyed garments from Bozrah?" In his coming to earth Christ will pass over Petra, descending from the east (Matt. 24:27), and the Jewish fugitives who are hiding there in the mountain fastness will see Him coming in the clouds of heaven with power and great glory. Then will the words of Isa. 42:11-13 be fulfilled, "Let the wilderness and the cities lift up their voice . . . let the inhabitants of the rock (Sela) sing, let them shout in the top of the mountains . . . The Lord shall go forth as a mighty man . . . He shall cry like a man of war . . . He shall prevail against His enemies." These passages, with Joel 3; Zech. 9:1-14:21; 2 Thess. 1:7-10; Rev. 14:14-20; 19:11-21, picture Armageddon when Christ delivers Israel from Antichrist.

2. **In the Psalms.** In Ps. 60:6-12 David encourages himself with the promises of God to give Israel the whole of Canaan, and speaks of Moab as being "my washpot"; i. e., personal property to be treated contemptuously as a vessel in which the conqueror's feet are washed. He continues, "Over Edom will I cast out my shoe" which is an idiom of taking possession, Ruth 4:7. This was spoken by David when he had conquered these countries and made them his servants, 2 Sam. 8:12-14. This passage prophetically shows their subjugation to Israel in the last days, Isa. 11:11-14; Jer. 48:47. Especially is Ps. 60:9-12 prophetical, "Who will bring me into the strong city (Petra)? Who will lead me into Edom? Wilt not thou, O God; which hadst cast us off?" It speaks of Israel's cry at the time the dragon persecutes the woman. The last verse of this passage conveys the same idea as Isa. 63:1-5, as explained above. See also Ps 108:8-13.

3. **In Ezekiel.** Ezek. 20:33-44 records another prophecy that God will bring Israel back from the nations in the last days and then will bring her "into the wilderness of the people, and there I will plead with you face to face. LIKE AS I PLEADED WITH

YOUR FATHERS IN THE WILDERNESS OF THE LAND OF
EGYPT, so will I plead with you, saith the Lord God. And I
will cause you to pass under the rod (judgment), and I will bring
you into the bond of the covenant: and I will purge out from
among you the rebels, and them that transgress against me
. . . and ye shall know that I am the Lord."

God will send the two witnesses with power to do miracles and
to bring Israel back to God and to literally fulfill this passage in
pleading with Israel like God pleaded with them by the hands
of the first two prophets—Moses and Aaron, in their first wilderness experience. At the time of the flight of Israel the two witnesses will appear and will do miracles in protecting them from
the Devil and Antichrist and they will lead them into Petra
and then bring them back to their God so that when Christ
appears over Edom in His descent to the earth they will look
upon Him whom they have pierced and will say, "Blessed is he
that cometh in the name of the Lord," Matt. 23:37-39; Rev. 1:7.

4. In Daniel. Dan. 11:36-45 reveals that at the time of the
conquests of Antichrist "many countries shall be overthrown:
but these shall escape out of his hand, even Edom and Moab, and
chief of the children of Ammon." If Edom and Moab are to
escape out of his hand this seems to be the only local place
where the Israelites in Judea can flee during the great tribulation. God will reserve these countries from Antichrist to use
them as a place of refuge for His people, and to show further
the "place prepared of God, that they (these countries) should
feed her there" for three and one-half years. This shows that
the feeding is not necessarily supernatural, but that the inhabitants of the wilderness will feed her.

5. In Hosea. Hosea 2:14-23 speaks of Petra or a place in the
wilderness to which Israel will flee for protection from Antichrist,
saying, "I will allure her, and bring her into the wilderness, and
speak comfortably unto her . . . at that day . . . thou shalt call
me Ishi (my husband); and shall call me no more Baali (my
Lord) . . . and I will betroth thee unto me forever."

6. In Matthew. Jesus predicted that at the time the abomination of desolation is set up, that is, when the Antichrist breaks
his seven years covenant with Israel and does away with their
daily sacrifices to God in their temple and sets himself and his
image in the holy of holies to be worshipped during the last half
of the Week, that the Jews "in Judea" will flee into the mountains and "there shall be great tribulation, such as was not since
the beginning of the world to this time, no, nor ever shall be,"
Matt. 24:15-22; Dan. 9:27; 2 Thess. 2:1-3; Rev. 13:1-18.

Thus we have many passages speaking of the persecution,
flight and protection of the woman in the wilderness. They all
refer to Israel, not to the Church, Christendom, or Gentiles, as
is clear in each passage.

Chapter Seventeen

THE MANCHILD—VARIOUS INTERPRETATIONS

"And she brought forth a man child, who was to rule all nations with a rod of iron: and her child was caught up unto God, and to his throne," Rev. 12:5.

We shall discuss only briefly the various interpretations of the manchild in this chapter. This is another symbol and must be treated as such. The following are four theories of the manchild and reasons why they could not possibly be the thought of the symbol.

I. The Manchild as Christ.

It is believed by some that the manchild is Christ because:

1. He came from Israel "concerning the flesh," Rom. 9:4, 5.

This argument is too general and proves nothing, for every son of Israel came from Israel according to the flesh. Upon this basis any one son of Israel could be taken as the manchild.

2. He is to rule with a rod of iron, Rev. 19:15; Ps. 2.

This is also no definite argument to prove the manchild to be Christ. The expression "rod of iron" means authority over the nations, and in this sense every redeemed (raptured) or resurrected saint will have such authority with Christ as is proved by the following Scriptures in both Testaments.

(1) The Old Testament saints will reign with Christ, Ps. 149:6-9; Dan. 7:18, 27; Matt. 8:11, 12; Jer. 30:9; Ezek. 34:24; 37:24, 25; Hos. 3:5.

(2) The Church saints will reign with Christ, Matt. 19:28; 20:20-28; Rom. 8:17; 1 Cor. 4:8; 6:2; 2 Tim. 2:12; Rev. 1:5, 6; 2:26, 27.

(3) The 144,000 Jews will reign with Christ, Rev. 7:1-8; 12:5; 14:1-5; Ps. 149:6-9; Dan. 7:18, 27.

(4) The tribulation saints will reign with Christ, Rev. 20:4-6.

Therefore, in view of the fact that all saints of all ages reign with Christ, we conclude that the phrase "rod of iron" in Rev. 12:5 does not prove that Christ is the manchild any more than it could be used to prove that any one of the above four companies of redeemed is the manchild. (See chapter nine, point 3, for proof that there are four different companies of redeemed.) All these saints will not have the same degree of rule, nor will it depend on whether they are in a certain company that they will rule, but all will be given authority to their degree of faithfulness in the service rendered here on earth. That will be determined at the judgment seat of Christ, Luke 19:11-27; Rom. 14:10; 1 Cor. 3:11-16; 2 Cor. 5:10, 11.

3. He was caught up to God's throne, Eph. 1:20.

This again is no definite proof that Christ is the manchild. The angel is not showing John the historical ascension of Christ, which he saw with his own eyes about sixty years previous, but a prophecy that will be fulfilled in the middle of the Week as revealed here, Rev. 1:19; 4:1. All raptured saints will be caught up to God and His throne, 1 Thess. 2:19; 3:13; 4:13-18; 5:23; Rev. 3:21; 4:4; 7:9-17; 14:1-5; 19:1-10.

4. He is called a man, 2 Tim. 2:5.

This does not prove that Christ is the manchild, for others are also called men in Scripture. The Church is called a man, Eph. 2:15; 4:13. Hence, we see that all these arguments are too general and cannot be used as proof that Christ, or any other individual, or group of individuals, is symbolized by the manchild.

This theory destroys the plain consecutive order of the book, disregards the natural divisions, and inserts historical events in this plain prophecy. If this theory be true, it would necessitate the fulfillment of all of Rev. 1:1-12:4 before the ascension of Christ. It has been abundantly proved that we are dealing with things in the middle of the Week and that all of Rev. 4-22 takes place after the Church Age. The plain statements concerning the woman and manchild could not possibly be harmonized with the lives and times of Christ and the virgin Mary. Therefore, we conclude that this theory is out of harmony with the intended thought of the "prophecy" and has no part in the "things which must shortly come to pass."

II. The Manchild as the True Church.

1. It is believed by some that the Church is the manchild, and the professing Christians are the woman. It is expected that the Church will be caught up out of the mass of Christian profession who will be left here to go into the wilderness, because the majority in Christendom are not in the Church, and therefore, not ready to go up in the rapture.

This argument is no proof that the Church is symbolized by the manchild and the mass of Christian profession, the woman. It will be noticed that there is no statement or indication to this effect in Scripture, else it would have been given by this school. Neither does such an argument prove that the Church is caught up in the middle of the Week. We have already proved in chapters six through eight that the Church will be raptured before the Week in Rev. 4:1. If this be true the Church cannot be caught up in the middle of the Week as will be the case with the manchild. This theory, like that of Christ above, is out of harmony with the plain revelation concerning the woman and manchild.

2. It is further believed that the sun with which the woman is clothed means the righteousness of Christ; that the moon symbolizes the Jewish ordinances superseded by the teachings of Christ; and that the twelve stars in her crown represent the twelve apostles.

This is also without scriptural foundation and really contradicts the argument above, for the woman cannot be the mass of Christian profession who are not ready to meet Christ or go up in the rapture and still be clothed with the righteousness of

Christ. If professing Christians were clothed with the righteousness of Christ, they would be Christ's, and if they were His, they would go in the rapture as well as all other Christians, 1 Cor. 15:20-23; 1 Thess. 4:16. Instead of clothing professors with His righteousness Christ condemns such to eternal damnation, Matt. 23; Rev. 3:14-17.

On the same grounds, the twelve stars cannot represent the twelve apostles, for they are the foundation of the true Church and not in the crown of backslidden Christian profession, Eph. 2:19-22. Such a theory would have us believe that Christ and the apostles sanctioned hypocrisy and a mere profession, but such they never did. God will never protect a body of professors who trample under their feet His Word any more than He will others who admit that they are sinners. It is beyond all reason that He would do this and on the other hand allow the godly tribulation saints to suffer martyrdom without such protection and care. However, in the case of Israel, God has sworn by Himself to protect her in the same manner that He is to protect this woman, as we have seen. God, to fulfill His covenants with their fathers, is obligated to protect Israel and bring her back to Himself. The primary purpose of the tribulation is to accomplish this.

3. It is argued that Christianity will travail in the middle of the Week because of the persecution of Christians by Antichrist.

This argument cannot be used of Christendom, for in no passage do we find any statement that Christendom will travail in the middle of the Week or any other time. If the woman is the mass of profession, she does not have real salvation, or she would be raptured, and such Christians must have if they undergo any serious persecution. This need not be the case with Israel, for Jews are to be persecuted in fulfillment of prophecy. They cannot escape the persecutions by denying some faith as will be possible with Christians during the Seventieth Week. That this married woman does not symbolize Christendom is proved in Rev. 17 where Christendom is symbolized by an unmarried woman, a great whore, who is destroyed by the Antichrist and the ten kings in the middle of the Week, Rev. 17:14-18. Christendom cannot be destroyed by the Antichrist and still be this married woman who escapes the Antichrist and is protected by God for three and one-half years.

4. Some think that the manchild is the Church because the seventh trumpet (11:14-13:18), according to their belief, is the same as the "last trump" which is blown at the rapture of the Church, 1 Cor. 15:51-58; 1 Thess. 4:13-18.

This association of the seventh trumpet with the "trump of God" does not prove that the Church is the manchild. There are many points of contrast between these trumpets as has been proved in chapter six, point I, 2. Even after this seventh or so-called "last trump" takes place there will be others sounded in the tribulation, Isa. 27:12, 13; Zeph. 1:16-18; Zech. 9:14, 15;

Matt. 24:31. Therefore, we conclude that the Church cannot be symbolized by the manchild, or Christendom by the woman.

III. The Bride Part of the Church as the Manchild.

This theory teaches that the manchild represents the "bride part" of the Church, and that the bride of Christ is not to be the Church, but merely a select company of believers, known better as full overcomers, out of the Church. This theory resolves itself into two questions:

1. **Are the body of Christ and the Church the same?** According to this theory they are not the same. However, three definite passages prove that they are the same, Eph. 1:22, 23; Col. 1:18, 24. These passages state that the body of Christ and the Church are the same. There is no plain passage that teaches a difference between the Church and a bride part of the Church. No Scripture ever mentions a difference between the body of Christ and the Church.

2. **Are there two classes of people in the Church, partial overcomers as the Church and full overcomers as the bride part of the Church?** This theory teaches that there are two classes, and attempts to create within the Church two groups of believers, those who partially live in sin and those who do not, those who partially overcome and those who fully overcome. This class of interpreters use the seven promises to the overcomer in Rev. 2, 3, claiming that the full overcomers form the bride who will receive rewards and reign with Christ, and that the partial overcomers are to be finally saved but have no part in Christ's reign. There is nothing promised to the one who does not overcome as is clear. Let us examine the New Testament books to determine whether there are two groups in the Church or not.

(1) Paul, in writing to the Corinthians, leaves no doubt with them as to whether or not they form a part of the body of Christ, saying, "For as the body is **one** (not two parts) and hath many members, and **all** the members of that **one** body, being many, are **one** body . . . by **one** Spirit are **we all** baptized into **one** body." If the body is not one then we might say that the Spirit is not one. If we can misconstrue such plain language and divide the one body, we can also divide the one Spirit on the same grounds, for the same terms are used of both. Paul continues, "Now **ye are the body** of Christ and members in particular. And God hath set some in **the Church**, first apostles," etc., 1 Cor. 12:12-28. This passage, at least, does not advance the above theory of two parts to the body of Christ.

The idea so often implied that one must be a special angelic sort of being in order to be a member of the body of Christ or qualify for the rapture is certainly rebuked by this epistle. A few glances at the common life of those Corinthians will soon dispel that false impression. Paul was writing to a sanctified church (1 Cor. 1:2) yet among those sanctified believers there were divisions and strife (1:10-17); carnal living (3:1-8; 4:18); unholy living unjudged (5:1-13); lawsuits (6:1-8); wrong ideas of marriage (7:1-40); disputes over doubtful things (8:1-10:33); disorders at the Lord's Table (11:1-34); abuse of spiritual gifts and ministries (12:1-14:40); wrong ideas of the resurrection and other doctrines (15:1-16:24); and still Paul stated "ye are Christ's" and "I have espoused you to one husband" (3:23; 2 Cor. 11:2) thus proving that he recognized them as part of the body of Christ.

Although this is true of these believers, it must be recognized that only those in this local congregation, as well as any other, that are saved and ready to meet God will be a part of the body of Christ. In this connection, there are many passages which teach that there is only one class of people in the Church and that these are the ones who overcome sin and live holy in this life. Of such there can be no two classes. Every Christian is an overcomer and no one is a Christian and saved who does not overcome, as is amply proved in John 3:8; Rom. 6:16; Gal. 5:17-21; 6:7,8; Heb. 12:14; Matt. 7:21-23; etc.

These passages clearly state that one is either righteous or unrighteous; saved or lost; holy or unholy; consecrated or unconsecrated. There are no half-breeds in the body of Christ. Jesus said, "No man can serve two masters" and if there were such a thing as a partial life for God and for the Devil at the same time, He would not have made this statement. If there were different degrees of overcoming in the sense the doctrine is taught, surely we should have some passage teaching it. To what degree must one overcome in order to be in the rapture and who is to set the standard and tell whether one is overcoming sufficiently or not if we hold any other standard than "without holiness no man shall see the Lord"? Not one passage holds any promise to those who do not overcome, and, on the contrary, there are numerous rebukes to people for their sins, showing that "they which do such things shall not inherit the kingdom of God," Gal. 5:17-21; 6:7,8; Rev. 3:15-19.

Paul further likens the Church to a human body with many members (1 Cor. 12:12-28) and it is just as unreasonable and unscriptural to argue that there are two parts to a human body, and that some members are not in the body because they are not as perfect or mature as some of the others, as to argue that about the Church. It is not a question as to degrees of overcoming according to human standards; it is whether one is walking in all the light he has and is in Christ. Every member has not the same function and therefore all do not have the same things to overcome.

(2) In Ephesians the Church **as a whole** is viewed as the body of Christ. The "Church" **which is his body** is what Christ is to present to Himself, Eph. 1:22,23; 5:26,27. In this letter, as always, Paul uses plural words "us," "we," and "all" in stating

truths about the Church, which is one. He speaks of the Ephesians as being "fellow citizens with **the** saints, and of the household of God . . . in whom **all** the building fitly framed together groweth into an holy temple in the Lord," Eph. 2:19-22. "To make in himself of twain (Jew and Gentile) **one** new man," Eph. 2:15; 3:6. "There is **one** body, and **one** Spirit . . . **one** hope . . . **one** Lord, **one** faith, **one** baptism, **one** God and Father of **all,** who is above **all,** and through **all,** and in you **all,**" Eph. 4:4-6. Paul speaks of the ministry being given "for the perfecting of **the** saints (not part of them) . . . Till we **all** come to the unity of the faith . . . unto a perfect man (not one perfect part and one imperfect part) . . . from whom the **whole body fitly joined together and** compacted by that which every joint supplieth, according to the effectual working in the measure of every part, maketh increase of **the body** unto the edifying of itself in love," Eph. 4:7-16. Those who belong to this body are those who are "created in righteousness and true holiness" and have put off the sins of the flesh, Eph. 4:17-32.

Continuing this subject, the author compares the relation of Christ and the Church to that of man and wife. "For the husband is the head of the wife (one wife, one body, or one part) even as Christ is the head of **the Church** and he is the savior of **the body.** Therefore as **the Church** is subject unto Christ, so let the wives be to their own husbands in everything. Husbands love your wives, even as Christ also loved **the Church,** and gave himself for **it;** that he might sanctify and cleanse **it** with the washing of water by the word, that he might present **it** to himself a glorious Church, not having spot, or wrinkle, or any such thing; but that **it** should be holy and without blemish . . . I speak concerning Christ and **the Church.**" Christ gave Himself to cleanse every man and if any individual fails to yield to the cleansing process and live in Christ "he is none of his" (Rom. 8:9; 2 Cor. 5:17) and therefore not a member of the Church. A study of other epistles reveals the same truths. However, this is sufficient to show that the Church and body of Christ are the same and that the one Church will be presented to Christ.

The arguments of this school are greatly composed of so-called Old Testament types, using marriages of some historical characters of the Old Testament, or they are based on the details of parables which have nothing to do with the subject. Such arguments are not sufficient. Therefore, we conclude that the Church and the body are the same and that there is no such thing as a bride part of the church, or two classes of saved men in Christ, and that the Church is not the manchild.

IV. The Holy Spirit Baptized People as the Manchild.

The theory teaches that the manchild represents only those Christians who have received the baptism of the Spirit, and that all other Christians compose the woman and the remnant who are left after the rapture to go through the tribulation. The attempted proof is found in the parable of the ten virgins, for which see chapter eight, and in 1 Cor. 12:12, 13, which we shall examine.

This passage does not and could not teach the baptism in the Holy Spirit but a baptism in the body of Christ, showing just how the body is constituted. It is the office work of the Spirit to bring the individual into the body of Christ, John 3:3-8; 16:7-11; Rom. 8:1-4, 9-13; 1 Cor. 6:11; 12:12, 13; Eph. 2:18; 4:4; Titus 3:5. While it is the office work of Christ to baptize the members of that body into the Spirit, Matt. 3:11; Mark 1:7, 8; Luke 3:16; John 1:33; 7:37, 38; Acts 1:5-8; 2:1-4; 8:15-19; 9:17; 10:44-48; 11:15; 19:1-6. If this passage meant the baptism in the Spirit," it would read, "For **by Jesus** are we all baptized **into one Spirit**," but it reads **"by one Spirit are we all baptized into one body."** The baptism of the Spirit does not place one in the body of Christ, neither does it cleanse from sin. One must be in the body before he can be baptized into the Spirit.

In 1 Cor. 12, 13, and 14 the subject is spiritual gifts or things concerning the Spirit, their meanings, manifestations, and operations in the body of Christ: hence 1 Cor. 12:12, 13, as proved by the context, does not refer to the baptism into the Spirit by Jesus, but the constitution of that body by the Spirit. We are baptized into the body by the Spirit in the sense of being immersed into Christ as a vital part of His body. 1 Cor. 12:12-28; Rom. 6:3-6; Gal. 3:26-28; Eph. 2:14-22; 4:1-16; 5:30. Therefore, we may conclude that this passage is no proof in the identification of the manchild with those baptized in the Holy Spirit. (See our book **The Truth About the Baptism in the Holy Spirit.)**

Thus, there are many interpretations of both the sun-clothed woman and the manchild, and all of them cannot be right; there must be a right understanding, and there is. One thing is certain: any intrepretation that brings the Church or Christendom into these "THINGS WHICH MUST BE HEREAFTER," that is, after the churches, cannot be right. The Church will have been raptured at least three and one-half years before the manchild will be caught up to meet God and to live in heaven. Both the woman and the manchild are Jewish, as we have already seen, and so we must interpret the manchild with Israel, not with Christ, or the Church, as we shall see further in the next chapter.

Chapter Eighteen

THE MANCHILD—THE TRUE INTERPRETATION

We believe that the manchild symbolizes the 144,000 Jews who are the "firstfruits" to God from Israel, after the rapture of all Jews of the Church and the Old Testament saints. **The reasons are:**

1. **It has been conclusively proved that the woman represents Israel.** Since this is true, it follows that Israel cannot bring forth a company of Gentiles. She is sure to bring forth a company of her own nationality, the Jews. She cannot bring forth an individual person. Only an individual can do that. **The manchild then can only represent a company of Jews out of Israel.** The woman represents a company. The "remnant" is a company, so the manchild must, of necessity, represent a company of Jews in order to fulfill the plain statements of Rev. 12. This alone would exclude the theory of Christ's being the manchild. There is no other company of Jews definitely mentioned in the fulfillment of Rev. 4-19 in Daniel's Seventieth Week besides the 144,000 and, as their salvation and sealing for protection through the trumpet judgments only are described, it seems clear that they are the ones to be caught up in the seventh trumpet as the manchild.

2. We have also seen that **the woman cannot be** the spirit of Christendom, or the Church, and that **the manchild cannot be** the Church, or overcomers out of the Church, or any Gentile Christians. Thus, by a process of elimination, we have left only one group of people, the Jews, from which to draw the personnel of the manchild, and what other company can be represented but the 144,000 of Rev. 7 and 14? The manchild must be limited to one of the four companies of redeemed heavenly saints who are saved in the scope of redemption from Adam to the first resurrection, as enumerated in chapter nine, point 3, for which see. These companies are saved, dispensationally, in the order in which we give them. When one company is complete then the gathering of the succeeding one begins.

3. **The manchild represents a company of living saints only,** for the woman will travail and bring forth the complete manchild in the middle of the Week. She cannot bring forth a partly dead and partly living child at this time. This seems clear from the very language of the chapter. The dragon will stand before the woman to devour her child **as soon** as it is born but the child will be immediately "caught up to God and to his throne."

How could the dragon **kill** the manchild if it were composed of dead, or even resurrected people? Such a thing is an impossibility. This proves that the manchild represents a company of living people only, who will be still in natural bodies with the possibility of being killed. This eliminates the Old Testament saints, the Church saints, and the tribulation saints. The only other company of redeemed left and the only one composed wholly of living saints is the 144,000 Jews who will be sealed to go through the first six trumpet judgments and who will be caught up under the seventh trumpet as the manchild. They are seen in heaven throughout the last three and one-half years so they must be raptured in the middle of the Week, Rev. 14:1-5. God will supernaturally protect the manchild or 144,000 of Israel from the dragon and Antichrist, when the latter breaks his covenant with Israel, in the middle of the Week, by catching them up to His throne.

4. **An examination of Rev. 7 and 14 shows the 144,000 of Israel to be the manchild.**

(1) **The companies in both chapters are the same because:**

A. Of the sealing in their foreheads, Rev. 7:1-3; 14:1.

B. Of the uniqueness of their number, Rev. 7:4; 14:1.

C. Their history is only complete when both chapters are considered. Together they show their destiny, time of rapture, place or position in heaven, and their occupation around the throne.

D. There is nothing to lead us to believe that the 144,000 of the two chapters are not the same; therefore, we naturally consider them the same.

(2) **The destiny of the 144,000 proves them to be the manchild.** They will appear "before the throne" in heaven and "before the four beasts and the elders" who are before the throne. It is expressly stated that they will be redeemed "**from** the earth" and "**from** among men." They, therefore, cannot be earthly people, who will go through the last three and one-half years of tribulation, and who will form the nucleus around which the twelve tribes will be gathered in the Millennium. The fact that they will be in heaven between the seventh trumpet and the first vial shows that they will have been raptured. When, if not as the manchild in the middle of the Week? The three messenger angels immediately following this vision of the 144,000 in heaven, will proclaim their particular messages from the middle of the Week onward. So it stands to reason that the vision will be fulfilled in the place it is given, which is immediately after the catching up of the manchild under the seventh trumpet, and before the vials and the ministry of the messenger angels.

(3) **The time of the rapture of the 144,000 shows them to be represented by the manchild.** If the 144,000 are seen on earth up to the middle of the Week, and in heaven immediately after the seventh trumpet which blows in the middle of the Week, then they are sure to be raptured as the manchild in the middle of the Week. We have seen that the Old Testament and the Church saints will be caught up to heaven before the Seventieth Week and that they will be with God in heaven, represented by the elders. We have also seen that the tribulation saints will be martyred principally after the rapture of the manchild, but not caught up until about the end of the Week. The only other

place for the insertion of the rapture of the 144,000 is in Rev.
12:5. Therefore, the manchild must be the 144,000 who will be
caught up under the seventh trumpet, for, immediately after
this trumpet they will be seen in heaven before God, Rev. 14:1-5.
If the 144,000 are not to be raptured as the manchild, then how
and when are they to be raptured? And where is the account of
their rapture? If the 144,000 are not the manchild, the history
of the manchild is incomplete, and if the catching up of the
manchild is not the rapture of the 144,000, then mystery shrouds
the rapture of the 144,000 and also the destiny and position of the
manchild around the throne. Once we believe that the 144,000
and the manchild are the same, that John saw the 144,000 caught
up to heaven as the manchild in Rev. 12:5 and that the history
of the manchild is completed in Rev. 14:1-5, all mysteries and
questions cease to be.

(4) **The place in which John saw the 144,000** further proves
that they will be in heaven before the second advent of Christ
to earth, and necessarily must be raptured before then. When,
if not as the manchild? John seemed to see this company at
two places; namely, on Mount Zion and in heaven before God.
Some argue that this Mount Zion is the earthly one and that
the whole scene (14:1-5) must be earthly, but we are convinced
that Rev. 14:1 is heavenly, and refers to the heavenly Mount
Zion because:

A. The rest of the verses refer to heavenly things. This cannot be disputed by reason of the plain language picturing scenes
in heaven. The throne, the living creatures, and elders all show
a heavenly setting. The throne seen here does not come down
to earth until after the Millennium, and then it is in the
heavenly Mount Zion and the New Jerusalem, Rev. 21:22; 22:3-5.
If these verses picture heavenly things then Rev. 14:1 does.

B. The "Lamb" seen on Mount Zion with the 144,000 is never
seen on earth in the Revelation, but always in heaven, as can be
verified by the reader himself. When Christ comes to the earth
He will not be pictured as a lamb but as a mighty conqueror
taking vengeance on the ungodly, Rev. 19:11-21.

C. All redeemed peoples who have part in the first resurrection will have their abode in the New Jerusalem, which is always spoken of in connection with heavenly, redeemed people,
Heb. 11:10, 13-16; John 14:1-6; Rev. 21, 22. Paul states in Heb.
12:18-24 that there is an heavenly Mount Zion, so if Rev. 14:2-5
speaks of heavenly things Rev. 14:1 does also.

D. The earthly tabernacle, candlestick, table of shewbread,
holy place, holy of holies, ark of the covenant, cherubims, mercy
seat, etc., were all patterned after "things in heaven," Heb. 8:1-5;
9:1-5, 23, 24. Is it unreasonable to believe that this Mount Zion
is the heavenly one? Certainly the heavenly patterns are just
as real and literal as the earthly things made from them.
Moses was not the only one to see the heavenly patterns, for John

in the Revelation describes what he saw of them. They are enumerated as follows, but studied elsewhere: the door to the heavenly tabernacle, throne, lamps, sea of glass, golden altar, golden censer, incense, temple and ark of the covenant. Therefore, we conclude that the heavenly Mount Zion is the place for the temple of God in heaven, as seen in Rev. 4, 5; 11:19; 14:15, 17; 15:5-8; 16:1, 17; 21:2-22:7.

(5) **The privileges of the 144,000 in heaven** show them to be a distinct company of redeemed from the earth who will have part in the first resurrection. When, if not as the manchild? They will form one of the wonderful choirs of heaven and sing a secret song that no man knows "but the hundred and forty and four thousand," Rev. 14:1-3. The thought is not that others will not understand the words of the song, but that they will not be able to sing its contents, not having had the particular experience it will describe. The song will be accompanied by harps and sung before the throne and all heavenly inhabitants, but, apart from this, we know nothing about it. This is the only mention of a song without reference to the words or the nature of it. It is to be a new song, by a new company and with a new theme, which further indicates that those who sing it are saved and translated as a living company after the rapture of the Church. They will have undergone the same trials, will have been protected from the same judgments, and will have been translated from the wrath of the dragon at the same time that the woman travails, in the middle of the Week. It is further stated of the 144,000 that they will "follow the Lamb whithersoever he goeth." This indicates their fellowship with Christ and the ability to follow Him anywhere in the universe as special "servants" of God, Rev. 7:3; 14:1-5.

(6) **The character of the 144,000** further shows them to be a special company of redeemed saints, saved and translated after the rapture of the Church, and before the dragon is cast out of heaven, in the middle of the Week, for this is the only time they are seen on earth. Whenever they are seen after this, they are in heaven before the throne of God. They "were not defiled with women: for they are virgins," Rev. 14:4. This has no reference to celibacy, but to the pollutions connected with the great religious system dominating the nations of Revised Rome during the first three and one-half years until Antichrist rises to absolute power over the ten kings who together destroy Mystery Babylon, in the middle of the Week, Rev. 17:14-18. The 144,000 will not be a company of natural virgins but, having abstained from the fornication of Mystery Babylon, will be recognized as pure virgins and chaste in the same sense as in 2 Cor. 11:2. They are not mentioned in connection with Antichrist or anything that he does in the last three and one-half years, which seems to indicate that they will be translated before the Antichrist makes war on the saints.

"In their mouth was found no guile: for they are without fault before the throne of God," Rev. 14:5. This passage shows that the 144,000 must abide by the same rule of conduct to which the Church and all other redeemed have been subjected, Eph. 5:26, 27; Phil. 4:8; Col. 3:5, 16; etc. This verse (14:5) can be taken literally while the verse above (14:4) cannot possibly be taken so because of its own statements which show that the 144,000 have not been defiled with women (indicating, if literal, that they were all men); for they are virgins (indicating, if literal, that they are women). Both cannot be true. The only other meaning must be the one above.

(7) **The 144,000 are "firstfruits unto God and the Lamb"** (14:4), which definitely proves their salvation and translation after the rapture of the Church. The "firstfruits" were always mentioned in connection with Israel in the Old Testament, speaking of the first gathering of the harvest, whether corn, wheat or anything. They were offered to the Lord together with the tithes, as a recognition of earthly blessings from the hand of the Lord, Num. 15:20; 18:12; Neh. 10:35-37; Prov. 3:9, 10. In the New Testament the first converts are spoken of as "firstfruits," 1 Cor. 16:15. James, in writing to the twelve tribes scattered abroad, says "that we should be a kind of firstfruits of his creatures," Jas. 1:1, 18. Christ is referred to as the "firstfruits" of the resurrection, 1 Cor. 15:20-23. From all these passages in both Testaments we gather that the "firstfruits" mean the first of vegetation gathered, or the first of mankind to experience something new. The 144,000 will be "firstfruits" and "of all the tribes of the children of Israel"; i. e., the first ones saved after the rapture.

Now comes the question as to how **the 144,000 will be firstfruits to God from Israel.** It has already been proved that they will be saved and sealed after the rapture of the Church and the Old Testament saints who will be caught up in Rev. 4:1. It cannot be denied that they will be living Jews all sealed in their foreheads after the sixth seal and before the first trumpet in the first three and one-half years as plainly stated in Rev. 7:1-8. If this is true, then they cannot be the firstfruits to God, from Israel of the Old Testament or the Church saints, for the first Jews saved in these companies will have died centuries before and will have been raptured at Christ's coming in the air, 1 Thess. 4:13-18. These 144,000 will be the first Jews saved between the rapture and the first trumpet, after all saved Jews are caught up in the rapture of the Church. The awful wars, bloody persecutions, devastating famines and noisome pestilences in the first six seals, together with the knowledge of God and of the rapture which has taken place, will serve as powerful incentives in converting thousands of Jews and Gentiles. Hence the 144,000 Jews and the great multitude, which will be two different bodies of people, are seen in Rev. 7 between the sixth and seventh seals, with the 144,000 being sealed for protection through the trumpet judgments and the great multitude suffering martyrdom in the tribulation.

If the manchild, which represents a company of Israelites, as is clear, were to be raptured before the 144,000 which is also a company of Israelites, then the manchild would be the "firstfruits" to God from Israel and not the 144,000. But such is not true, for it is the 144,000 who are firstfruits to God from Israel. This proves that the 144,000 are the ones symbolized by the manchild, for the manchild will be the first company raptured after the Church is raptured in Rev. 4:1. There is only one company of believers raptured after the Church until the rapture of the tribulation saints at about the end of the tribulation, and that company is symbolized by the manchild. Therefore, since the manchild and the 144,000 are both Israelitish, since there is but one rapture for both, and since they are both seen in heaven before the throne immediately after the seventh trumpet, they must be identical.

The 144,000 will be the firstfruits to God from Israel while the real harvest of Israel will be at the end of the tribulation when the nation is born at one time, Isa. 66:7, 8; Rom. 11:26, 27. Since the firstfruits of the harvest in the Old Testament belonged to God and were used at His discretion, so these firstfruits of all Israel are dedicated especially to God and His service. The harvest after the gathering of the firstfruits, was left to sustain natural life so God will likewise leave the harvest of Israel as an earthly people, to serve as a factor in the sustenance of natural life on earth forever, Isa. 9:6, 7; Luke 1:32-35; Rev. 21, 22.

Thus all the facts concerning the 144,000 in Rev. 7 and 14 seem to require their oneness with the manchild. If they are to be caught up before the manchild they must be translated after the fifth and sixth trumpets, for they will still be on earth and protected during their fulfillment. If they are not the same, then there are two translations and the first or 144,000 is not seen while the other is. The history of the 144,000 is resumed while the other is not. Thus mystery after mystery appears unless the 144,000 are recognized as the manchild.

5. **The 144,000 will be sealed for the purpose of being protected through the trumpet judgments only,** for immediately after the seventh trumpet, which includes the last verse of Rev. 13, we see them in heaven as in the first five verses of Rev. 14. It was said to the first four trumpet angels, who are to hurt the earth, trees and seas, "Hurt not the earth, neither the sea, nor the trees, till we have sealed the servants of our God (144,000) in their foreheads," Rev. 7:1-3. After they are sealed the trumpets will begin. They will be immune from the first four plagues. They are not mentioned in connection with that time, but, in the fifth trumpet or first woe, special direction is given to the demons of that woe not to hurt the 144,000, Rev. 9:4. This also plainly applies to the demons of the sixth trumpet or second woe which

immediately follows. The way God will protect them under the seventh trumpet or third woe, which is the casting out of Satan from heaven, will be by translating them to thwart the dragon in his purpose of devouring the manchild "as soon as it is born." The dragon will be full of wrath because God will have protected them from the first six trumpet plagues so he will try to destroy them. But he will be defeated by God, who will translate them to His throne. Then the dragon will turn on the woman who will have brought forth the manchild, but God will defeat him in all his machinations as we have already seen. We find no mention of the 144,000 on earth after the trumpets and the very next view places them in heaven, 14:1-5. Therefore, they are the company symbolized by the manchild who will be protected from the wrath of the dragon, Antichrist and vial plagues of the last three and one-half years of the Week by being translated.

6. **It seems clear from the previous studies that the woman, manchild, and the remnant of the woman are all Jewish,** and that these three are the only companies in Revelation that are Jewish. If this is true then the 144,000 must be one of the three since they are Jewish. They are not mentioned separately from them, but are mentioned as being "of all the tribes of the children of Israel" thus indicating that if they were not of the three they would also be mentioned in connection with the three which go to make up all Israel before the middle of the Week. Since they are one of the three, which one? **They cannot be symbolized by the woman and cannot be the remnant because of the following contrasts:**

(1) The woman will be national Israel or all the Jews in Judea in the last days, while the 144,000 will form a group sealed out of Israel.

(2) The woman and remnant will be earthly peoples while the 144,000 will be heavenly.

(3) The woman and remnant will be in travail while the 144,000 will not be.

(4) The woman will bring forth the manchild, while the 144,000 will not.

(5) A company will be taken out of the woman but not out of the 144,000 for they themselves are a company taken out of the woman.

(6) The woman will flee to the wilderness and the remnant will be left in Judea while the 144,000 will be taken up to heaven before the throne.

(7) The remnant will be left on earth after the flight of the woman while the 144,000 will be taken to heaven as "firstfruits" of the woman before she flees. They will be the first of Israel to be translated to heaven during this period.

(8) Neither the number of the woman nor of the remnant is given while it is in the case of the 144,000.

(9) Neither the woman nor the remnant will be sealed for protection while the 144,000 will be, Rev. 7:1-8; 9:4.

Now therefore, since the woman or the remnant cannot be the 144,000 or the manchild, the 144,000 and the manchild must be identical. The 144,000 are the only company that can possibly fill the requirements of the language of Rev. 12. The manchild represents a small company of Israelites out of all Israel. The 144,000 are a company from all Israel. The manchild is caught up to the throne. So are the 144,000. The manchild is delivered from the dragon at the time of the travail of the woman. So are the 144,000. The manchild is the object of the vengeance of the dragon. So are the 144,000, else they would not be protected by God from the demons, Rev. 9:4. The manchild is not mentioned on earth after the seventh trumpet. Neither are the 144,000. The manchild is to rule the nations. So are the 144,000 as well as all saints, as we have seen in chapter seventeen, theory I. The manchild is an heavenly company. So are the 144,000. The manchild is a baby in size compared to the woman. So are the 144,000 compared to all Israel. These and other reasons of harmony between the two seem to prove that the manchild and the 144,000 are the same.

7. **Daniel also pictured the rapture of the manchild saying,** "**At that time** (beginning of the great tribulation) **shall Michael stand up** (as in Rev. 12:7-12 when the manchild is delivered), the great prince **which standeth for the children of thy people** (Israel): and there **shall be a time of trouble** (three and one-half years of Dan. 12:7-13; Rev. 11:1-3; 12:5, 6, 14-16; 13:1-7), **such as never was since there was a nation** (Matt. 24:15-26; Jer. 30:7) even to that same time; and at **that time** (that Michael stands up to cast out Satan and deliver the manchild) **thy people** (Israel) **shall be delivered** (from Hebrew **malat,** meaning "to escape, to be rescued," implying a translation to Israel), **every one** (144,000) that shall be found written in the book," Dan. 12:1. Such passages as Exod. 32:32, 33; Ps. 56:8; 69:28; Isa. 4:3; Ezek. 13:9; Luke 10:20; Rev. 3:5; 13:8; 17:8; 20:11-15 show that the reference to those found written in the book of life among Daniel's people at the middle of the Week will escape the great tribulation. Christ plainly reveals to John that there will be 144,000 written in the book of life at that time.

8. In Isa. 66:7, 8 we have another definite passage showing that Israel is to bring forth a manchild before she herself is delivered at the end of the Week. This passage reads, "Before she (Israel) travailed (for her own deliverance at the end of the Week, Zech. 12:10-14), she was delivered of a man child," verse 7. That the pain and travail of Israel here is the one which results in her own deliverance at the end of the Week is the one referred to is clear from verse 8 which reads, "Who hath heard such a thing? . . . shall a nation be born at once? for as soon as Zion travailed, she brought forth her children." But before

this birth of a nation in one day (Rom. 11:25-27) "she brought
forth a man child." Who is the manchild that Israel is to bring
forth before her own deliverance if it is not the 144,000 or "every
one found written in the book" among Israel in the middle of the
Week as in the above passages in Dan. 12:1 and Rev. 7:1-8; 12:5;
14:1-5? The manchild in Isaiah must be the same as the one in
Revelation, for both passages are fulfilled at the same time and
concern the same class of people. Since both passages refer
to Israel as a whole and to the manchild as being a smaller group
out of Israel and since the woman or the remnant of the woman
cannot be the manchild, the only others left to make up the
manchild are the 144,000 Jews out of Israel. Therefore, we conclude that the manchild referred to in Isaiah and Revelation is
a symbol of the 144,000 Jews who are caught up to God as an
heavenly people in the middle of the Week.

As we have seen, the 144,000 are a special company from Israel who
are to have a special mission. They are a separate and distinct company
of redeemed eternal rulers who help God, with all other redeemed men
and faithful angels, to administer the affairs of the vast universe of God
— even His creations in infinite outer space, far beyond what we now
know to be in existence.

Since the manchild truly represents a group of people who will be
alive, on earth, after the rapture and will fulfill prophecies of the
"THINGS WHICH MUST BE HEREAFTER," that is, after the
churches, then it is definitely clear that the manchild refers to the
144,000 Jews who are protected from the judgments of the trumpets in
the first half of the Week, Rev. 7:1-8; 9:4, and are caught up to heaven
as the manchild in the middle of the Week (Rev. 12:5), where they are
seen before God in heaven, having been redeemed from the earth, Rev.
14:1-5.

This being true, we must keep in mind that the word "manchild" is
never used in connection with the Church, or with Gentiles in any age
from Adam until now. The word is used only with Israel in prophecy,
and only with Israel will it be fulfilled.

THE DRAGON, WAR IN HEAVEN, AND THE REMNANT

I. The Dragon.

"And there appeared another wonder (sign) in heaven; and behold a great red dragon, having seven heads and ten horns, and seven crowns upon his heads. And his tail drew the third part of the stars of heaven, and did cast them to the earth: and the dragon stood before the woman which was ready to be delivered, for to devour her child as soon as it was born," Rev. 12:3, 4.

The word "dragon" is used thirteen times and only in Revelation. It is a symbol of Satan, the chief adversary of God, Rev. 12:9. This is the first time he is mentioned in Revelation. We must distinguish between the symbol and the thing symbolized, as in all other symbols. The "great red dragon" is a fitting symbol of Satan in his role as the relentless persecutor and murderer of multitudes of unfortunate people, John 8:44. In Job 41 and Isa. 27:1 he is portrayed as "leviathan, the piercing serpent . . . That crooked serpent . . . the dragon that is in the sea."

The seven heads and ten horns symbolize the same seven world kingdoms as the seven heads and ten horns on the beast out of the sea in Rev. 13:1-4; 17:1-18, and all have been or will be used by God in His purpose in judging Israel from the beginning of her history to Christ's coming. They are Egypt, Assyria, Babylon, Medio-Persia, Greece, Rome and the ten kingdoms of Revised Rome as we shall see in our study of Rev. 17. The heads being crowned shows that Satan has reigned and will reign over these seven kingdoms. He has tried to destroy Israel under the first six kingdoms and will try to do so under the seventh or Revised Rome, but he will meet defeat by God as on all previous occasions.

The beast out of the sea will have his ten horns crowned, but not his seven heads, showing that he is to be new in existence and that he has not lived through the length of these seven empires, but will come in the future and conquer the ten horns or the seventh kingdom, reign over it and become the last kingdom before Christ's coming. These facts further prove that Israel is the one represented by the woman, for she is the only company of people that has existed throughout the length of these seven kingdoms except the Gentiles and they compose these kingdoms themselves. The Church has existed through only part of Old Rome and will be translated before Revised Rome has finished its course. Such a symbol can never be used in connection with the Church for that reason.

This symbol is also seen in heaven and is represented as drawing one-third of the stars from heaven and casting them to earth. The stars have reference to the angels of God, and the casting down refers to one-third of God's angels who fell with Satan as recorded in Isa. 14:12-14; Ezek. 28:11-17; Luke 10:18. These "stars" are called "his angels" in Rev. 12:7-12. In the New Testament both men and angels are called stars, Rev. 1:20; 9:1; 12:3-9.

The reference cannot be of literal stars, for they are generally larger than our earth, hence the stars seen in the universe could not fall to the earth.   The tail pictures Lucifer's power and influence in causing the angelic rebellion.

"The dragon stood before the woman which was ready to be delivered (literally, 'is about to bring forth, showing that the manchild is delivered in the middle of the Week, and therefore, cannot possibly refer to the historical ascension of Christ), for to devour (same word as in Rev. 20:9 and 'eat up' in Rev. 10:9, 10) her child **as soon as it was born."** The dragon will try first to destroy the manchild before he turns on the woman.   The following outlines briefly the actions of the dragon in Revelation after he is cast to the earth at the rapture of the manchild.

The first thing he does is to league with Antichrist and give him his power, throne, and great authority (13:1-4), and then they both will turn on the woman which brings forth the manchild.   By this action Satan will continue his age-long animosity toward Israel.   He will make war on her and she will flee into Edom and Moab with the armies of the dragon and Antichrist after her.   God will intervene and the pursuing armies will be swallowed by the earth.   This will aggravate the dragon and he will come back to war with the remnant of her seed, or the remaining Jews who do not flee into the wilderness.   But God will intervene again and stir up enemies in the North and East of the kingdoms of the old Roman Empire, who will at this point submit to the Antichrist, who will keep Antichrist occupied in war for the last three and one-half years.   However, he will finally conquer them about the end of the Week and lead them against Jerusalem as he intended to do in the middle of the Week.   Then he will meet defeat at the hands of Christ who will come at that time to deliver Israel and set up His earthly kingdom.   Satan will be in full co-operation with the Antichrist and back his every move in the destruction of men throughout the last three and one-half years and, at the end, will inspire the nations to fight against Christ, Rev. 16:13-16.   At Armageddon he will be taken and thrown into the bottomless pit for one thousand years to deceive the nations no more until the thousand years are fulfilled.   Then he is to be loosed for a little season to deceive the nations again, leading them in rebellion against God.   They will try again to destroy the Holy City and the saints, but fire will come down out of heaven and will devour his armies.   He will then be taken and cast into the lake of fire where he will be tormented for ever and ever, Rev. 20:1-10.   This will end Satan's career on earth as the enemy of God and man.

II.   The War in Heaven.

"And there was war in heaven: Michael and his angels fought against the dragon: and the dragon fought and his angels, and prevailed not; neither was their place found any more in heaven.   And the great dragon was cast out, that old serpent, called the Devil, and Satan, which deceiveth the whole world: he was cast out into the earth, and his angels were cast out with him. And I heard a loud voice saying in heaven, Now is come salvation, and strength, and the kingdom of our God, and the power of his Christ: for the accuser of our brethren is cast down, which accused them before our God day and night. And they overcame him by the blood of the Lamb, and by the word of their testimony; and they loved not their lives unto the death. Therefore rejoice, ye heavens, and ye that dwell in them. Woe to the inhabiters of the earth and of the sea! for the Devil is come down unto you, having great wrath, because he knoweth that he hath but a short time," Rev. 12:7-12.

The heavens are peopled with multitudes of spirit beings of different orders and kinds, such as seraphim (Isa. 6:1-8), cherubim (Ezek. 1:4-25; 10:1-22), living creatures (Rev. 4:6-8), spirit horses and chariot drivers (2 Kings 2:11-13; 6:13-17; Zech. 1:8-11; 6:1-8; Rev. 19:11-14), common angels (Heb. 1, 2) archangels (Isa. 14:12-14; Ezek. 28:11-17; Jude 9), etc. Principalities, powers, age rulers of darkness, wicked spirits, demons, unclean spirits, thrones, dominions, fallen angels, spirits in prison, etc., are also mentioned which require acknowledgement of many other kinds of spirit beings than are mentioned in a definite way in Scripture, Eph. 6:11-18; Col. 1:15-18; 2 Pet. 2:4; Jude 6, 7; 1 Pet. 3:18-20; 1 Tim. 4:1; Psa. 89:6; Job 1, 2; 38:1-7; etc. **These beings are apportioned into three classes:**

1. God's subjects, Heb. 1, 2.
2. Satan's angels who are loose with him, Rev. 12:7-12.
3. Fallen angels who are bound in tartarus, 2 Pet. 2:4; Jude 6, 7.

This war in heaven will be the last desperate struggle between spirit beings in the heavenlies for and against the majesty and kingdom of God. It will be the culmination of the struggle in heaven between God and Satan. It first began when Lucifer attempted to exalt his kingdom above the angels of God and dethrone God from His universal kingdom over all other kingdoms in the universe. In his rebellion against God and in his ascension into heaven and above the clouds from the earth (Isa. 14:12-14) he was cast out of heaven back down to the ground and was dethroned. Although deprived of his kingdom and exalted position he was not deprived of the power which was his by nature and gift for he still has great power in the heavenlies and over the earth that was usurped from Adam, Eph. 2:2; 6:12; John 12:31; 14:30; 16:11; Matt. 4:1-11. He still has access to heaven and accuses the saints before God day and night, Job 1, 2; Rev. 12:10-12; Zech. 3:1. (See our book, God's Plan for Man, Lesson Seven. for Satan's rebellion.)

Facts Concerning War in Heaven, Rev. 12:7-12.

1. **There is to be a war in the middle of the Week,** Rev. 12:7.
2. The **place** of the war will be heaven, Rev. 12:7.
3. The **combatants** will be Michael, the archangel, in command of the angels of God, arrayed against Lucifer, the archangel, in command of his angels that fell with him when he sinned and was dethroned. How angels fight is not known but surely this will be a real combat. How an angel could wrestle with Jacob;

how angels could take hold of Lot and family and pull them out of the city of Sodom; how an angel could have a sword drawn and meet Joshua in the plains of Jericho; how one angel with a sword could slay 185,000 Assyrians in one night; how angels observe us in all we do; how they protect us from material harm; how they separate people at the judgment of the nations; how they eat like physical men; how they gather Israel back; how they fight with Christ at Armageddon against physical men and do many other things, as plainly stated in Scripture, is not clearly revealed, but the facts are that they do them and that is enough.

This, to my mind, proves that angels have bodies that are of material substance, but in an incorruptible, immortal, indestructible and glorified spiritual state, something like the body of Christ after the resurrection and like our bodies after they will have been glorified. Did not men handle the body of Christ after the resurrection while at the same time it could appear and disappear at will? The same then can be said of the angels else they could not fight against one another as here stated. If they are not objects that can be pushed back by another, how could Satan and his angels be cast down to the earth by the force of other beings of like nature? There may be other ways of war between angels and spirit beings but it cannot be denied that the above is possible. One angel will take Satan, put a chain on him, and bind him in the pit for a thousand years, then loose him, Rev. 20:1-3. The same angel will loose four others that are now bound in the river Euphrates, Rev. 9:14. The angels in tartarus are also bound in chains, 2 Pet. 2:4; Jude 6, 7. Demons are bound in the pit, Rev. 9:1-21. Satan, angels, demons, and wicked men can and will all be confined in the lake of fire forever, Matt. 25:41-46; Rev. 19:20; 20:10-15. How spiritual beings can be bound in chains and be confined to a material place in the earth is not beyond us, for we believe it, and think we understand it, because we can see that they have bodies that are capable of such treatment. (See our book, God's Plan for Man, Les. 4 for a study of spirit bodies.)

With these facts in mind we can better understand the war between these two armies of angelic hosts which prevail one against another. Michael, at the head of God's army, is mentioned in Dan. 10:13, 21; 12:1 and Jude 9 from which we must gather all our information about him, except what we gather from statements made of other angelic beings of the same order. The word "prevailed" (12:8) implies strength to wrestle or struggle against one another (Acts 19:16) thus showing actual combat.

4. **The result of the battle will be** that the Devil and his angels will be thrust down to the earth never to have access to heaven again, Rev. 12:8, 9.

5. **A voice from heaven will cry the following because of the defeat of Satan:**

(1) To God he will state, **"Now** is come salvation, and strength, and the kingdom of our God, and the power of his Christ," Rev. 12:10. Cf. 11:15.

(2) To the saints on earth he will state that "the accuser of **our** brethren (this voice is one of a redeemed man, for he classes himself with other redeemed) is cast down which accused them before our God day and night," Rev. 12:10. This gives the reason for Satan's present access to God, Job 1, 2. Next, he states the method of overcoming Satan. It is the same used to overcome him while on earth as well as in heaven, that is, "by the blood of the Lamb, and by the word of their testimony" and loving "not their lives unto death," Rev. 12:11. These overcomers are not those of the Church, for they have all been raptured, but are those of the Jews and Gentiles who have been saved since the rapture of the Church in Rev. 4:1.

(3) To the inhabitants of heaven he will cry, "Rejoice, ye heavens, and ye that dwell in them" because of the casting out of Satan, Rev. 12:12.

(4) To the inhabitants of the earth· he will say "Woe to the inhabiters of the earth and of the sea! for the Devil is come down unto you, having great wrath, because **he knoweth** he hath but a short time," Rev. 12:12. This third woe will no doubt affect men in a physical way as much as the first two woes, Rev. 9:1-21. This seems to be required by Rev. 8:13; 12:12. He will vent his wrath on the woman, remnant, and many other classes of people during the last three and one-half years. His wrath will be great for he knows he will have but a short time.

III. The Remnant of the Woman.

"And the dragon was wroth with the woman, and went to make war with the remnant of her seed, which keep the commandments of God, and have the testimony of Jesus Christ," Rev. 12:17.

We have already discussed the remnant in connection with the woman and manchild so little needs to be said here. The remnant is not a personage or a symbol, but literally some Jews who will be saved after the rapture of the manchild and who do not flee into the wilderness when the woman or main body of Israel does. In nearly all previous invasions of Judea and Jerusalem there has been a remnant left and the same is to be true at the future time in the middle of the Week when the dragon and Antichrist determine to destroy Israel. The word "remnant" in Scripture is never used of the Church or Gentiles, but contrarily, always of Israel. Isa. 1:9; 10:20; 11:16; Joel 2:32; Micah 2:12; 5:3-9; Zech. 8:6-12; Rom. 11; etc. The remnant was not saved at the time the manchild or 144,000 Jews were translated, or those of the remnant would have been translated also (Dan. 12:1), but they get saved after the rapture of the 144,000 and during the flight of Israel into the wilderness, hence they are saved by the time the dragon wars on them after he fails to destroy Israel that flees.

Chapter Twenty

THE BEAST OUT OF THE SEA

"And I stood upon the sand of the sea, and saw a beast rise up out of the sea, having seven heads and ten horns, and upon his horns ten crowns, and upon his heads the name of blasphemy. And the beast which I saw was like unto a leopard, and his feet were as the feet of a bear, and his mouth as the mouth of a lion: and the dragon gave him his power and his seat (throne), and great authority. And I saw one of his heads as it were wounded to death; and his deadly wound was healed: and all the world wondered after the beast. And they worshipped the dragon which gave power unto the beast; and they worshipped the beast, saying, Who is like unto the beast? Who is able to make war with him? and there was given unto him a mouth speaking great things and blasphemies: and power was given unto him to continue forty and two months. And he opened his mouth in blasphemy against God, to blaspheme his name, and his tabernacle, and them that dwell in heaven," Rev. 13:1-6.

It is claimed that the pronoun "I" of Rev. 13:1 is Satan speaking, but such a theory is false because John is referred to forty times before this and thirty-five times after this by the same pronoun. Such would contradict the plain language of the rest of the passage which shows that John is the one seeing this vision. Rev. 13 gives the effects upon earth of the casting out of Satan.

First let us examine this passage to see what it has to say about the beast out of the sea. This is a symbol and must be treated as such. For the explanation of the beast with its heads, horns, crowns, names of blasphemy, feet, head wounded to death, etc., see chapters thirty to thirty-five.

The sea is symbolic of peoples, Dan. 7:2, 3; Rev. 17:1, 15. The beast in Revelation refers to the rise of a kingdom, and more particularly to the Antichrist, the earthly head of this kingdom. It also symbolizes a supernatural spirit out of the abyss as we shall later see. Beasts as symbols symbolize either the kingdom or king (Dan. 2:38, 39; 7:2-7 with 7:17, 23), as well as supernatural powers which control the kingdom. The personal Antichrist, his power, source of power, worship, mouth, exaltation, wars, characteristics, titles, reign, length of reign, etc., are the subject of this passage. They are briefly dealt with as follows:

1. **Who is he?** At the present time (1948) this question cannot be answered. The question is unsolved and will be until the Antichrist personally makes the covenant with Israel for seven years, Dan. 9:27. Many today, as ever, are speculating on the pope, Stalin, a magician in Syria and others as the Antichrist. Much harm has been done to the subject of prophecy by this for many thinking people have become disgusted and many have turned their faces against the inspiration of prophecy by just such unfounded speculation. The points which follow prove that no man now prominent in world affairs could possibly be the Antichrist.

2. **From where does he come?** This question is fully answered in the book of Daniel. In Dan. 2 and 7 we have two visions that cover the Gentile world powers from Daniel's day to the second coming of Christ. The "head of gold" on the image (Dan. 2:32, 35, 38) and the "lion" (Dan. 7:4, 12, 17) symbolize Babylon,

Nebuchadnezzar's kingdom (Dan. 2:37, 38; Jer. 15:4; 24:9; 25:11, 12; 29:18). The "breast and arms of silver" on the image (Dan. 2:32, 35, 39) and the "bear" (Dan. 7:5, 12, 17) symbolize Medo-Persia, which followed Babylon in the punishment of Israel (Dan. 2:39; 5:24-31; 6:1-28; 8:1-4, 20; 10:1-20; 11:1-3; 2 Chron. 36:22; Ezra 1:1-3). The "belly and thighs of brass" on the image (Dan. 2:39) and the "leopard" (Dan. 7:6, 12, 17) symbolize the old Grecian Empire of Alexander the Great that followed Medo-Persia in the times of the Gentiles (Dan. 2:39; 8:20, 21; 11:1-4). The "legs of iron" on the image (Dan. 2:33-35, 40) and the nondescript "beast" (Dan. 7:7, 8, 17-27) symbolize the old Roman Empire that followed the Grecian Empire and its four divisions in the persecution of Israel (Dan. 2:40; 7:23-25; 9:26; Luke 2:1; John 11:48; Matt. 24:1, 2; Luke 21:20-24; Acts 16:21; 22:25-29). The "feet and toes" of iron and clay on the image (Dan. 2:33-35, 41-44) and "the ten horns" on the nondescript beast (Dan. 7:8, 20-24) symbolize ten kings who will head ten separate governments from ten separate capitals inside the old Roman Empire in the days of the second coming of Christ (Dan. 2:31-44; 7:23-25; Rev. 12:3; 13:1-4; 17:8-17).

Men call these ten kingdoms the Revived Roman Empire, but to be technical, there is no such thing as the Roman Empire being revived. This would require the old Roman territory to be formed into one empire again and be ruled by one man from Rome, but this the Bible does not teach. It teaches ten kingdoms inside of this territory instead of one empire (Dan. 2:44; 7:23, 24; Rev. 17:8-17). It would be best to call these ten kingdoms the "Revised Roman Empire" due to the fact that they will be formed inside the old Roman territory, but there will be ten kingdoms instead of one empire as is generally taught.

Daniel did not see a little toe growing out of the ten toes in Dan. 2, but in Dan. 7 he did see a "little horn" growing out of the ten horns, which plucked up three of the ten horns by the roots (Dan. 7:7, 8). This is explained in Dan. 7:23, 24 thus: "The fourth beast shall be the fourth kingdom upon the earth (the old Roman Empire, which followed Babylon, Medo-Persia, and Greece from Daniel's day on), which shall be diverse from all kingdoms. . . . the ten horns OUT OF this kingdom are ten kings that shall arise: and ANOTHER shall rise AFTER THEM; and he shall be diverse from the FIRST (the ten), and he shall subdue three kings (of the ten)." This will give him four of the ten kings. The other six of the ten will agree to give their power to this little horn and he will then form the eighth kingdom of Rev. 17:8-17.

It is clear that this "little horn" arises "AFTER" the ten kingdoms and not "BEFORE" them and that he does not have anything to do with the rise of the ten kingdoms. He does not come until "AFTER" they are fully formed and exist for a "short space," Dan. 7:8; Rev. 17:9-11. If men would have believed the simple statements of the Bible on these questions we never would have had the foolish speculations on Mussolini, Hitler, Stalin, the pope, and others as being the future Antichrist. The sensational writings of many trying to prove who the Antichrist will be has caused much confusion and the sooner such guessing is stopped the better off the subject of prophecy will be in the eyes of intelligent people. The "little horn" as well as the "ten horns" are all yet future, for in Rev. 13:1-8; 17:9-17 it is clear that the ten kings give their power and kingdom to the beast for forty-two months and together they will fight against Christ at Armageddon.

In Dan. 8 we have a vision of a ram and an he-goat. The ram symbolizes Medo-Persia the same as the silver in the image of Dan. 2 and the bear of Dan. 7. The he-goat symbolizes the Grecian Empire the same as the brass in the image of Dan. 2 and the leopard of Dan. 7. The he-goat had a notable horn between its eyes, which was broken off, and in its place grew four horns and "OUT OF" one of them came forth the little horn." The interpretation of these things is given as follows: "The ram which thou sawest having two horns ARE THE (two) KINGS OF MEDIA AND PERSIA. And the rough goat IS THE KING (kingdom) OF GRECIA: and the great horn that is between his eyes IS THE FIRST KING (Alexander the Great who founded the old Grecian Empire). Now that being broken (Alexander having died), whereas four stood up for it (that is, four horns grew on the he-goat instead of the great horn), FOUR KINGDOMS SHALL STAND UP OUT OF THE NATION (the Grecian Empire shall be divided into four kingdoms), but not in his (Alexander's) power. And IN THE LATTER TIME OF THEIR KINGDOM, when the transgressors are come to the full, A KING OF FIERCE COUNTENANCE, AND UNDERSTANDING DARK SENTENCES, SHALL STAND UP (that is, the little horn shall come out of one of these four divisions of Greece in the last days of the existence of these four kingdoms) . . . He shall also stand up against the Prince of princes (Jesus Christ); but he shall be broken without hand" by Christ at His second advent. These four divisions of Greece would be known today as Greece, Turkey, Syria and Egypt. Four of Alexander's generals divided his empire after his death. Cassander took Greece and Macedon, Lysimachus took Asia Minor or present Turkey and Thrace, Seleucus took Syria and Babylonia, and Ptolemy took Egypt. (This can be verified by anyone who will get an ancient history and see the map of the old Grecian Empire and its four divisions after the death of Alexander.)

In Dan. 8:9 it is definitely stated that "the little horn" will come from one of the four horns, "OUT OF ONE OF THEM came forth a little horn, which waxed exceeding great, toward the south (Egypt), and toward the east (Syria and Babylonia), and toward the pleasant land (Palestine)." This verse is interpreted in verse 23 as "IN THE LATTER TIME OF THEIR KINGDOM (the existence of Greece, Turkey, Syria, and Egypt), when the transgressors are come to the full, A KING OF FIERCE COUNTENANCE, and understanding dark sentences, SHALL STAND UP" and fight against "THE PRINCE OF PRINCES" at his second advent.

The purpose of Dan. 8 over Dan. 7 is to narrow down the coming of the Antichrist geographically from the ten kingdoms of the future Revised Roman Empire to four of the ten kingdoms, and reveal that Antichrist will come from either Greece, Turkey, Syria or Egypt, not from the Vatican, Italy, France, Spain, Germany, Russia, or some other place in the world. We must now forget any place outside the four divisions of the old Grecian Empire as being the place from which Antichrist must come. He will come from one of these four divisions of Greece and will overthrow the other three, thus reviving the Grecian Empire, which will become the eighth or leopard kingdom of Rev. 13:1-18; 17:1-17.

In Dan. 11 we have a vision of wars between two of the four divisions of the Grecian Empire, Syria, and Egypt, which were fought over a period of about 150 years ending with Antiochus Epiphanes who reigned about 165 B. C. Then the prophet skips over to the end time and pictures the last war between Syria and Egypt, with the result that Syria will finally overthrow Egypt. Egypt is called "the king of the south" and Syria "the king of the north" in this vision.

Dan. 11:36-12:13 definitely identifies the Antichrist as "the king of the north" (Syria) at "the time of the end." The whole purpose of the vision was to show "what shall befall thy people (Israel) in the latter days" (Dan. 10:14). The purpose of this vision over Dan. 7 and 8 is to narrow down the coming of the Antichrist geographically from the ten kingdoms of Dan 7, and from the four kingdoms of Dan. 8 to the one kingdom of Dan. 11, the Syrian division of the old Grecian Empire, thus teaching that the Antichrist will come from Syria at the end time. If the whole vision of Dan. 11 concerns only Egypt and Syria showing the latter-day war between them with the result that Egypt will be finally overthrown by Syria, then it proves that he will come from Syria and not Egypt, Greece or Turkey, the other three divisions of the old Grecian Empire.

"The king of the north" is the same as the "little horn" of Dan. 7 and 8, "the prince that shall come" of Dan. 9:26, 27, "the son of perdition" and "man of sin" of 2 Thess. 2:1-12, and "the beast" of Rev. 13 as proved by the following:

(1) All do according to their will for the same length of time, Dan. 7:25; 8:14; 11:36; 2 Thess. 2:10-12; Rev. 13:5-7.

(2) All will exalt themselves above every god, Dan. 7:25; 8:25; 11:36, 37; 2 Thess. 2:4; Rev. 13:1-18.

(3) All are conquerors in the same territory at the same time, Dan. 7:8, 20-24; 8:23-25; 11:40-45; Rev. 13:1-18.

(4) All speak blasphemies against God at the same time, Dan. 7:8, 11, 20-25; 8:23-25; 11:36; 2 Thess. 2:4; Rev. 13:5.

(5) All prevail against the saints and Jews during the tribulation, Dan. 7:21-26; 8:24; 11:40, 41; 12:1, 7; Matt. 24:15-22; Rev. 13:1-18; 14:9-11; 15:1-4; 20:4-6.

(6) All come out of the ten kingdoms of Revised Rome and get power over the ten kingdoms and reign over them until all of them are destroyed at Armageddon, Dan. 7:7, 8, 23, 24; 8:9, 22-25; 11:40-45; Rev. 13:1-4; 17:9-17; 19:19-21.

(7) All change the times and laws for a time, Dan. 7:11, 21-27; 8:22-25; 11:35-45; 12:7; 2 Thess. 2:1-13; Rev. 13:1-8.

(8) All reign "UNTIL" the second coming of Christ, Dan. 2:44; 7:11-14, 18, 21-26; 8:23-25; 9:27; 11:36-45; 12:7-13; 2 Thess. 2:8-12; Rev. 17:9-17; 19:19-21.

(9) All continue the same length of time, Dan. 7:21-26; 8:22-25; 9:27; 11:40-45; 12:7-13; 2 Thess. 2:8-13; Rev. 13:5; 17:9-17; 19:19-21.

(10) All will be alive when the God of heaven comes to set up His kingdom, Dan. 2:44; 7:11-14, 18-26; 8:22-25; 9:27; 11:40-45; 12:7-13; 2 Thess. 2:8-13; Rev. 17:14; 19:19-21; 20:1-10.

(11) All cause the greatest tribulation that ever will be on earth, Dan. 7:21-27; 8:19, 24, 25; 9:27; 12:1, 7; Matt. 24:15-22; 2 Thess. 2:1-12; Rev. 7:14; 13:1-18; 14:9-11; 15:2-4; 20:4-6; Jer. 30:3-7.

(12) All will do away with the Jewish daily sacrifices in the future temple and cause the abomination of desolation, Dan. 7:25; 8:11-14; 9:27; 11:35-45; 12:11; Matt. 24:15-22; 2 Thess. 2:4; Rev. 13:1-18.

(13) All will reign in the Jewish temple in Jerusalem, Dan. 8:9-14; 9:27; 11:45; 12:7; 2 Thess. 2:4; Rev. 11:1, 2; 13:1-18.

(14) All will disregard the God of the fathers, Dan. 7:11, 19-25; 8:22-25; 9:27; 11:38, 39; 2 Thess. 2:1-12; John 5:43; Rev. 13:1-8.

(15) All will honor the Devil and get their power from him, Dan. 8:24; 11:35-45; 2 Thess. 2:9; Rev. 13:1-4.

(16) All will come to the same end and be slain by Christ at the second advent and then be cast into the lake of fire, Dan. 2:44, 45; 7:11, 21-26; 11:45; 2 Thess. 2:8-12; Rev. 19:19-21.

3. **When is he to be revealed or when is he due to come into prominence in world affairs?** This question is also clearly answered in Scripture:

(1) In Dan. 7:24, we have definite proof that Antichrist cannot be revealed and be prominent in world affairs, until **after** the ten kingdoms are formed inside the Roman Empire, as seen in point 2. According to this verse, the ten kingdoms must first be formed and exist for some time as the seventh kingdom or Revised Rome. The Antichrist will arise and gain the whole ten in the first three and one-half years of the Week. By the middle of the Week he will be seen as the beast of Rev. 13 coming out of the sea of humanity already with the seven heads and ten

horns, which he will have conquered before the middle of the Week. His coming out of the sea in the middle of the Week will be simply the recognition of his power by the ten kingdoms and his acceptance of them from the ten kings and the dragon, Rev. 13:2-4; 17:12-17. This verse further teaches, because of his rise out of the ten kingdoms, that he is to come out of obscurity and that his rise to power will be quick. Daniel saw the "little horn" rising so suddenly among the ten that he was bewildered about it, Dan. 7:7, 8, 19-24. Therefore, no man can determine definitely who the Antichrist will be until **after** the ten kingdoms are formed.

(2)   The Antichrist cannot be revealed until after the rapture as proved in 2 Thess. 2:6-8, for which see point 9, chapter seven.

4. How long is he to reign?   He will reign over one of the ten kingdoms from the beginning of the Week, but he will reign over all the ten kingdoms only the last three and one-half years, Rev. 13:5; Dan. 7:25; 12:7. It is in these last three and one-half years that he will exalt himself above every God to be worshipped by all, Rev. 13:4-18; Dan. 8:25; 11:36-45; 2 Thess. 2:4.

5. Where is he to reign?   During part of the last three and one-half years he will reign in Jerusalem "in the glorious holy mountain" where the temple will be rebuilt, Dan. 11:45. He will sit "in the temple of God, showing himself that he is God," 2 Thess. 2:4. This temple is where the abomination of desolation will be placed, Dan. 9:27; 12:7-13; Matt. 24:15-22; Rev. 11:1, 2; 13:12-18. Babylon, and not Rome, will be his place of reign until then as we shall see in chapter thirty-seven. The fact that there will be ten separate kingdoms with ten separate capitals and ten separate kings in the first three and one-half years shows that up to the middle of the Week the Antichrist will have no one place of reign over the ten kingdoms, for they will not yet be under him. Rome will be just one of the ten capitals and her king will reign over the territory of Italy and her possessions and not over all of Revised Rome. It is only when Antichrist becomes head of the ten kingdoms by the middle of the Week that he will establish one central throne for all the newly formed empire. Even then, the ten kings will continue as kings under him, Rev. 17:9-17.

6. The power of the Antichrist.   The power of the Antichrist will come from Satan, the spirit of the abyss, and the ten kings. His power has already been decreed of God, who will see that it is duly given him. It is God who will permit Satan and his agents to give their power to the beast and inspire him in his evil designs, Dan. 8:24; 2 Thess. 2:8-12; Rev. 13:1, 2. It is God who will put it into the hearts of the ten kings to give him their power for the purpose of destroying Mystical Babylon, Rev. 17:12-17. It is the satanic prince out of the abyss (Rev. 11:7; 17:8) who is the executive of Satan's power to the beast and who will inspire and back the Antichrist in all his diabolical activities, as will be seen in chapter thirty-two. Satan will give to Antichrist what he offered Christ. Antichrist will accept it; Christ did not. Antichrist must fight to possess it even as Christ would have had to do and will yet have to do. Antichrist will succeed in this world conquest by conquering the Revised Roman Empire by the middle of the Week and all the northern and eastern countries of Asia and Europe by the end of the Week; also by getting the co-operation of many other nations, through the ministry of the three unclean spirits, who will help him against the Jews and Christ at the second advent. After his defeat at Armageddon by Christ, Antichrist will be cast into the lake of fire. The kingdom of Christ will succeed his kingdom and extend throughout all the earth. **The power of the beast may be summarized as follows:**

(1)   To blaspheme God, Dan. 7:8, 11, 20, 25; 11:36; Rev. 13:5, 6.

(2)   To overcome saints, Rev. 7:9-17; 14:13; 15:2-4.

(3)   To overcome the Jews, Dan. 7:21; 12:7; Rev. 13:7, 15.

(4)   To conquer many nations (Dan. 7:8, 20-24; 11:36-45; Ezek. 38, 39) and rule them as he wills, Rev. 13:7.

(5)   To destroy Mystery Babylon, Rev. 17:12-17.

(6)   To overcome and kill the two witnesses, Rev. 11:7.

(7)   To change times and laws, Dan. 7:25.

(8)   To understand mysteries, Dan. 8:23.

(9)   To protect the Jews as long as he desires, and also to do as he desires against them, Dan 9:27; 2 Thess. 2:4; Rev. 11:1, 2.

(10)   To work signs and wonders, Dan. 8:24; 2 Thess. 2:8-12; Rev. 13:1-18; 19:20.

(11)   To cause craft to prosper, Dan. 8:25.

(12)   To control money and riches in his own realm, Dan. 11: 38-43.

(13)   To cause great deceptions, 2 Thess. 2:10-12; John 5:43; Dan. 8:25; Rev. 13:1-18.

(14)   To do according to his own will, Dan. 11:36.

(15)   To control religion and worship, Dan. 11:36; 2 Thess. 2:4; Rev. 13:1-18; 14:9-11; 16:2.

(16)   To control the lives of all men in his realm, Rev. 13:12-18.

(17)   To control kings as he wills, Rev. 17:12-17.

(18)   To make all the other nations fear him, Rev. 13:4.

(19)   To fight against Christ, Rev. 19:11-21; Dan. 8:25.

(20)   To reign forty-two months, Rev. 13:5.

7. The Titles of the Antichrist.

(1)   **"Antichrist."** This is the most common one we use in speaking of him for he is to be the great opposer of Christ at the end of the age. The word occurs only four times in the Bible (1 John 2:18, 22; 4:3; 2 John 7), but the studies above and below show him to be the one to have that title more than any other and is to be the one expressly stated to come in these passages.

(2)   **"The Assyrian,"** Isa. 10:20-27; 30:18-33; 31:4-32:20; Mic. 5:3-15. These prophecies were directed against the Assyrian king in the days of the prophets but a study of them reveals that

they have a latter-day fulfillment in the future Assyrian king who is to oppress Israel just preceding her final restoration. The Assyrian territory will be part of Antichrist's kingdom and in that sense he is the king of Assyria.

This first passage (Isa. 10:20-27) refers to the "remnant" of Rev. 12:17: "IN THAT DAY the remnant of Israel . . . shall NO MORE again stay (Hebrew, look for support) upon him (Antichrist) that smote them; but shall stay (Hebrew, lean upon, rely) upon the Lord . . . O my people THAT DWELLEST IN ZION, be not afraid of THE ASSYRIAN: he shall smite thee with a rod . . . yet a little while (1,260 days, Rev. 12:6, 14-17; 13:5), and the indignation (Hebrew, God's anger and wrath, the day of vengeance in the tribulation, as in Isa. 26:20; Dan. 8:19; 11:36) shall cease, and MINE ANGER IN THEIR DESTRUCTION . . . IN THAT DAY his burden shall be taken away from off thy shoulder . . . the yoke shall be destroyed BECAUSE OF THE ANOINTING." The Hebrew root for "anointing" is shawman, to shine, and no doubt refers to the brightness of Christ's coming in 2 Thess. 2:8, 9.

The second passage (Isa. 30:18-33) refers to Israel's final restoration under the Messiah, as is clear: "Therefore will he (the Lord) be exalted . . . the people shall dwell in Zion at Jerusalem: thou shalt weep NO MORE . . . IN THE DAY that the Lord bindeth up the breach of his people . . . the name of the Lord cometh from far, burning with his anger . . . to sift the nations . . . with the flame of a devouring fire, with scattering, and tempest, and hailstones. For through the voice of the Lord shall THE ASSYRIAN BE BEATEN DOWN."

This is also referred to in Isa. 31:4-32:20, "Like as the lion roaring on his prey . . . shall the Lord of hosts COME DOWN TO FIGHT FOR MOUNT ZION . . . As birds flying, so will the Lord of hosts DEFEND JERUSALEM; defending also HE WILL DELIVER IT; and PASSING OVER HE WILL PRESERVE IT . . . For IN THAT DAY every man shall cast away his idols . . . THEN shall THE ASSYRIAN FALL WITH THE SWORD, not of a mighty man (but by Christ, 2 Thess. 2:8, 9) . . . a king shall reign in righteousness . . . And my people shall dwell in a peaceable habitation, and in sure dwellings, and in quiet resting places."

The last passage (Mic. 5:3-15) definitely speaks of Israel being given up "UNTIL the time that she which travaileth hath brought forth (Israel has brought forth the manchild, as we have seen in chapters sixteen through eighteen): THEN the remnant of his brethren shall return unto the children of Israel. And he (Christ, verses 1, 2), shall stand and feed in the strength of the Lord . . . now shall he be great UNTO THE ENDS OF THE EARTH. And THIS MAN shall be the peace, WHEN THE ASSYRIAN (Antichrist) SHALL COME INTO OUR LAND: and WHEN HE SHALL TREAD IN OUR PALACES (Dan. 9:27; 11:40-45; 2 Thess. 2:3, 4;

Rev. 13:8, 11-18) . . . thus shall he deliver us from THE ASSYRI-AN . . . I will execute vengeance in anger and fury upon the heathen, such as they have not heard."

(3) **"The king of Babylon,"** Isa. 14:4. This passage is in a prophecy of Babylon which had a partial fulfillment in the overthrow of Babylon by the Medes and Persians, Isa. 13:17. The complete fulfillment will be in the last days under Antichrist, as is proved by the mention of "the day of the Lord" and the restoration of Israel, which will occur when Christ comes to earth in the days of the reign of Antichrist, Isa. 13:6-16, 19-22; 14:1-8, 18-27. All this has never been fulfilled as stated here. Antichrist will be the king of Babylon in the same sense he will be the king of Assyria, in that Babylon will be under his jurisdiction in the last days. (See chapter thirty-seven.)

(4) **"The spoiler"** and **"the extortioner,"** Isa. 16:1-5. (For a latter-day fulfillment of this passage see chapter sixteen, point III, 1.)

(5) **"Gog, the chief prince of Meshech and Tubal,"** Ezek. 38, 39. These two chapters will be fulfilled at Armageddon, as seen in chapter forty.

(6) **The "little horn,"** Dan. 7:8, 24; 8:9, 23. (See point 2, page 162.)

(7) **"A king of fierce countenance,"** Dan. 8:23. (See point 2, page 162.)

(8) **"The prince that shall come,"** Dan. 9:26, 27. This refers to the "little horn" from the ten kingdoms of Revised Rome that will make the seven years covenant with Israel and then break it in the middle of the Week and cause the abomination of desolation in the Jewish temple at Jerusalem, as seen in chapter five.

(9) **"The king of the north,"** Dan. 11:36-45. This is the king of the Syrian division of the old Grecian Empire as we have seen in point 2 on page 162. He is called this because he will be from the northern division of old Greece, that is, north of Palestine. Many Bible teachers say the Antichrist will come from Russia and use this term to prove it, but this will be disproved in chapter twenty-one, point 6. If "the king of the north" refers to Russia, then what countries are there north of Russia that could fight against Russia as required in Dan. 11:44? There are none, so this title applies to the future king of Syria—the northern division of the four divisions of the old Grecian Empire out of which Antichrist must come, Dan. 8:8, 9, 20-25.

(10) **"The man of sin,"** 2 Thess. 2:1-12.

(11) **"The son of perdition,"** 2 Thess. 2:1-12.

(12) **"The wicked"** and **"that wicked,"** Isa. 11:4; 2 Thess. 2:1-12. These last four phrases picture the Antichrist in his role as the most sinful and wicked man of his time and perhaps all time, for he will literally murder multitudes who do not conform to his every desire (Rev. 7:9-17; 13:16-18; 15:1-3; 20:4-6). For this wickedness he is "the son of perdition," because he is destined to perdition or destruction and eternal hell.

The theory that Antichrist is "the mystery of iniquity" or Satan manifest in the flesh as Jesus was "the mystery of godliness" or God manifest in the flesh; that Antichrist will be "the son of perdition" or "the son of Satan" by a woman as Jesus was "the Son of God" by a woman; and that Antichrist is the opposite of Christ in every detail is not taught in Scripture. That Antichrist is a "mysterious personage" and will be such a man of mystery in all that he does is false. Not one statement about him is mysterious or teaches that he will be a supernatural, or an immortal man from the abyss and an incarnation of the Devil, or a natural son of the Devil, as we shall see in chapters thirty through thirty-five.

The phrase "mystery of iniquity" literally means the invisible spirit of lawlessness or the evil spirit forces that cause men to sin (John 8:44; 14:30; Eph. 2:1-3; 1 John 3:8; Eph. 6:10-18; 2 Cor. 4:3, 4). The same men that teach Antichrist is the mystery of iniquity teach that he is the beast now bound in the abyss and will come out again as the Antichrist. They teach that this spirit is Judas who will be reincarnated, and their main proof is that Judas and Antichrist are both called "the son of perdition" (John 17:12; 2 Thess. 2:1-4). As we shall see in chapter thirty-one, no human being ever goes into the abyss and therefore Judas could not be in the pit to come out. The expression "the son of perdition" literally means "the son of destruction," because both Judas and Antichrist are destined to destruction, not because they are natural sons of Satan. They could not be sons of Satan and be incarnations of Satan at the same time.

In the Greek it reads "the son of the destruction" just as it reads "the man of the sin." This last phrase does not limit the Antichrist as being the only man of sin and the former phrase does not limit him to be the only son of destruction. The Hebrews and Greeks called any man who was subject to a particular evil or thing, the son of that thing, as "sons of Belial" (1 Sam. 1:16; 2:12; 25:17, 25; 1 Kings 21:10); "child of the devil" (Acts 13:10); "children of the wicked one" (Matt. 13:38); "children of the devil" (1 John 3:10); children of "wisdom" (Luke 7:35); "children of the world" (Luke 16:8); "children of light" (Luke 16:8; John 12:36); "children of disobedience" (Eph. 2:1-3; 5:6-8; Col. 3:6). Also anyone who was destined to some particular thing was called the child of that destiny, as "children of the kingdom" (Matt. 8:12); "children of wrath" (Eph. 2:1-3); "children of the resurrection" (Luke 20:36). So it would be only natural to call both Judas and Antichrist "the son of perdition" or destruction, for both are destined to destruction in hell, because of their sin.

The word "perdition" is used only eight times and is from the Greek **apoleia,** meaning ruin, loss, destruction, perdition, and perish. It is never used as a name of the Devil; hence to call Judas and Antichrist sons of the Devil by a woman is not Biblical. In no Scripture is it stated that Judas ever was or ever will be, or that the future Antichrist will ever be a direct and literal child of the Devil by a woman. That is as far from truth as the Devil himself. Try to substitute the word Devil for perdition in all other places where it is found, and see if it makes sense, Phil. 1:28; 1 Tim. 6:9; Heb. 10:39; 2 Pet. 3:7; Rev. 17:8, 11. The Greek **apoleia** is translated "destruction" (Matt. 7:13; Rom. 9:22; Phil. 3:19; 2 Pet. 2:1; 3:16); "damnation" (2 Pet. 2:3); "die" (Acts 25:16); "perish" (Acts 8:20); and other ways, but it never means the Devil, hence "son of perdition" does not mean "son of the Devil."

All other statements about the Antichrist coming in his own name (John 5:43); exalting himself (2 Thess. 2:4); being worshiped (Rev. 13:8); being cast into hell (Rev. 19:20); doing his own will (Dan. 11:36); destroying men (Dan. 8:24); being wicked (2 Thess. 2:3-8); and other facts about him do not prove he is such a super being and a mystery as men teach. All these things can be understood in connection with a natural and mortal man, as we shall see. If Antichrist is the mystery of lawlessness, then he has been here all the time and he cannot come from the pit, for Paul said this mystery was already working in his day, 2 Thess. 2:7. Men try to find so many hidden meanings in the Bible and spend lifetimes trying to make the Bible a mystery instead of taking it as a simple book as it really is. All such interpretations must be rejected for the sake of simple truth.

The Devil is never going to have a natural son by a woman. Gen. 3:15 certainly does not teach such a thing. The seed of the serpent is plainly understood to be the children of the Devil by service, not by natural birth (Matt. 13:38; 1 John 3:8-10; John 8:44). This last passage is taken by some to mean Antichrist will be a natural seed of the Devil, "Ye are of your father the devil . . . When he speaketh a LIE, he speaketh of his own; for he is a LIAR, and the father of IT." It is claimed that the word "IT" refers to one particular son of the Devil, the Antichrist, but this is not only proved false by the same passage that speaks of all men being "of your father the devil," but it is also proved ridiculous by the same passage. The "LIE" refers to a literal lie and not to a natural son of the Devil by a woman. If telling a lie can be turned into a natural son in this passage then we can make natural sons in Acts 5:3; Rom. 1:25; Ps. 78:36, and all other places in Scripture where lies were spoken. If the "LIE" here means the Devil is going to have a natural son by a woman, then he is going to "speak" this son into existence and if this be true, then he could not be a natural son by a woman or an incarnation of himself. If he could do this he would be speaking enough sons into existence to fill the earth, so he would have a better chance to defeat God. Such teaching is plain foolishness.

It is also argued that Judas was the only one ever called a "devil," thus proving further that he was the Devil incarnate, or the mystery of iniquity and son of perdition (John 6:70, 71; 17: 12). It is claimed the definite article is used thus making Judas "the devil," but the definite article is not in the Greek at all and means "a devil." The Greek for "devil" is **diabolos** and means "adversary or slanderer" and is used of other men who are called "false accusers" (2 Tim. 3:3; Tit. 2:3) and "slanderers" (1 Tim. 3:11). Since the word is used of other men, Judas is not the only one it is used of, as is claimed. The word never implies an incarnation as some argue. If so, then these other men were also incarnations of the Devil. The Devil never incarnates himself in the Antichrist any more than he did Judas, for the dragon is always seen as a separate person outside the beast.

If Judas were the Devil incarnate then the Devil was the son of Simon, a human being, so he could not have been created of God and could not have existed until the time of Christ (John 6:70, 71). Then it was the Devil that betrayed Jesus (Matt. 10:4); that Jesus chose as one of His own trusted disciples and planned to give a throne in the eternal kingdom (Matt. 10:1-8; Luke 22:28-30); that received power from the Holy Spirit through Jesus to cast out himself and his demons and to destroy his own work (Matt. 10:1-21); that did cast out himself and destroy his own work (Mark 6:7-13); that followed Jesus and had fellowship for over three years with Him (Ps. 41:9; 55:12, 13); that had a place in the bishopric and fell from it by transgression (Acts 1:15-25;Ps. 109:8); that lost his name out of the book of life (Acts 1:20 with Ps. 69:25-28); that entered into himself to betray Jesus (Luke 22:3); that carried the bag and was the trusted treasurer of the apostolic band (John 13:29); that repented himself of selling Jesus (Matt. 27:3-10); and that hanged himself and had his bowels gush out and was buried in a potter's field (Matt. 27:5; Acts 1:17-20). Who could believe these things happened to the Devil?

If Judas were the Devil incarnate then it was Judas that was a created being and an angel that ruled the earth before Adam and that invaded heaven and was cast out (Isa. 14:12-14; Ezek. 28:11-17; Luke 10:18); that opposed Israel and smote Job with boils and that has present access to heaven (1 Chron. 21:1; Job 1:6-2:7); that stood at his own right hand to betray Jesus and became childless ever afterward (Ps. 109:6-20); that tempted Christ (Matt. 4:1-11); that used Peter as a tool (Matt. 16:23); that caused all the sickness in men (Acts 10:38; Luke 13:16); that was still alive and worked against early believers after he committed suicide (Acts 5:3; 26:18); and that does all the things that the Devil does in all Scriptures.

If the Antichrist is going to be the Devil incarnate, then we would have to conclude that the Devil has not yet come (1 John 2:18; John 5:43); that he will not come until after ten kingdoms are formed inside the Roman Empire (Dan. 7:24) and after the rapture of the Church (2 Thess. 2:7, 8; chapter seven, point 9); that he will only continue forty-two months when he does come (Rev. 13:5); that the Devil is a "man" (Rev. 13:18); that this man is in heaven now accusing the saints and will be cast out in the middle of the Week (Rev. 12:7-17; 13:1-8); that the dragon is not a separate person outside the beast as he is pictured as being in all passages on the subject (Rev. 13:2-4; 16:13-16; 19:20; 20:10); that the Devil is to be "slain" by Christ at His second advent (Dan. 7:11; Isa. 11:4; 2 Thess. 2:8, 9); that he is put into two different places during the Millennium, for the beast is in the lake of fire and the dragon is in the abyss (Rev. 19:20; 20:1-3); that the Devil is still in the lake of fire while he is loosed at the end of the Millennium and that he will be again cast back where he already is and has always been since Armageddon (Rev. 19:20; 20:1-10); and that the Devil has died once and will die two times in the future.

We would also have to believe that Judas became his own father when he incarnated himself in a woman and was born; that he died and will become incarnated again in a woman in the latter days and will become a second incarnation of the Devil, or himself. How could any person become nothing but a seed in a woman twice and grow from nothing but a seed to a full grown man two times? How could the Devil as an immortal angel be a man and die three times? How could he be the Devil outside of both Judas and Antichrist and still be an incarnation of the Devil in both? How could the Devil enter into Judas if he were Judas? How could he give his power to the Antichrist and be a dragon outside of him and still be the Antichrist? How could he be the beast in the lake of fire and still be himself in the pit? These and other ridiculous things we would have to believe if we accepted as truth what some men teach on the subject of Antichrist. These teaching are not the truth about Judas or the Antichrist or the head wounded to death as we shall see in chapters thirty through thirty-five.

(13) **"The beast,"** Dan. 7:11; Rev. 13:1-18; 14:9-11; 15:2, 3; 16:2, 10; 17:1-18; 19:19-21; 20:2-4, 10. This beast is fully explained in chapters thirty through thirty-six.

8. His Person. All the above studies prove that the Antichrist is to be a real person and not a system or the successive head of some system as the pope, and that he is yet future and will literally carry out all the prophecies concerning himself. His character and characteristics are clearly implied in the points above, which reveal that he will be a man who will possess the talent and leadership of all previously gifted conquerors and leaders. In addition to these natural gifts, he will possess the miraculous power of attracting people of every class, fascinating them with his marvelous personality, successes, wisdom, administrative and executive ability, and bringing them under his control through his well-directed flattery and masterly diplomacy. He will be endued with the power of Satan in the exercise of these gifts until the world will wonder after him and many will worship him as God. Some of his titles, the operations of his power, his wars, and other points of interest concerning him will be given in chapters thirty to thirty-nine.

THE EXTENT OF ANTICHRIST'S REIGN

"And it was given unto him to make war with the saints, and to overcome them: and power was given him over all kindreds, and tongues, and nations. And all that dwell upon the earth shall worship him, whose names are not written in the book of life of the Lamb slain from the foundation of the world. If any man have an ear, let him hear. He that leadeth into captivity shall go into captivity: he that killeth with the sword must be killed with the sword. Here is the patience and faith of the saints," Rev. 13:7-10.

The question often arises, "Will the Antichrist have power over **all** kindreds, tongues, and nations, and will **all** that dwell upon the earth worship him?" It is generally answered in the affirmative but that depends upon what is meant by "all." If it means "all" in the most inclusive sense and includes every individual in the known world today, we can say that he will not have this power, but if it is taken to mean "all" that God has in mind— the ten kingdoms of old Rome—we can say that "all" means "all" as far as a decree is concerned. The following points from Scripture prove that **Antichrist will not rule America or be a world-wide dictator as our modern prophetical students teach.**

1. The word **all** in Rev. 13 is simply part of the figure of speech called "synecdoche" in which a part is put for a whole and a whole for a part. It is frequently used in Scripture as in the following examples:

(1) "I, even I, do bring a flood of waters upon the earth, to destroy **all flesh,** wherein is the breath of life, from under heaven; and **EVERY THING that is in the earth shall die,**" Gen. 6:17. If we took this as literal as men do Rev. 13, we would have Noah and his family and all the animals in the ark dead, for they were also under heaven and in the earth and yet they did not die.

(2) "And they utterly destroyed **ALL that was in the city,** both men and women," referring to the people in Jericho when the wall fell, but the "all" here must be understood in a limited sense, for Rahab and her people were spared, Josh. 6:21-25.

(3) "David and **ALL the house of Israel** played before the Lord" and "brought up the ark" (2 Sam. 6:5, 15), yet not all Israel did this, for many did not know how to play instruments and many were too young and still many were not even gathered at that one place.

(4) "Six months did Joab remain there (out of his own country) with **ALL Israel,** until he had cut off every male in Edom" (1 Kings 11:16, 17). The "ALL Israel" referred to here is part of the army of Israel.

(5) "So when **ALL Israel** saw that the king hearkened not unto them . . . see to thine own house, David. So Israel departed unto their tents. But as for the children of Israel which dwelt in the cities of Judah, Rehoboam reigned over them," 1 Kings 12:16-19. Here "ALL Israel" means only part of Israel which rebelled against Rehoboam. See also 1 Chron. 10:6; 2 Chron. 10:1, 3, 16; 11:16, 17; 12:1; 13:15; 16:6; Ezra 10:5; Ezek. 21:4; etc.

(6) It is spoken of Nebuchadnezzar that God made him ruler over **ALL men,** but ancient Babylon ruled only over part of the earth (Dan. 2:37, 38; 4:1, 11, 12, 20). He never reigned over Greece, Rome, and many other lands at this time. In Dan. 2:39 Greece is spoken of as ruling "over **ALL the earth,**" but Greece never reigned over Italy, Spain, and many other countries at this time. In Dan. 7:23, Rome is spoken of as ruling over the "whole earth" but we all know that did not include many tribes even in Europe and Asia which later overran the Roman Empire. Neither did any of these kingdoms rule the peoples of North and South America, the greatest part of Asia and Africa, the northern part of Europe, any part of Australia, or the many islands of the seas, so "all" in these passages simply means all the peoples ruled by these kingdoms.

(7) In Matt. 3:5, 6 we read, "Then went out to him **Jerusalem, and ALL Judea,** and **ALL the region round about Jordan,** and **were baptized of him** (John) in Jordan, confessing their sins," but we know that the Pharisees, the Sadducees, and many in all these parts were not baptized of John. Many women, children, the sick, and others of all classes never even saw John, much less were baptized by him in Jordan.

(8) In Luke 2:1-3 we read that Caesar Augustus made a decree that "**ALL** the world should be taxed . . . And **ALL** went to be taxed, every one to his own city." We all know that any law made by a Roman emperor did not affect the many countries outside of his empire, so **"all"** here must be understood only in connection with the old Roman Empire that was under Caesar Augustus.

(9) In Rom. 1:8 Paul said, "Your faith is spoken of throughout the **WHOLE world,**" but we know that he meant only that the local church at Rome was known by many in the various parts of the Roman Empire. Multitudes outside of Rome, and even many inside of the Empire had never yet heard of the Christian faith, much less of the local church at Rome. The same thing is true of Col. 1:23 where we read that the gospel had been "preached to **EVERY CREATURE under heaven**" and in Rom. 10:18 it was preached "into **ALL the earth**" and "**UNTO THE ENDS OF THE WORLD.**" The gospel has not yet been taken to all nations, so we know the whole world was not evangelized in Paul's day.

(10) In Acts 11:28 we read of a drouth **"THROUGHOUT ALL the world"** which came to pass in the days of Claudius Caesar. That drouth did not cover every part of the Roman Empire much less all continents and islands of the world.

Many hundreds of examples could be given to demonstrate that the word **"all"** is used in a figurative sense of a part, so we do not need to believe that Rev. 13 means that the Antichrist of the future will literally reign over all the earth and kill everyone who does not take a mark. What are all the writers in the above examples trying to convey? It is evident that if we take what they literally say that we would have to disbelieve what they say, for the empires mentioned above did not rule all the earth, John did not baptize all in all the regions round about, and the gospel has not yet been preached to all the world as Paul said. Should we discount these Bible writers and call them false teachers? Or, should we get the literal truths conveyed by their figures of speech and believe them? Can we not understand them like we do today when men use such figures of speech? Shall we condemn them for using human language as we all do in our everyday life?

If one should say of some great gathering of people, "Everyone in town" or "the whole county" or "ALL the people in the country were there last night," we would understand that he is expressing what a great crowd was at the meeting. If the United States lawmakers would make a law that "all kindreds, and tongues, and nations" and "all that dwell upon the earth" must register on a certain day, we would naturally understand that it refers only to the kindreds, tongues, and nations that are under the government of the United States, not the same kindreds, tongues and nations that are under other governments. Or, if they would make a law that "all men and women" must register on a certain day, we would understand this "all" to refer to the men and women who are subjects of the government of the United States, and not to all other men and women under other governments in other parts of the world.

We must, therefore, understand the word "all" as it is supposed to be understood in a particular Scripture. If it means "all" in the all inclusive sense then there will be no limitations to it in the passage itself or in other Scriptures on the same subject. If it means "all" of what it is talking about and it is clear that it means a part of something and this is made clear in the passage itself or in other passages on the same subject, then we must be sensible and recognize this fact. For example, when Paul said of God that it was His will that "ALL men come to the knowledge of the truth" (1 Tim. 2:4), we know that this means "all men" without exception. But when we read of "ALL" men being baptized of John in the same passage and in other passages on the subject, it is clear that many were not baptized, then we take it as a figurative statement expressing that a great many in the region were baptized of John.

We have seen in both Testaments that God used universal terms in speaking of the extent of certain kingdoms and the power of certain kings. We have also seen that these terms express that only a great part of the earth was ruled by these kings and empires, so we must conclude that the extent of Antichrist's kingdom and power could likewise be limited to a part of the world. If we find a number of Scriptures limiting his power and authority to a part of the earth and if they plainly tell us what part will be under him and what parts will not be under him, then we must limit the "all" of Rev. 13 to what it is talking about and not make it as universal as many prophetical students do.

2. Rev. 13 itself limits the kingdom of the future Antichrist to ten kingdoms that are yet to be formed inside the old Roman Empire. "The ten horns which thou sawest are ten kings (that will be formed inside the old Roman Empire just before the second advent of Christ to the earth to set up His kingdom, Dan. 7:23, 24), which have received no kingdom as yet; but receive power as kings one hour (Greek, **hora** meaning a period of time as in some places, John 16:2, 4, 25; 1 John 2:18; Rev. 14:15; Rom. 13:11) WITH the beast. These (ten only) . . . shall give their power and strength unto the beast. These shall make war with the Lamb (at Christ's second coming, Rev. 19:11-21), and the Lamb shall overcome them. . . . And the ten horns which thou sawest upon the beast, these shall hate the whore (of Rev. 17:1-7, that sits on the "many waters" or peoples that make the beast or the eighth kingdom), and shall make her desolate and naked, and shall eat her flesh, and burn her with fire. For God hath put in their hearts to fulfill his will, and to agree, and to give their kingdom (the ten kingdoms) unto the beast, until the words of God shall be fulfilled," Rev. 17:8-18.

If the "beast" has only "ten horns" and they are ten kings over ten kingdoms, then this is the extent of the reign of the Antichrist. We are then to understand that the "all kindreds, and tongues, and nations" that Antichrist will be given power over, refers to the kindreds and tongues and nations in the ten kingdoms and not to the same peoples that are in other countries. The "all" that worship him refers to a great many in the ten kingdoms and the "all" that receive his mark refers to a great many in the ten kingdoms that are under him. Rev. 13 predicts that he will make a law that all in his ten kingdoms must worship him and take his mark or be killed but it does not say that this law becomes literally enforced even in the ten kingdoms, as we shall see below.

3. In Dan. 7:7, 8, 17-27, we have statements limiting the Antichrist's kingdom to the ten kingdoms that will yet be formed inside the old Roman Empire. In verses 7, 8, this is symbolized by a beast with ten horns and another little horn which comes out of the ten horns and subdues three of them. All eleven horns come out of the head of the same beast and from within it.

In verses 19-22 we have the record of Daniel's inquiry as to the meaning of the fourth beast, the ten horns, and the little horn. Daniel said he saw the little horn come up out of the head of the fourth beast and among the ten and after the ten horns were already grown out of the head.

He also saw the little horn pluck up three of the ten and then make war on the saints "UNTIL" three things happened: the ancient of days came (from heaven to earth to give to the Son of man a kingdom over all nations, verses 9-14), and judgment was given to the saints of the most High; and the time came that the saints possessed the kingdom and ruled instead of the little horn (verses 18, 22; Zech. 14:1-21; Matt. 24:29-31; 25:31-46; 2 Thess. 1:7-10; 2:8-12; Rev. 1:5, 6; 5:10; 19:11-21; Jude 14).

Not one of these three things has taken place yet, so they remain to be fulfilled in the future. If the little horn is destroyed by the coming of the God of heaven to the earth to put a stop to the war on His saints and if the saints have not yet taken the kingdoms of this world to judge men in the eternal kingdom, and if there is no such man now making war on the saints, then the little horn is yet future as well as are the other events in connection with the ten horns and the little horn.

The ten horns and the little horn are explained to Daniel thus: "The ten horns OUT OF THIS KINGDOM (the fourth kingdom, the old Roman Empire) are ten kings that shall arise: and ANOTHER (the eleventh horn, the little horn) shall rise AFTER THEM; and he shall be diverse from the first, and he shall subdue three kings. And he shall speak great words against the most High (Rev. 13:5, 6), and shall wear out the saints of the most High (Dan. 7:21, 22; Rev. 13:7), and think to change times and laws: and they shall be given into his hand UNTIL a time and times and the dividing of time (three and one-half years, 1,260 days (Dan. 12:7; Rev. 11:2; 12:6, 14; 13:5). But the judgment (of Dan. 7:9-14; Matt. 25:31-46) shall sit, and they shall take away his dominion, to consume and to destroy it UNTO THE END (2 Thess. 1:7-10; 2:7-12; Rev. 19:11-21; Zech. 14). And the kingdom under the whole heaven, shall be given to the saints of the most High, whose kingdom is an EVERLASTING KINGDOM, and all dominions shall serve and obey him." Dan. 7:21-27; 2:44, 45; 8:25; 11:45; Zech. 14; Ezek. 38, 39; Joel 2, 3; Luke 1:32-35; Matt. 25:31-46; 2 Thess. 1:7-10; 2:7-12; Jude 14; Rev. 19:11-22:5.

In point 2 on page 142 we have seen that only "ten kings" will give their power unto the beast and continue as kings "WITH the beast" for a period of time, or forty-two months. In the above passages in Daniel 7, we see where the ten kingdoms will be located. They come "out of this kingdom," the old Roman Empire, so the extent of Antichrist's reign, at the time he makes a law that all must worship him and take his mark or be killed, is over ten kingdoms within the old Roman Empire.

America and all other countries outside the old Roman Empire will naturally not be affected by this law and will not be ruled by the Antichrist, because they are not inside the old Roman territory ruled by the ten kings. If God said that the ten kingdoms are "out of this kingdom" or within the old Roman Empire, then that settles the question for those who believe that God knew what He was talking about. If God said ten horns only would be on the beast and He tells us exactly where the ten kingdoms will be located, then it is very unwise of anyone to paste fifty or more other horns on the beast and suddenly extend the ten kingdoms of the old Roman Empire territory over the whole world. What is to be gained by such contortion of Scripture? Would it not be best to believe what God said in preference to interpretations of men? Could not prophecy be fulfilled just the same if this is the way it is to be? Do we have to quit preaching on prophecy if the Antichrist's kingdom is to be limited to where God said it would be? No statement in Scripture ever changes the ten horns to sixty-five horns.

4. In Dan. 11:40-45 it is plainly stated that when Antichrist breaks his seven years covenant with the Jews (Dan. 9:27), and enters Palestine in the middle of the seven years, and is given power over the ten kingdoms, and makes a law that all must worship him, that "many countries (not all) shall be overthrown: but these SHALL ESCAPE out of his hand, even Edom, and Moab, and the chief of the children of Ammon." If these countries escape the Antichrist and they are bordering states to Palestine where he has his capital during the last three and one-half years of this age (Dan. 11:45; Rev. 11:1, 2), then it is certainly conceivable how other countries across the vast oceans and that were never in the old Roman Empire will also escape him.

5. The main part of the nation of Israel in Judea will flee from the Antichrist when he breaks his covenant with them in the middle of Daniel's Seventieth Week, Dan. 9:27. They will flee into Edom and Moab where they have a "place prepared of God" where they are protected from the Antichrist during the time all men are supposed to be under him, according to some students. (See chapter sixteen.)

6. In Dan. 11:44, 45 we have another definite prophecy foretelling of other nations that will not be under the Antichrist when power is given him over all nations of the ten kingdoms. After Antichrist has conquered "many" countries and has seized Palestine, "tidings out of the east and out of the north shall trouble him: therefore he shall go forth with fury to destroy, and utterly to make away many." It is clear here that "many" countries of the north and east of the ten kingdoms of the old Roman Empire will wage a war against the Antichrist and the ten kingdoms, and therefore will not be under him, or will not take his mark. (See chapters thirty-five and forty.)

7. Zechariah the prophet also teaches that many people, even many of the ten kingdoms, will not take the mark of the beast and still will not be killed. He speaks of a battle between the Jews at Jerusalem and many nations under the Antichrist the very day Christ comes with the armies of heaven to deliver Israel and set up a kingdom in the world, Zech. 14:1-5. Zechariah said, "And it shall come to pass, that every one THAT IS LEFT of all the nations which came against Jerusalem shall even go up from year to year to worship the King, the Lord of hosts, and to keep the feast of tabernacles. And it shall be, that whoso will

not come up of **ALL THE FAMILIES OF THE EARTH** unto Jerusalem to worship the King, the Lord of hosts, even upon them shall be no rain.   And if **THE FAMILY OF EGYPT** go not up, and come not, that they have no rain. . . . This shall be the punishment of **EGYPT**, and the punishment of **ALL NATIONS** that come not up to keep the feast of tabernacles.   IN THAT DAY shall there be upon the bells of the horses, HOLINESS UNTO THE LORD. . . . Yea, every pot in Jerusalem and in Judah shall be HOLINESS UNTO THE LORD OF HOSTS," Zech. 14:16-21.

This is proof that even in the ten kingdoms under the Antichrist that all will not take the mark or be killed.   In Dan. 11:40-45 we read that "the land of Egypt shall not escape" him, so if Egypt is under the Antichrist and there are some Egyptians left to go into the Millennium, they have not taken the mark of the beast, for it is definitely stated in Rev. 14:9-12 that everyone who does take the mark will be damned to eternal hell when Christ comes.   The fact that they are left and are permitted to go up from year to year to worship at Jerusalem proves that they have not taken the mark and that they have escaped death also.   This is true of some of all the families of the earth, even all nations that were under the Antichrist.

8.   The truth is that the Antichrist will make a law that all in his ten kingdoms must take a mark and worship him or be killed, but there is the war with the countries of the north and east that keeps him so much occupied that he cannot enforce such a law in such a vast territory in such a short time as three and one-half years.   Then, too, there will be ways of avoiding this law in certain localities as there are concerning any law man has ever made.   Local officials, relative pulls, money, and many ways will be found to escape this law.   Also, from the standpoint of not being able to reach every person in the mountains, deserts, rural sections of the vast empire there will be many who will escape taking the mark of the beast.

Not only this, but in all lands outside of the ten kingdoms under the Antichrist, there will be all nations, kindreds, and tongues who will not be affected by this law.   Even if Antichrist ruled all the world, as many Bible scholars teach, it can be understood that it would be utterly impossible to enforce such a law in every part of the earth in forty-two months or three and one-half years.   Whole tribes of people in the interior of Tibet, China, Africa, Australia, South America, Mexico and other parts of the earth never would get to hear about the Antichrist, much less be conquered and be forced to take a mark and change their religion in such a short time.

Multiplied thousands have not yet heard of Jesus Christ, the first and second world wars, and many other things that the civilized part of the earth has known.   The same will be true in the days of the Antichrist, for he will reign only over the old Roman Empire which will cover only the northern part of Africa, the southern part of Europe, and the western part of Asia, and which will then be formed into ten kingdoms.

The Bible teaches that even in the Millennium there will be multitudes of people who have never heard of God through Jesus Christ, and who will never have seen the glory of God until the Jewish missionaries go out from Jerusalem telling them that Christ is reigning in Jerusalem and then many peoples will go and see for themselves that this is true (Isa. 2:2-4; 40:9; 52:7; 61:6; 66:18-21; Zech. 8:23; 14:16-21). If nations have not heard of Jesus Christ in over nineteen hundred years, then it is certain that many in all parts of the earth will not hear of Antichrist in three and one-half years.

9. If all people of all nations co-operate with the Antichrist in the destruction of Israel during the tribulation, there would not be any "sheep" nations to enter the Millennium under Christ, as taught by Christ in Matt. 24, 25. "When the Son of man shall come in his glory, and all the holy angels with him, THEN shall he sit upon the throne of his glory: and before him shall be gathered ALL NATIONS: and he shall separate them one from another, as a shepherd divideth his sheep from the goats: and he shall set the sheep on his right hand, but the goats on the left. THEN shall the King say unto them on his right hand, Come, ye blessed of my Father, inherit the kingdom prepared for you from the foundation of the world. . . . THEN shall he say also unto them on the left hand, Depart from me, ye cursed, into everlasting fire, prepared for the devil and his angels," Matt. 25:31-41.

This takes place at the second advent of Jesus from heaven with the armies of heaven to set up a kingdom in the world. It is "immediately after the tribulation" of the last three and one-half years of this age when Antichrist reigns and tries to exterminate the Jewish race, Matt. 24:15-31; Jer. 30:3-11; Dan. 9:27; Zech. 12:10-14:21; Rev. 12:1-17. It is after the one-day battle of Armageddon between Christ and His heavenly armies and the Antichrist and his earthly armies the day Christ comes to earth, Zech. 14:1-9, 14-21; Isa. 63:1-7; Joel 3; 2 Thess. 1:7-10; 2:8-12; Jude 14; Rev. 14:14-20; 16:13-16; 19:11-21; 20:1-3.

Immediately following the one-day battle of Armageddon the Lord will gather the living nations and judge them on the basis of their treatment of His "brethren," the Jews, as in Matt. 25:31-46. Some of all nations will be called "blessed of my Father" and will "inherit the kingdom" thus proving that they have not taken the mark of the beast and yet they will escape being killed because they did not take the mark. These include some inside the kingdom of Antichrist as well as those outside of his kingdom. Such kind treatment of Israel could not be possible if they worshipped the beast and were directly under his control, for his main purpose is to exterminate Israel and be worshipped by all men on earth. He is defeated in his purpose by the return of Christ when not all of Asia is conquered, much less all other lands that are not near his empire.

10. Rev. 13:4 proves that there are nations that are not ruled by Antichrist, for it would be foolish for his followers to say, "Who is like unto the beast? Who is able to make war with him?" if there were no other governments to compare his power to.

11. Rev. 16:13-16 also cannot be understood if all the earth is to be under the Antichrist. What would be the need of unclean spirits coming from "the dragon," (the Devil, Rev. 12:9), "the beast," and "the false prophet" to endue with power false prophets to be sent to the kings of the earth to get their co-operation at Armageddon, if all were directly controlled by the Antichrist and if they all loved him enough to worship him and take his mark?

As we have seen above, the beast has only ten kingdoms that have given their power to him, so such a program of supernatural powers will be necessary to get the co-operation of other kings of the earth at Armageddon. The Devil and the beast know when Christ is coming (Rev. 12:12; 19:19), so they put forth every effort to mobilize the nations and their vast armies to be present to stop Christ and His armies the day He appears. Thus, we see that many kings of the earth will not be under the Antichrist and the ten kings under him, so will need such supernatural powers to get them to co-operate with them at Armageddon.

12. It is definitely stated in Rev. 14:9-12 that every person without exception that takes the mark of the beast and worships him will be damned to eternal hell. If, as our prophetical teachers tell us, every person on earth must either take the mark of the beast and worship the Antichrist or be killed, and if everyone who does take it is confined eternally to hell when Christ comes, then who will be left on earth for Christ and the righteous resurrected saints to reign over in the Millennium and forever? It is certain according to Ps. 2; Isa. 2:2-4; 9:6, 7; Zech. 14:16-21; Dan. 2:44; 7:13, 14, 18, 27; 12:12, 13; Rev. 1:4-6; 2:26, 27; 5:10; 11:15; 20:1-10 and many other Scriptures that all nations will be ruled by Christ and the saints forever, so if all are to be killed by the Antichrist who do not take the mark, or be sent to hell by Christ if they do, from where are these nations coming to populate the earth when Christ comes to reign?

If the Antichrist were to kill every person in the whole world who would not worship him, then he would contact every person on earth, and thereby do more in three and one-half years than God, Christ, and the whole Church have done in over 1900 years.

We conclude that the Antichrist will be limited in his power over only a part of the earth and that there will be plenty of people who will not be under him and who will not take the mark of the beast and worship him. It is these people that will be left here for Christ and the saints to reign over forever.

Seeing the Antichrist only reigns for three and one-half years over the ten kingdoms that are yet to be formed inside of the old Roman Empire, we conclude that America will not be ruled by the Antichrist and that he will not be a world-wide dictator.

Chapter Twenty-two

THE BEAST OUT OF THE EARTH

"And I beheld another beast coming up out of the earth; and he had two horns like a lamb, and he spake as a dragon. And he exerciseth all the power of the first beast before him, and causeth the earth and them which dwell therein to worship the first beast, whose deadly wound was healed. And he doeth great wonders, so that he maketh fire come down from heaven on the earth in the sight of men, and deceiveth them that dwell on the earth by the means of those miracles which he had power to do in the sight of the beast; saying to them that dwell on the earth, that they should make an image to the beast, which had the wound by a sword, and did live. And he had power to give life unto the image of the beast, that the image of the beast should both speak, and cause that as many as would not worship the image of the beast should be killed. And he causeth all, both small and great, rich and poor, free and bond, to receive a mark in their right hand, or in their foreheads: And that no man might buy or sell, save he that had the mark, or the name of the beast, or the number of his name. Here is wisdom. Let him that hath understanding count the number of the beast: for it is the number of a man; and his number is six hundred three score and six," Rev. 13:11-18.

The above individual, or second beast is here mentioned for the first time and all that is given concerning him in the Bible is recorded in Revelation. He is called "the false prophet" (Greek, **pseudoprophetes**) in Rev. 16:13; 19:20; 20:10, which are the only other passages that mention him. He is to be a prophet, but a false one; a prophet of Antichrist, not of Christ. In Rev. 16:13 he is seen with the beast and dragon as sending forth the demon spirits to gather the nations to Armageddon. In Rev. 19:20 he is seen as being the miracle-working co-laborer and leader of the nations along with the first beast as he comes against Christ at Armageddon. The doom of this second beast will be torment in the lake of fire forever along with the first beast, the dragon, and all rebellious creatures, Rev. 20:10. The facts concerning him and his ministry in Rev. 13:11-18 are:

1. **He is seen coming on the scene of action by John after the vision of the first beast,** Rev. 13:11. He is called "another" beast from Greek **allos**, meaning "another of the same kind," denoting numerical distinction; the second of two where there may be more, as in Matt. 10:23; John 18:15. Therefore, this beast is the second one in this chapter and cannot possibly be the same as the first beast of Rev. 13:1-10. If there were only one beast there would not be two descriptions and statements concerning two different beasts. This point is so clear in this passage that we need not take up the many points of contrast between the two beasts.

2. **This beast is seen coming up "out of the earth," Rev. 13:11.** The word "earth" is the same as "world" in Rev. 13:3 and "earth" in Rev. 13:12. Here it symbolizes the peoples on the earth, as in Dan. 7:1-7. The word "sea" is also used in a symbolical sense of peoples in Rev. 13:1; 17:1, 15; Dan. 7:1-7. The phrase "out of the earth" is the same in meaning as "out of the sea" as is proved by a similar construction in Dan. 7:3 and 17 where four beasts came up "out of the sea" and in the interpretation they are stated to be four kingdoms coming up "out of the earth." There is no intimation that this beast comes out of the under-

world of spirits and is a resurrected or reincarnated man that has lived on the earth before, as is taught by some. Some say that he is Judas who will come up out of the underworld, because his characteristics are like those of Judas in that he will be a leader in worship, be idolatrous, and work miracles as Judas did. These arguments based upon similar acts in the lives of these men are not sufficient proof of this. Others claim that the first beast will be Judas from the underworld, but, as we shall see in chapter thirty-one, no human being can come up from the underworld and fulfill the office of either of these beasts. The beasts symbolize two natural men as the sea and earth symbolize peoples. They are yet future and will be born and live a natural life like all other men and rise in power out of the peoples of the earth to carry out their intended mission of these prophecies in the will of God.

3. **The second beast has two horns making him look like a lamb but he speaks as a dragon.** His lamb-like appearance will make him a fit man for his office, thus causing him to be looked upon as a wonderful prophet and man of religion. Combined with this lamb-like appearance will be his dragon or serpent-like deceiving speech. This, and a few miracles, will complete his method of deception. The expression "spake as a dragon" should best read "was speaking as a dragon" showing that when John saw him coming out of the mass of humanity he was speaking and that was one of the most conspicuous things about him.

4. **He will exercise all the power of the first beast before him and cause the earth to worship the first beast, whose deadly wound will be healed,** Rev. 13:12. He will be the executive of Antichrist and exercise Satan's power, which will be given to the first beast, Rev. 13:2-4; 2 Thess. 2:8-12. The length of the existence of this second beast in power is not stated but he is not to rise until after the first one does, so it cannot be for more than three and one-half years. He will exercise this power "before" or in the presence of the Antichrist. He is never mentioned apart from the Antichrist, so it must be that the two will work in close union and perhaps withstand the two witnesses as Jannes and Jambres withstood Moses in power and miracles, 2 Tim. 3:8.

5. **"He doeth great wonders, so that he maketh fire to come down from heaven on the earth in the sight of men,"** Rev. 13:13. The word "wonders" comes from the Greek **semeion.** Its meaning and usage are explained at the beginning of chapter sixteen. The purpose of these signs wrought by the false prophet is to deceive men to accept the Antichrist as God. He "deceiveth them that dwell on the earth by the means of those miracles which he had power to do in the sight of the beast," Rev. 13:14. Satan has continually deceived the whole world (12:9), but here he has planned the worst deception ever known, which is to be permitted of God, because men receive not the love of the truth that they might be saved, 2 Thess. 2:8-12; Rev. 9:20, 21; 13:3,

12-18; 14:9; 16:2; 1 Tim. 4:1-3. He will deceive and use these signs to impress his deception, for miracles alone are no complete and definite proof of a divine mission. Just as the Lord's signs were for the purpose of impressing the people and causing them to ponder, so these also will be to impress those who may not be ready to believe in the beast.

6. **He will tell the earth dwellers to make an image to the first beast.** The image will be made and set up in the temple of God to be worshipped, Matt. 24:15. He will have the power to give life to this image that it should both speak and cause all who will not worship it to be killed. This will be a wonderful sign in itself; that a material image should be given power to speak and act, Rev. 13:14, 15.

7. **The second beast will cause all classes to receive a mark in their right hands or in their foreheads, that no man might buy or sell except those who have it,** Rev. 13: 16-18. This will result in the martyrdom of most of the "great multitude, which no man could number, of all nations," Rev. 7:9-17; 13:7; 14:13; 15:2, 3; 20:4. In the worship of the first beast and his image, men will be so devoted as to say, "Who is like unto the beast? Who is able to make war with him?" Showing perhaps the worship to be both political and religious, Rev. 13:4. It will not be a willing worship on the part of many, for force will be used to make them worship. The worship will be of such an apostate nature as to pronounce eternal doom to all who partake, Rev. 14:9-11. Many men will throw overboard all faith in God and Christ, become servants of the Devil, and be controlled by demon spirits to such an extent as to be past redemption.

The three brands that followers of Antichrist may choose are:

(1) **"A mark," or in the Greek, "the mark."** That this is different from either the name or the number of his name is clear from the following passages where the three are enumerated, Rev. 13:16-18; 14:9; 15:2-4; 20:4. What kind of mark it will be is not revealed, but it is to be a literal mark in the flesh, Rev. 13:16; 14:9. Perhaps it will be the emblem of the kingdom of the Antichrist.

(2) **"The name of the beast";** i. e., of the first beast, Rev. 13:17. His name is not found in Scripture, so it cannot be known.

(3) **"The number of his name,"** Rev. 13:17, 18; 15:2. This will be "the number of a man." There are many Greek and Hebrew names that have a numerical value of 666. Especially is this true of foreign names which are transliterated into Hebrew or Greek. There is no hidden meaning to the number, for the very expression "Here is wisdom" (native insight, understanding) shows that it is easy to understand, for it is given here as 666 and anyone can understand this. It is trying to learn the name and the mark by the number that is all foolish speculation and it should not be indulged in at all. (See chapter one, point VIII, 3.)

The brands of the beast cannot be taken until the last three

and one-half years of this age or in the great tribulation. Therefore, it is impossible for one to take any of his brands, or worship
him today, for he is not now on the scene. When he does come
and these things begin to be fulfilled those who take any one
of the brands or worship him will be doomed to eternal hell
forever, and in this life, will be plagued by the vial plagues,
Rev. 14:9-11; 16:1-21. No man will ever know what the mark
or the name of the beast will be until after he comes, which will
be after the rapture and after ten kingdoms are formed inside
the old Roman Empire, as seen in chapter twenty.

No Satanic Trinity

In the sense of making Satan the opposite of God, the Father, in
work and position, the Antichrist the opposite of Jesus Christ as to
birth, incarnation, life, work, death, and resurrection, and the false
prophet the opposite of the Holy Spirit as the executive of Satan and
Antichrist, there is no teaching of such a parallel in the Bible. But,
regarding these three persons being three separate and distinct persons,
about this there is no question, for it is plainly shown in all of the
Revelation where they are mentioned, Rev. 12:3, 7-17; 13:1-18;
16:13-16; 19:20; 20:1-10. In Bible history there are other examples of
three persons who could be called a satanic trinity because of their close
co-operation and work together against God. There were: Satan, Nadab
and Abihu (Lev. 10:1-10); Satan, Hophni, and Phinehas (1 Sam. 2:12;
4:11); Satan, Ananias, and Sapphira (Acts 5:1-11); and others, but their
relationship did not in any case make them a special satanic trinity as
some teach regarding Satan, Antichrist, and the false prophet. There is
no ground for, and no need for such speculation as a satanic trinity, and
it certainly is no explanation of any detail of the book of Revelation.

Mystery Babylon Destroyed

It is at this particular time in the fulfillment of the Revelation that
the ten kings will turn on the great whore of Rev. 17 and destroy her
and give their kingdoms to the beast (Antichrist) for the last three and
one half years of this age (Rev. 17:12-17), so that the Antichrist can be
worshipped as God in the temple of God at Jerusalem, Dan. 9:27; 12:7;
Matt. 24:15; 2 Thess. 2:3-12; Rev. 13:1-18; 14:9-11; 15:2; 16:2;
19:20; 20:4-6. Antichrist could never be the sole object of worship in
the last 42 months or 1260 days of this age until Mystery Babylon, the
great whore, is destroyed. Since he is to be worshipped at this time,
then it has to be that her destruction, as stated in Rev. 17:12-17, will
take place at this particular time, that is, in the middle of Daniel's 70th
Week.

Chapter Twenty-three

THE SEVEN PARENTHETICAL STATEMENTS, Rev. 14:1-20

This sixth parenthetical passage contains seven statements which come between the seventh trumpet and the.first vial as to reception, but not necessarily in fulfillment. The first five are necessary at this time to explain certain things which are to transpire between the seventh trumpet and the end of the Week.

I.   The Lamb on Mount Zion With the 144,000 Jews.

"And I looked, and lo, a Lamb stood on the mount Sion, and with him an hundred forty and four thousand, having his Father's name written in their foreheads. And I heard a voice from heaven as the voice of many waters, and as the voice of a great thunder: and I heard the voice of harpers harping with their harps and they sung as it were a new song before the throne, and before the four beasts, and the elders: and no man could learn that song but the hundred and forty and four thousand, which were redeemed from the earth. These are they which were not defiled with women; for they are virgins. These are they which follow the Lamb whithersoever he goeth. These were redeemed from among men, being the firstfruits unto God and to the Lamb. And in their mouth was found no guile: for they were without fault before the throne of God," Rev. 14:1-5.

These 144,000 have been discussed in detail in chapter eighteen, for which see. This passage shows what the manchild is doing before the throne in heaven and proves that the 144,000 are no longer on earth after this time. The following three parenthetical statements concern three messenger angels who will go forth from the middle to the end of the Week during the reign of Antichrist. They will announce certain commands and events as follows:

II.   The First Messenger Angel: The Everlasting Gospel.

"And I saw another angel fly in the midst of heaven, having the everlasting gospel to preach unto them that dwell on the earth, and to every nation, and kindred, and tongue, and people, saying with a loud voice, Fear God, and give glory to him; for the hour of his judgment is come: and worship him that made heaven, and earth, and the sea, and the fountains of waters," Rev. 14:6, 7.

The "everlasting gospel" which will be the subject of the first messenger angel in the great tribulation, is used only here and has reference to the eternity of the message past, present, and future. Its message and scope takes in all the intelligent creatures in the universe. Its message is threefold: first, "fear God"; secondly, "give glory to him for the hour of his judgment is come"; thirdly, "worship him that made heaven, and earth, and the sea, and the fountains of waters." This message will have particular significance at this time, for it will be proclaimed immediately after the rise of the beasts out of the sea and out of the earth, who will deceive men by reason of the supernatural powers invested in them. God will counteract these deceptions by the ministry of the two witnesses, the multitudes of saints who will be saved and indued with miraculous powers after the rapture, the Jewish people, the Holy Spirit who will exercise His present office work as before, the judgments of God, and by the appearance of angels in the heavens preaching their respective messages. God will permit the deceptions of Satan; yet in the face of them, He will still be faithful to warn men and use all legitimate means to turn men from such falsehoods which will seal their eternal doom.

The theme of this eternal message is that the Creator alone is to be feared and worshipped and that He alone will be the final judge of all. This gospel has been preached to all creatures since the creation of free moral agents who were capable of a law and to whom God must of necessity reveal His will and also the blessings of obedience and punishment of disobedience to that will. It will also be preached to all creatures who shall come into existence in all future ages, of whatever nature they may be. This message, although an eternal one, will have an additional incentive in the great tribulation, for the angel announces, "the hour (period) of His judgment is come," or is already manifest, referring to the judgments of God which will be poured out during this time. This will indeed be glad tidings to those oppressed by the Antichrist, but fear and condemnation to him and his followers. Hence, the special preaching of it at this time.

III.   The Second Messenger Angel: The Fall of Babylon.

"And there followed another angel, saying, Babylon is fallen, is fallen, that great city, because she made all nations drink of the wine of the wrath of her fornication," Rev. 14:8.

This angel will also fly in mid-heaven proclaiming the fall of literal Babylon, that great city, which is to be destroyed under the seventh vial at the end of the Week, Rev. 16:17-21; 18:1-24. Such an anticipative message at this time is in keeping with God's dealings with any city or nation. God always warns of impending judgment, thus giving the guilty a chance to repent, and avert the judgment.

For the fall of literal Babylon and the difference between the Babylons of Rev. 17 and 18 see chapters twenty-six and thirty-seven.

IV.   The Third Messenger Angel: Doom of the Beast Worshipers.

"And the third angel followed them, saying with a loud voice, If any man worship the beast and his image, and receive his mark in his forehead, or in his hand, the same shall drink of the wine of the wrath of God, which is poured out without mixture into the cup of his indignation; and he shall be tormented with fire and brimstone in the presence of the holy angels, and in the presence of the Lamb: and the smoke of their torment ascendeth up for ever and ever: and they have no rest day nor night, who worship the beast and his image, and whosoever receiveth the mark of his name. Here is the patience of the saints: here are they that keep the commandments of God, and the faith of Jesus," Rev. 14:9-12.

The third messenger angel also will fly in mid-heaven during the great tribulation announcing the fact that if any man worship the beast and his image or receive his mark he will be doomed to eternal torment. This torment will be with fire and brimstone, in the presence of the angels and the Lamb. It is called the "wine of the wrath of God" which will be poured out undiluted upon all that commit this great sin. The above is one of the most solemn messages in the Bible and is an unanswerable argument on the reality and eternity of hell. So awful will be this sin and so terrible its consequences that God will send an angel to warn men continually during this period of beast-worship.

It appears that if a man takes the mark he will likely first make a shipwreck of his conscience and faith in God, yield to the possession of demons and sell his soul to the Devil, and become the habitation of all that is foul and unclean. It also appears that this message will be given in sufficient time to warn men not to take the mark. If this be true, then it will be given in the middle part of the Week or in the early part of the last three and one-half years.

The three messages will go forth at about the same period of time. All three will serve as anticipative warnings to men of the consequences of their sin and rejection of God. If this is true of the ministry of the three angels in the middle of the Week, then the first passage about the 144,000 must be fulfilled before their ministry or at the same time, thus further proving that the 144,000 are to be caught up to heaven as the manchild. The above message seems to be also one of comfort to those who do not take the mark and worship the beast but who receive his persecution, for it ends with "Here is the patience of the saints: here are they that keep the commandments of God and the faith of Jesus." Cf. Rev. 12:17; 13:10.

V. The Blessed Dead

"And I heard a voice from heaven saying unto me, Write, Blessed are the dead which die in the Lord from henceforth: Yea, saith the Spirit, that they may rest from their labours: and their works do follow them," Rev. 14:13.

Following the messages of the three angels "a great voice from heaven" told John to write the above statement concerning the dead that die "henceforth"; i. e., during the great tribulation of the last three and one-half years. These dead referred to are those who will be martyred because they will not worship the beast and his image or receive his mark. They are the same as those referred to in Rev. 7:9-17; 13:5-7, 15; 15:2-4; 20:4. This message of encouragement will be needed at that time by these saints to help them to be true in their trials. What a contrast between this message and the doom spoken by the third messenger angel concerning the beast worshippers! Their "labours" and "works" probably refer to their ceaseless opposition to Antichrist and the prevailing corruption of this time, and to the trials and hardships they are to undergo in the persecution from the beast. These blessings will be only to those who "die in the Lord from henceforth."

This is the tenth time John is told to "write." The voice is perhaps the voice of Christ that told him to "write" on all other occasions, Rev. 1:11, 19; 2:1, 8, 12, 18; 3:1, 7, 14. The Spirit is the one imparting this to Christ in His reception of it from the Father, Rev. 1:1. The clause, "Yea, saith the Spirit" has been expressed seven times before, "He that hath an ear let him hear what the Spirit saith unto the churches." There are only two other persons in the Revelation who tell John to write and they are the redeemed prophet who is showing John these Revelations (1:3; 19:9, 10; 22:8, 9) and God the Father (21:5). There are only two more times that John is told to "write," once by God and once by the above prophet, Rev. 19:9, 10; 21:5.

VI. The Harvest of the Earth: Armageddon.

"And I looked, and behold a white cloud, and upon the cloud one sat like unto the Son of man, having on his head a golden crown, and in his hand a sharp sickle. And another angel came out of the temple, crying with a loud voice to him that sat on the cloud, Thrust in thy sickle, and reap: for the time is come for thee to reap; for the harvest of the earth is ripe. And he that sat on the cloud thrust in his sickle on the earth: and the earth was reaped," Rev. 14:14-16.

This "harvest of the earth" will not be the above martyrs who "die in the Lord." This is entirely a different message. The one above pictures the martyrs who will die for the sake of Christ while this pictures those who will die for the sake of Antichrist at Armageddon. John saw the Son of Man (Christ) sitting on a cloud, which is associated with His coming to the earth, Rev. 1:7; 10:1, 2; Matt. 24:27-31; Acts 1:9-11. This passage reminds us of the parables of the wheat, tares, and dragnet (Matt. 13:24-30, 36-43, 47-50) and certainly is a reference to the same future time as a comparison will reveal. This is the last occurrence of the title "Son of Man," for which see chapter three. **There are several reasons why this harvest pictures Armageddon and not the tribulation martyrs as is often thought:**

1. "The Son of Man" is to reap this harvest; i. e., He is the one who will execute the judgment upon the people represented by this figure. This He does not do in the case of the tribulation martyrs.

2. Here Christ has a "golden crown" which indicates kingship and a kingdom. He will receive the kingdom from the Father at the second advent, Rev. 19:12; Dan. 7:13, 14. This seems to show that the passage is anticipative and parenthetical and will not be fulfilled until Armageddon.

3. The harvest will be reaped after the fall of Babylon, as announced by the second messenger angel and fulfilled under the seventh vial, Rev. 16:17-21. If it were to be reaped before the destruction of Babylon, it surely would have been placed before the message of that fall. Even in the parenthetical passages each separate event is in consecutive order in fulfillment, unless stated otherwise.

4. The "sharp sickle" is the same as that mentioned in Joel 3:9-14 in picturing the destruction of the hosts of Armageddon. Therefore, the scene must be of Armageddon and not of the righteous martyrs. Cf. Rev. 19:21; Isa. 11:4; Matt. 13:30, 39; Jer. 51:33; Hos. 6:11; 2 Thess. 2:8.

5. The expression, "time is come for thee to reap," shows that Christ has delayed reaping and that now the time is approaching

for Him to take vengeance on them which dwell on the earth as foretold by the prophets in connection with Armageddon, Isa. 34:8; 59:17; 61:2; 63:4; Jer. 46:9, 10; 2 Thess. 1:8. Therefore, martyrs cannot be the thought of the vision. In obedience to the cry of the angel, Christ will thrust in His sickle into the earth and reap, which action is pictured in the above passages. (See chapter forty.)

VII. The Vintage of the Earth: Armageddon.

"And another angel came out of the temple which is heaven, he also having a sharp sickle. And another angel came out from the altar, which had power over fire; and cried with a loud cry to him that had the sharp sickle, saying, Thrust in thy sharp sickle, and gather the clusters of the vine of the earth; for her grapes are fully ripe. And the angel thrust in his sickle into the earth, and gathered the vine of the earth, and cast it into the great winepress of the wrath of God. And the winepress was trodden without the city, and blood came out of the winepress, even unto the horse bridles, by the space of a thousand and six hundred furlongs," Rev. 14:17-20.

The vision of "the vine of the earth" is the same in theme as "the harvest of the earth" above. The "harvest" and the "vintage" are both judicial and are anticipative of the future Battle of Armageddon. In this vision "another angel" is the one to reap, thus showing that the angels will have a part in the Battle of Armageddon, 2 Thess. 1:7-10.

The vine of the earth will be cast into the "great winepress of the wrath of God." The winepress will be trodden "without the city," referring to the place just outside of Jerusalem where Armageddon will be fought. Blood will flow out of the winepress even up to the horses' bridles as far as sixteen hundred furlongs or nearly two hundred miles. This is definite proof that the gathering of the vintage refers to the gathering of the nations to Armageddon by the ministry of the three unclean spirits (16:13-16) to fight against Christ at His coming. The winepress with the blood flowing out of it refers to the destruction of these nations when blood will flow as pictured here. This same scene is spoken of in Rev. 19:11-21; Isa. 34:1-8; 63:1-5; Joel 3:1-21; Ezek. 38-39; Zech. 14:1-21; Matt. 24:29-31, 30-43; Luke 17:23-37; Jude 14-15.

In these and other scriptures there is a detailed description of the battle of Armageddon, as symbolized in the above pictures of the harvest and the vintage. Christ is pictured as treading the winepress of the fierceness of the wrath of Almighty God, having blood sprinkled all over His white garments.

THE SEVEN ANGELS, SEA OF GLASS, AND HEAVENLY TABERNACLE

This passage (15:1-16:1) contains the necessary introduction to the terrible vial judgments of the last part of the Week.

I. The Seven Angels.

"And I saw another sign in heaven, great and marvelous, seven angels having the seven last plagues; for in them is filled up the wrath of God . . . And the seven angels came out of the temple, having the seven plagues, clothed in pure white linen, and having their breasts girded with golden girdles. And one of the four beasts gave unto the seven angels seven golden vials full of the wrath of God, who liveth for ever and ever," Rev. 15:1, 6, 7.

For the meaning of the word "sign" see chapter sixteen. The rest of this passage is clear as to the seven angels, their reception of the vials, and what they contain. The expression "seven last plagues" indicates there will have been plagues preceding these. When, if not under the sixth seal and seven trumpets which shall have contained the first of God's wrath?

These seven angels will not be ordinary ones but seven redeemed men who will be already in heaven with glorified bodies at the time of this fulfillment of the book. Such is entirely possible as proved in chapter two, point 5, and chapter nine, point 3. According to Rev. 17:1, one of these angels showed John the judgment of the great whore and the beast that carrieth her. In Rev. 21:9, one of them, perhaps the same one, came to show John the Holy City. After showing him the Revelation, John fell down at his feet to worship him, but was told "See thou do it not: for **I am thy fellowservant,** and **of thy brethren the prophets** and **of them which keep the sayings of this book:** worship God," Rev. 19:9, 10; 22:8, 9. This proves that one of them is a redeemed man, for he is expressly called "a man" in Rev. 21:17; and if one of them is a man, the other six must be also. It seems entirely reasonable that God would permit redeemed men to take part in executing His vengeance upon His enemies.

II. The Sea of Glass.
(Parenthetical, Rev. 15:2-4)

"And I saw as it were a sea of glass mingled with fire: and them that had gotten the victory over the beast, and over his image, and over his mark, and over the number of his name, stand on the sea of glass, having the harps of God. And they sing the song of Moses the servant of God, and the song of the Lamb, saying, Great and marvelous are thy works, Lord God Almighty; just and true are thy ways, thou King of saints. Who shall not fear thee, O Lord, and glorify thy name? for thou only art holy: for all nations shall come and worship before thee; for thy judgments are made manifest," Rev. 15:2-4.

This "sea of glass" is the same as that seen by John when he was first caught up to heaven, Rev. 4:1-6. It is a literal pavement before the throne, like unto crystal mingled with fire. It was unoccupied in Rev. 4 while here it is occupied by the tribulation martyrs.

These saints will have "harps of God" and sing the song of Moses and the Lamb, thus implying that this company will have already been victorious and resurrected. The song of Moses and of the Lamb is one of victory. This does not indicate that they will sing the same words as did Moses and the Lamb, for a study of their song as compared with that of Moses (Exod. 15:1-19; Deut. 32:1-43) will disprove this. We do not know the exact words of the song of the Lamb, but we know that its theme is one of victory. Compare the words these martyrs sing with Ps. 86:9-12; Isa. 66:15, 16, 23; Zeph. 2:11; Zech. 14:16, 17.

This is the sixth parenthetical passage and shows the position in heaven of those who get the victory over the beast. The expression, "for thy judgments are (were) made manifest" seems to show that the scene will be fulfilled after the judgments are finished. If this is true then the passage is parenthetical and anticipative of the coming time when the martyrs will have been slain and will have obtained the victory and will be on the sea of glass.

The message concerning the seven angels is broken into here by this passage and such would not be the case if it were not parenthetical. In Rev. 15:1 the seven angels are spoken of, then abruptly left and not mentioned again until after this picture of the saints on the glassy sea, Rev. 15:6-16:1. This further shows that this passage has something to do with the introduction of the seven vials and that it cannot be inserted among them. The purpose of the vials is to judge the men who have taken the mark of the beast, hence this picture at this juncture to show the blessedness of those who do not worship the beast and who get the victory over him.

III. The Heavenly Tabernacle.

"And after that I looked, and behold, the temple of the tabernacle of the testimony in heaven was opened . . . . And the temple was filled with smoke from the glory of God, and from his power; and no man was able to enter into the temple, till the seven plagues of the seven angels were fulfilled. And I heard a great voice out of the temple saying to the seven angels, Go your ways, and pour out the vials of the wrath of God upon the earth," Rev. 15:5, 8; 16:1.

In this passage, the vision of the seven angels and the heavenly tabernacle is resumed, after being broken into by the vision of the tribulation saints upon the sea of glass. The temple in heaven is mentioned twelve times in Revelation and each reference indicates a literal temple in which God sits on a throne. The words "temple" and "temples" are used 206 times and the words "tabernacle" and "tabernacles" are used 339 times in both Testaments. The same words that are used of earthly temples and tabernacles are used of the heavenly without any word of explanation that there is any difference in the nature of them. **There are two Hebrew words for our English word "temple."**

1. **Haykawl** means "a large public building" such as a palace or temple. It is used seventy-six times in reference to an earthly building and one time of an heavenly building, Isa. 6:1.

2. **Bahyith** means "a house" in the greatest variety of applications. It is used only eleven times and every time of the temple of

the Lord on earth.

There are three Greek words for our English word "temple."

1. **Hieron** means "a sacred place, sanctuary, or temple of worship." It is used seventy-one times, always of a literal earthly building.

2. **Naos** means "dwelling, a shrine, or a temple." It is used forty-six times and always of a building made with hands except in John 2:19, 21; 1 Cor. 3:16, 17; 6:19;2 Cor. 6:16; Eph. 2:21; Rev. 21: 22, where it is used of the Church, body of man, and Christ. In John 2:19-21, we have an example of the natural meaning of the word as well as an example of God's principle of always explaining the meaning of a word which is not used according to· ordinary usage. This is the word used in Rev. 3:12; 7:15; 11:19; 14:15, 17; 15:5, 8; 16:1, 17 of the temple of God in heaven. The same word is used in 11:1, 2 of the earthly temple. Thus we have conclusive proof that there is a material temple in heaven.

3. **Oikos** means "home, household, or temple." It is used one time of an earthly temple, Luke 11:51.

There are two Hebrew words for our English word "tabernacle."

1. **Ohel** means "a tent, covering, house or tabernacle." It is used about two hundred times and is interchangeable with the temple and tabernacle of God on earth.

2. **Mish-kawn** means "residence, shepherd's hut, animal's lair, temple, dwelling, tent, or tabernacle." It is used 117 times and its meaning is always clear in the passages themselves.

There are three Greek words for our English word "tabernacle."

1. **Skene** means "habitation or tabernacle." It is used eighteen times. In Heb. 8:2-5; 9:2-11; 13:10 it is the word describing both the earthly and heavenly tabernacles. This is the only word in Revelation translated "tabernacle," Rev. 13:6; 15:5; 21:3.

2. **Skenonia** means "encampment, man's body, or idol temple." It is used three times, Acts 7:43, 2 Pet. 1:13, 14.

3. **Skenopegia** means "festival of tabernacles or a temporary home." It is used only one time, John 7:2.

Every time these words are used they are to be taken in their plain natural sense unless there is an explanation that they are used differently. What kind of temple would the heavenly one be if not a literal, material one? If this be not the meaning of these passages, then upon what basis can there be any other meaning? These facts with those in chapter nine should prove conclusively that the temple and all things seen in heaven are just as real as those on the earth. The fact that the temple will be opened at different times and that beings will come out of it, shows that the temple is literal. Cf. 4:1; 11:19. The Greek word **ek** translated "out" in Rev. 14:17, 18; 15:6; 16:1-17; etc., denotes motion from the interior and means "out from" as distinguished from "away from." Such could not be possible if there were no temple and if it were impossible to go into and out of it as with any other building.

The temple will be filled with the smoke of the glory of God and His power after the seven angels come out of it with the seven vials which are to be poured out upon the earth, and no man will be able to enter the temple until the seven vials are completed, Rev. 15:8. Smoke, in connection with the glory of God, generally, if not in every case in the Bible, means judgment. It is used ten times in Revelation, and always in connection with judgment, Rev. 8:4; 9:2, 3, 17, 18; 14:11; 15:8; 18:9, 18; 19:3. Next, John heard "a great voice out of the temple" saying to the seven angels, "Go your ways, and pour out the vials of the wrath of God upon the earth." This indicates that they knew just what to do and when to do it.

As a final proof that there is a literal temple in heaven, let us rememeber that both the tabernacle of Moses and the temple of Solomon were patterned after the temple in heaven. See Exod. 25:9, 40; Num. 8:4; 1 Chron 28:11-19; Heb. 8:5; 9:23.

Chapter Twenty-five

THE SEVEN VIALS AND THE THREE UNCLEAN SPIRITS,
Rev. 16:2-21

The seven vials and their contents are just as literal as the seals and trumpets and their contents. They will be poured out only upon the kingdom of the beast during the last half of the Week, and will complete the wrath of God upon men for their persecution of Israel. They are not to be confused with any historical event or with the seals and trumpets in any respect. They cannot begin until after the seals and trumpets are finished. They will be the last events of the "things shortly to come to pass" before the second coming of Christ. Just such plagues as these are promised upon Israel's enemies in the last days, Deut. 30:1-10; Isa. 51:23. Four of these plagues in a lesser degree have been poured out upon Egypt. The very language describing them proves that they will be literal and fulfilled in the order in which they are given. This forms the only true basis of understanding.

How long any one of them lasts is not revealed, but judging from the length of those in Egypt, and the seals and trumpets, most of them are not to be long in duration. If they last over the whole last three and one-half years then smoke will fill the temple in heaven and no man will be able to enter it that long, Rev. 15:8. These plagues are for the purpose of punishing men for their worship of the beast, and hardness against God and those things must become well established before the plagues begin so that men will realize the purpose of them. All in Rev. 13:1-14:13 takes place between the middle of the Week to the time the plagues begin.

1. The First Vial: Boils.

"And the first went, and poured out his vial upon the earth; and there fell a noisome and grievous sore upon the men which had the mark of the beast, and upon them which worshipped his image," Rev. 16:2.

This first vial is a repetition of the plague of boils sent upon the Egyptians, Exod. 9:8-12. It is clear that this plague falls upon only those people who have the mark of the beast and who worship him. If this is true of this one plague, it is also true of all the others, for they are all for the same purpose. It is clear that these seven plagues will be from heaven, directly sent from God, and that they will have a supernatural cause, just like the ones sent upon the land of Egypt. It will be divine judgment, not nature's judgment. We cannot help recognizing the supernatural in these plagues for the vials contain the completion of the wrath of God.

When the angel pours out his vial, boils will immediately break out on the followers of Antichrist. This humiliating and torturing malady will be upon the highest as well as the lowest. They, no doubt, like Pharaoh's magicians, will be unable to maintain an erect posture owing to the unbearable pains in the joints and limbs, and thus will be forced to lick the dust of the earth. Instead of their giddy pleasures and pursuits of evil they will seek incurable remedies for their mortifying sores and corruption. This will be a great hindrance in their bowing the knee to worship Antichrist.

The word "fell" refers to anything suddenly falling and shows that the plague is a sudden one causing men, before they can hardly realize it, to break out with sores and ulcers. The word "sore" is used only here and in Rev. 16:11 and Luke 16:21. The words "noisome" and "grievous" are from two Greek words meaning "depraved, bad in nature" and "full of labours and pains in working mischief" and are used here to show that the ulcers will be very painful and corrupt. The expression "them which worshipped his image" literally is "those worshipping his image." Perhaps it means that, while in the act of prostration to the image, the sores will suddenly break out upon them as a sign of God's displeasure of their willful image worship and as punishment for their rejection of plain light concerning the will and worship of the true God, who is to be heralded by angels as well as by men during this time.

2. The Second Vial: The Sea to Blood.

"And the second angel poured out his vial upon the sea; and it became as the blood of a dead man: and every living soul died in the sea," Rev. 16:3.

At the blowing of the second trumpet, one-third of the sea will become blood (8:8, 9), but here under the second vial all the sea will become blood. This does not mean that all the oceans will become blood for "the sea," which is a definite sea, as mentioned in the Bible many times, is the reference. It is the Mediterranean, around which is the kingdom of Antichrist that is to receive all these plagues. This does not mean that the sea will become the actual blood of dead men but "as the blood of a dead man," such as came through supernatural power in the land of Egypt and under the second trumpet in the first part of the Week. As the waters are changed and corrupted, all the creatures in the sea will die and the surface of the sea will be strewn with dead bodies of the finny family.

This will perhaps result in a pestilential odor that will make it impossible for human life to be near, and the waters will perhaps become so clogged that ships will remain immovable as if icebound. It is impossible to imagine such foul conditions. One could only expect disease and starvation if caught out on the sea at that time. Previously, in the second trumpet, one-third of the ships will have been destroyed, and here all the ships are likely to be destroyed, for judgment will be over all and not over one-third of it.

3. The Third Vial: The Rivers to Blood.

"And the third angel poured out his vial upon the rivers and fountains of waters: and they became blood. And I heard the angel of the waters say, Thou art righteous, O Lord, which art, and wast, and shalt be, because thou hast judged thus. For they have shed the blood of saints and prophets, and thou hast given them blood to drink; for they are worthy. And I heard another out of the altar say, Even so, Lord God Almighty, true and righteous are thy judgments," Rev. 16:4-7.

The third vial will be a repetition of the first plague upon Egypt, Exod. 7:19-24. When the waters of Egypt and the sea in the second trumpet and second vial are turned to blood, the fish will die but here there is no statement that the fish will die. Still it is reasonable to think that they will die, for they cannot live in impure waters. Not only will the rivers be turned to blood, but also the fountains of waters and the drinking places of both man and beast. What a terrible plague when men and beasts will be made to drink bloody water!

After seeing the rivers and fountains turned to blood, John heard the angel of the waters; i.e., the angel that has the third vial which turns the waters to blood, give thanks to God and ascribe to Him righteousness because he had thus judged. Then the angel of the altar in heaven sanctioned the judgment of God and the praise to Him given by the angel of the waters. God always has been, is, and always will be just to all His creation. Any judgment He sends is just and has not been sent before His mercy and longsuffering have been futile. The men who will drink these bloody waters will have shed the blood of saints and prophets and unmercifully tortured God's own people in the earth, and He will be causing them to reap what they have sowed. They will have shed blood so they will deserve blood!

But what a difference between the two classes of sufferers! One will suffer for Christ's sake and be given sufficient grace from God to do so. After the suffering those of that class will enter into eternal rewards and bliss, while those of the other class will suffer for their own sins and have no grace from God to make the suffering light. After this particular suffering they will suffer through all eternity in the lake of fire. God rewards all men for their deeds whether they be good or bad.

4. The Fourth Vial: Great Heat.

"And the fourth angel poured out his vial upon the sun; and power was given unto him to scorch men with fire. And men were scorched with great heat, and blasphemed the name of God, which hath power over these plagues: and they repented not to give him glory, Rev. 16:8, 9.

Under the fourth trumpet, one-third of the sun, moon, and stars will be stricken with darkness so that one-third part will be darkened (8:12), while here, under the fourth vial, the heat of the sun will be increased to such an extent that men will actually be scorched by it, until, in misery and torment, they will blaspheme God whom they recognize as the cause of the heat.

This plague is called "great heat." Men fret and groan under heat from the sun when it is 90 to 110 degrees but what will they do under such intense scorching heat at this future time? This passage shows that God has power over "these plagues" and that men recognize it. In Egypt, when the plagues became so great as to be unbearable, the magicians could not imitate them, so they told Pharaoh that they were the "finger of God." Thus we have

in these first four vials, the earth, the sea, the rivers and fountains, and the planets all adding their quota of torment to men.
Yet these same men will be so degraded and degenerated that
they will not repent. The plagues upon Egypt had the effect of
hardening the hearts of evil men; even so these plagues will hard-
en the followers of the Antichrist and make men rather wish to
die than serve God. The Greek word for "repent" here means to
change one's mind, always for the better and morally, Matt. 3:2;
4:7; Acts 2:38; 3:19. It means not merely to forsake sin but to
change one's attitude regarding it. This, men will not be willing
to do, so they will receive judgment for their sins until the judgment becomes unbearable, so they will blaspheme God for such
treatment.

5. The Fifth Vial: Darkness.

"And the fifth angel poured out his vial upon the seat of the beast;
and his kingdom was full of darkness; and they gnawed their tongues
for pain. And blasphemed the God of heaven because of their pains
and their sores, and repented not of their deeds," Rev. 16:10, 11.

The fifth vial is a repetition of the ninth Egyptian plague, Exod.
10:21, 22. All these plagues that are similar to those which have
been poured out before, seem to be much more intense than those
of Egypt. After the sun has been shooting its rays of intense heat
in torrents of torment upon the followers of Antichrist it will undergo a sudden change in that part of the earth. The change will
be from one extreme to another—from fiery, piercing, blinding
brightness and heat to impenetrable darkness. The beast and his
followers will be overwhelmed with fresh horror to such an extent
that they will gnaw their tongues in pain. Such a condition cannot be pictured with words. One has only to look upon a person
who may be suffering convulsions and gnawing the tongue to
have some idea of what this suffering will be.

The beast and his followers will have been tormenting God's
people and in their hideous unmerciful attitude will have laughed
at the cries and pains of the saints, so God will reward them
doubly for their sins. This plague will be poured out upon the
"seat" or throne of the beast and "his kingdom will be full of
darkness." This further indicates the extent of these plagues. All
kingdoms outside of his kingdom will escape these plagues just as
all peoples outside of Egypt did. Further than that, there seems
to be no doubt but what God's people (Jews and Gentiles) in this
kingdom will escape these plagues as they did in Egypt. That is
plainly stated in the first vial, as well as in this one.

It is not known how long the plagues last, but when this vial
comes men will still have their ulcers received in the first vial.
They also will have their pains, or the effects of the other vials.
They will not repent even under such a plague as this, but will
blaspheme "the God of heaven." Men will have deepened in their
wickedness and rebellion and will likely continue to do so more
and more with each additional plague, as was the case of Pharaoh
and his servants in Egypt. The main purpose of these plagues is

punishment for their continued rebellion against God and "their deeds" which have become as unbearable to God as in the days of Noah and Sodom.

6. The Sixth Vial: The Euphrates Dried Up.

"And the sixth angel poured out his vial upon the great river Euphrates; and the water thereof was dried up, that the way of kings of the east might be prepared," Rev. 16:12.

This is just as literal as any one of the other plagues. It will take place at the very last of the great tribulation, just before Armageddon, and after the Antichrist has been successful in conquering the countries of the North and East. Then he will gather these newly conquered nations and those which he will have conquered in the first three and one-half years, together with others which will co-operate with him, to fight against Christ at Armageddon. The drying up of the Euphrates will prepare the way for those who will come from the East. **There are many interpreters who symbolize this passage as the drying up of the Turkish Empire** from the great Empire that it once was to the small state that it is today, thus making this vial to be already fulfilled. **This is utterly unscriptural as is proved by the following:**

(1) Such an interpretation takes the passage out of its proper setting and destroys the literal meaning. If it refers to the past breaking up of an empire, then it would stand to reason that all the seals, trumpets, and first five vials have already been fulfilled. In that case we should now be living during the time of the fulfillment of the gathering of the nations to Armageddon by the three unclean spirits. However, we are sure that such is not the case, for we have not seen the fulfillment of any of these terrible events recorded in Revelation, either before or after the breaking up of the old Turkish empire in our day.

(2) Just because the Turkish Empire has dwindled down almost to nothing as compared to what it used to be is no proof that this is the fulfillment of the sixth vial any more than the diminishing of some other empire. It is clear from prophecy that the four kingdoms that were formed out of Alexander's Empire will exist as four separate kingdoms in the future and that the old Roman Empire will exist again as ten separate kingdoms in the last days. For this to be made possible, the Turkish Empire had to lose its grip over these peoples so that they could gain their independence, but it cannot be proved that this is the drying up of the great river Euphrates. There is no association between the two events whatsoever. The Turkish Empire and its being broken up is necessary for the formation of the ten kingdoms. That is one thing and the drying up of the river Euphrates is another thing.

(3) If we should take any one of the twenty-one passages in the Bible where "the river Euphrates" is mentioned or any one of the five passages where "the great river Euphrates" is mentioned and substitute "the Turkish Empire" there would be no reasonable meaning to the passage. "The river Euphrates" refers to the same

place in both Testaments. It means a literal river in Asia. It never symbolizes anything in the Bible.

(4)   All the other vials as well as the judgments of the seals and trumpets are literal; why not this one?

(5)   No oriental kings from the rising of the sun have ever come over the broken-up Turkish Empire as yet, and we have no record in Scripture that such will be the case. On the contrary, the kings of the East and North will fight with Antichrist, who will control most of the old Ottoman Empire, and war will be waged between them during the last three and one-half years until Antichrist becomes conqueror. Then he will lead them against Christ at Armageddon. If the literal river Euphrates is not dried up to prepare the way for the kings of the East and their armies to cross the river bed in their effort to help Antichrist against Christ at Armageddon, then we can find no interpretation with sufficient proof as to the meaning of the sixth vial.

(6)   The drying up of the Jordan and the Red Sea were literal so that men walked over dry shod. Why should not this also be literal as a great aid to these eastern kings and their armies in coming to Jerusalem to fight against Christ? This is not the same as the drying up of the Red Sea called the "Egyptian Sea" but it is the same as the drying up of "the river" as prophesied in Isa. 11:15, 16. This shows that at the regathering of Israel from the different countries these waters of Egypt and Assyria will be dried up. After the drying up of this river under the sixth vial it will remain dry at least until the gathering of Israel. The annual rise of the river is from March to May. The average depth of the upper river is eight feet and the lower river twenty to thirty feet. It is navigable for twelve hundred miles from Sumeisat in the Taurus to the Persian Gulf. Its width varies from two hundred to four hundred yards. One can see what a wonderful benefit the drying up of this river will be to the kings of the East.

The wrath is not upon the river, for it is harmless, but it is for the purpose of preparing the way for the kings of the East to come to the determined and predestined wrath of God upon the nations at Armageddon, upon whom God desires to take vengeance for their part in the persecution of His people during the last days.

The Three Unclean Spirits.
(Parenthetical, Rev. 16:13-16.)

"And I saw three unclean spirits like frogs come out of the mouth of the dragon, and out of the mouth of the beast and out of the mouth of the false prophet. For they are the spirits of devils working miracles, which go forth unto the kings of the earth and of the whole world, to gather them to the battle of that great day of God Almighty. Behold, I come as a thief. Blessed is he that watcheth, and keepeth his garments, lest he walk naked, and they see his shame. And he gathered them together into a place called in the Hebrew tongue Armageddon," Rev. 16:13-16.

This is the seventh parenthetical passage and is usually admitted as such. It is inserted between the sixth and seventh vials and has its fulfillment in the part of the Week in which it is given. This tells how the kings of the earth, who are not under the control of Antichrist and who do not form a part of his kingdom will be gathered to the Battle of Armageddon. These three unclean spirits will have shapes like frogs and come out of the mouths of the dragon, beast, and false prophet. They are to be demon spirits who will go forth working miracles, inspiring the nations, and mobilizing them into vast armies which will march from all directions and from all countries for the purpose of preventing the establishment of the kingdom of Christ upon earth.

These lying spirits, speaking and working through the medium of false prophets, will enable them to do miraculous wonders and cause the nations to co-operate with the Antichrist at Armageddon. They will inspire the nations with the faith that by a united effort they can defeat the armies of heaven and dethrone God and reign supreme forever. This is the attitude of certain nations today as pictured in Ps. 2. Just as the crusaders of the middle ages were allured to their destruction at Jerusalem and just as Ahab was incited to go up and fall at Ramoth-gilead (2 Chron. 18: 18-22), so the nations at this time will be led in vain hope that with one great united effort they can defeat Christ and His armies, but the end will be utter destruction. The false prophets who will be used in this false deception are referred to in Matt. 24:24-26; 1 Tim. 4:1.

The source of these spirits is clear. They will come out of the dragon and the two beasts which are symbols of the three leaders against Christ at His coming. In this vision John saw them come out of the mouths of these symbols, but in the fulfillment it could be that these spirits will go from these three persons according to word of command. The beasts symbolize two earthly men who will be possessed with demons by the legions and these demons could come out of them, but whether we can say that Satan is possessed with demons is another question. He is prince of the demons (Mt. 12:24) and not controlled by them, so the thought seems to be that these demons go from these three persons by word of command.

The purpose of their going forth unto the kings of the earth is to "gather" them to the battle of "that great day of God Almighty." This gathering of the nations is the same as the gathering mentioned in Matt. 24:40-42 which is fully explained in chapter eight. This passage (Rev. 16:13-16) shows what part other nations, outside of Antichrist's kingdom, will have in the affairs of the last days in the fulfillment of prophecy and in connection with Antichrist and Israel.

These nations will be gathered into one place called Armageddon, which is the same as the valley of Jehoshaphat near Jerusalem. Therefore, Armageddon will be fought in Palestine and not in Europe, Joel 3; Zech. 14. It is the time when Christ will come "as a thief" to bring sudden destruction upon the world of the ungodly, 1 Thess. 5:1-11; 2 Thess. 1:7-10. There is a blessing pronounced upon all those living at that time who are faithful to Christ, eagerly watching for Him, and taking heed as to their walk before the ungodly, Rev. 16:15.

7. The Seventh Vial: A Great Earthquake and Hail.

"And the seventh angel poured out his vial into the air; and there came a great voice out of the temple of heaven, from the throne, saying, It is done. And there were voices, and thunders, and lightnings; and there was a great earthquake, such as was not since men were upon the earth, so mighty an earthquake, and so great. And the great city was divided into three parts, and the cities of the nations fell: and great Babylon came in remembrance before God, to give unto her the cup of the wine of the fierceness of his wrath. And every island fled away, and the mountains were not found. And there fell upon men a great hail out of heaven, every stone about the weight of a talent: and men blasphemed God because of the plague of the hail: for the plague thereof was exceeding great," Rev. 16:17-21.

This passage is by no means all that is pictured under the seventh vial, for what happens under it is continued in Rev. 18: 1-24 after the parenthetical section, Rev. 17, on "Mystical Babylon." However we shall limit our remarks on the seventh vial to this passage until we first consider the parenthetical passage. After that we shall resume our study of the destruction of the Babylon that is scheduled to be destroyed under the seventh vial as fully elaborated upon in Rev. 18. Under the seventh vial the wrath of God will be completed, and therefore, must also, for this reason, include the coming of Christ to earth. It will be fulfilled at that time, thus ending the Seventieth Week of Daniel and beginning "the day of the Lord." When the seventh angel poured out his vial into the air, the first thing John heard was a "great voice (perhaps God's) out of the temple of heaven from the throne, saying, It is done." This has reference to the completion of God's wrath during the seventh vial, Rev. 15:1; 16:1.

The result of this earthquake will be that "the great city" (Jerusalem, Rev. 11:8) will be divided into three parts. Many of the large cities of the nations will be destroyed as well as "great Babylon." Besides the total and partial destruction of many cities, the moving of mountains and islands and great changes in the surface of the earth in certain places, there will be "great hail" out of heaven upon men. Each hail will weigh 56 to 114 pounds, according to the weight of different talents in the New Testament. This last plague will be so terrible that men will again blaspheme God because of it. The hail will perhaps be the same as that mentioned in Ezek. 38:21-23 in connection with Armageddon. This is a repetition of the seventh Egyptian plague, but on a much larger scale. Cf. Exod. 9:13-36; Josh. 10:11. Thus God will complete His wrath begun under the sixth seal in the first part of the Week, Rev. 6:12-17.

MYSTICAL BABYLON, Rev. 17:1-18

(Parenthetical, Rev. 17:1-18.)

"And there came one of the seven angels which had the seven vials, and talked with me, saying unto me, Come hither; I will shew unto thee the judgment of the great whore that sitteth upon many waters: With whom the kings of the earth have committed fornication, and the inhabitants of the earth have been made drunk with the wine of her fornication. So he carried me away in the spirit into the wilderness: and I saw a woman sit upon a scarlet coloured beast, full of names of blasphemy, having seven heads and ten horns. And the woman was arrayed in purple and scarlet colour, and decked with gold and precious stones and pearls, having a golden cup in her hand full of abominations and filthiness of her fornication: And upon her forehead was a name written, MYSTERY, BABYLON THE GREAT, THE MOTHER OF HARLOTS AND ABOMINATIONS OF THE EARTH. And I saw the woman drunken with the blood of the saints, and with the blood of the martyrs of Jesus: and when I saw her, I wondered with great admiration. And the angel said unto me, Wherefore didst thou marvel? I will tell thee the mystery of the woman, and of the beast that carrieth her, which hath the seven heads and ten horns," Rev. 17:1-7.

Rev. 17 is the eighth parenthetical passage and is an account in some detail of Ecclesiastical Babylon, her identification, character, power, wickedness, judgment and destruction by the Antichrist and the ten kings, as well as an explanation of the beast and its seven heads and ten horns. **We believe this passage is parenthetical for the following reasons:**

1. It is dislocated from its proper place as to fulfillment and is inserted here as explanatory matter between the **fact** of the destruction of literal Babylon of the seventh vial (16:17-21), and the complete **description** of that destruction in Rev. 18:1-24. The placing of it here is to show the contrast between Mystical Babylon and Literal Babylon, rather than to show its sequence of fulfillment. Its fulfillment is not contained in the vials, and therefore, is not a part of them. The seven vials, and, in fact, all of the events of the last three and one-half years will be fulfilled after the destruction of Mystical Babylon. The doom of Mystical Babylon by the Antichrist and the ten kings will transpire in the middle of the Week that the beast and his image may be the only objects of worship for the last three and one-half years, Dan. 9:27; Matt. 24:15; 2 Thess. 2:4; Rev. 13:1-18; 14:9-11.

2. If this chapter is not parenthetical and its Babylon is the same as that which is destroyed under the seventh vial and as described in Rev. 18, and if both are the continuation of the seventh vial, then this Babylon cannot be destroyed by the beast and the ten kings in the middle of the Week. But the Babylon of Rev. 17 must be destroyed in the middle of the Week according to Rev. 17:14-17. The ten kings will give their kingdoms to Antichrist for the purpose of destroying her at this time, while the destruction of the Babylon of Rev. 18 is supernatural, according to Rev. 16:17-21 and 18:1-24. This destruction will be through the means of an earthquake. Surely earthquakes will not be in the power of the ten kings and the Antichrist. If, on the other hand, there will be two Babylons, and the one of Rev. 17 is to be destroyed by the beast and the ten kings as

in 17:14-17, and this takes place in the middle of the Week when the ten kings give their kingdoms to the beast as in Rev. 13:1-10, then she will not be destroyed three and one-half years later by the earthquake under the seventh vial. Therefore she cannot be the same as the Babylon of Rev. 18:1-24.

3. This Mystical Babylon will dominate the ten kings and even the beast himself for the first three and one-half years until they together will receive power sufficient to destroy her. They will burn her with fire in the middle of the Week. The Antichrist will have all power during the last three and one-half years. Such could not be if he were to be dominated by her during his entire reign. The Babylon of Rev. 17 will dominate the same kings in the first three and one-half years that the beast dominates during the last three and one-half years. Certainly both cannot be dominant or be the supreme objects of worship at the same time. This then proves that Rev. 17:1-18 is parenthetical and that this judgment of the whore will take place in the middle of the Week when Antichrist will come into power over the ten kings in her stead. It further proves that this event will happen before the vial judgments which fall upon the beast and his kingdom, rather than on the great whore.

4. Her identity is entirely different from the Babylon of Rev. 18 as is proved below in a comparison of the two chapters. Rev. 18 is the continuation of the seventh vial. Rev. 17 breaks into the message of the seventh vial at Rev. 16:21. In Rev. 18 the Babylon that is destroyed under the seventh vial (16:17-21) is taken up in detail as to her destruction. If Rev. 17 were removed from this place and put in its proper place as to fulfillment with Rev. 10-13, which deal with the middle of the Week, Rev. 18 would be a continuation of the seventh vial of Rev. 16:21, showing just how and why Literal Babylon is destroyed. However, this would complicate the understanding of the two Babylons for some, more than ever.

5. Rev. 17, as can readily be seen, is foreign in its subject matter to the destruction of the Babylon in Rev. 16:17-21 and 18:1-24, and is thus recognized as an alien passage, inserted between the two passages, and used to describe Mystical Babylon and "the beast that carrieth her." In Rev. 13:1 we see the beast coming up out of the sea. Rev. 17 must be parenthetical because no revelation concerning the beast could be given before the rise of the beast, nor could the woman ride upon the beast until it appeared. In other words, the beast and the great whore both will have existed before the rise of the beast out of the sea. The revelation of the beast in this new form of seven heads and ten horns could not be given to be fulfilled before the middle of the Week, because the beast will not be given power over the seven heads and ten horns until then. Therefore, no revelation of the woman could be given in connection with the beast and its seven heads and ten horns until it ap-

peared, so this chapter must be parenthetical in order to show the revelation of both. If the woman were to be revealed in the middle of the Week when the sun-clothed woman is to be revealed, much confusion might arise over the two women, but, as it is, there need be none, because the time of the fulfillment of Rev. 17 is very clear as taking place in the middle of the Week when the beast comes to power over the ten kings, Rev. 13:1-7; 17:12-17; Dan. 7:23, 24.

6. There is nothing in the chapter, or elsewhere, to refute our parenthetical claim; contrarily, there are many facts which prove that the woman here will be destroyed in the middle of the Week and that the destruction of Literal Babylon under the seventh vial will take place at the end of the Week.

Points of Contrast Between the Two Babylons of Rev. 17 and 18.

1. One of the "seven angels" shows John the complete mystery of the woman (17:1, 7), while "another angel" begins the other message, Rev. 18:1.

2. The woman and the beast are symbolic in Rev. 17:1-18. Nothing is symbolic in Rev. 18:1-24.

3. Everything is explained in Rev. 17:1-18. Everything is clear in Rev. 18:1-24, and therefore needs no explanation.

4. The woman and the beast are mysteries in Rev. 17:7. Nothing is mysterious in 18:1-24.

5. In Rev. 17 the angel talks to John, while in chapter 18 he simply hears various voices announcing certain facts, Rev. 18:1, 2, 4, 10, 16, 18, 21. This would be entirely out of place if the two Babylons were to be the same, for the angel in Rev. 17 promised John this: "I will tell thee the mystery of the woman."

6. In Rev. 17 only one angel speaks, 17:1, 3, 7, 15. In Rev. 18 both men and angels speak, Rev. 18:1, 2, 4, 10, 16, 18, 20. If the two Babylons are the same why did not the angel of Rev. 17 continue speaking to John in Rev. 18, especially so, when he said, "I will tell thee the mystery of the woman?"

7. The Babylon in Rev. 17 will dominate the nations (17:1, 9, 15, 18), while the Babylon of Rev. 18 will not.

8. One is called "the woman"; the "great whore"; etc. The other is not.

9. One is on a scarlet colored beast. The other is not.

10. Names are written on the forehead of one, but not on the other, for one is symbolized by a woman and the other is not.

11. John wonders "with great admiration" over the one (17:6, 7), because he has never seen nor heard of her before, while there is no such wonder over the other. (He was well acquainted with the existence of the literal city of Babylon.)

12. There is no announcement in Rev. 17 of the fall of Mystical Babylon, while there is of Literal Babylon in both Testaments, revealing its complete destruction in the latter days, Isa. 13:19-22; 14:4; 21:9; Jer. 50:39-41; 51:6-11, 24-29, 36-57; Rev.

14:8; 16:17-21; 18:1-24.

13. No merchants are to be enriched through the commerce of one, while they are with the other, Rev. 18:3, 9-19. Cf. 17:4.

14. No voice will warn people to come out of one. But a warning will be given of the other, Rev. 18:4.

15. There is no boasting by one, while there is by the other, Rev. 18:7.

16. Plagues, mournings, famine, and fire **from God** are not to be in one. They are in the other, Rev. 18:8. Cf. 17:16, 17.

17. Men do not stand afar off for fear of the destruction of one, while they do of the other, Rev. 18:8. Cf. Rev. 17:16, 17.

18. Merchandise is not described in one. It is in the other, Rev. 18:11-14.

19. No definite period of destruction is mentioned of one, while it is of the other, Rev. 18:8, 10, 17-19.

20. Man destroys one, Rev. 17:16, 17. God destroys the other, Rev. 18:5-8, 20.

21. God will put it into the hearts of the ten kings to give their kingdoms to the beast for the purpose of destroying Mystical Babylon (17:14-17), while this is not true of the other.

22. The beast and the ten kings will rejoice over the destruction of Mystical Babylon, Rev. 17:16, 17. They will mourn over the destruction of the other, Rev. 18:9-19.

The woman and the beast are fully explained in Rev. 17 and the revelation of these things is completed before the description of Literal Babylon is begun. In Rev. 18 there is another separate and distinct description of another thing entirely. This is proved by the expression "after these things" clearly referring to the things after the complete revelation of the woman and the beast. This does not mean that Rev. 18 is in immediate fulfillment after "these things," but that it was received by John in the Revelation after them. (See this phrase and its usage under "The Heavenly Door" in chapter nine.) Most of the things that are spoken concerning the woman in Rev. 17 do not and cannot apply to a literal city, and the things spoken of the city in Rev. 18 cannot possibly apply to the same thing that the woman symbolizes. If the two Babylons were one and the same they would be destroyed together, but we have seen above that they are to be destroyed at different times, and by different persons and for different causes.

Points of Similarity of the Two Babylons.

1. Both commit fornication with kings of the earth; one in a religious way, the other in a commercial way, 17:2; 18:3, 9; 19:2.

2. Both shed the blood of saints, 17:6; 18:24.

3. Both have a cup of abominations, 17:4; 18:6.

4. Both are called a city, 17:18; 18:10, 16, 18, 19-21.

5. Both are made desolate, 17:16, 17; 18:19.

6. Both are called "Babylon the Great," 17:5; 18:2.

THE IDENTITY OF MYSTICAL BABYLON

There are many marks of identification proving Mystery Babylon to be a great religious system, but these marks do not conclusively prove it to be Roman Catholicism as various Bible students have taught down through the centuries. The commonly accepted theory is that Roman Catholicism is the mother of harlots and the harlots are the many branches of Christianity, all of whom will become linked together again in the last days to fulfill Rev. 17. These scholars believe that Romanism will control the ten kings of Revised Rome and will dominate the beast for a short time during his rise over the ten kings and until the middle of the Week. Then, the beast and the ten kings will destroy her so that the beast may be worshipped the last three and one-half years of this age, Rev. 17:9-17.

The scholars point out that the "whore" is not a political organization, but a religious one with political aspirations. Having a present program to rule the world, she has always satisfied herself with the power of dictation through kings rather than by the direct ruling of kingdoms.

Those who claim that the great whore is the Roman Catholic Church give the following arguments to prove their claims:

I. The Whore Is Identified by Her History.

The whore is identified as Roman Catholicism by her history, from her inauguration some centuries after John until the present day. The history of Romanism is that of Christendom from its beginning, through the gathering of local churches into an organization, and culminating into the one great religious apostate system known today as the Roman Catholic Church.

During the first century the churches were composed of small groups of believers in a heathen community. Most of them were poor, outside the local congregation at Rome, which included believers of the higher social rank. Everywhere Christians were distinguished from the heathen by their brotherly love, moral earnestness and purity, confident gladness in Christian teachings, hope of the Lord's coming, etc. They were hated for these differences and from the time of Nero (54-68 A.D.) the Roman Government was hostile to them and tried suppression. Their worship was informal and was generally held in private houses. In the public meetings the services were carried on by the people, who took part as the Spirit moved them. Prayers, testimonies, singing of psalms, reading of the Old Testament and the writings of the apostles were all a part of the worship. Sometimes there was such eagerness to take part that disorder resulted. They often had a love feast or a common meal, the symbol of brotherly love, from which the unbeliever was barred. They did not have creeds or formal statements of belief. The so-called Apostle's

Creed was not used before the second century. All Christians held that they belonged to the universal church, for all were one in Christ. There was no general organization having control of the scattered churches. The apostles exercised certain authority over them but it was not formal or official as in an organization. Each congregation managed its own affairs. The churches had elders and presbyters, sometimes called bishops, meaning one who has oversight, whose duties were the pastoral care, discipline, and financial affairs. They also had deacons which performed subordinate services of the same kind.

During the second and third centuries prior to the reign of Constantine, Christianity spread in many places and among all classes and ranks, through the medium of traveling missionaries, apologists or literary defenders of the Christian religion, teachers, and Christians generally. The Christians were persecuted in the first three centuries by the Roman Government, not only for their clean lives which were a standing condemnation of the prevalent religious customs and moral conduct, but also because they would not honor the state religion by paying worship to the statutes of the emperors. The churches went through ten persecutions until the time of Constantine who established religious liberty, chiefly for the benefit of Christians. He caused a radical change in Christianity, raising its position in the empire and changing the standard of admission to the churches until thousands of pagans were admitted with all their pagan ideas and superstitions. Through this supposed liberation of Christianity by the emperor, who entered actively into the affairs of the churches, endeavoring to settle doctrinal disputes, and exercising authority among Christians, certain errors crept into the churches.

Rise of the Roman Catholic Church.

The churches by this time had become organized so that Constantine could deal with an organization. In the second century, a loose federation of churches sprang up, having one form of belief, expressed in confessions much like the Apostles Creed, and one form of local church government. These churches in this federation called themselves the Catholic Church—Catholic meaning universal. There were many churches which differed from this Catholic Church in belief and government. The statement of faith became the test of membership. The test of man's Christianity became, not so much his loyalty to Christ as his agreement with the church as to doctrine.

Distinction between the clergy and laymen, unknown in the apostolic age, was marked. Bishops, presbyters, and deacons were separated from the members of the churches. As the sacrificial idea of the Lord's Supper grew, the clergy were more and more called "priests." The office of bishop was magnified and those in that office sometimes thought they had authority from God to correct error and to forgive sins. The idea that asceticism was the way to holiness grew and led them to believe that the clergy ought not to marry. Later came the idea that when several churches were established in one town they should be under a bishop and naturally, the bishops of larger towns rose to importance over those of the smaller towns. They were called "Metropolitans" and each of them began to rule over several bishops and their districts or dioceses. By a further centralization, five bishops rose to a higher rank, that of patriarchs. These were the bishops of Rome, Constantinople, Alexandria, Jerusalem, and Antioch.

In the fifth century, Augustine taught his doctrine of the nature of the Catholic Church, which was generally accepted. He believed that the first bishops of the church were appointed by the apostles, that the apostles received from Christ the gifts of the Holy Spirit for the care of the church, who, in turn gave them to their first successors, the first bishops; that the successors of the first bishops held the original faith and could give Christian teaching which brought salvation; that only in the Catholic Church, the Church of these bishops in apostolic succession, was there salvation. Augustine was not the first to teach these ideas but he worked for their acceptance more than anyone before him.

There came another step in the centralization of the government of the Catholic Church. Among the five patriarchs, the two most prominent were those of Rome and Constantinople, the two principal cities of the world. Several causes concurred to raise the Roman bishop to the higher place, the greatest being the fact that he was bishop of the ancient capital of the world. For centuries Rome had ruled the world. The bishop of Rome naturally had an authority that none other had, or could have. Another cause was the custom which sprang up making the bishop a court of appeal in church disputes. This was brought about by the influence of the emperors of Rome who encouraged the centralization of the church in Rome. From the fifth century, the so-called Petrine claim was accepted, which made the bishop at Rome head of the church by divine right, since he was supposedly the successor to Peter, the first universal head of the church. The general acceptance of this made it as certain as if it were really true. Then the policy of the Roman bishops of holding all the authority that this claim bestowed upon them and claiming still more, and taking every opportunity to use this power to further the elevation of the Roman bishop over all others was carried on. Leo I, sometimes called the "first Pope" (444-461) asserted his universal authority in the strongest terms and claimed the right to give commands to bishops everywhere. His claims were denied by the bishop at Constantinople and were resisted somewhat in the West, but opposition helped to increase his power as the universal bishop. The word "pope" was used in the fourth and fifth centuries as the title of any bishop, but it gradually came to be reserved for the bishop at Rome.

The full title of "Roman Catholic Church" did not come into use until the power of the Roman bishops as the universal head of the church was fully recognized. Thus, out of the independent churches of the apostolic age, grew the Catholic Church, having its complete graded organization, its clergy possessing spiritual authority over the people together with a definite creed calling those who would not accept their rule, heretical. This Catholic Church later became the Roman Catholic Church, completely dominated by the bishop of Rome.

The centralization of the church continued toward Rome until about 600 A.D. Gregory I was crowned and recognized the first universal bishop and pope. The popes were for some time chosen by the emperors, but that order was changed when Hildebrand procured the establishment of the college of cardinals with power to elect the pope. The power of the emperor diminished so much as to be negligible from 1058-1061 A.D. Hildebrand also conceived the idea that the pope should be the supreme temporal ruler of the world as well as the absolute head of the church. The Roman Church reached the height of its power during the jurisdiction of Innocent III, who made and set aside rulers and did according to his will in the affairs of all the kingdoms of western Europe.

During the thirteenth century the church became master of the Holy Roman Empire and ruled without a rival. In 1294 A.D., after the papacy had lost much influence, Boniface VIII came to the throne. He attempted to surpass Hildebrand and Innocent III in manifestation of his power, endeavoring to excommunicate Philip of France, who answered him by sending men-of-arms and taking him prisoner for three days. This act of flagrant rebellion and humiliation broke the temporal power of the papacy and the popes went into "Babylonish Captivity" for sixty-nine years at Avignon, which is just across the Rhone River from French territority. Then the pope went back to Rome and the French cardinals elected a pope who set up his court at Avignon and two popes occupied the papal chair for a period of thirty years, being in opposition to each other during that time. A meeting for reconciliation was held and a new pope was elected, but the other two indignantly refused to resign and so there were three popes for a short time. The general council called at Constance, five years later, deposed two, caused the other to resign, with a closed breach resulting. Martin V was elected and acknowledged by the whole church in 1414 A.D.

The popes continued to wield an influence upon temporal rulers until the reformation gained such headway that the Emperor Charles V came to Germany to settle the religious dispute. He failed and despairing of a doctrine of love, at the Diet of Augsburg, 1530, the Roman Catholic majority decreed that the Protestant cause should be put down by war. The war started in 1546 and the emperor was victorious on all sides until Maurice drove him out of Germany. Then the emperor gave the German affairs of the empire into the hands of his brother Ferdinand, who made peace at Augsburg in 1555. The reformation spread to many lands until today practically all lands are blessed with freedom of worship.

The opening of the nineteenth century saw the papacy in great humiliation. In 1801 Napoleon, then ruler of France, concluded a concordat with pope Pius VII, which was a treaty defining the relations of the Roman Catholic Church and the government in France. By this "the church was harnessed to the state" being made in part subject to the government, yet also supported by it. These terms involved a serious loss of authority for the pope, but he was helpless before the all-powerful Napoleon. When the pope, as sovereign of the Papal States, disobeyed his wishes in a matter of European policy, Napoleon entered Rome with an army, annexed the Papal States and made the pope a prisoner in 1809. After Napoleon's downfall (1814) pope Pius VII returned to Rome and re-established the Papal States.

The rulers then controlling Europe were favorable to the church which seized upon this opportunity to acquire much power. The church set its face against all modern progress and attempted to develop its medieval elements. The order of the Jesuits, the soldiers of the papacy, strove to gain the absolute supremacy of the pope and was successful. Pope Pius IX (1846-1878) outlined the policy of the Roman Church which exists today, assuming with gross bigotry, that limitless authority was his by divine right. He thus took upon himself the power and right to define doctrine, which, in the past had been exercised only by the general councils. The Council of Trent (1545) determined the complete statement of doctrine for the church. The Vatican Council was the next held (1870) which added more decrees and gave the pope unlimited and immediate authority in every part of the activities of the church and made him infallible in defining the doctrines and morals of the church.

In 1848 a movement began to free Italy from the papal supremacy and bring her under one standard. By 1860 both the northern and southern parts of Italy came under the rule of an Italian king, Victor Immanuel, of Piedmont. The Italians recognized that there could be no united Italy as long as the pope held full sway over the Papal States, stretching from sea to sea and with a population of 3,000,000. In 1870 the king added Rome and the Papal States to his domain, thus uniting the whole of Italy.

The pope was no longer the temporal ruler of Rome. Since then, it became the policy of the popes to remain voluntary prisoners in the Vatican and never walk the streets of Rome, for to do so, it was said, would be recognizing the claims of the government that ruled. Much was said and done concerning the restoration of the Papal States and finally on February 11, 1929, the Lateran Treaties were signed, the ceremony taking place at the Vatican Palace, which ended the long conflict between Italy and the Holy See and freed the popes from voluntary imprisonment.

One treaty, solving and eliminating the "Roman Question," which had existed since the loss of temporal power in 1870, and a second, a concordat designed to regulate the relations of the church and state in Italy, were signed. The canon law which is the subject of three of the four parts of the concordat was completed in 1917. It contains 2,417 canons, or rules regulating faith, morals, conduct, and discipline of church members, which have been gradually added by the church throughout the centuries. These treaties were ratified May 14 and 25 and became effective June 7, 1929.

The pope is again temporal ruler and sovereign over a territory the size of a town of 20,000 people, known as the Vatican State or State of Vatican City. It now has power to coin money, issue bank notes, postage stamps and do as any other sovereign state. The pope has his own railway station, wireless station, aviation field, army and navy, etc. He is to receive indemnity from the Italian government of $87,500,000. This is a great boon to Romanism, for she now has a "free" pope to enter personally into world affairs. **The Holy See maintains diplomatic relations with many nations.**

"Father" Phelan in a recent sermon on the greatness of Romanism said, "The Catholics of the world are Catholics **first and always:** they are Americans, they are Germans, they are French, or they are English **afterwards.**" The political aspirations of the pope and his legions are known to every thinking person. Even in this country, preparation for the impending conflict is being made through which it is hoped that the schools, and every vestige of human rights and liberties will be destroyed.

According to "Father" Chiniquy, the Jesuits have organized many secret Catholic societies into military ones which are scattered over the United States. They number nearly 1,000,000 soldiers, who under the name of United States Volunteer Militia, are officered by some of the most skilled officers of this Republic.

Stores of ammunition are laid away in secret places for use when necessary. Many boastful statements may be found in Catholic papers for which there is not space to mention, but these few facts will suffice to show the purpose of this great whore in all lands. Whether she will be successful in other lands or not, we do know from Rev. 17 that she will be master once more of the nations of Revised Rome and those the whore will control until the middle of the Week when she will finally be destroyed by these nations.

Chapter Twenty-eight

THE IDENTITY OF MYSTICAL BABYLON, Continued

II. The Whore Is Identified by Her Names.

1. She has a name on her forehead, "MYSTERY, BABYLON THE GREAT," Rev. 17:5. This name is surely appropriate as far as Romanism is concerned. Paul called the Church a "mystery" because it was unknown to the Old Testament prophets, Eph. 3:1-12; 5:23-32. So here this apostate religious system is called a "MYSTERY" because she was not known before her revelation to John. Some have tried to make a comparison between this whore and the Church, calling one the bride of Christ and the other the bride of Antichrist, but a vital truth has been overlooked in this. Antichrist has never wanted this whore. He tolerates her only until he has gained sufficient power to destroy her. He does not seek for her, love her, and nourish her as Christ does the Church, so there can be no comparison. In the second place, the Church is not the bride of Christ. (See chapter forty-five.)

It is said that the papal crown bore the word "MYSTERY" on its frontlet for some time, but it was removed by Julius III, after having his attention called to the accusation of this passage. The Roman Church has always shrouded herself in mystery. The mystery of baptismal regeneration, the mystery of miracle whereby the literal bread and wine are supposedly changed into the actual blood and body of Christ, the mystery of holy water and of the lights on altars, the mystery of plays, confession, and other rites and ceremonies, mumbled in a language that tends to be mysterious all go to help us to understand that this system is Babylon in mystery. These ordinances were unknown in John's day but they are recognized now by all as part of the Catholic ceremony of mystery, thus identifying her as Mystery Babylon, and the only one that will meet the requirements of this prophecy in the last days. Even Catholic divines admit that this description fits their church. For instance, Cardinal Ballarmine says, "St. John, in his Apocalypse, calls Rome (the priestly term for the Roman Church) Babylon." The celebrated French Prelate, Boussuet, in his exposition of Revelation says, "The features are so marked that it is easy to decipher Rome under the figure of Babylon."

The Ancient Babylonian Cult.

Since this is true, what is the historic relation of Babylon to the city of Rome and the Roman Church, and why should Romanism be called Babylon in mystery? That the cities of Rome and Babylon were related seems to have been well known in the earlier days. **It is simple to trace in the archives of history the relation of Babylon to Rome and of Rome to the Roman Church.** Let us look at the history of ancient Babylon.

This city was built by Nimrod, the mighty hunter, Genesis 10:8-10. It was the seat of the first great apostasy against God

after the flood. Here the "Babylonian Cult" was invented by
Nimrod and his queen, Semiramis. It was a system claiming the
highest wisdom and ability to reveal the most divine secrets. This
cult was characterized by the word "MYSTERY" because of its
system of mysteries. Besides confessing to the priests at admission, one was compelled to drink of "mysterious beverages,"
which, says Salverte (Des Sciences Occultes, page 259) "was indispensable on the part of those who sought initiation into these
mysteries." The "mysterious beverages" were composed of wine,
honey, water, and flour. They were always of an intoxicating
nature, and until the aspirants had come under the influence of
it and had their understanding dimmed they were not prepared
for what they were to see and hear. The method was to intro-
duce privately, little by little, information under seal of secrecy
and sanction of oath that would be impossible to reveal otherwise. This has been the policy of the Roman Church and the
secret of the power of the priests over the lives of men whom
they could expose to the world for their sins that have been
confessed to them. Once admitted, men were no longer Baby-
lonians, Assyrians, or Egyptians, but were members of a mystical
brotherhood, over whom was placed a Supreme Pontiff or High
Priest whose word was final in all things in the lives of the
brotherhood regardless of the country in which they lived.

The ostensible objects of worship were the Supreme Father,
the Incarnate Female, or Queen of Heaven, and her Son. The
last two were really the only objects of worship, as the Supreme
Father was said not to interfere with mortal affairs. Nimrod
III, page 239. This system is believed to have come from fallen
angels and demons. The object of the cult was to rule the world
by these dogmas.

How the Ancient Babylonian Cult Spread.

In the days of Nimrod this cult secured a deep hold on the
whole human race for it was of one language and all were one
people. Nimrod gained the title "Mighty Hunter" and "the Apostate" because of his success in building cities with walls to free
men from the ravages of wild beasts which were multiplying
against men, and because of his freeing men of the idea of God
and His wrath. As a great deliverer and protector of the people
and the head of the godless civilization at that time he would
naturally have great influence upon the people. He led them
astray to such an extent that they gloried in the fact that they
were free from the faith of their fathers.

All tradition from the earliest time bears witness of this great
apostasy, which continued to such proportion that people defied
God to send another flood to destroy men by building a tower
to escape such. The result was that God confused their language
and scattered them throughout the earth. This Babylonian system was the one which the Devil had planned to counteract the
truth of God. From Babylon it spread to the ends of the earth

and we have record that Abraham was chosen of God from all these idolatrous nations to represent the true God. Through him God planned to bring man back to Himself. This explains how the different nations of the world have traditions and religions somewhat similar, with changes suitable to the individual nation.

After the nations were scattered abroad, Babylon continued to be the "seat of Satan" until it was taken by Xerxes in 487 B.C. The Babylonian priesthood was then forced to leave Babylon, so it moved to Pergamos, which was the headquarters for some time. When Attalus, the Pontiff and King of Pergamos, died in 133 B.C. he bequeathed the headship of the Babylonian priesthood to Rome. When the Etruscans came to Italy from Lydia (the region of Pergamos) they brought with them the Babylonian religion and rites. They set up a Pontiff who was the head of the priesthood and had the power of life and death over them. Later, the Romans accepted this Pontiff as their civil ruler. Julius Caesar was made the Supreme Pontiff of the Etruscan Order in 74 B.C. In 63 B.C. he was made Supreme Pontiff of the Babylonian Order, thereby becoming heir to the rights and titles of Attalus, who had made Rome his heir by will.

Thus, the first Roman emperor became the head of the Babylonian priesthood and Rome became the successor of Babylon with Pergamos as the seat of this cult. Henceforth, Rome's religion has been that of Babylon. In the year 218 A.D. the Roman army in Syria, having rebelled against Macrinus, elected Elagabalus emperor. This man was High Priest of the Egyptian branch of Babylonianism. He was shortly afterward chosen Supreme Pontiff by the Romans, and thus the two Western branches of the Babylonian apostasy centered in the Roman Emperors who continued to hold this office until 376 A.D. when the Emperor Gratian, for Christian reasons refused it because he saw that by nature Babylonianism was idolatrous. Religious matters became disorganized until it became necessary to elect someone to fill the office.

The Babylonian Religion and Roman Christendom United.

Damascus, Bishop of the Christian Church at Rome, was elected to this office. He had been bishop for twelve years, having been made such in 366 A.D. through the influence of the monks of Mount Carmel, a college of the Babylonian religion originally founded by the priests of Jezebel and continued to this day in connection with Rome. So, in 378 A.D., the Babylonian system of religion became part of the Christian Church, for the bishop of Rome, who later became the supreme head of the organized church, was already Supreme Pontiff of the Babylonian Order. All the teachings of pagan Babylon and Rome were gradually interspersed into the Christian religious organization. Soon after Damascus was made Supreme Pontiff, the rites of Babylon began to come to the front. The worship of the Roman Church became

Babylonish, and under him the heathen temples were restored and beautified and the rituals established. Thus, the corrupt religious system under the figure of a woman with a golden cup in her hand, making all nations drunk with her fornication, is divinely called "MYSTERY, BABYLON THE GREAT."

The Effects of This Union Upon Organized Christianity.

The changes that transpired in the doctrines and practices of the Roman Church by this union did not come all at once. The Roman Church of today is purely a human institution; her doctrines, which militate against God's Word, were never taught by Christ nor the apostles. They crept into the church centuries afterward. It can be seen how easily the Babylonish rites were introduced into, and made a part of this church, when the greatest influence in it became the Supreme Pontiff of the Babylonian Order. The adherents of each religion would not compromise so a union of the two was the outcome. **The following points in conjunction with the above history of the rise of the Catholic Church will show some of the pagan elements that entered into the church,** many of which were taken from the Babylonian religion:

(1) The first after this union was the introduction of the worship of the saints, especially of the virgin Mary. Thousands of pagans entered the church in those times who were accustomed to worshipping the gods of towns and places, and who were not thoroughly Christianized. The veneration of saints and holy men became a worship. Saints were considered lesser deities, whose intercession availed with God. Places connected with the lives of holy men were considered sacred and pilgrimages resulted. Relics or bones of saints were believed to have miracle working power. The worship of the virgin Mary was set up in 381 A.D., three years after Damascus became head of the Babylonian Cult.

Just as the Babylonian Cult worshipped the "Queen of Heaven" and her "Son" and did not worship the "Supreme Father" because He, supposedly, did not interfere with mortal affairs, so the Roman Church has a similar worship in that they worship Mary as the "Mother of God" and her "Son." The image of mother and child was an object of worship in Babylon long before Christ. From Babylon this spread to the ends of the earth. The original mother was Semiramis, the beautiful queen of Nimrod, who was a paragon of unbridled lust and licentiousness.

In the "mysteries" which she had the chief part in forming, she was worshipped as "Rhea" (**Chronicon Paschale,** Vol. 1, page 65), the great "Mother of the Gods" with such atrocious rites as identified her with Venus, the mother of all impurity. She raised Babylon, where she reigned, to eminence among the nations as the great seat of idolatry and consecrated prostitution. (**Hesiod, Theogonia,** Vol. 36, page 453). The apocalyptic emblem of the harlot with cup in hand was one of idolatry derived from ancient Babylon, as they were exhibited in Greece, for thus the Greek

Venus was originally represented. (**Herodotus, Historia,** Book 1, cap. 199, page 92).

The Roman Church has taken this as her emblem. In 1825 a medal was struck bearing the image of Pope Leo XII on one side and on the other side Rome symbolized by a woman with a cross in her left hand and a cup in her right hand and a legend around her "Sedet Super Universum"; i.e., "The whole world is her seat."

From this original, practically all nations have copied a similar worship and in each land the same figure is carried out under different names. In Egypt the mother and child are known as Isis and Osiris; in India, Isi and Iswara; in Eastern Asia, Cybele and Deoius; in pagan Rome, Fortuna and Jupiter-puer; in Greece, Ceres or as Irene with Plutus in arms, etc. In Thibet, China, and Japan the Jesuits were surprised to find the counterpart of the madonna (the Italian name for virgin) and her child as devoutly worshipped as in Rome itself. Shing Moo, the mother of China, is represented with child in her arms and a glory around her exactly as if a Catholic artist had painted her. Where did these nations get this common worship if not from Babylon before the dispersion in the days of Nimrod? Thus the worship of Mary in connection with her Son is of Babylonish origin for there is no such worship in Scripture.

(2) Our next allusion is to the supremacy of the pope over all moral and religious affairs of the church, and unlimited and immediate authority over the lives of all as was true of the Babylonian Pontiff, as we have seen in chapter twenty-seven.

(3) The worship and veneration of images was begun early. It was first decreed by the Second Council of Nice, 787 A.D. In the ninth century certain emperors attempted to abolish such worship but it was so rooted in the people and the attempt was so resisted by the ignorant and the monks that the emperors gave up their persecutions and in 869 A.D. a synod at Constantinople declared in favor of them. Image worship is purely pagan and came from Babylon.

(4) Private confession to a priest grew from a small beginning in the second and third centuries to an elaborate system in the time of Innocent III, 1215 A.D., but it was not decreed by council until the Council of Trent, 1551. People were compelled to confess to a priest at least once a year and to do penance according to the degree of sins committed. Penances were fastings, scourgings, pilgrimages, etc. Without confession no one had a right to the sacraments. This is the same system Babylon had, which bound the people to the priest by fear of exposure or divine wrath.

(5) The "Sign of the Cross" had its origin in the mystic "Tau" of the Babylonian Cult. It came from the letter "T," the initial letter of Tammuz (Ezek. 8:14), but better known in the classical writings as "Bacchus," "The Lamented One" who was Nimrod, the son of Cush.

(6)   The "Rosary" is of pagan origin. It is used for the same magic purposes in Romanism for which it was used in the Babylonian mysteries.

(7)   The "Order of Monks" and "Nuns" was borrowed from the Babylonian Cult. The latter is an imitation of the "Vestal Virgins" of Pagan Rome, copied from Babylon.

(8)   The outstanding festivals of Romanism, such as Christmas, Easter, St. John's Day, Lady Day, Lent, etc., are Babylonian and have no relation to Christ and the Bible. None of them were celebrated in Christendom for two hundred years after Christ. Note the following:

A. **Christmas,** literally "Christ-mass," was copied from a heathen festival observed on December 24 and 25 in honor of the son of the Babylonian Queen Astarte, and was kept centuries before Christ. The Chaldeans called it "Yule Day" or "Child Day." The Christmas tree so well known now was equally pagan and was common to all the heathen in those lands. According to a legend, on the eve of the day we call December 24 the "yule-log was cast into a tree" from which divine gifts from the gods were taken to bless men in the new year. This tree was common in the days of Jeremiah who warns Israel to flee from this heathen custom, Jer. 10:1-9.

There is no warrant that Christ was born on December 25. On the contrary it seems that He was born during warm days, for He was born in a manger and in the cold months from December to February the winters are too severe for one to be traveling to pay tax as Joseph did with his family. Shepherds were in the field when Christ was born and it was not customary for them to stay with their flocks in the open from October to February. The winters of that land are so severe that Christ said, "Pray that your flight be not in winter, Matt. 24:15-22. The only thing given in Scripture whereby we are to remember Christ is the Lord's Supper.

The apostles did not observe such a day as is common to us. Tertullian, writing about 230 A.D., lamented the fact that Christians were beginning to observe the custom of the heathen and said, "Gifts are carried to and fro, new year's day presents are made with din, and sports and banquets are celebrated with uproar; how much more faithful are the heathen to their religion, who take special care to adopt no solemnity of the Christians." The church after Constantine, full of pagans, became so corrupt that, in order to conciliate the heathen and swell the ranks of nominal Christians, adopted this heathen festival on December 25 and gave it the name of Christ-mass. It is not known when this was officially done but it was not observed as a ritual of the church until the fourth century. (See the International Encyclopedia on this subject.)

B. **Lady Day** is observed on March 25 and is also of Babylonian origin. It is the supposed day of the miraculous conception of Mary, while, among the heathen, it was observed as a festival in honor of Cybele, the Mother of the Babylonian Messiah. In Rome, Cybele was called Domina, or Lady, hence, Lady Day.

C. **Easter** also sprang from the fountain of Babylon. It is not a Christian name, since its derivation is from Ishtar, one of the Babylonian titles of the Queen of Heaven. It was the worship of this woman by Israel which was such an abomination in the sight of God, 1 Sam. 7:3; Jer. 44:18. Round cakes, imprinted with the sign of the cross, were made at this festival, the sign being, in the Babylonian mysteries, a sign of life. This day was observed centuries before Christ and is possibly a factor in the origin of our Easter and hot-cross buns. (See Mosheim's **History of the Church** 1, page 370.)

The Easter eggs which play a great part in this day's celebration were common in heathen nations. The fable of the egg affirms that "an egg of wondrous size fell from heaven into the river Euphrates; the fishes rolled it to the bank, where the doves settled upon it and hatched it and out came Astarte, or Ishtar, the goddess of Easter." The word "Easter" is used one time in the Bible (Acts 12:4) and should be translated "passover" instead, as elsewhere in Scripture.

D. **Lent** which is observed for forty days, ending with Easter, is derived from the Babylonian system of mysteries. It is also observed today by devil worshippers of Kurdistan, who obtained it from the same source as did Rome. Humboldt found it practised among the pagan Mexicans and Wilkinson informs us that it was a custom in ancient Egypt. Both Easter and Lent were introduced into the church 519 A.D. A writer of this time says, "The observance of Lent had no existence so long as the Church remained inviolate."—Cassianus. At the same time of the year that Romanism observes it the heathen observe it for a different purpose—as a celebration of the "rape of Proserpine" in which is culminated a period of unbridled lust after forty days of enforced abstinence in preparation therefor. How well does God liken Romanism to a whore, who professes to be the sole spotless bride of Christ, but in reality is the final great apostate religious system linked with the world and exercising power over the nations of the world under the ten kings until Antichrist comes to full power and destroys her in the middle of the Week.

Chapter Twenty-nine

THE IDENTITY OF MYSTICAL BABYLON, Continued

2. **She has a name on her forehead** "THE MOTHER OF HAR-LOTS," Rev. 17:4. This name is also appropriate to Romanism and means "one who has forsaken the true God and His worship, to follow idols and false gods." During the rise of the Catholic Church there were many churches who would not line up with this organization because of doctrinal views and racial and political differences. These were condemned by the organized church who tried to force them into the church. Then in the sixth century the eastern part of the church began to be estranged from the western part and in 1154 they were completely divided, each claiming to be the true Catholic Church, and refusing recognition of each other. From the twelfth century to the Reformation there were many dissenters from Romanism, such as the Petrobrusians, Cathari, Albigenses, Waldenses, Brethren, Lollards, Bohemian Brethren, etc. Then came the Reformation which has resulted in hundreds of different branches of Christianity.

The "HARLOTS" in this name no doubt refer to these many branches of Christendom who, in the last days, will affiliate themselves with Romanism and together make the "MOTHER" and "HARLOTS" of this symbol in one religious system dominating the ten kings before and during the rise of the Antichrist to full power over the ten kings. When every believer "in Christ" is taken out of the world it will not take long for this union to be made. All signs point more or less to a union of different denominations and when that is formed they will not be far from Romanism. Many churches of today are denying the gospel and its power and have only "a form of godliness" as foretold in 2 Tim. 3:1-5. Upon becoming apostate and extremely liberalistic they become "HARLOTS" as much as their "MOTHER." They become linked with the world and favorable toward union with others who can lay aside all parts of the gospel that may prevent a common union of all churches. The spirit of the age is to depart from the faith and "get together" in one union which will prove to the world that there is no difference among churches. This condition, the most ignorant among us recognize.

There is a widespread movement on foot today among the leaders of the large denominations to unite all religions in one. One who reads and is acquainted with current events is well informed of this movement and of its great strides along this line. In the last few years there have been several conferences of all world religions for the purpose of coming to a perfect understanding and putting forth a united effort to make all religions one. During the last few decades many branches of Protestantism have united, as is common knowledge to all, so space will not be taken to list the many recent unions of churches.

The slogan of world churchmen is "We are out for all kinds of union with all kinds of followers of Christ" and they will get it.

The churches are becoming more like Rome in form every year. Conferences have already been held by representatives of larger denominations and Rome, thus demonstrating that the "HARLOTS" want to conclude some sort of agreement with the "Mother Church" who has dogmatically given them to understand that they will have to come back without compromise.

3. **She has a name on her forehead** "THE MOTHER OF THE ABOMINATIONS OF THE EARTH," Rev. 17:5. This, too, is very appropriate of Romanism. The word "abomination" in Scripture means anything hateful and detestable. Here it seems to be the evil doctrines and practices of a great religious system. This name is easy to comprehend after we have examined her history. The many abominations of the earth of today had their start in Babylon and are now practiced by this woman. She is the "MOTHER OF ABOMINATIONS" in the sense that she mothers and shelters the principles of doctrine and practice of ancient Babylon and of paganism. She is recognized as the mother of abominations in the same sense that the blood of all slain on earth is found in Literal Babylon and that the blood of the prophets was required of the Jews of the first century (Matt. 23:29-34; Rev. 18:24); i.e., she has exceeded them in all abominations and therefore will be held more accountable.

LIST OF HERESIES
Adopted and Perpetuated by the Roman Catholic Church in the course of 1,600 years.

These dates are in many cases approximate. Many of these heresies had been current in the church years before, but only when they were officially adopted by a Church Council and proclaimed by the pope as dogma of faith did they become binding on Catholics.

At the Reformation in the sixteenth century these heresies were repudiated as having no part in the religion of Jesus as taught in the New Testament.

1. Of all the human inventions taught and practiced by the Roman Catholic Church, which are contrary to the Bible, the most ancient are the prayers for the dead and the sign of the cross. Both of these began 300 years after Christ.

2. Wax candles were introduced in churches about 320 A.D.

3. Veneration of angels and dead saints began about 375 A.D.

4. The Mass as a daily celebration was adopted in 394 A.D.

5. The worship of Mary the mother of Jesus and the use of the term "Mother of God" as applied to her originated about 381 A. D., but was first decreed in the Council of Ephesus in 431 A. D.

6. Priests began to dress differently from the laity in 500 A.D.

7. The doctrine of purgatory was first established by Gregory the Great about the year 593 A.D.

8. The Latin language as the language of prayer and worship in churches was also imposed by pope Gregory I in the year 600 A. D.

9. The Bible teaches that we pray to God alone. In the primitive church never were prayers directed to Mary or to dead saints. This practice began in the Roman Church about 600 years after Christ.

10. The papacy is of pagan origin. The title of pope, or universal bishop, was first given to the bishop of Rome about 600 A. D.

Jesus did not appoint Peter to the headship of the apostles and expressly forbade any such notion, Luke 22:24-26; Eph. 1:22, 23; Col. 1:18; 1 Cor. 3:11.

11. The kissing of the pope's feet began in the year 709 A. D.

It had been a pagan custom to kiss the feet of emperors. The Word of God forbids such practices, Acts 10:25, 26; Rev. 19:10; 22:9.

12. The temporal power of the popes began in the year 750 A. D.

Jesus expressly forbade such a thing and He Himself refused worldly kingship, Matt. 4:8, 9; 20:25, 26; John 18:36.

13. Worship of the cross, images, and relics was authorized in 787 A.D. Such practice is called idolatry in the Bible, and is severely condemned, Exod. 20:2-6; Deut. 27:15; Ps. 115.

14. Holy water, mixed with a pinch of salt and blessed by the priest, was authorized in the year 850 A. D.

15. The veneration of St. Joseph began in the year 890 A. D.

16. The baptism of bells was instituted by pope John XIV in 965 A. D.

17. Canonization of dead saints, first by pope John XV in 995 A. D.

Every believer and follower of Christ is called "saint" in the Bible, Rom. 1:7; 1 Cor. 1:2, etc.

18. Fasting on Fridays and during Lent was imposed in the year 998 A. D. by popes said to be interested in the commerce of fish. See Matt. 15:11; 1 Cor. 10:25; 1 Tim. 4:1-3; Col. 2:14-17; Rom. 14:1-23.

19. The Mass was developed gradually as a sacrifice and attendance made obligatory in the eleventh century.

The gospel teaches that the sacrifice of Christ was offered once and for all, and is not to be repeated, but only commemorated in the Lord's Supper, Heb. 7:27; 9:26-28; 10:10-14.

20. The celibacy of the priesthood was decreed by pope Hildebrand and Boniface VII in the year 1079 A. D.

Jesus imposed no such rule, nor did any of the apostles. On the contrary, Peter was a married man, and Paul says that bishops were to have a wife and children, 1 Tim. 3:2-5, 12; Matt. 8:14, 15.

21. The rosary, or prayer beads, was introduced by Peter the Hermit in the year 1090 A. D. This was copied from Hindoos and Mohammedans.

The counting of prayers is a pagan practice and is expressly condemned by Christ, Matt. 6:5-13.

22. The inquisition of heretics was instituted by the Council of

Verona in the year 1184 A. D. Jesus never taught the use of force to spread his religion.

23. The sale of indulgences, commonly regarded as a purchase of forgiveness and a permit to indulge in sin, began in the year 1190 A. D.

The Christian religion, as taught in the gospel, condemns such a traffic, and it was the protest against this traffic that brought on the Protestant Reformation in the sixteenth century.

24. The dogma of transubstantiation was decreed by pope Innocent III in the year 1215 A. D.

By this doctrine the priest pretends to perform a daily miracle by changing a wafer into the body of Christ, and then he pretends to eat Him alive in the presence of his people during Mass. The gospel condemns such absurdities; for the Holy Communion is simply a memorial of the sacrifice of Christ, Luke 22:19, 20; John 6:35; 1 Cor. 11:26.

25. Confession of sins to the priest at least once a year was instituted by pope Innocent III in the Lateran Council, in the year 1215 A. D.

The gospel commands us to confess our sins direct to God, Ps. 51; Isa. 1:18; Luke 7:48; 15:21; 1 John 1:8, 9.

26. The adoration of the wafer (host) was invented by pope Honorius in 1220.

So the Roman Church worships a god made by hands. This is plain idolatry and absolutely contrary to the spirit of the gospel, John 4:24.

27. The Bible was forbidden to laymen and placed in the index of forbidden books by the Council of Toledo in 1229 A. D.

Jesus and Paul commanded that the Scriptures should be read by all, John 5:39; 2 Tim. 3:15-17; 2 Tim. 2:15.

28. The scapular was invented by Simon Stock, an English monk, in 1287.

It is a piece of brown cloth, with the picture of the virgin and supposed to contain supernatural virtue to protect from all dangers those who wear it on naked skin. This is fetichism.

29. The Roman Church forbade the cup to the laity, by instituting the communion of one kind in the Council of Constance in 1414 A. D.

The gospel commands us to celebrate Holy Communion with bread and wine, Matt. 26:27; 1 Cor. 11:26-29.

30. The doctrine of purgatory was proclaimed as a dogma of faith by the Council of Florence in 1439 A. D.

There is not one word in the Bible that would teach the purgatory of priests. The blood of Jesus Christ cleanseth us from all sins, 1 John 1:7-9; 2:1, 2; John 5:24; Rom. 8:1.

31. The doctrine of Seven Sacraments was affirmed in 1439 A. D.

The gospel says that Christ instituted only two sacraments, baptism and the Lord's Supper, Matt. 28:19, 20; 26:26-28.

32. The Ave Maria, addition of part of the last half, in 1508 A. D.

It was completed fifty years afterward and finally approved by pope Sixtus V, at the end of the sixteenth century.

33. The Council of Trent held in the year 1545 declared that tradition is of equal authority with the Bible.

By tradition is meant human teachings. The Pharisees believed the same way, and Jesus bitterly condemned them, for by human tradition they nullified the commandments of God, Mark 7:7-13; Col. 2:8; Rev. 22:18.

34. The apocryphal books were added to the Bible also by the Council of Trent in 1545. See Rev. 22:18, 19.

35. The creed of pope Pius IV, was imposed as the official creed in 1560.

True Christians will retain the Holy Scriptures as their creed. Hence, their creed is fifteen hundred years older than the creed of Roman Catholics. See Gal. 1:8; Rev. 22:18, 19.

36. The immaculate conception of the virgin Mary was proclaimed by pope Pius IX in the year 1854 A. D.

The gospel states that all men, with the sole exception of Christ, are sinners. Mary herself had need of a Saviour, Rom. 3:23; 5:12; Ps. 51:5; Luke 1:30; 46, 47.

37. In the year 1870 pope Pius IX proclaimed the dogma of papal infallibility.

38. Pope Pius X, in the year 1907, condemned, together with "modernism," all the discoveries of modern science which are not approved by the church. Pius IX had done the same thing in the syllabus of 1864.

39. In the year 1930 Pius XI condemned the public schools.

40. In the year 1931 the same pope Pius XI reaffirmed the doctrine that Mary is "the Mother of God."

This doctrine was first decreed by the Council of Ephesus in the year 431. This is a heresy contrary to Mary's own words, Luke 1:46-49.

What will be the next invention? The Roman Church says it never changes; yet it has done nothing but invent new doctrines which are contrary to the Bible, and has practiced rites and ceremonies taken wholly from paganism. At least 95 per cent of the rites and ceremonies of the Roman Church are of pagan origin.

Cardinal Newman, in his book **The Development of the Christian Religion** admits that . . . "Temples, incense, oil lamps, votive offerings, holy water, holidays and seasons of devotions, processions, blessing of fields, sacerdotal vestments, the tonsure (of priests and monks and nuns) and images are all of pagan origin," page 359.

The above chronological list of human inventions and "abominations" disproves the claim of the priests of the Roman Church that their religion was taught by Christ and that the popes have been the faithful custodians of that religion.

4. She is called "the Great Whore."

"And there came one of the seven angels which had the seven vials, and talked with me, saying unto me, Come hither; I will shew unto thee the judgment of the great whore that sitteth upon many waters: With whom the kings of the earth have committed fornication, and the inhabitants of the earth have been made drunk with the wine of her fornication," Rev. 17:1, 2.

The waters are explained in Rev. 17:3, 11, 15 as being "a scarlet colored beast" and the eighth kingdom made up of "peoples, and multitudes, and nations, and tongues." These peoples are mentioned in this passage as "kings of the earth" and "inhabitants of the earth" whom the great whore will make drunk with the wine of her fornication. This shows the exercise of her future power over many nations and kings in holding them duped under her own power as has been demonstrated for centuries in the past. But this influence will not continue long, for these kings and peoples whom she intoxicates will become sober and see her in her true light as a domineering, selfish religious system whose only purpose is to get rich from the ignorance and superstition of her adherents. Her bold, dictatorial manner will cause her to overreach herself in her greed for more power and the ten kings will suddenly turn on her and give their kingdoms to Antichrist that they may destroy her in the middle of the Week.

The word "fornication" refers to her illicit practices and superstitious pagan ceremonies appealing to the religious nature of men which give her influence over the many peoples. She has long kept people in drunkenness of superstition and ignorance of the true teachings of Christ and held an unbelievable influence over the masses, who are afraid of eternal damnation without her blessing. This term not only refers to physical, but also to spiritual harlotry, Jer. 3:6-9; Ezek. 16:32; Hos. 1:2; Rev. 2:22. This woman is the peerless harlot, "THE MOTHER OF HARLOTS AND ABOMINATIONS OF THE EARTH."

This passage is for the purpose of showing John "the judgment of the great whore that sitteth upon many waters." The very ones whom she has kept in superstition are to turn on her and destroy her; they will leave her and unite with Antichrist and his cause, Rev. 17:14-17.

5. She is called "the Woman" which identifies her with the Roman Church, Rev. 17:3, 4. This usage is closely akin to "the great whore" above, so needs no special comment.

6. She is called "That Great City."

"And the woman which thou sawest is that great city, which reigneth over the kings of the earth," Rev. 17:18.

This is the last title she is known by in this chapter and it brings out a different phase of truth about her in emphasizing her identification. It has to do with her headquarters from which she rules many kings and nations. This verse literally reads: "And the woman whom thou sawest is the city the great, which has a kingdom over the kings of the earth." This clearly shows that she is not a political power, but a system whose kingdom dominates political kingdoms of the earth, and the place of her headquarters is "the city the great."

Must we not look for a literal city according to this one verse, since that is what is plainly stated and implied? This does not contradict all the above truths of a religious system but merely shows the seat of the system. If the "great city" is not an explanation of the woman then it is symbolical and one symbol is explained with another and thus we are more confused than ever. However, once we see that not only a vast religious system is in the symbol but also a literal city where she reigns, then the whole passage is clear in every detail. If we recognize only a literal city we have conflict with other parts of the explanation and if only a religious system we have conflict with this one statement. Cannot both be in the one symbol even as three things must be seen represented by the beast to harmonize all passages concerning him as we shall see in the next chapter?

All other parts of the angel's explanation have been from the symbolical to the literal and why not this? It is not likely that a great religious system would reign over the kings of the earth from a desert cave. It would be necessary for her to have headquarters in some city. She not only represents a great city but she **has a kingdom** over other kingdoms. There are many cities that are the centers of kingdoms today but we must find one which "has a kingdom" over all the other cities and kingdoms. This city will hold control over the kingdoms of the earth, not by her superior military and naval powers, but by her deceptive doctrines and practices. That this kingdom is an ecclesiastical or church kingdom is further shown by the fact that she will have unlawful alliance with the kings of the earth who themselves will be the heads of the kingdoms, and who will be made drunk by "the wine of her fornication."

There is only one city that can possibly fulfill these details and that is Rome, the seat of the whore . The Roman Church claims to be the kingdom of Christ on earth with power to rule the wills of men and dictate to kings of the earth. Cardinal Manning, in his work entitled **The Temporal Power of the Vicar of Jesus Christ,** says, "It is a kingdom, it has a **legislature;** the line of its councils for eighteen hundred years has sat, deliberated, and decreed with all the solemnity and the majesty of an **imperial parliament.** It has an **executive** which carries out and enforces the decrees of those councils with all calmness and all **pre-emptory** decision of an **Imperial will.** The Church of God (Roman), therefore, is an **empire** within an empire; and the governors and princes of this world are jealous for that reason. . . . Thus he (pope) is in himself a personal **sovereign,** and can be subject to none . . . a divine authority over all other powers . . . the whole world is in his hands . . . to enforce, obedience to the faith . . . to judge . . . nations and their princes." Pages 48-50, 124-126, 155-156, 181-182.

Israel many times was spoken of under the figure of a city or country, but it was the people who lived in that city or country, to whom God spoke. Both were in view. So it is in this symbol, both the system and the seat of the system are seen in the symbol and both are clearly explained so that we cannot mistake their identification. One literal city with its inhabitants cannot reign over many kings, but a religious system with sufficient following and influence can, and that system must have some city as its base of operation. The kings will have control of their kingdoms and have the power to throw off the woman any time they unite to do so, as is clearly implied in that this very thing will be done. This woman is not necessarily desirous of becoming queen of the nations but merely dictator to them in their affairs, which will be tolerated only until Antichrist gains sufficient power to destroy her. Thus it is evident that only a religious system will meet the requirements of this prophecy in every detail.

III. The Whore Is Identified by Her Attire.

"And the woman was arrayed in purple and scarlet colour, and decked with gold and precious stones and pearls, having a golden cup in her hand full of the abominations and filthiness of her fornication," Rev. 17:4.

This is a divine portrait of the colors and riches of this religious system. Scarlet is the color of Romanism, being reserved for the pontiff and cardinals. The inner surface of the popish cloak is scarlet, his carriage is scarlet, the carpet on which he treads is scarlet. The hats, cloaks, and stockings of the cardinals are scarlet. Five of the various articles of attire which the pope wears upon installation are scarlet. Scarlet color upon the woman is the same in meaning as upon the seven headed beast, and symbolizes her murderous sins in bringing all under control even by punishment of death. The woman is to be drunk with the blood of the saints, Rev. 17:6. Purple is also a papal hue and represents dignity and rulership.

This religion is the richest in existence as pictured here under the figure of a woman "decked with gold, and precious stones and pearls." At the coronation of the pope, a vest covered with pearls, and a mitre adorned with gold and precious stones are worn. She is also seen as having a golden cup "full of the abominations and filthiness of her fornication" which has already been dealt with.

IV. The Whore Is Identified by Her Drunkenness.

"And I saw the woman drunken with the blood of saints, and with the blood of the martyrs of Jesus; and when I saw her, I wondered with great admiration. And the angel said unto me, Wherefore didst thou marvel? I will tell thee the mystery of the woman," Rev. 17:6, 7a.

This finger of accusation is no mere accident. While this refers more particularly to the future persecutions of saints, who are saved after the rapture, still who does not know of the persecutions of saints by Romanism in all past ages? It has been estimated Rome has slain more than 200,000,000 people in the past because they would not conform to her system of religion and yield to the supremacy of the pope over their wills. One has but to turn to the pages of history to be convinced. Through the Papal Inquisition, multitudes disappeared. It was with a thrill of horror that Europe read of the opening of the dungeons of the Inquisition in Spain and of how enraged the populace was when, breaking into the monasteries, they found their way with torches into underground caverns, and discovered, chained to walls, human beings stark naked with long matted hair and nails like bird claws. Some of them were quite mad; others went raving mad when brought into the light.

These conditions will again exist when the beast comes and when the woman gets control of the nations of Revised Rome. She is the one who will cause the death of the martyrs of the fifth seal. She has almost stamped out Protestantism in Spain and Italy and is gaining influence and power in many other lands. Even in our own country she is reaching out through propaganda and elections in the hope that she may eventually put down all "heretics" who will not conform to her wishes in all matters.

The Romanists in the past have been bold in their boasts of using the "secular arm" to "punish" all "heretics" until the nations "grew refractory toward the church" and refused to "repress and punish heretics." Equally as bold are the public statements today in that they declare if ever they get control again all heretics must be brought into the "Mother Church" or else pay the penalty of excommunication and death.

V.   The Whore Is Identified by Her Destiny.

"And the ten horns which thou sawest upon the beast, these shall hate the whore, and shall make her desolate and naked, and shall eat her flesh, and burn her with fire. For God hath put in their hearts to fulfill his will, and to agree, and give their kingdom unto the beast, until the words of God shall be fulfilled," Rev. 17:16, 17.

Romanism is to reap what she has sowed and will sow. She is to be destroyed in the middle of the Week by the ten kings of the Revised Roman Empire and by the Antichrist who will rise to power over them by the middle of the Week. These will hate the whore, thus showing that the time of her future supremacy over the nations is to be short and that her policies and domineering attitude towards the nations will soon make them tire of her and cause them to turn on her, make her desolate, and burn her with fire. This shows further that the ten kings will have power enough in their kingdoms to do as they will when they choose. This alone is proof enough that the woman is to be a religious organization that deceives the nations, for kings will not permit a political system to dominate them if they had the power to resist such a system. But they would permit a religion to dominate as has been proved in the past. Therefore, many men conclude that Romanism is the great whore of Rev. 17.

To say the least, all the above arguments are enlightening as to the history of the Roman Catholic Church, but they do not really prove that the great whore is a symbol of Roman Catholicism. They leave too many questions unanswered. Why would the city of Rome be called

Babylon when there is no connection between them? They are over 2,000 miles apart and furthermore, whereas Rome is not once mentioned in prophecy, Babylon is so mentioned scores of times — six times in Revelation alone. Apart from prophecy Rome is mentioned only nine times, as compared to the 294 times Babylon is named throughout Scripture. And the Roman Catholic Church is not mentioned once in the entire Bible, so why bring her into the picture at all?

The often repeated idea that Rome is a city on seven hills, which can be what Christ meant when He mentioned the seven heads on the beast as being seven mountains does not hold up in the light of all that is said in the passage (Rev. 17:9-12) on the subject.

This could not be the intended thought, for the explanation makes it clear that five of these mountains had been in existence before John's time, only one was in existence when he saw the Revelation, and the seventh was yet to come. Then, there was to be an eighth — and this would completely do away with Rome and her so-called seven hills, as a fulfillment of the passage.

Regarding any points of similarity between the religion of Rome and that of Babylon, this would not prove them to be one and the same city any more than points of similarity between two men would prove them to be one and the same person. With two cities to consider and their two religions with some points of similarity, which one could we logically say was referred to as Mystery Babylon in Rev. 17? The one whose actual name is called in Rev. 17 — or another? Babylon, being a city, as it is stated, and her future religion must be the reference of Scripture, instead of Rome and her religion.

How could the so-called mysteries of the Roman Church, as listed in chapters 27-29, cause Rome to be Babylon? Actually, they are not mysteries at all but rather unscriptural practices that are plain to all. Any number of practices adopted from Babylon by Rome could not make Rome to become Babylon, herself. And, the same is true regarding the splitting up of Christians into many branches, as well as the present trend toward church unions — these do not prove Romanism to be the mother of harlots of Rev. 17.

How could the terms "the great whore" and "the woman" prove Babylon to be Rome? The fact is, these terms are used in Scripture in connection with Israel, Babylon, and various pagan nations with whom Israel committed fornication long before there were Christians (Isa. 13:8; 54:6; Jer. 3:9; 4:31; 6:2, 24; 13:27; 22:23; Lam. 1:17; Ezek. 16:17-36; 20:30; 23:3-44; 43:7-9; Hos. 4:10-12; Zech. 5:5-11); but they do not prove the identity of any one more than another. Neither can these terms identify Babylon as Rome or Roman Christendom, for not once are they used of professing Christians in any sense or degree. Persons professing to be Christians are never called Babylon, Rome, a whore, a woman, or anything else of the feminine gender, as a group in particular. The true church, being the body of Christ who was a man, is therefore called a "man" in Scripture instead of a woman, Eph. 2:14-15; 4:13.

Truly the religion of witchcraft, demon worship, and demon manifestations, as mentioned in Rev. 9:20-21; 13:2. 12-18; 16:13-16; 18:2; 19:2; Dan. 11:37-38; Matt. 24:24; 2 Thess. 2:8-12 best describe the religion of Babylon in the days after Antichrist. Such demon religion headed by Satan will be given to Antichrist and he will become the object of worship in the last three and one-half years of this age, 2 Thess. 2:3-4, 8-12; Rev. 13; 17:12-18; chapter Twenty-two.

None can deny that the great whore is a religious system with headquarters in a well known city. In this all scholars agree. And so, the only points we could differ on are: which city — Rome or Babylon? and which religion — Christianity or ancient magism, spiritism, witchcraft, sorcery, idolatry, and paganism?

It cannot be denied that Roman Catholicism is basically a Christian religion with a firm faith in God, Christ, the Holy Spirit, the virgin birth, the death, burial, resurrection, and ascension of Jesus Christ to sit on the right hand of God, the blood atonement for sins, the forgiveness of sins by God through Jesus Christ, and other basic Christian doctrines and biblical facts. Therefore, Romanism as now constituted, even though it has some ancient Babylonian rituals and rites intermingled throughout, could not be Mystery Babylon of Rev. 17. To become the great whore or Mystery Babylon and the kind of religion prevailing after the rapture of the Church, she would need to give up all of her true Christian truths and rites — and regarding this we have no proof that it will happen.

The religion of Mystery Babylon will be anti-God; and this cannot be said of Roman Catholicism. The same is true of Mohammedanism, the prevailing religion of most of the eastern countries of the old Roman empire; they are not anti-God. And so, we cannot consider either one of these to be the religion spoken of in Rev. 17.

It must be remembered that, as we have so often emphasized, the "THINGS" of Rev. 4-22 "MUST BE HEREAFTER," — after the churches — therefore, we have to understand Rev. 17 as referring to the religion of Babylon in the future, after the rapture of the church. What then, could this religion possibly be?

The word "HARLOTS" could very easily be understood as referring to the many branches of ancient demonism that were practiced among many nations, beginning with Babylon. The word "ABOMINATIONS" is used many times in Scripture, and long before the times of Christianity, of idolatry and whoredoms associated with demon worship and the sorceries and witchcraft of all kinds that were practiced by many pagan nations, Deut. 18:9-12; 29:17-18; 32:16-17; 1 Kings 14:24; 2 Kings 16:3-4; 17:1-25; 21:2-11; Ezek. 16:22-58; etc.

15 Reasons   Babylon is the city referred to:

1. Literal Babylon is definitely the subject of Rev. 16:17-21 and 18:1-24, not Rome.

2. Mystical Babylon is another subject inserted between these two passages, a parenthetical one to explain the religious aspect of Babylon. See 22 points of contrast, p. 187, and 30 facts about Babylon, chapter 37.

3. The fact that the great whore is called "mystery Babylon" proves a connection with literal Babylon, Rev. 17:5.

4. Literal Babylon was the site of the first great rebellion against God after the flood of Noah (Gen. 11) and it will be the site of the last great rebellion, Rev. 14:8; 16:17-21; 18:1-24.

5. Literal Babylon is always associated with demon religions and idolatry in Scripture, Isa. 21:9; 47:9-10; Rev. 18:2-3, 23.

6. Many prophecies concerning literal Babylon in both testaments are yet unfulfilled (Isa. 13:1-22; 14:1-27; 43:14; 47:1-15; 48:20; Jer. 50-51; Zech. 5:5-11; Rev. 14:8; 16:17-21; 18:1-24); whereas, Rome is not mentioned in any prophecy either fulfilled or unfulfilled.

7. Of all the empires taking part in the times of the Gentiles — Egypt, Assyria, Babylon, Medo-Persia, Greece, Rome, Revised Rome and Revived Greece, the capital city of only one is mentioned in prophecy with a latter day fulfillment — Babylon.

8. Never has it been necessary to re-identify any city named in prophecy. Predictions in Scripture about Sodom, Gomorrah, Ninevah, Tyre, Sidon and others have been fulfilled regarding cities by said names as in the various passages.

9. Literal Babylon is the only city called "the lady of kingdoms," Isa. 47:5, 7.

10. Babylon is the only city of the last days that will be the headquarters for every demon and unclean spirit (Rev. 18:2), the only one to be the center of sorceries, enchantments, etc., Rev. 18:23; Isa. 47:9-10, 12-13. This being true, then neither Rome nor any city other than Babylon will be the center of false religions fulfilling prophecy.

11. Babylon is the only city named as making all nations drunk with the wine of her fornication (Rev. 18:3), and the great unnamed whore is the only other Babylon causing nations to be drunk with the wine of fornication (Rev. 17:2). Therefore, the reference must be to the same city -- Mystery Babylon being the religious aspect of literal Babylon, Rev. 17:2.

12. Babylon is the only named city which is singled out as the object of God's wrath and plagues, Rev. 16:19; 18:4, 6. Rome was well known at the time John wrote the book of Revelation; and so, its absence from the prophecy indicates further that Babylon instead of Rome was to be the great city fulfilling the predictions.

13. Babylon is the only city God commanded His people to come out of, in the last days, Rev. 18:4; Jer. 50:4-9; 51:4-8, 45.

14. Babylon is the only city named which is to be judged in the last days for martyrdoms, Rev. 18:24. Both mystery and literal Babylons martyr saints, and so, there must be a relationship. If two different cities as far from each other as Rome and Babylon were to be guilty of this after the rapture, then two would have been mentioned instead of one only as in Rev. 18:24.

15. Antichrist will be king of Syria with Babylon as his capital (Isa. 14:4), and this will fulfill Dan. 8:8-9, 20-25; 11:35-45. The great whore will ride the beast (Antichrist's kingdom) in his rise to power over the ten kingdoms, Rev. 17:3, 7. It should be recognized then, that she symbolizes a religion in his capital even before he gets power over the ten kingdoms of Revised Rome, Rev. 17:12-17.

Babylon's could be a new religion entirely, or a revival of ancient sorcery, witchcraft, enchantments, and astrology which characterized the ancient city. It is clear that such will be the prevailing religion of the entire Roman Empire territory in the last days, as in point 10, above. Jesus predicted the coming of many false prophets who would show great signs and wonders to deceive men just prior to His coming to earth again, Matt. 24:24. Paul predicted the coming of Antichrist with all power, signs, and lying wonders by the power of Satan (2 Thess. 2:8-12; Rev. 13:1-18; 19:20). All nations will be deceived by the sorceries and manifestations of demon powers concentrated in future literal Babylon, Rev. 9:20; 14:8; 16:13-16, 19; 18:23; Isa. 47:9-10, 12-13.

If Antichrist can start a religion and martyr millions during the last three and one-half years of this age (Rev. 7:9-17; 13:1-18; 14:9-11; 15:2, 6; 16:13-16; 19:20; 20:4-6), then it stands to reason that Mystery Babylon as a revival of ancient magism backed by a concentration of demon powers dominating the nations of the old Roman Empire territory, from Babylon, could martyr many saints of Jesus during the first three and one-half years of Daniel's 70th Week, and until Antichrist comes to full power over the ten kingdoms of Revised Rome, Rev. 17:1-2, 5-6, 12-17.

It should be understandable that, if Antichrist in a period of three and one-half years, can start a new religion with worship of himself as God (2 Thess. 2:3-4; Rev. 13:1-18), killing multitudes who do not worship him and take his mark, then another religion with headquarters at Babylon could fulfill Rev. 17 during the few years when Antichrist is coming into full power over the ten kingdoms. Both the religions of Babylon and Antichrist, with headquarters at Babylon and Jerusalem, will be demon endued. Satan and demons will give their power to Antichrist for the purpose of such worship and to fulfill Dan. 9:27; 11:37-38; 12:7; Matt. 24:15-28; 2 Thess. 2:1-12; Rev. 13:1-18; 14:9-11; 15:2; 16:2; 18:2, 20:4-6.

Chapter Thirty

THE BEAST THAT CARRIETH HER, Rev. 17:1, 3, 7-17

"And there came one of the seven angels which had the seven vials, and talked with me, saying unto me, Come hither; I will shew thee the judgment of the great whore that sitteth upon many waters: So he carried me away in the spirit into the wilderness: and I saw a woman sit upon a scarlet coloured beast, full of names of blasphemy, having seven heads and ten horns. And the angel said unto me, Wherefore didst thou marvel? I will tell thee the mystery of the woman, and of the beast that carrieth her, which hath the seven heads and ten horns. The beast that thou sawest was, and is not; and shall ascend out of the bottomless pit, and go into perdition: and they that dwell on the earth shall wonder, whose names were not written in the book of life from the foundation of the world, when they behold the beast that was, and is not, and yet is. And here is the mind which hath wisdom. The seven heads are seven mountains, on which the woman sitteth. And there are seven kings: five are fallen, and one is, and the other is not yet come; and when he cometh he must continue a short space. And the beast that was, and is not, even he is the eighth, and is of the seven, and goeth into perdition. And the ten horns which thou sawest are ten kings, which have received no kingdom as yet; but receive power as kings one hour with the beast. These have one mind, and shall give their power and strength unto the beast. These shall make war with the Lamb, and the Lamb shall overcome them: for he is Lord of lords, and King of kings: and they that are with him are called, and chosen, and faithful. And he saith unto me, The waters which thou sawest, where the whore sitteth, are peoples, and multitudes, and nations, and tongues. And the ten horns which thou sawest upon the beast, these shall hate the whore, and shall make her desolate and naked, and shall eat her flesh, and burn her with fire. For God hath put in their hearts to fulfill his will, and to agree, and give their kingdom unto the beast, until the words of God shall be fulfilled," Rev. 17:1, 3, 7-17.

The symbol of the beast is mentioned in the eleventh to the twentieth chapters of Revelation but explained fully in the seventeenth. The descriptions in all these chapters combine to give a thorough understanding of the beast, and its seven heads and ten horns. The Greek word **therion** translated "beast" is used thirty-seven times in this book in connection with this symbol, and designates a wild, untamed, and dangerous animal. It is a fitting symbol of the powers to be arrayed against Christ in the last days.

Sixty Historical and Prophetical Fundamental Facts.

There are sixty historical and prophetical facts given in the book concerning the beast and its seven heads and ten horns which serve as fundamental truths, without which no true and complete understanding of the future beast and its seven heads and ten horns can be had. **All statements concerning the subject must harmonize with these facts, else they are based upon false principles.** The historical facts are given to enable the student to comprehend the prophetical facts governing the reconstruction of the last Gentile kingdom in "the times of the Gentiles" under the direction of the last earthly sovereign, the Antichrist.

The purpose of the vision is not to reveal history, but to enable us to identify the eighth and last kingdom, which will be formed after the rapture. We must not interpret any event of Rev. 4-22 as being fulfilled in past history for they are all yet future after the rapture as proved in chapters one and seven. It is not violating any prophetical principle to predict something future and at the same time give a retrospective of things leading up to that future event. In order for us to properly identify the eighth kingdom of the future, the seven kingdoms that precede the eighth, are mentioned to show that the last one will reign over all the peoples and territories of the preceding ones. **The sixty statements concerning the symbol of the beast in Rev. 11:7-20:10 are as follows:**

1. He is to come out of the bottomless pit, Rev. 11:7; 17:8.

2. He will make war on the two witnesses during the last part of the Week, Rev. 11:7.

3. He will finally overcome and kill them, Rev. 11:7.

4. He will come from the sea of humanity, Rev. 13:1; 17:1, 3, 11, 15.

5. He has seven heads and names of blasphemy written on them, Rev. 13:1; 17:3, 7-11.

6. He has ten horns and on them ten crowns, Rev. 13:1. Cf. Rev. 12:3; 17:12-17; Dan. 7:7, 8, 19-25.

7. He is like a leopard, Rev. 13:2; 17:3. Cf. Dan. 7:6.

8. He has the feet of a bear, Rev. 13:2. Cf. Dan. 7:5.

9. He has a mouth of a lion, Rev. 13:2. Cf. Dan. 7:4.

10. The dragon gives him his power, and his seat (throne), and great authority, Rev. 13:2. Cf. Dan. 8:24; 2 Thess. 2:7-12.

11. One of his heads has been wounded and it will be healed, Rev. 13:3, 12, 14.

12. All the world will wonder after him, Rev. 13:3; 17:8.

13. Many will worship the dragon which will give power to the beast, and they will worship the beast, saying, "Who is like unto the beast? Who is able to make war with him?" Rev. 13:4, 8, 16-18; 14:9-11; 15:2-4; 20:4-6.

14. He will be given a mouth to speak great things and blasphemies, Rev. 13:5. Cf. Dan. 7:8, 11, 20; 11:36.

15. He will be given power for forty-two months, Rev. 13:5.

16. He will blaspheme God, His name, His tabernacle, and those that dwell in heaven, Rev. 13:6.

17. He will make war on the saints, Rev. 13:7. Cf. Dan. 7:19-22.

18. He will overcome the saints and kill them, Rev. 13:7; 14:9-11; 15:2-4; 20:4-6.

19. He will be given power over all the peoples of the ten kingdoms, Rev. 13:1, 7; 17:12-17. Cf. Dan. 7:23, 24, and see chapter twenty-one.

20. Saints are commanded to have patience and faith and not to repay him evil for evil, Rev. 13:10.

21. He will have a co-worker and religious leader in the false prophet who will exercise his power and cause men to worship him, Rev. 13:11-18; 16:13-16; 19:20; 20:10.

22. Miracles will be done in his sight to get the world to worship him, Rev. 13:12-14.

23. An image will be made of him to be worshipped, Rev. 13:14, 15.

24. His image will be given life to speak and cause men to be killed if they refuse to worship the beast and his image, Rev. 13:15.

25. He will have a name, which at present is not known, Rev. 13:17, 18; 15:2.

26. He will have a mark, which at present is not known, Rev. 13:17; 14:9; 15:2; 16:2; 20:4-6.

27. His number, not his mark, or his name, is 666, Rev. 13:16-18; 15:2.

28. These three things—his mark, or his name, or the number of his name—will be forced upon men who must take any one of them in the right hand or forehead, or they will be boycotted and killed, Rev. 13:16-18; 14:9-11; 15:2-4; 20:4-6.

29. He is A MAN, Rev. 13:18; 16:13-16; 19:19-21; 20:10. Cf. Dan. 7:7, 8, 19-27; 8:9, 20-25; 9:26, 27; 11:36-45; Isa. 11:4; 2 Thess. 2:1-12; John 5:43. (See chapter twenty.)

30. Men will be warned by literal angels flying in mid-heaven not to take his mark, or his name, or his number, or they will suffer eternal hell, Rev. 14:9-11.

31. His worship will be so apostate in nature that all who do worship him or take any one of his three brands will be damned in hell forever, Rev. 14:9-11.

32. Many will get the victory over his worship and brands, Rev. 15:2-4.

33. His followers will partake of the vial plagues, Rev. 16:2, 10.

34. He has a throne and a kingdom, Rev. 16:10.

35. He will be in league with, and be possessed with demon powers, to gather the nations who are not under him to Armageddon, Rev. 16:13-16.

36. He carries the woman or great whore, Rev. 17:3, 7.

37. He "was" or had been on the earth before John's day, Rev. 17:8.

38. He "is not," that is, he was not on the earth, but was in the bottomless pit during John's day, Rev. 17:8.

39. He "shall ascend out of the bottomless pit," Rev. 17:8.

40. He will then "go into perdition," or be destroyed at the second advent, Rev. 17:8; 19:19-21; 20:10.

41. "The seven heads are seven mountains, on which the woman sitteth. And there are seven kings" or kingdoms, Rev. 17:9.

42. "Five are fallen"; that is, the first five of these seven kingdoms had passed away before John saw the Revelation, Rev. 17:10. They are Egypt, Assyria, Babylon, Medo-Persia, and Greece.

43. "One is"; that is, the sixth of these seven kingdoms, or the old Roman Empire, was in existence in John's day, Rev. 17:10.

44. "The other is not yet come; and when he cometh he must continue a short space"; that is, the seventh of these seven kingdoms which will be made up of the ten kingdoms inside the old Roman Empire has not yet come, and when the ten kingdoms

are formed they will continue a short time before the "little horn" will arise from among them to get power over them, Rev. 17:10. Cf. Dan. 7:7, 8, 19-27.

45. "The beast that was, and is not, even HE IS THE EIGHTH"; that is, when Antichrist comes out of the ten kingdoms he will get power over them by the middle of the Week and he will form the eighth kingdom, which continues forty-two months, Rev. 17:11; 13:5.

46. He "is of the seven and goeth into perdition"; that is, he is one of the seven, not necessarily of the seventh, Rev. 17:11. He must be of one of the first five that had fallen before John, either of Egypt, Assyria, Babylon, Medo-Persia, or Greece, for the beast "was" or had been before the sixth that was in existence in John's day, and he becomes the eighth following the seventh, which was to come between the sixth and the eighth. It is the eighth kingdom that will fight against Christ at Armageddon and will be destroyed.

47. The ten horns "are ten kings," Rev. 17:12. Cf. Dan. 2:44; 7:7, 8, 19-24.

48. They "have received no kingdom as yet," Rev. 17:12. Cf. Dan. 7:23, 24.

49. They "receive power as kings one hour (Greek, **hora,** hour or period) WITH the beast," Rev. 17:12. Cf. Rev. 13:5.

50. "These have one mind, and shall give their power and strength UNTO THE BEAST," Rev. 17:13, 16, 17. (See chapter twenty-one.)

51. "These shall make war on the Lamb, and the Lamb shall overcome them" at the second advent, so they must all be in existence at that time, Rev. 17:14; 19:19-21. Cf. Dan. 2:44; 7:23-27; 8:20-25; 11:45; 12:7.

52. "These shall hate the whore, and shall make her desolate and naked, and shall eat her flesh, and burn her with fire," Rev. 17:16.

53. "For God hath put in their hearts to fulfill his will, and to agree, and give their kingdom unto the beast, UNTIL the words of God shall be fulfilled," Rev. 17:17.

54. The beast is the commander-in-chief of all armies of the kings of the earth at Armageddon, Rev. 19:19. Cf. Ezek. 38, 39.

55. He mobilizes the armies of the nations to fight against Christ and the armies of heaven at the second advent, Rev. 19:19. Cf. Zech. 14:1-5; Rev. 16:13-16; Ezek. 38, 39.

56. The beast will be "slain" by Christ at His coming, thus proving him to be a mortal man at that time, Rev. 19:20. See Dan. 7:11; Isa. 11:4; 2 Thess. 2:8, 9.

57. He and the false prophet will both be cast into the lake of fire, Rev. 19:20.

58. His armies will be destroyed by Christ and his armies, Rev. 19:20, 21; 17:14. Cf. Ezek. 38:17-21; 2 Thess. 1:7-10; Joel 3.

59. Those whom he kills for not worshipping him will be resur-

rected in the first resurrection and will reign with Christ, Rev. 20:4-6.

60. He and the false prophet will be in the lake of fire for one thousand years before the Devil is cast into that lake and all will "be tormented day and night for ever and ever," Rev. 20:10.

It is clear from these statements that **the beast is not a symbol of only one thing, but of several.** The heads, horns, feet, body, mouth, wounding of one of the heads, etc., are symbolic of different things. The beast itself is entirely different from the seven heads and ten horns which are upon it. Failure to make a distinct difference between him and his heads and horns will lead to the wrong understanding of the beast. That which is represented by the seven heads and ten horns will have passed when the beast appears, for they are upon the beast when he rises, and shows the succession of seven world kingdoms from the first to the last of the history of Israel, before the eighth kingdom comes.

The Beast Symbolizes Three Things:

1. **A human being,** the Antichrist, or beast out of the sea, as dealt with in chapter twenty. Such facts above as in points 4, 10, 12-35, 49-60 prove that a human being is seen in the symbol. He is definitely called "a man," so no true understanding can be had of the beast without recognizing this fact.

2. **A supernatural being,** the beast out of the abyss, as will be dealt with in the following chapters. Such facts as in points 1-3, 35, 37-40, prove that a satanic prince is seen in the symbol.

3. **An empire,** the eighth kingdom, which immediately succeeds the seven heads or kingdoms. Such facts as in points 5-9, 11, 36-38, 41-46, prove that a kingdom is also symbolized by the beast.

Some interpreters have made the mistake of recognizing only a kingdom and not a human, or a supernatural person in the beast. Others recognize only a human being while still others recognize only an earthly king and kingdom and not the satanic powers controlling the kingdom. All these errors have led men to disregard some of the previously mentioned plain facts concerning the beast. When all three things are seen in the symbol and the passages which clearly refer to the one or to the other are distinguished, then a clear understanding of all the facts is gained. The basis of discriminating these three things is taking each passage as applicable to the one which will make the reading most clear. Some passages apply to all three things, while others apply to one or two. Hence, the beast out of the abyss, the beast out of the sea, and the beast as the eighth kingdom are all different things, but all three are to be recognized in the one symbol, the beast.

Chapter Thirty-one

THE BEAST OUT OF THE ABYSS

"And when they (two witnesses) shall have finished their testimony, the beast that ascendeth out of the bottomless pit shall make war against them, and shall overcome them, and kill them. . . . And the angel said unto me, Wherefore didst thou marvel? I will tell thee the mystery of the woman, and of the beast that carrieth her, **which hath** the seven heads and ten horns. The beast that thou sawest was, and is not: and shall ascend out of the bottomless pit, and go into perdition: and they that dwell upon the earth shall wonder, whose names were not written in the book of life from the foundation of the world, when they behold the beast that was, and is not, and yet is (shall be)," Rev. 11:7; 17:7, 8.

Many hypotheses have been advanced concerning the identity of the beast out of the abyss. Some hold that he is a human spirit who is now confined there and who will come out and exist again as the Antichrist. Others hold that he represents a revival of a kingdom once existent, and which will exist again. But the Scriptures indicate something more than a mere revival of a certain kingdom. How could a kingdom be confined to the abyss for centuries and come out again as a kingdom and go into destruction a second time? Only a person can be the reference in such statements as quoted above. If this is true then it lies between a human or a supernatural spirit who has once existed on earth, who is at present confined in the abyss, and who will exist again on the earth in the last days. Those who believe that the beast is a human spirit now in the abyss advance almost as many different men as there are interpreters.

It is believed by this school of interpreters that when this human spirit (whoever he may be) is reincarnated as the Antichrist, he will grow to maturity; that in the middle of the Week he will be slain by an assassin; that his body will lie in state for three days and then be raised from the dead; and that Satan at that time will incarnate himself in this man who will then become an immortal being. This, they claim, will be Satan's imitation of the resurrection of Christ and proves that Antichrist will not be an ordinary mortal during the last three and one-half years, and further shows why he was cast "alive" into the lake of fire.

However, it cannot be proved from Scripture that any one of these men will be the beast out of the abyss, nor can it be proved that any one of them will be the Antichrist. Neither the beast of the abyss nor the Antichrist will be a reincarnated human being or any other kind of reincarnated being. **It may be well at this time to prove that the beast of the abyss and the Antichrist are two distinct persons.** If this can be done then all the arguments of the above school are of no value in identifying the beast of the abyss, and there is no ground for believing that the Antichrist will be a reincarnation of some historical man and that he will be assassinated and resurrected as an immortal being. **The following points prove that the beast out of the abyss and the Antichrist are two distinct persons:**

1. It has been proved by the sixty facts of the previous chapter that the symbol of the beast represents three things: first, a

human being who is the beast out of the sea of humanity; secondly, a supernatural being who is the beast out of the abyss; thirdly, an empire which is the eighth kingdom composed of many peoples, Rev. 17:1, 3, 7, 9-11, 15. Thus, the beast out of the abyss and the Antichrist are not required by Scripture to be the same person.

2. The Antichrist is to be an ordinary mortal throughout his life until the Battle of Armageddon when he will be killed as other men by Christ at His coming to the earth. The following quotations prove this: "He (Christ) shall smite the earth with the rod of His mouth, and with the breath of His lips shall He slay the wicked," Isa. 11:4. "I beheld even until the beast was **slain**, and his **body destroyed**, and given to the burning flame," Dan. 7:11; Rev. 19:20. "He (Antichrist) shall be **broken** (slain as in Dan. 8:8, 22; 11:4, 22) without hand," Dan. 8:25. "And then shall that wicked (Antichrist) be revealed, whom the Lord shall **consume** (Greek, destroy) with the spirit of his mouth, and shall **destroy** (Greek, to cut or split in two; to halve; divide) with the brightness of his coming," 2 Thess. 2:8. Antichrist must be a mortal in order to fulfill these statements. He is expressly called "a man" in Rev. 13:14-18; 2 Thess. 2:3, 4.

3. The doctrine of reincarnation is not taught in Scripture. Certainly such a doctrine cannot be based upon the mere fact that a spirit is to come out of the abyss. To be reincarnated one must go through the process of a rebirth and growth to maturity as he did when he was born before. This would make Antichrist a baby at least twice, and if he were to die by an assassin in the middle of the Week and also be slain by Christ, he would have to die at least three times. These ideas contradict Scripture, for "it is appointed unto men once to die, but after this the judgment," Heb. 9:27. This passage does not teach that after death there can be a reincarnation and another death. The men mentioned previously are no exception to this divine rule. The only exception to this rule will be those who are to be raptured without seeing death at the first resurrection, 1 Cor. 15:51-58. After death comes the resurrection when the individual will be raised just as full grown as he was at death, and when that is done he will have an immortal body and cannot die, 1 Cor. 15:20-23, 34-51; John 5:28, 29. Hence, there is no room for a doctrine that a mature human spirit can become a baby spirit again, and be born in the flesh and grow to maturity a second time and die again. If Antichrist were to be a baby and grow to maturity in his second life on earth what would be the purpose of his being another person reincarnated? Why could not any baby grow to maturity and fulfill the same things that a reincarnated baby could, seeing his success does not depend upon past maturity and experience? If this one human can be reincarnated then it stands to reason that others can also be and, if we admit the doctrine of reincarnation, we need not condemn the Hindu and others

who believe in such. Therefore, we believe that the Antichrist is a mere man who will be born on earth in the last days for the first time, and that he will not be the beast out of the abyss.

4. It is clear from the Scripture that the abyss is not the place for departed human spirits; therefore, a human spirit cannot come out of the abyss. The abyss is the prison of demon spirits. Luke 8:31; Rev. 9:1-21. It is also the place of the present confinement of certain satanic princes, Rev. 9:11; 11:7; 17:8. How many other angels are there is not known. It will be Satan's prison for one thousand years, Rev. 20:1-10. Judging from these Scriptures it seems clear that the abyss is reserved for Satan and his demon and angelic following, but never as the place for human spirits. Human spirits went into paradise and hell before the resurrection of Christ, Luke 16:19-31; Ps. 16:10; Luke 23:43; Rev. 20:11-15. At the resurrection of Christ He led all righteous souls out of paradise under the earth and took them into heaven with Him, so when a Christian dies now he goes to be "with Christ" until the first resurrection, Eph. 4:7-11; Heb. 2:14; Phil. 1:21; 2 Cor. 5:8; Rev. 6:9-11. The wicked human spirits still go to hell as before and Judas or no other man is excepted. From this, we conclude that no human spirit is now in the abyss to come out as the beast.

5. There is no Scripture to prove that the Antichrist will be different from any other natural man as to his being, birth, death, etc. He will merely be used by satanic powers in the last days. Neither God nor Satan will have to call back from the dead any man who has lived in order to fulfill prophecy. If some man in history could fulfill the necessary requirements why could not some future man do so? No reincarnation has ever been necessary for the operation of supernatural powers in the world. Neither will such be necessary in the future. The only necessary thing will be complete submission to the will of the operator.

6. That Antichrist is to be assassinated in the middle of the Week and rise from the dead as an immortal being and an incarnation of Satan is unscriptural. The wounding of one of the heads on the beast and its being healed again does not teach this. One vital thing which some interpreters have failed to see is that it was one of the seven heads on the beast that was wounded to death and not the beast itself. The angel explained to John that the seven heads were seven kingdoms and that they all were to precede the beast itself, which is the eighth kingdom ruled by the Antichrist and the satanic prince of the abyss, Rev. 17:9-11. Thus we see that the Antichrist who is the king of the eighth kingdom will not be assassinated at all, and therefore, cannot be resurrected in the middle of the Week. Antichrist will never be an incarnation of Satan, for we see the dragon or Satan as a separate being from the Antichrist throughout the period he is supposed to be incarnated in Antichrist, 2 Thess. 2:8, 9; Rev. 13:1-4; 16:13-16; 20:10. Hence, Satan could not be incarnate in Antichrist and exist as a separate being outside of him.

Chapter Thirty-two

IDENTIFICATION OF THE BEAST OUT OF THE ABYSS

We firmly believe that the beast out of the abyss represents a mighty supernatural satanic prince and not a human spirit. We do not believe that this spirit is to be incarnated in any human body and become the Antichrist, but that he will be the ruling prince under the guidance of Satan, dominating the Antichrist and exalting him as the earthly king over the eighth and last kingdom at the end of the age. We further believe that he ruled one of the first five kingdoms, which had fallen before John's day and is represented by the first five heads on the beast; that when his kingdom fell, he was cast into the abyss and confined there during the sixth kingdom (the Roman Empire), which was the one that existed in John's day; that he will still be confined there until the formation of the ten kingdoms as the seventh kingdom; that he will be loosed out of the abyss during the existence of the seventh, cause the rise of Antichrist out of the ten kingdoms, and revive the kingdom of Greece he ruled before the sixth and seventh; and that this kingdom will become the eighth and last kingdom headed by Antichrist who will fight with Christ at Armageddon.

This is what the angel meant when he said that the beast "was (had existed on earth before John), and is not (on the earth in John's day); and shall ascend out of the bottomless pit (in the last days to revive the kingdom he ruled before he was confined to the abyss) and go into perdition." This spirit will control the Antichrist through demons, thus making him the embodiment of wickedness and the manifestation of satanic power. It is represented by the symbol of the beast out of the abyss which will cause the rise of Antichrist, who in turn is symbolized by the beast out of the sea of humanity, reviving and forming the beast, the eighth kingdom. This kingdom is also symbolized by the beast. All three things make up the powers represented by the one symbol

It is the beast out of the abyss that will make war on the two witnesses through Antichrist. In this fact we see the cruel operations of satanic powers through the Antichrist and his kingdom by the combination of human and supernatural powers. But only when their testimony is finished will God remove His protecting hand from them. Kingdoms of this world have always been controlled by supernatural powers and the things which transpire on earth are really the result of what transpires in heaven in the battles lost or won between the good and bad spirits of Satan and God. The Devil controls the kingdoms of this world. He offered them to Christ, who did not deny this claim of Satan, Luke 4:5, 6. God, during this present time, interferes with the plans of Satan in the kingdoms of this world to make possible the fulfillment of His prophetic word which Satan and evil forces are continually longing to see fail, hence, the battles in the heavenlies.

The battle between Satan and God can be traced throughout the Bible from Genesis to Revelation. God is trying to bring men back to the place where they were before they fell and in order to do so must continually counteract the powers of Satan who tries in every conceivable way to hinder this plan. The battle in general throughout the Old Testament was over the coming of the seed of the woman and the fulfillment of God's purpose concerning Israel, Gen. 3:15; 12:1 and throughout the Old Testament. The great weapon used by the Devil was the kingdoms of this world whom he inspired time and again to destroy Israel from the face of the earth that Christ should never come pronouncing doom upon him.

From the beginning of Israel's history in Genesis 12 on through the Old Testament there were five great kingdoms which were used of Satan for this purpose. However, God took advantage of Satan's efforts and used these same nations to chasten Israel when it became necessary to bring her to repentance. When one of them overstepped itself in God's plan for His people, God had to overthrow it by another, and in order to do this, had to deal with Satan in the heavenlies. These five kingdoms were Egypt, Assyria, Babylon, Medo-Persia and Greece and its divisions, making up the five that had already fallen before John. The sixth was the Old Roman Empire which existed at the time of John and which scattered Israel to the four winds of heaven. The seventh will be that same empire in the form of ten kingdoms. It will also persecute Israel. The beast will be the eighth immediately succeeding the seventh and will become the greatest and most bitter persecutor of Israel of all the eight kingdoms. It will try to carry out Satan's original plan to destroy Israel and thwart God's eternal purpose concerning them and the earth as promised to their fathers.

In every time of crisis in the history of Israel and these kingdoms, God has intervened at the proper moment. Thus, Israel has been spared and preserved in the past and will also be preserved in the future as God has promised. Satan, besides using kingdoms to destroy and oppress Israel and to thwart God's promise, has also caused Israel to sin so that God Himself has at times cursed them. But it has been during these times that God has made the very tool, which the Devil used to destroy Israel, to chasten them and bring them to repentance. Such will be the case in the final repentance of Israel in the tribulation.

One can readily see these facts illustrated in the history of Israel as found in the Pentateuch and the historical books of the Old Testament, and especially in the prophecies, where God tries by the mouths of His servants, to bring Israel to repentance by threatening punishment by the goad of foreign foes. In the Bible we have numerous passages showing the operation of satanic powers over the different kingdoms of the world in attempts to thwart God's eternal purpose in the earth concerning

Israel. Also we have the record of the opposition of God's spirit
forces toward these satanic powers in carrying out His purpose in
the earth, Isa. 14:4-21; 24:21-23; 25:7; Ezek. 28:11-17; Dan. 2:19-
23, 28, 31-45; 4:25-37; 5:18-31; 7:1-28; 8:1-26; 9:24-27; 10:1-12:13;
Joel 3; Zech. 14; Luke 4:5, 6; John 12:31; 2 Cor. 4:4; Eph. 2:2;
6:11-17; 2 Thess. 2; Rev. 11:15; 13:1-18; etc. These are just a
few references clearly setting forth this truth. This is plainly illustrated and the beast out of the abyss is plainly identified in
the book of Daniel in conjunction with Revelation. In this book
we see the rise and fall of several empires which were used to
carry out God's purpose in chastening or delivering Israel from
Daniel's time to the coming of the Messiah. When one kingdom
fails to carry out God's purpose He then chooses another as illustrated in 2 Kings 23:29-24:10. In Dan. 2; 7; 8; 9; 10-12, we
have really six world kingdoms which were used to oppress Israel: Babylon as the head of gold and the lion; Medo-Persia as
the silver, the bear and the ram; Greece as the brass, the
leopard and the he-goat; Rome as the iron and the terrible
beast; Revised Rome as the ten toes and the ten horns; and Revived Grecia as the kingdom of the little horn out of the ten
horns of Dan. 7 and out of the four horns of Dan. 8, and as the
king of the north (Syria) in Dan. 11.

In Dan. 10:1-11:1 we have the pivot passage of all the Bible concerning the supernatural princes under Satan who rule different
kingdoms, and concerning God's method of overruling the rulers
of these kingdoms to fulfill prophecy. This clearly shows how and
why the spirit in the abyss was confined there and incidently
gives his identity. This is not the final reason for this conclusion
but it does settle the fact that there are such supernatural princes
over the different kingdoms. Whatever we may conclude about
the beast out of the abyss we must associate him with one of the
first five kingdoms symbolized by the first five heads on the
beast. This in itself excludes Judas, Nero, Nimrod, Napoleon, and
many other men whom some advance as the beast of the abyss.
This spirit, then, must be one who has ruled either Egypt, Assyria,
Babylon, Medo-Persia or Greece, for they are the first five heads
on the beast. Let it be remembered that he was on earth before
the sixth, was not on earth during the sixth, that he will come
out of the abyss during the seventh and that he will revive a kingdom he once controlled which will become the eighth and the succession of the seventh kingdom.

Gabriel, who was sent to show Daniel the vision of the kingdom
that was to oppress Israel in the last days, was hindered by the
spirit ruler of the kingdom of Persia, the fourth head on the
beast, which was in existence at the time of this vision. Gabriel
said to Daniel, "From the first day that thou didst set thy heart to
understand, and to chasten thyself before thy God, thy words
were heard, and I am come for thy words. But THE PRINCE OF
THE KINGDOM OF PERSIA withstood (detained) me one and

twenty days: but, lo, MICHAEL, ONE OF THE CHIEF PRINCES
(of God), came to help me: and I remained there with the KINGS
OF PERSIA" (until Michael delivered me), Dan. 10:12-14.

In Dan. 10:20, 21 there is another indisputable reference to supernatural princes over kingdoms. If this is true of these few
mentioned, surely it is true of all other kingdoms and principalities
in the world that have existed or will exist until all "the kingdoms
of this world" become the kingdoms of Christ at His coming. The
same angel that was detained by "the PRINCE OF THE KING-
DOM OF PERSIA" said to Daniel, "Knowest thou wherefore I
come to thee? and now will I return to FIGHT with THE PRINCE
OF PERSIA: and when I am gone forth, lo, THE PRINCE OF
GRECIA will come. But I will shew thee that which is noted in
the Scripture of truth: and there is none that holdeth with me in
these things, but MICHAEL YOUR (Israel's) PRINCE."

The eleventh chapter, a continuation of the angel's message,
reads, "Also I (Gabriel) in the first year of Darius the Mede (five
years before this) even I, stood to confirm and to strengthen him
(Michael was the prince of Israel who overthrew the prince of
Babylon in order that the prince of Persia might come, whose
kingdom was to deliver the Israelites and permit them to return
to their own land)," Dan. 11:1. This last verse shows that Michael
was not the prince to withstand the prince of Persia, but that
Gabriel was the choice this time. Gabriel had helped Michael
overthrow the prince of Babylon in order to fulfill the prophecy of
the overthrow of the Babylonian Empire and the establishment of
the Persian, as was previously revealed to Daniel and Nebuchadnezzar, so in turn Michael helped him in his responsibility of opposing the prince of Persia. This further emphasizes the fact that
different good and bad angels have under their control certain
responsibilities in certain kingdoms. Note the divine and angelic
appearances in the book of Daniel, which show what kind of
princes these are: Dan. 3:25; 4:13, 17, 23; 6:22; 7:17; 8:13, 14, 16-
26; 9:21; 10:4-8, 10, 16, 18, 20, 21; 11:1; 12:1, 5, 6.

These passages show that God ordains certain angels and sends
them forth to cause the rise and fall of certain kingdoms in order
to fulfill prophecy. They also reveal that Satan's princes over
these kingdoms try to hinder the rise and fall of kingdoms to hinder God's plan. Dan. 10:12-14 shows that there was a war in
heaven between the prince of Persia and Gabriel and that Gabriel
was detained twenty-one days and could not get through to
Daniel until Michael, the prince that protects Israel, came to help
him. Together they defeated the prince of Persia. If there was
such a war, of twenty-one days in length, over a mere answer to
prayer, what kind of wars and how long must they be over the
overthrow of a kingdom?

This passage first speaks of one "prince of Persia"; then it
speaks of "kings of Persia." The difference between these two

terms is easily explained, for the Hebrew word **sar** generally rendered "prince" and "princes" in this book as in Dan. 1:7, 8, 10, 11, 18; 8:11, 25; 9:6, 8; 10:13, 20, 21; 11: 5, 8, 18, 22; 12:1 means a head person of any rank or class, a captain, chief, master, ruler, prince, etc. The prince of the kingdom of Persia has reference to the one satanic spirit ruler who was chief of the whole kingdom and as such was responsible to Satan. The Hebrew word **melek** means king, royalty and could mean in this case subordinate princes under the chief prince, or it could refer to the prince of the Medes and the prince of the Persians who were over the dual kingdom, the prince of Persia being the greater of the two, as was the case in the earthly kingdom. Another translation of the kings of Persia is "I remained there with the royalty of Persia," for it was the prince of Persia that detained him during the twenty-one days.

Not only does the Bible teach that over every kingdom there are good and bad spirits, but also over each individual person on earth there are good and bad spirits who are trying to dominate his life for good or bad, Ps. 78:49; 91:11; Matt. 18:10; Rom. 8:38; Heb. 1:14; Eph. 2:2; 6:12; etc.

Dan. 10:20, 21 brings out the same thought of only one chief ruler or prince over each kingdom and further enables us to ascertain whether there was more than one prince of the kingdom of Persia. Here Gabriel, after being delivered from the royalty of Persia and fulfilling his mission to the prophet, said, "And now will I return and fight with THE PRINCE OF PERSIA: and when I am gone forth (to overthrow the prince of Persia in order that the next empire that was to succeed Persia might come), lo, THE PRINCE OF GRECIA shall come"; i.e., when I conquer the spirit prince that controls the kingdom of Persia under Satan, the spirit prince that controls the kingdom of Grecia under Satan shall come and rule these territories and shall fulfill "the Scripture of truth."

The Scripture of truth concerning the overthrow of Persia by Grecia was given during the third year of the reign of Belshazzar, the vicegerent of the king of Babylon, Dan. 8:1-26. At the time of this prophecy (Dan. 10:1-12:13) in the third year of Cyrus, king of Persia, Gabriel told Daniel that Persia was soon to fall, that Grecia would come, and that the one helping him in the fulfillment of these things was none other than "MICHAEL, YOUR PRINCE"; i.e., the prince of Israel, Dan. 12:1; Rev. 12:7. Gabriel further told Daniel how many kings were to reign in Persia before the kingdom was to be overthrown, Dan. 11:2. The mighty king of Dan. 11:3 was Alexander the Great, who overthrew the Persians so easily because it was God's time to fulfill prophecy and because the satanic power ruling Persia had been defeated by Gabriel and his hosts in the heavenlies.

It is doubtless clear to the reader that a mighty satanic prince is to work as a colleague of the earthly Antichrist in the future as has been the case of all mighty rulers of kingdoms in times past.

We conclude, therefore, that the beast of the abyss is this satanic prince of Grecia who will inspire the Antichrist and use him in the formation of the eighth kingdom, which will be a revival of the kingdom he controlled before he was defeated in the heavenlies and cast into the abyss.

We affirm that the beast out of the abyss is "THE PRINCE OF GRECIA" and advance the following points as proof:

1. The last visions of Daniel concern the Grecian Empire, its four divisions, and the rise of the Antichrist out of one of them. Out of the 155 verses of Daniel describing "the times of the Gentiles," from Daniel's time to the coming of Christ, 125 are devoted to the Grecian Empire. In the vision of Dan. 2, of the fourteen verses speaking of Babylon, Medo-Persia, Greece, Rome, and Revised Rome, six speak of Greece. In the twenty-eight verses of Dan. 7, only three speak of Greece, but nine speak of the "little horn" which will be the future king of Revised Grecia. In the twenty-seven verses of Dan. 8, the "he-goat" or Greece, and the king of Greece in the last days are the main objects of the vision. The purpose of the whole chapter is to show the overthrow of Persia and the existence of Greece in the last days under four divisions with the Antichrist coming out of one of these divisions. The seventy-nine verses of Dan. 10-12 are all devoted to show that the Antichrist will come from one of the four Grecian divisions and they show just which one; namely, the Syrian. These facts are no mere accidents and go far to prove that the prince of Grecia will be the spirit out of the abyss and that the eighth kingdom will be Revived Greece under the Antichrist.

2. The fact that the Antichrist, who is the earthly head of the eighth kingdom, will come out of the Syrian division of Greece seems conclusive proof that the prince of Grecia is the spirit out of the abyss and not the Egyptian, Assyrian, Babylonian, and Persian princes. Since there is no intimation that the first four kingdoms will be revived as in the case of Greece, and since the spirit out of the abyss could not have been the prince of Rome, because of his presence in the abyss during the existence of Rome, it follows that he will be the prince of Grecia.

3. The body of the beast is "like a leopard." In Daniel, the leopard symbolizes the Grecian kingdom, showing that the kingdom of Antichrist, or the eighth and last kingdom, is basically Grecian in character and policy and in its attitude towards Israel as foretold of the Syrian division in Dan. 8:9-14, 20-25; 9:27; 11:21-12:7; Rev. 13; etc. If it is true that the beast is Grecian, being "like a leopard" then it must be true that the spirit of the abyss is the prince of Grecia.

4. In Joel 3:6 and Zech. 9:13 we have two definite prophecies of the Grecian Empire in the last days under Antichrist and at the time of the deliverance of Israel from the nations at the return of Christ. These passages require the existence of Greece as an empire under Antichrist.

Chapter Thirty-three

THE SEVEN HEADS UPON THE BEAST

"And here is the mind which hath wisdom. The seven heads are seven mountains, on which the woman sitteth. And there are seven kings: five are fallen, and one is, and the other is not yet come; and when he cometh, he must continue a short space. And the beast that was, and is not, even he is the eighth, and is of the seven, and goeth into perdition," Rev. 17:9-11.

In explaining the seven heads on the beast according to the R. V., the angel says, "The seven heads are seven mountains on which the woman sitteth, and they are seven kings." This rendering is also that of many other versions which are in harmony with the literal translation as follows, "The seven heads are seven mountains ... and are seven kings." Then the seven heads symbolize seven mountains and the seven mountains, seven kingdoms. If the seven kings are not a further explanation of the seven heads and mountains, then they have been thrust into the interpretation of the seven heads and have no connection with the subject at all. Then in that case, all that follows concerning the seven kings is no part of the explanation which the angel promised John of the seven heads.

We have in these verses the divine explanation of the seven heads which are seven kings or kingdoms. The words "kings" and "kingdoms" are used interchangeably in Scripture, Dan. 2:37, 38 with 2:39; and 7:3, 23, 24 with 7:17. This excludes the idea that the seven heads are seven literal hills on which literal Rome is built.

If these seven heads are seven hills on which the city Rome is built we would have to believe that five of these hills had flattened out before John, for "five are fallen." Rome was on only one hill in John's day, for only "one is," and that hill was to be flattened out and Rome was to be moved on to the seventh hill and then after that was to be moved on to the eighth hill, for "the beast is the eighth." Rev. 17:9-11.

Such an idea is foreign to every phrase of language used in this explanation. Mountains in symbolic passages refer to kings and kingdoms, Jer. 51:25; Dan. 2:35, 45. **We advance the idea that the seven heads are Egypt, Assyria, Babylon, Medo-Persia, Greece, Rome and the future Revised Roman Empire, and that the beast itself is the eighth and final empire, which will be the Revived Grecian Kingdom** immediately following the Revised Roman Empire. **We give the following points as proof:**

1. There are no other kingdoms capable of fulfilling the requirements in the sixty previous statements about the beast and its seven heads, as can readily be seen by choosing any other set of seven kingdoms in an attempt to harmonize them with these statements.

2. All admit that the rise of the lion, bear, leopard, and terrible beast out of the sea in Dan. 7 symbolizes the birth of four great world kingdoms through the medium of supernatural powers working in and through human leaders. The ribs in the mouth of

229

the bear, the four heads on the leopard, the ten horns on the terrible beast and the little horn coming up among them, etc., are all different from the beasts themselves. If this is true of these beasts in Daniel, why not of the beast with its seven heads and ten horns in Revelation?

The fact that the beast was "like a leopard" and had the stamp of the lion and bear shows that at its rise it will have the elements of Babylon, Medo-Persia, and Greece, but that it will be mainly Grecian. This further proves that these cannot be certain kingdoms over which the whore has ruled since John. Why should we pick out seven of the many kingdoms over which the pope has ruled, when they are wholly alien to Israel, and the fulfillment of prophecy, and are not even mentioned in Scripture? We find the above kingdoms mentioned in Scripture and so have a more sure foundation.

When we see the mention of a leopard, a lion, a bear, horns, etc., in the New Testament as the symbol of a kingdom and its ruler, we should immediately look back to the meaning of the same things in the Old Testament. Especially, should we do this when Daniel portrayed the very empires that were to be from his time on to the Millennium. The lion of Dan. 7 had only one head which shows only one kingdom, while the leopard had four heads showing the formation of four kingdoms out of that one. The terrible beast had one head, but ten horns, showing the coming of ten kingdoms out of that one kingdom. Since this is true, and is recognized by prophetical students, the same can also be easily seen in the seven heads and ten horns that the beast of Revelation has.

There is, however, this difference. Since the beast will be the eighth and the succession of the seventh, he will not be the first of a succession of eight kingdoms, but the last. Therefore, his heads and horns are historical in that they represent kingdoms before him while those on the beasts of Daniel were to follow the beasts themselves and were prophetical of kingdoms after them. The beast of Revelation as a leopard or Grecian kingdom must be a revival of Greece or one of the seven heads, while the beasts of Dan. 7 were not revivals of their heads, but the sources of them.

3.   The entire ten kingdoms, which make the seventh head, will be given to the Antichrist whose kingdom becomes the eighth. This seventh kingdom will be a revised form of the sixth. The eighth would surely not be a revival of the one already revised, so it must be a revival of one of the five before the sixth, which was the one in existence in John's day. The sixth, seventh, and eighth being identified as great world kingdoms opposing Israel, the first five must also be of the same nature and not therefore five over which the whore has reigned since the sixth or Old Rome. We must look then for five world kingdoms before Rome and the only five there could possibly be either in history or in Scripture whom God has used to chasten Israel, were the successive king-

doms of Egypt, Assyria, Babylon, Medo-Persia, and Greece which were fallen before John's day, and before the sixth or Rome which was in John's day.

This tracing of the heads back to Egypt is not violating one fundamental principle of prophetic interpretation since the angel explained to John that the beast will be the eighth and the last of a succession of eight world kingdoms. This symbol of the beast and its seven heads depicts all the Gentile world kingdoms in the whole length of "the times of the Gentiles." These times of the Gentiles do not begin with Babylon and Nebuchadnezzar as is generally taught, but they go back to the first oppression of Israel in Egypt. Daniel saw only "the times of the Gentiles" from his time onward as he was picturing what was to befall Israel after this day, but there is no hint that he saw all "the times of the Gentiles."

4. The other explanation of the seven heads advanced by the historical school is given as follows. The Lord desired to portray seven successive kingdoms, each rising out of the territory of its predecessor, each distinct in language and laws as was Egypt, Assyria, etc. These kingdoms have all existed since John and have carried the women in their turn. The woman (Romanism) did not come into existence until a few centuries after John, so the seven heads could not have existed before.

The first kingdom to carry her was that of Justinian or the eastern part of the Roman Empire from 533-38 A.D. and when that kingdom betrayed her she entered her first valley with no government supporting her. The second head was the Holy Roman Empire under Charlemagne who was crowned by the pope, 800 A.D. When this one declined she was in the valley again. The third head was the kingdom of Otto the Great, who was crowned by the pope, 962 A.D. The third valley was a great struggle between the pope and certain kings. The pope came out victorious over Frederick II, 1230 A.D., the fourth head. This kingdom fell and the woman was again in the valley. Charles V was crowned in 1520 when the woman ascended the fifth kingdom. The fifth kingdom received the "deadly wound" at the hand of the Protestants and the woman was again in the valley. The sixth kingdom was Austria who carried the woman. The seventh was to "continue a short space" and was fulfilled in the brief support of the church by Napoleon and then the woman was in the valley the seventh time. The eighth kingdom is yet future and will be a revival of the fifth or the German Empire of Charles V who will fight against Christ at Armageddon.

If these interpreters are to be accepted as right then we are compelled to believe that the kingdoms of Justinian, Charlemagne, Otto the Great, Frederick, and Charles V existed before John received the Revelation because the angel said to John, "Five are fallen." We must also believe that the sixth or Austrian kingdom was in existence in John's day for "one is." And we must further admit that the seventh or the kingdom of Napoleon was the only one to exist after John's day for "one is not yet come and when he cometh he must continue a short space."

These facts given by the angel are utterly irreconcilable with the above theory as well as many other theories concerning the beast. Again, the Bible contradicts the fact that the eighth head is to be a revival of the kingdom of Charles V because the eighth kingdom is to be a revival of one of the five kingdoms that had "fallen" before John's day, or before the Old Roman Empire which ruled the world in John's day, while Charles V reigned about fourteen centuries after John. Then too, the ten kings, who will give their power to the beast for forty-two months, 1,260 literal days, or three and one-half years, are to rise out of the Old Roman Kingdom and form the kingdoms from which Antichrist is to arise, whose kingdom will immediately become the eighth. The Bible does not concern itself with kingdoms appearing between the old Roman and Revised Roman Empires.

The main argument of this school lies in the fact that the woman rides each head in succession, and therefore, since she did not come into existence until after John, the seven heads must also be since John. This is logical if it were true that she rides each head, but that is not true. The woman sits on the heads only in the sense that they are upon the beast, or the symbol of the eighth kingdom, upon which she really will sit. In Rev. 17:1 she is sitting upon "many waters" which are explained in Rev. 17:15 as being many nations, which are in turn explained to be the "scarlet coloured beast . . . that carrieth her, which hath the seven heads and ten horns," Rev. 17:3, 7. When she sits on the beast, which has the seven heads she also sits upon the heads, which will be the structure of the eighth kingdom at that time.

Jesus Christ is not showing John that the woman and the beast have both existed throughout the length of the seven kingdoms. He is revealing the fact that the beast is the eighth in a succession of eight kingdoms in the whole length of the times of the Gentiles (Rev. 17:11); that the woman is a great religious system with headquarters in Babylon; and that she will dominate the future ten kingdoms of Revised Rome after the rapture of the Church and during the first half of the Week, while the eighth kingdom is being formed by the Antichrist, Rev. 17:1, 3, 7, 12-17. He is showing John what will happen after the rapture of the Church when the "THINGS WHICH MUST BE HEREAFTER" the churches will be fulfilled, and not a single detail of what will happen between the great whore and the beast prior to the rapture.

The ten horns on the dragon are not crowned, but those on the beast are, which clearly reveals that the Devil will give his power over the ten kings of Revised Rome to the Antichrist who will rule these kingdoms for the last three and one-half years of this age, Rev. 13:2, 5; 17:8-17; 2 Thess. 2:8-12; Dan. 8:24; 11:38. Neither the beast as the eighth kingdom, nor its king, the Antichrist, has existed throughout the length of all these seven kingdoms. The ten kings of the seventh kingdom, and the Antichrist of the eighth kingdom, as well as the domination of the ten kings by the whore, and her destruction by the ten kings and the Antichrist are future and all these "THINGS" will be fulfilled after the rapture, unless it be that the ten kingdoms should be formed before the rapture. We cannot be certain about this last point because the rapture can take place any moment without any sign coming to pass or any prophecy being fulfilled. It can happen either before or after the formation of the ten kingdoms, this being the only limitation, that it must happen before the revelation of the Antichrist and the Seventieth Week of Daniel 9:27, as we have already seen.

5. The fact that the dragon and the beast will in the future put forth every effort to destroy Israel seems to prove that Egypt, Assyria, etc., are the seven heads. This will be the last and final super-effort of the dragon to carry out his agelong purpose of destroying Israel which began with these seven kingdoms. These are the only kingdoms mentioned in the Bible as carrying out the dragon's purpose along this line.

6. The fact that the clay, iron, brass, silver, and gold in the image will be destroyed together at the return of Christ shows that elements of all those kingdoms symbolized by those metals in Dan. 2 will be inherent in the beast which will go "into perdition" or destruction. That they will be destroyed together is further proved by the destruction of the beast and its seven heads and ten horns together, by Christ at His coming. From these facts also, we conclude that the seven heads of the symbol represent Egypt, Assyria, Babylon, Medo-Persia, Greece, Rome, and Revised Rome, all of which are required to run their course before the beginning of the beast or eighth kingdom ruled by Antichrist and the spirit of the abyss, and that they are the only kingdoms which will harmonize with the revelation of the beast and its heads.

7. "The name of blasphemy" further identifies the seven heads and the beast itself. In Rev. 13:1 we read "upon his heads the name (names) of blasphemy" and in Rev. 17:3 we read that the beast itself was "full of names of blasphemy." These two verses show that all eight kingdoms were and will be blasphemous kingdoms or controlled by blasphemous kings. One can readily see from Bible history the blasphemous attitude of Egypt, Assyria, Babylon, Medo-Persia, Greece, and Rome, and from prophecy one can see the same characteristic in the future Revised Roman and Revived Grecian kingdoms. Practically all kings of the six kingdoms of the past have assumed the title of God and have been worshipped as God. This was common according to the history of the political and religious worship of these kingdoms. See Rev. 13:5, 6; Dan. 7:9, 11, 20, 25; 11:36; 2 Thess. 2:4 for prophecy of this in the life of Antichrist.

Chapter Thirty-four

THE SEVEN MOUNTAIN KINGDOMS AND ISRAEL

The seven kingdoms represented by the seven heads on the beast and the dragon are seven kingdoms coexistent with Israel from her beginning until the existence of the beast or eighth kingdom. These are not only mentioned in conjunction with Israel as her oppressors but without fail, the existence of every one of the seven, as well as the eighth, is foretold to be in the last days in connection with Israel. This further helps us to understand how all seven will be in the eighth as to territory and peoples.

I. The First Mountain Kingdom and Israel.

Egypt was the first world kingdom to oppress Israel in "the times of the Gentiles," which is that period beginning with Israel's history in Egypt and continuing to the coming of her Messiah.

The words "Egypt" and "Egyptian," are found in the Bible about 731 times. Practically every time, they are used in connection with Israel. Even until the establishment of Rome, Egypt was Israel's most bitter enemy, with intermittent periods of friendship. The following are the main points in history and prophecy concerning Egypt and Israel.

1. Egypt was the place for the multiplication and first oppression of Israel, Gen. 15:13, 14; Gen. 37 to Exod. 15.

2. Egypt received mention in Solomon's time, six hundred years after the exodus, 1 Kings 3:1-3; 9:16; 11:1-40; 12:1-34.

3. Egypt was used to chasten Judah in Rehoboam's time, 1 Kings 14.

4. Egypt soon after this invaded Judah, 2 Chron. 14:9-12; 16:7-9.

5. Both Israel and Judah trusted Egypt for help in times of oppression from other nations, 2 Kings 17; 18:21-19:38; Isa. 30, 31.

6. Egypt again invaded Judah, 2 Kings 23:28-37.

7. Egypt again was the refuge of Israelites, 2 Kings 25:25, 26.

8. In Ezek. 29-32 there are prophecies of the downfall of Egypt because of the oppression of Israel. In them are many references concerning the latter days, Ezek. 29:5, 6, 21; 30:2, 3.

9. Egypt is to be in the kingdom of Antichrist, Dan. 11:42, 43. It will be one of the four divisions of Greece and one of the ten of Rome in the last days, Dan. 7:24; 8:21-25.

10. Egypt will be in the Millennium with Israel, Isa. 11:11-16; 19:23-25; 27:12, 13; Zech. 10:10, 11; 14:18, 19.

II. The Second Mountain Kingdom and Israel.

Assyria was the second world kingdom to oppress Israel in "the times of the Gentiles." Assyria was founded in the days of Nimrod, Gen. 10:8-12. It was an inferior kingdom during the thirteen hundred years Egypt was being used of God to chasten Israel. The words "Assyria" and "Assyrian" are found in the Bible about 141 times and in nearly every case in connection with Israel. The following points in history and prophecy summarize the scriptural relation of Assyria to Israel in the past and future.

1. Assyria is first mentioned as oppressing Israel in the reign of Menahem when Israel was put to tribute, 2 Kings 15:16-20.

2. Assyria later invaded Israel, 2 Kings 15; 1 Chron. 5.

3. Assyria invaded Israel again, 2 Kings 16; Isa. 7.

4. Assyria formed an alliance with Judah against Israel, 2 Kings 16.

5. Assyria invaded Judah after the fall of Israel, 2 Kings 18, 19.

6. Next came wars between Egypt and Assyria for supremacy. During this time, Judah again fell into the hands of Egypt, 2 Kings 23:28-24:7. Assyria oppressed Israel and Judah, more or less, for about 175 years.

7. In the prophecies of the downfall of Assyria because of her oppression of Israel, there are many references to Assyria as being, in the last days, an enemy of Israel, Isa. 10:20-27; 14: 25; 31: 4-9; Mic. 5:5, 6. See chapter twenty, 6 (2).

8. Israel at the coming of Christ will be regathered from Assyria, Isa. 11:10-16; 27:12, 13; Zech. 10:10, 11; Matt. 24:31.

9. Assyria is to be blessed in the Millennium with Israel, Isa. 11:16; 19:23-25. Thus, we see Assyria in the beast or eighth kingdom as to territory and peoples.

III. The Third Mountain Kingdom and Israel.

Babylon was the third world kingdom to oppress Israel in "the times of the Gentiles." It is the first one mentioned in Daniel in "the times of the Gentiles," although both Egypt and Assyria oppressed Israel before Babylon did. The following points summarize the history and prophecy of this kingdom in connection with Israel in the past and future.

1. Babylon, as an inferior kingdom under Assyria, helped her at certain times against Israel and Judah, 2 Kings 17:24-30; 2 Chron. 33:11.

2. Babylon is prophesied as being Judah's captor, 2 Kings 20.

3. She was chosen of God to chasten Judah, 1 Chron. 9; Jer. 25; 28.

4. Judah was made captive to Babylon for seventy years, Jer. 25:9-14.

5. Babylon was punished after this, Jer. 25:9-14; Dan. 5.

6. Babylon as the oppressor of Israel is symbolized in Dan. 2 and 7 as "the head of gold" and "a lion."

7. Babylon will be under Antichrist at the time of Christ's coming, which will begin "the day of the Lord." (See chapter thirty-seven for a full explanation of Babylon in the future.)

IV. The Fourth Mountain Kingdom and Israel.

Medo-Persia was the fourth world kingdom to oppress Israel in "the times of the Gentiles." It is the second one recorded in the book of Daniel. Medo-Persia helped Babylon in the overthrow of Assyria. When God finished with Babylon in His purpose concerning Israel He chose this kingdom to succeed Babylon in His dealings with Israel and to liberate them from captivity. The words "Mede" and "Persian" are used only fifty-eight times in the Bible, but it is clear that this kingdom is one of the heads of the beast. The main points in the history and prophecy of this kingdom and Israel in the past and future are:

1. At the captivity of the ten tribes some Medes peopled the cities of the land of Israel, 2 Kings 17:6; 18:11.

2. The Medes are mentioned as the instrument of chastening upon Babylon for their treatment of Israel (Isa. 13:17), which was fulfilled over two hundred years later, Dan. 5.

3. Medo-Persia is symbolized in Dan. 2 as the "breast and his arms of silver"; in Dan. 7 as "a bear" and in Dan. 8 as "a ram." It is also mentioned in Dan. 10:13, 14, 20, 21 as being ruled by satanic princes. In Dan. 11:1, 2 the angel explains to Daniel how many kings were yet to be in Persia before the rise of "a mighty king" (Alexander the Great) of the realm of Grecia, Dan. 11:3.

4. Cyrus, the Persian, is mentioned in prophecy as liberating Israel from Babylon and making a decree for the rebuilding of the temple and city (Isa. 44:28-45:1), which was fulfilled over two hundred years later as in 2 Chron. 36:10-23; Ezra. 1:1-8.

5. Cambyses, the son of Cyrus, stopped the work on the temple and the city, and Israel again was oppressed by this kingdom, Ezra 4-6.

6. Darius I of profane history re-confirmed the decree of Cyrus and the work on the temple and city was begun again and Israel encouraged, Ezra 6.

7. Artaxerxes permitted Ezra to return with other captives, Ezra 7:1-9:9.

8. Nehemiah was sent over with other captives to restore the city fully, Neh. 1-13.

9. The book of Esther records persecutions of Israel under Persia.

10. Persia is mentioned as being under Antichrist and one of the oppressors of Israel in the last days, Ezek. 38:5, 8-23; 39:1-28. The fact that the beast has "the mouth of a lion" and "the feet of a bear," which animals in Daniel symbolized Babylon and Medo-Persia, shows that both will be ruled by Antichrist in the last days.

V. The Fifth Mountain Kingdom and Israel.

Greece was the fifth world kingdom to oppress Israel in "the times of the Gentiles." It is the third one mentioned in the book of Daniel. This kingdom has a threefold relationship with Israel: first, with Israel under the old Grecian Empire; secondly, with Israel under the four divisions of the old Grecian Empire; thirdly, with Israel under the Revived Grecian Empire.

1. We shall first consider Israel under the old Grecian Empire. Greece was the kingdom that existed between the close of the Old Testament canon and the rise of Rome; hence it is mentioned

in the Old Testament but twelve times under various names. There are many prophecies which concern Greece in Daniel and Revelation but which do not mention it by name.

(1)   There are scores of references concerning Israel's oppression by this kingdom and two of its divisions in the Old Testament apocryphal books, 1 Macc. 1:1-10; 6:2; 8:9; 2 Macc. 4:1-15, 36; 6:1; 9:15; 11:2; 13:2; etc.

(2)   It is symbolized in the image as a "kingdom of brass, which shall bear rule over the whole earth," including Israel, Dan. 2:39. This was fulfilled in Greece over 250 years after this vision.

(3)   It is symbolized by "a leopard" with "four heads" showing the kingdom itself and its four later divisions, two of which oppressed Israel, Dan. 7:6.

(4)   It is symbolized by "an he-goat" with "a notable horn between his eyes," Dan. 8:5-9, 20-25; 11:1-3. When this "notable horn" was broken off (Alexander died) "four notable ones" (kings) came up in his stead. This refers to the division of Alexander's vast empire into four parts headed by his four best generals, two of whom oppressed Israel.

2.   Let us next consider Israel under the divisions of the Grecian Empire. Two of these four divisions of Greece, Syria and Egypt, form a very important part in prophecy. It is necessary to mention only these two, for they were the only ones connected with Israel. The old Grecian Empire before its division never openly persecuted Israel as did these two divisions. Alexander made Palestine part of his empire but, after his death, it became a sort of buffer state between Egypt under the Ptolemies on the South, and Syria under the Seleucids on the North. These two divisions are prophesied about in Dan. 11, 12 as persecuting Israel both in that day and in the last days. In Dan. 11:5-34 we have a continued prophecy of these two divisions covering their history of approximately 150 years, from about 312-165 B.C., beginning with the reigns of Ptolemy I, king of Egypt, and Seleucus I, king of Syria, and ending with Antiochus Epiphanes, the Syrian king in this prophecy, who fulfilled Dan. 11:21-34 and who is a foreshadow of the future Syrian king, the Antichrist.

The purpose of the prophecy of these two sets of kings is to show us from which one of the four divisions of Greece Antichrist will come. After continuing the history of Antiochus Epiphanes in Dan. 11:21-34 the prophet skips over to the last days and shows us the work of the Antichrist. Daniel, in continuing the record of the wars between Egypt and Syria in the last days, states in Dan. 11:40-45 that the king of the north will come against the king of the south and the king of the south will come against the king of the north, but the king of the north, or Antichrist, will be the victor, will overthrow Egypt and many other countries, and will oppress Israel in the last days as we shall see below.

In this passage (Dan. 11:35-45) some have tried to insert a third king into the prophecy and teach that Antichrist is not the king

238   Revelation Expounded

of the north or Syria, and that he will be the king of Greece or the king of Turkey who will overthrow both the king of the north, or Syria, and the king of the south, or Egypt. But we reply, why should we insert a third king into the prophecy when the prophet is dealing with only the two divisions of Greece, Syria, and Egypt, down to these verses? The prophet does not insert a third king in this passage, or at least we have no indication of such. Surely, if the prophet had seen a third king in the vision after dealing with only the kings of Syria and Egypt in all previous verses, he would have made such clear. What would be the purpose of dealing with these two divisions as they appear centuries before the Antichrist, and then skipping over to the end time and picturing the same two divisions fighting in the last days if not to locate definitely the division from which Antichrist is to come? Greece or Turkey is not once mentioned in the whole chapter, so we have but to understand the prophecy as we naturally would if there were no third king to insert into the prophecy. The passage is best understood to mean that Syria and Egypt will war in the last days as they did in former days, with the result that Syria will be victorious over Egypt. This requires that Antichrist come from Syria, for he is the subject of all of Dan. 11:35-12:13, as we have already seen.

3. As to Israel under the Revived Grecian Empire and the Antichrist, the following passages refer to this kingdom and Antichrist's persecution of Israel. In Dan. 8:8, 9, 17-26 we have the four Grecian divisions as existing in the last days or "at the time of the end" and "in the latter time of their kingdom ... a king of fierce countenance ... shall stand up. And his power shall be mighty, but not by his own power (2 Thess. 2:8, 9; Rev. 13:2) ... and shall destroy the mighty and holy people (Israel) ... he shall stand up against the Prince of princes; but shall be broken without hand," Dan. 7:11; Rev. 19:11-21; Isa. 11:4; 2 Thess 1:7-10; 2:8, 9. There can be no question but what this is a reference to Antichrist and his persecution of Israel in Revived Grecia as well as Dan. 7:17-27; 9:26, 27; 11:35-45; 12:1-13; Ezek. 38, 39; Zech. 9:7-13; 12:4-14; 13:1-9; 14:1-9; Rev. 12:6, 14-17; 13:1-18. The language and time of fulfillment expressed in these passages prove that. These first five mountain kingdoms are the ones mentioned as the five heads on the beast that had "fallen" before John's day. This fifth mountain kingdom is the head that was "wounded to death; and his deadly wound was healed," or will be revived as the eighth kingdom.

VI. The Sixth Mountain Kingdom and Israel.

Rome was the sixth world kingdom to oppress Israel in "the times of the Gentiles" and the fourth mentioned in Daniel. This was the kingdom symbolized on the beast by the head "that was" at the time of John. The following prophecies concern this kingdom.

1. In Dan. 2:31-45 the Roman Empire is seen as the "fourth kingdom ... strong as iron." It succeeded Egypt, Assyria, Babylon,

Medo-Persia and Greece as the oppressor of Israel in furthering God's purpose in the earth. The legs of iron on the image represent the eastern and western divisions of this kingdom.

2. In Dan. 7:7-27 the kingdom is seen as the "fourth beast, dreadful and terrible, and strong exceedingly ... and it had ten horns ... and behold, there came up among them another little horn." This passage will be explained in the next chapter.

3. In Dan. 9:26, 27 there is another allusion to Rome as the destroyer of Jerusalem and the temple. This is referred to by Jesus in Matt. 24:1-3; Luke 21:20-24 and fulfilled in 70 A.D., when Titus, a Roman general, came against Jerusalem with 100,000 men, and, after four months' siege, completely destroyed the city and the temple, slew 1,000,000 Jews, and took 97,000 captive. Twenty years earlier than this, Rome came against Jerusalem and killed 30,000 Jews. Four years earlier, Titus with 66,000 men met the Jewish army and slew 40,000 and subjugated Galilee. Thousands of other Jews perished in other ways. Again, in 135 A.D., the Jews rebelled and 580,000 were killed and Palestine made utterly desolate. The Jews were forbidden to enter the land again. Since that time until recent years, Jews have been few in the land.

VII. The Seventh Mountain Kingdom and Israel.

The Revised Roman Empire is the only one of the seven kingdoms that is yet future. It will become a relentless persecutor of Israel under the leadership of the great whore, which will rule the ten kingdoms of Revised Rome until the middle of the Week. Mystery Babylon, the great whore, will seek to suppress every religion that is not her own, and will murder the saints of Jesus until she will be drunk on their blood during the first three and one-half years of the Week. We have many scriptures revealing the persecution of Christians and Israel by the great whore and the ten kings before Antichrist gets full power over them, Matt. 24:4-13; Mark 13:4-13; Rev. 6:9-11; 17:3-6. Antichrist will continue the persecution of Christians, and will break his seven-year covenant with Israel, being determined to exterminate them from the earth, Dan. 7:21-22; 8:24-25; 9:27; 12:1, 7; Matt. 24:15-31; Rev. 7:9-17; 13:1-18; 14:11-13; 15:2; 20:4-6. This seventh kingdom, as a revised formation of kingdoms inside the old Roman Empire, will be studied next.

Chapter Thirty-five

THE TEN HORNS AND THE BEAST ITSELF

"The fourth beast shall be the fourth kingdom upon the earth (from Daniel's time to Christ's coming) which shall be diverse from all kingdoms, and shall devour the whole earth ... And the ten horns out of this kingdom are ten kings that shall arise: and another shall rise after them; and he shall be diverse from the first (ten) and shall subdue three kings (of the ten, which are the other three divisions of Greece besides Syria, the one Antichrist shall come from) ... And the ten horns which thou sawest are ten kings, which have received no kingdom as yet; but receive power as kings one hour (period) with the beast. These have one mind, and shall give their power and strength unto the beast. These shall make war with the Lamb, and the Lamb shall overcome them: for he is Lord of lords, and King of kings: and they that are with him are called, and chosen, and faithful. And he said unto me, The waters which thou sawest, where the whore sitteth, are peoples, and multitudes, and nations, and tongues. And the ten horns which thou sawest upon the beast, these shall hate the whore, and shall make her desolate and naked, and shall eat her flesh, and burn her with fire. For God hath put in their hearts to fulfill his will, and to agree, and to give their kingdom unto the beast, until the words of God shall be fulfilled," Dan. 7:23, 24; Rev. 17:12-17. See also Dan. 2:40-45; 7:7-27; 8:8, 9, 17-25; 9:26, 27; 11:1-45; 12:1-13; Rev. 12:3; 13:1-3; 17:8-11; 19:11-21.

The following points deal with Revised Rome composed of ten kingdoms as the seventh head on the beast.

I. The Ten Horns—The Seventh Kingdom or Revised Rome.

1. **Is Rome to be revived? If so, in what form is she to exist?** The above quotations without comment, prove that there will never be a Revived Roman Empire as a single empire ruled by one man as in Old Rome, but there will be ten separate governments formed inside Rome as the seventh head on the beast. It could best be called a Revised Roman Empire. **The following facts prove** that Rome is to exist in the form of ten kingdoms in the last days before the revelation of both Christ and Antichrist. They will still be in existence during the appearance of both and will be overthrown by them, first by Antichrist and then by Christ.

(1) In Dan. 2:40-45 we have the first picture of Rome under the figure of two legs of iron and ten toes of iron and clay. Rome never has existed yet as separate kingdoms, as symbolized by the ten toes, so in order for all the prophecy to be fulfilled it must exist as such. Rome has existed as one kingdom, however, symbolized by the lower part of the body, where the legs are joined to the body. Then too, Rome has existed in the form of two divisions as symbolized by the two legs of iron, representing the eastern and western divisions of the empire. The time of the existence of the ten kingdoms is clearly stated in this passage by "in the days of these kings shall the God of heaven set up a kingdom, which shall never be destroyed." God has not yet set up His kingdom and will not do so until the coming of His Son, Jesus Christ, who will reign forever, Isa. 9:6-7; Rev. 11:15. This proves that Rome will exist again in a new form of ten kingdoms at the time of the second advent, which will succeed old Rome as Rome did the first five heads or kingdoms. The ten toes out of the two feet on the two legs represent ten kingdoms from the eastern and western divisions of Rome, five from one and five from the other. The phrase "the kingdom" is used twice in this passage and shows the unity of the ten kingdoms in some kind of loose federation.

240

(2)   Dan. 7:7-27 shows that there will come out of Rome ten kingdoms which will exist at the same time as the above ten kings. The additional prophecy given here is that "another little horn," called "the beast" in Dan. 7:11, will arise **"after them"** and overthrow three others. This little horn will continue "until the Ancient of days" comes, and judgment is given to the saints of the Most High; and the time arrives for the saints to possess the kingdom. This relates to the coming of Christ to destroy Antichrist and the ten kings and to set up His kingdom, and proves that these ten kings and the eleventh king will all exist at the time of the coming of Christ. The ten will give their kingdoms to the eleventh or the beast, and they together will destroy the whore or the great whore in the middle of the Week, and then three and one-half years later, they will fight Christ at Armageddon, Rev. 17:12-17. This beast of Dan. 7:11 is to be slain like the one in Rev. 19:20. Thus, we see that Rome is to be revised and exist in the form of ten separate kingdoms. Some have supposed that the ten kings have existed in succession as the seven heads have done but such is not stated of them as of the heads. **The following points prove the ten toes and ten horns of Dan. 2 and 7 are to be the same as the ten horns and ten kings of Rev. 12, 13, and 17 and that all of them will exist at the second coming of Christ and be destroyed at that time.**

A.   The number is the same, Dan. 2:40-45; 7:7-27; Rev. 12:3; 13:1; 17:12.

B.   They will all exist together and fight with Christ at His coming to earth, Dan. 2:34, 35, 44, 45; 7:8-14, 21-27; Rev. 17:14; 19:17-21.

C.   They will all exist **after** the "fourth kingdom" or Rome, and be a revision of that kingdom, Dan. 2:40-45; 7:7, 8, 23, 24; Rev. 17:12-14.

D.   They will all be connected with the same beast at the same time, Dan. 7:8, 11, 21-27; Rev. 17:8-17; 19:11-21.

E.   The beast or "little horn" will be an individual as much as any one of the "ten horns" and will arise **"after them"** according to both books; therefore, the two accounts must be identical, Dan. 7:8-24; Rev. 17:12-17.

F.   They all will become subject to the same beast, Dan. 7:23, 24; Rev. 13:1-10; 17: 12-17.

G.   They will all be coexistent at the time God sets up His kingdom, which immediately succeeds theirs, Dan. 2:40-45; 7:7-27; Rev. 17:12-17; 19:11-21. If they were to exist as a succession of ten kingdoms, then they surely would have risen one at a time as the four beasts did, and Daniel would not have seen them rise and exist at once on the head of the terrible beast of Dan. 7:7, 8. Neither could the "little horn" rise among all of them if only one were to be in existence at the time he arose. Nor could the "little horn" overthrow three of them if they were not in existence at the same time. The "little horn" of Dan. 7:7-11, 23-27 will exist at the same time, and in the same connection with the ten horns and continue the same length of time as does "the beast" of Rev. 13: 1-8; 17:8-17; 19:11-21 as proved by these passages.

H.   The "fourth kingdom" of Dan. 2 and 7 is the same as the sixth head of Rev. 17, and the ten horns in both passages succeed each so they must be the same. The seventh head of Rev. 17 and the ten horns will be identical. The ten horns of Dan. 7 were to be the next kingdom after Rome and be formed inside Rome. It is the only kingdom mentioned as yet future, besides the "little horn" and his kingdom composed of the ten. The only kingdom seen in Rev. 17 that was yet future from John's day besides the beast was the seventh head, which was to exist for a short space and then give its kingdom to the beast. Since the ten kings in both books are all to exist at the same time, are to form the next kingdom succeeding old Rome immediately preceding the beast, are to become subject to him, are to help form the eighth kingdom, and are to fight under the beast against Christ, they must be the same.

I.   The ten kings in both books are to reign both before and after the beast or "little horn." Their reign before him is to be different from that after him. Before the beast rises, they will control their own kingdoms, but after he comes they will be subject to his supreme will. They will control the seventh, he will control the eighth. Therefore, we conclude that the ten horns in both books are the same.

Thus, we see that Rome is to be revised and exist in the form of ten kingdoms before the rise of Antichrist. Then Antichrist will rise out of the ten kingdoms and in three and one-half years gain all ten kings. He will then form the eighth kingdom composed of all the ten, as well as perhaps a few other parts of the Old Grecian Empire, which were not under the Roman jurisdiction. Antichrist will come out of Syria and overthrow the other three Grecian divisions, which make four of the ten of Revised Rome, thus reviving Greece and bringing the territory of both Greece and Rome under him as the eighth kingdom. The Revised Roman Empire will be composed of ten kingdoms throughout its short existence, while the Revived Grecian Empire will not only be composed of the same ten kingdoms, but also others which it will add to its domain during its short time of existence, as we shall see below.

2.   **When is Rome to be revised?** The ten kingdoms are to be formed in the near future. Just what time is not known. Rome must be revised and exist as ten kingdoms before Antichrist can arise, for he is to come up **"after them"** and **"among them,"** Dan. 7:8, 24.

3.   **How long is Revised Rome to exist?**   Revised Rome is to exist as the seventh head only a "short space." The exact time is not known for it cannot be known just how long it will be revised before the Seventieth Week. It appears that soon after it is revised the Antichrist will arise and begin to conquer some of the ten kingdoms. This war will continue the first part of the Week

until Antichrist is given full power over the ten kingdoms thus forming his kingdom—Revived Grecia.

4. **How is Rome to be revised?** The ten kingdoms will be formed through wars and agreements. We must look for the ten kingdoms to come only out of the territory of old Rome, Dan. 7:19-27. Generally speaking, we may say that **Egypt,** the first head, was the smallest of these seven mountain kingdoms in territory, having ruled from Egypt to Syria. **Assyria,** the second head, ruled from Egypt to Armenia, part of Asia Minor, all of Babylon and the countries of Media and Persia. **Babylon,** the third head, ruled over Egypt and all the Syrian countries west of the Tigris. **Medo-Persia,** the fourth head, ruled over a greater territory than any of the preceding heads, ruling from the Indus river on the east, to a part of Thrace and Macedonia on the west, and from the Caspian and Black Seas on the north, to all of Egypt and part of North Africa. **Greece,** the fifth head, conquered all of the Medo-Persian territory and added to it Greece, Macedonia, and Thrace, thus becoming the largest territory of all the first five heads on the beast. **Rome,** the sixth head, reigned over all the territory of Greece except the countries east of the Caspian Sea and the Persian Gulf, and added to this vast possession west to the Atlantic, from the northern part of Africa on the south, to the Rhine and Danube rivers on the north and, in some parts, north of the Danube, taking in Dacia and including England. Wherefore, it is from this territory that we are to look for the rise of ten kingdoms. The kingdom of the Antichrist, which will be the eighth kingdom and will succeed these ten kingdoms, will embrace not only all this territory, but also the far eastern parts of the Grecian territory and whatever countries these ten kingdoms will control outside the old Roman Empire.

In 1948 we count no less than twenty-six separate states inside the old Roman Empire territory — England, Holland, Belgium, Luxembourg, France, Switzerland, Spain, Portugal, Italy, Austria, Hungary, Yugoslavia, Romania, Bulgaria, Albania, Greece, Turkey, Syria, Lebanon, Iran, Irak, Morocco, Algeria, Tunisia, Lybia, and Egypt. Though Israel was ruled by the Old Roman Empire, it will not be considered as part of the future ten kingdoms. This is clear from the fact that the Syrian kingdom of ten will make a seven-year covenant with them to guarantee their peace and security as a separate state, Dan. 9:27. Also, Trans-Jordan will not be a part of the ten kingdoms, because she will protect Israel from the Antichrist when he breaks his seven-year covenant with Israel, and the Jews have to flee into the wilderness, as seen in Chapter Sixteen.

For the fulfillment of prophecy the above named states will need to be reduced to ten kingdoms in number, or at least ten kingdoms will have to be formed inside this territory of the old Roman Empire in the final fulfillment of Dan. 7:7-8, 23-24; 8:8-9, 20-25; 9:26-27; 11:36-45; Rev. 12:3; 13:1; 17:8-17.

One thing is clear and that is Greece, Turkey, Syria, and Egypt must be four of these ten kingdoms in order to fulfill Dan. 8 and 11, for Antichrist comes out of one of these four original Grecian divisions in the latter time of their kingdom, and he will revive the old Grecian Empire. Another thing is also clear and that is Palestine must regain its independence and become a Jewish homeland to fulfill Ezek. 22:17-22; 37:1-39:29; Dan. 7:26, 27; 11: 40-12:7; Joel 3; Mic. 5:1-15; Zech. 12:4-14:21; Rev. 11:1, 2; etc. Palestine will not be one of the ten kingdoms as it was not one of the four divisions of Greece. It was a buffer state between Syria and Egypt as revealed in the wars of Syria and Egypt, as we have seen.

One thing is not definitely clear, however, and that is whether or not the ten kingdoms will have to give up all the lands outside the old Roman Empire that these twenty-six governments now control. They may or may not have to be separated from the ten kingdoms in the final formation of Revised Rome; this remains to be seen. The one necessary thing is that ten must be formed INSIDE Rome. It is valueless to speculate as to how these lands will become ten kingdoms, so we will not do so. In general, we can say that there will be five kingdoms in the eastern division and five in the western division of Rome to fulfill the prophecy of ten toes, five on each foot, and that is as far as we can state if we want to be backed by Scripture in all we say.

II. The Beast Itself—the Eighth Kingdom.

As we have seen in chapter thirty-three, the seven heads and the ten horns on the beast are entirely different from the beast itself. The beast is the eighth of a succession of world powers from the beginning of Israel as a nation in Egypt to the second advent when Israel will be delivered from the Gentiles and "the times of the Gentiles" end. The beast as the eighth kingdom will be ruled by the personal, visible, and mortal human being, the Antichrist, and the personal, invisible, and immortal angel, the prince of Grecia. As we have also seen, this prince of Grecia will be liberated out of the pit during the existence of the ten kingdoms and will cause the human Antichrist to rise to power over the original four Grecian divisions, thus reviving the Grecian Empire, which was not in John's day, and which had been before his day, and which will become the eighth in the day of the second advent.

This Revived Grecian Empire will engulf the whole ten kingdoms of the Revised Roman Empire during the first part of the Week. Then by the end of the last half of the Week, it will engulf the countries of the east and north of the ten kingdoms. But before Antichrist goes further in his world conquests he is defeated by Christ at Jerusalem, Zech. 14. Thus, the Antichrist's kingdom will be the greatest of all the eight Gentile world powers, but he will come short of total world conquest like all others before him.

Will Russia, Antichrist, or Christ Rule the Whole World?

With the above facts in mind, one can safely say that the present effort of Russia to rule the whole world will come to an end in due time. Communism will never rule the world as a whole and neither will any other ism. No earthly man will become the world-wide dictator before Christ comes to reign. Antichrist will come nearer to it than anyone, but before he even conquers all of Asia, Europe, and Africa, he will come to an end and none shall help him, Dan. 11:45; Zech. 14. Jesus Christ will be the world's first literal world-wide dictator or ruler. He will be the one who will bring universal peace and prosperity and not Antichrist. Before this universal peace and prosperity, certain wars must come to fulfill prophecy.

There MUST BE at Least THREE MORE EUROPEAN WARS before the Second Advent.

1. The first war will be to form the ten kingdoms. Twenty six governments cannot be brought down to ten by any other method. Sovereign states are not in the habit of giving up without a struggle. At least this is true of so many that are now inside the old Roman Empire. Much speculation as to a United States of Europe is now being discussed, but we can be scripturally safe in concluding this mere speculation. There will never be any such thing as ten kingdoms in Europe, for the ten must be formed of parts of three continents—Europe, Asia, and Africa.

We have seen the folly of guessing how and by whom certain prophecies would be fulfilled, so we had better not speculate as to how and by whom the ten kingdoms will be formed. Thousands of prophetical students during both World Wars I and II were sure that these wars would fulfill what they called the Revived Roman Empire, but both times they have been proved to be wrong. It is enough to say with a definite "thus saith the Lord" that the ten kingdoms will be eventually formed **inside** and **not outside** the Roman Empire. This is the next thing on schedule as far as a definite prophecy being fulfilled, unless it be the rapture of the Church. That a war is necessary to form the ten kingdoms is clear from the fact that at least twenty six states must be brought down to ten, Dan. 7:24.

When the ten kingdoms are formed they will exist as independent kingdoms and be ruled by ten kings for "a short space" before the Antichrist arises to make war on them to get power over the whole ten kingdoms, Rev. 17:10. If this short space is the same as "a short time" in Rev. 12:12, they will be independent kingdoms only for about three and one-half years, Rev. 11:2; 12:6, 14; 13:5.

2. **After** the ten are formed, THEN AND THEN ALONE will the Antichrist arise out of the ten, and in his rise to power he will overthrow three of the ten, Dan. 7:8, 24. This will be another war. It takes Antichrist at least three and one-half years, or the first part of the Week, to get power over the ten kingdoms by overthrowing three and causing the others to submit to him.

3. The third war will be a war the last half of the Week between the ten kingdoms under the Antichrist and the countries

of "the east and of the north" of the ten kingdoms to fulfill Dan. 11:44. This war will be fought until about the end of the Week when Antichrist will have conquered these northern and eastern countries. Then he becomes the chief prince of Meshech and Tubal of Ezek. 38, 39. He will then lead the ten kingdoms and the newly conquered countries of the north and east, together with other nations who co-operate with him by the ministry of the three unclean spirits, against Jerusalem and the Jews and especially against Christ at Armageddon. Antichrist will then be defeated before he takes all of Jerusalem, much less the rest of the world, Zech. 14:1-21.

Three Defeats of Russia

There will be three future defeats of Russia in the fulfillment of prophecy:

1. Russia will have to be defeated in the formation of the ten kingdoms, for she must lose her hold on Hungary, Romania, Bulgaria, and other parts of the old Roman Empire which she now controls. Russia, herself never was a part of the old Roman Empire and cannot be one of the ten kingdoms which must be formed therein to fulfill prophecy, but she has control over some who will be a part of that territory, Dan. 2:39-45; 7:7-8, 19-24; Rev. 13:1; 17:9-17. It being inconceivable that Russia would let these holdings go, without a war, it can be expected that a war will break out in Europe, Asia, and Africa which will result in defeat to Russia and the formation of these ten kingdoms.

2. Russia will again be defeated when the Antichrist arises out of one of the ten kingdoms (after a short space as independent kingdoms), when he overthrows three of the ten kingdoms in a period of three and one-half years, causing the other six to submit to him without further struggle, Dan. 7:8, 19-24; Rev. 17:8-17. A war will then break out between the ten kingdoms under Antichrist and Germany, Russia, and the other countries in the north and east of the ten kingdoms which will last about three and one-half years, Dan. 11:44. In this war, Russia and her allies being defeated, the Antichrist will then become the ruler of Russia also. He will proceed to lead his ten kingdoms, together with the newly conquered countries of the north and east, along with other nations who, though not yet conquered will co-operate with him through the ministry of the three unclean spirits — and they will all go as a united force against the Jews in an effort to exterminate them, Ezek. 38-39; Zech. 14. With half of Jerusalem taken and the Jews almost destroyed, Christ and the armies of heaven will suddenly appear in the clouds of heaven to defeat the armies of the earth in one day's battle and then set up a kingdom in the world forever, Zech. 14; Matt. 24:27-31; 25:31-46; 2 Thess. 1:7-10; 2:8-12; Jude 14; Rev. 19:11-21; 20:1-7.

Thus Antichrist will become the chief prince of Meshech and Tubal and the Gog of Ezek. 38-39 by conquest, not because he will come from Russia. This is the war that some scholars claim will take place in Palestine before the battle of Armageddon, but in this they are mistaken because the ten kingdoms must first be formed and be conquered by the Antichrist from Syria before the war with Russia takes place. This war will not be fought in Palestine, but in the countries to the north and east of the ten kingdoms (Dan. 11:44), and then will come the invasion of Palestine under Antichrist, at the very close of the age, as shown in all the above scriptures.

3. Russia will be defeated at last by Jesus Christ and the armies of heaven, and Judah, at Jerusalem, Zech. 14:14; Ezek. 38-39; Rev. 19:11-21. At that time Russia will be under Antichrist; she will not be the leader of the nations at Armageddon. This war will be fought in Palestine, not in the countries north and east of the ten kingdoms as the war in point 2 above, Ezek. 38-39; Zech. 14. Thus, Russia will never fulfill many of the predictions some of the scholars claim she will. Actually, Antichrist from Syria will fulfill these many scriptures they refer to, and Russia will merely be one of many allies of Antichrist after he conquers her as in the second war, above.

No World Peace and Prosperity Under Antichrist.

Thus, the old theory of the Antichrist being a man that will miraculously bring world peace and prosperity is unscriptural. He is a man of war from the time he comes until he is destroyed at Armageddon. The only peace he will cause is with the Jews for seven years and then he breaks this covenant in the middle of this period and "by peace shall destroy many" Jews, but among the Gentiles it is war all the time, Dan. 8:25; 9:27.

What Part Will the Americas Have in These Wars?

What part the Americas will have in these latter-day wars is not known, so we will let the many Bible speculators settle this question, for many of them seem to be able to get more out of what the Bible does not say than what it does say. The reason some nations are not definitely referred to in these events is that they are so far from the land of the Jews where these prophecies center.

Two Kingdoms Yet Future—Not One.

1. The first future world empire will be the seventh kingdom of chapters 34 and 35. This will be the ten-kingdom empire formed inside the old Roman Empire territory, Dan. 7:8-9, 19-24, Rev. 17:9-17. It will continue "a short space" before Antichrist comes to form the eighth and last kingdom in the times of the Gentiles.

2. The second and last future world empire of man will be the same ten kingdoms, as in point 1, above, except that the ten kings will cease to be independent of the Antichrist. They will submit to him and be

under him the last three and one-half years of this age, Dan. 7:7-8, 19-24; 8:9-25; Rev. 13:1-5; 17:9-17. This last empire will continue only 42 months (Rev. 13:5), 1260 days (Rev. 11:2; 12:6), a time, times, and a half, Rev. 12:14; Dan. 7:25; 12:7. It is during these 42 months that the great tribulation of the future will run its course and multitudes of Christians — people who will have become converted after the rapture — will be killed, Rev. 7:9-17; 12:1-17; 15:2-3; Rev. 20:4-6. This will also be the time of Jacob's trouble when Israel will experience a three and one-half year period of the greatest trouble that any nation has ever gone through, or ever will go through, Jer. 30:1-11; Dan. 7:25; 8:24; 9:27; 11:40-45; 12:1, 7; Zech. 13:9; Matt. 24:15-31; Rev. 11:1-11; 12:6, 14-17; 15:2-3; 20:4-6.

The beast will be the eighth and last of the eight kingdoms of Rev. 17:9-17 — Satan's last effort to destroy Israel and defeat God and Christ and the Holy Spirit as they take over the kingdoms of this world, Rev. 11:15; Dan. 7:18, 27. Thus, the beast is not any one of the seven heads or ten horns, but rather the successor of all these heads and horns. This eighth and last kingdom of man will be destroyed in one day, giving way to the eternal kingdom of God on earth, which kingdom could be called the ninth world empire, Dan. 2:44-45; 7:18, 22, 27; 8:24-27; Zech. 14; Matt. 25:31-46; Rev. 11:15; 20:1-10; 22:4-5.

We do not mean to say that God's kingdom is begun for the first time, after the above eight empires, but simply that it is established on the earth again, the rebellion that has existed since the days of Lucifer and Adam having been put down. Counting the pre-Adamite probationary period as the first dispensation and adding the seven dispensations of Adam's race which will end with the Millennium, it could be said that this ninth kingdom will be the ninth and last dispensation of men and angels on earth. It will be eternal (Rev. 21-22).

Chapter Thirty-six

THE TIMES OF THE GENTILES, Luke 21:24; Rom. 11:25

I. The Meaning of the Word "Gentiles."

The word "Gentiles" in the Old Testament is from the Hebrew **goy**, meaning "a foreign nation, a non-Israelite." It is used thirty times. In the New Testament it is from **hellen**, meaning "Grecian, a Greek-speaking person, a non-Jew" (used two times), and from **ethnos**, meaning "race or tribe, heathen, nation, people or non-Israelite." It is translated "nation" sixty-one times; "people" two times; and "heathen" five times.

II. The Source of the Different Nations.

The flood ended all the different families of the earth. Those of the earth today came from the three sons of Noah—Shem, Ham, and Japheth—as recorded in Gen. 10; 1 Chron. 1. Before Abraham, the whole race was one, and all had one language. At the confusion of tongues, God scattered the race abroad. Men began to separate into nations having their own territories and rulers. From the call of Abraham, God began to make a difference between certain families. Abraham's race became the chosen one through whom God planned to evangelize all other nations. There became two classes of people dealt with in Scripture—the Hebrews, Israelites, or Jews, and the non-Israelites called Gentiles. When the Church of the New Testament was started, there became three classes dealt with in Scripture—the Jews, the Gentiles, and the Church which is made up of Jews and Gentiles, 1 Cor. 10:31, 32.

III. What Is Meant by "The Times of the Gentiles"?

"The times of the Gentiles" (Luke 21:24) refers to that period of time from the beginning of the history of Israel to the second coming of Christ, during which time Israel has been more or less oppressed by the Gentiles. It is not to be understood in connection with any capture of Jerusalem, or salvation of Gentiles, but in connection with the oppressions of Israel, whether in the land or not. If the term be understood in connection with Israel in the land only, then the times of the Gentiles could not be from Nebuchadnezzar or Titus, 70 A.D., to our day, for the Jews have not been in the land during most of this time. We conclude, therefore, that it means that period of time from Israel's first to her last oppression by the Gentiles, whether in the land or not.

"The times of the Gentiles" means the same as "the fulness of the Gentiles" mentioned in Rom 11:25. Both end at the same time. "The fulness of the Gentiles" could not refer to the end of the salvation of the Gentiles for they will be saved all through the tribulation and the Millennium, Acts 2:16-21; Rom. 10; Rev. 6:9-11; 7:9-17; 15:2-4; 20:4-6; Isa. 2:2-4; 52:7; 66:19-24.

IV. The Length of "The Times of the Gentiles."

It is generally believed that the length of the times of the Gentiles is 2,520 years but this has already been disproved in chapter one, point VIII, 1, for which see.

Just because there have been about 2,500 to 2,600 years from
Daniel to our day, is no proof that these times are 2,520 years
long. Neither does the fact that Daniel pictured Gentile oppression from his day on prove that they are 2,520 years long. All
Daniel did was to prophesy from his day to the coming of Christ.
He could not have foretold what was already history concerning
the Gentile oppression of Israel before his day. The length of the
times of the Gentiles is much longer than 2,520 years.

Since Israel was oppressed by Egypt a much longer time than
by Babylon, since Assyria took the ten tribes captive before Babylon took the two tribes captive, and since no Scripture says that
the times of the Gentiles began with Babylon or that Daniel saw
all the times of the Gentiles, we naturally include the first two
kingdoms of the eight of Rev. 17 in the times of the Gentiles, for
they also oppressed Israel as much as any Gentile power.

V. When Do the Times of the Gentiles Begin and End?

John on Patmos pictures the whole length of the times of the
Gentiles. The dragon and the beast of Revelation had seven heads
and ten horns. The seven heads and the beast itself are explained
to be eight world kingdoms to oppress Israel from the Egyptian
bondage to the second coming of Christ as proved in chapter
thirty-four. The times of the Gentiles began with the oppression
of Israel in Egypt and will continue through the kingdom of Antichrist and end at the second coming of Christ. If the term refers
to that period in Israel's history when she is oppressed by the
Gentiles, then we should **begin with the first oppression of Israel
in Egypt** and forget about setting dates and the time element in
connection with the subject. **These times end with the last oppression of Israel by the Gentiles.**

The Scriptures are very clear that they end at the second coming of Christ to the earth to set up the kingdom and not at any
date that any man has yet set, Dan. 2:44, 45; 7:13, 14, 18-27; 8:20-
25; Zech. 14:1-21; Isa. 9:6, 7; Luke 21:24; Rom. 11:25; Rev. 11:1, 2;
11:15; 19:11-21; 20:1-10. In Rev. 11:1, 2 we have the fact that Jerusalem will be trodden down the last forty-two months of this
age or during the three and one-half years of the reign of the
Antichrist over the nations of old Rome. If this is true, "the times
of the Gentiles" must end at the conclusion of the forty-two
months. They cannot possibly end until the end of the Seventieth
Week of Daniel which has not yet begun. There must be a least
seven more years then before they can end. How many more years
there will be before this Week begins and Antichrist is revealed,
is not clear, so all date-setting and speculation is valueless. The
whole length of "the times of the Gentiles" will be more than
3,800 years and has run through the Egyptian, Assyrian, Babylonian, Medo-Persian, Grecian, and Roman empires and will continue
through the two empires that are yet future—the Revised Roman
and the Revived Grecian.

Chapter Thirty-seven

LITERAL BABYLON, Rev. 18:1-24

The word "Babylon" is used 283 times in Scripture and generally always in connection with Israel. (See chapter thirty-four, point III.) Only once is it used of a symbol and that is in Rev. 17:5. Many arguments can be presented to prove that Babylon is to be rebuilt and exist as a literal city in the last days. Those who do not agree with this can also present arguments, but there is this vital thing lacking in all of them—definite Scripture reading to that effect. The main arguments of the latter class are that Babylon has been destroyed as stated in the Old Testament prophecies, that it is in ruins today, and that the Babylon in Rev. 18 is the same as that in Rev. 17, which is not a literal city.

As to the first line of argument, it is insufficient in that it does not prove it to be impossible for Babylon to be rebuilt and destroyed again. As to the second line of argument, it is true that the Babylon in Rev. 17 is not a literal city, but this does not prove that the Babylon of Rev. 18 is the same as that of Rev. 17, nor does it yet prove that Babylon could not be rebuilt and destroyed again. There is to be a destruction of a literal city called Babylon under the seventh vial (16:19), for no earthquake could destroy a religious system. All the other cities destroyed under this vial are literal so why should not Babylon be literal? **We have the firm foundation of the Word of God as to the rebuilding of Babylon in the land of Shinar.**

Thirty Scriptural Proofs that Babylon Will Be Rebuilt Again.

1. Babylon will be overthrown as God overthrew Sodom and Gomorrah, Isa. 13:19; Jer. 50:40. This has never been fulfilled.

2. Babylon will never be inhabited after its final overthrow, Isa. 13:20; Jer. 50:39, 40; 51:29, 37, 43.

3. Arabs will never dwell there again, Isa. 13:20.

4. Shepherds will never dwell there, Isa. 13:20.

5. The final overthrow must be immediately followed by blessings on Israel, Isa. 13:6-17; 14:1-7; Jer. 50:4-7, 17-20, 33-35; Rev. 18-20.

6. The stones of Babylon were not to be used for building purposes again, Jer. 51:26. They are being used today to build with.

7. Babylon must be in existence in the future "day of the Lord," Isa. 13:6-13; Rev. 16:17-21; 18:1-24; 19:1-3.

8. Babylon must be destroyed under the seventh vial and at the second advent of Christ or in "the day of the Lord" by a supernatural destruction, Isa. 13:6-13; Jer. 50:20, 40; 51:8; Rev. 16:17-21; 18:8, 10, 17, 19, 21.

9. Babylon is to be destroyed at the end of the great tribulation when the planets are affected, Isa. 13:9-13; Matt. 24:29-31; Rev. 16:17-21.

10. Babylon is to be totally desolate and all sinners destroyed out of it forever, Isa. 13:9, 19-22; Jer. 50:3, 23, 39, 40; 51:26, 29, 37,

43; Rev. 18:19, 21-24; 19:3.

11. Babylon is to be destroyed at the time the world is punished for its sins at the second advent, Isa. 13:11; Rev. 18:1-24.

12. Babylon is to be destroyed when Christ comes with the armies of heaven to fight at Armageddon, Isa. 13:1-5, 11-13; 14:5, 25-27; Rev. 16:17-21; 18:8; 19:1-3, 11-21.

13. The site of Babylon is to be one of the openings of hell on earth where men will see the wicked in everlasting burnings— thus, the site of both the first and last great apostasy against God, as well as all rebels of all ages, will be everlasting monuments of God's wrath, Isa. 14:9-17; 66:22-24; Rev. 19:3.

14. On the desolate edges of this hell-hole will dwell the wild creatures of the desert, Isa. 13:21, 22.

15. Babylon is to be destroyed in the day of Israel's final restoration and blessing at the second advent, Isa. 13:12; 14:1-8; Jer. 50:4-7, 19, 20; 51:50; Rev. 18:17-19.

16. Israel is to rule over her oppressors in the day of Babylon's final destruction, Isa. 14:1-4.

17. The generation of Israel who enters the Millennium will sing a triumphant song over the future king of Babylon, the Antichrist who will have persecuted them, Isa. 14:3-27.

18. Babylon is to be "suddenly" and in "one hour" destroyed, Isa. 13:19; Jer. 50:40; 51:8; Rev. 18:8, 10, 17, 19.

19. Babylon is to be a world commercial center after the rapture of the Church (Rev. 4-22 are all fulfilled after the churches), Zech. 5:5-11; Rev. 18:3-19. The thirty items of commerce mentioned here could not be figurative.

20. Babylon must again be a world political center, Rev. 18:3-10.

21. Babylon must again be a world religious center, Rev. 18:2-10.

22. Babylon's latter-day sorceries will deceive much of the world, Rev. 18:23; 2 Thess. 2:9-15.

23. Orders for the martyrdom of saints during the great tribulation will be from this city, Rev. 18:24.

24. Babylon must be burned with fire, Rev. 18:8-10, 18; 19:3.

25. Babylon must be destroyed by an earthquake, Rev. 16:17-21.

26. Babylon must be thrown down with violence, Rev. 18:21.

27. Babylon must never be found after her destruction, Rev. 18:21.

28. Babylon must sink into the earth, Jer. 51:62-64; Rev. 18:21.

29. Babylon must be destroyed by God, not by man, Rev. 18:20.

30. Babylon's destruction must be followed by the Millennial reign of Christ, Rev. 19, 20.

None of these scriptures have been fully fulfilled.

Such passages as Isa. 13:6, 9-14, 19-22; 14:1-27; Jer. 50:4-20; 51:5-10 refer to a latter-day fulfillment of Babylon and Israel in "the day of the Lord" as is clear from reading these passages. These statements have never been literally fulfilled and must be if they are true predictions. When will they be fulfilled if not in connection with the events of Rev. 6:1-19:21 during the future tribulation?

In Zech. 5:5-11 we have a prophecy of the rebuilding of Babylon. The prophet saw an ephah, which is about a three-peck measure. It was "going forth" and contained a woman who was called "wickedness" or "the lawless one." There was also lifted up a talent of lead (about 158 pounds) for the prophet to see, and then it was cast back into the ephah. Both the talent and the woman (wickedness) were in the measure. There was also a stone or weight of lead upon the mouth of the measure besides the talent of lead inside it. The measure, talent, woman, and lid were being carried by "two women" who had wings like a stork (an unclean bird) and the wind was in their wings carrying them along with the ephah. The prophet asked, "Whither do these bear the ephah?" The answer was, "To build it (her, the woman in the ephah) an house in the land of Shinar (Babylon, Gen. 10:10; 11:2; 14:1, 9; Josh. 7:21; Isa. 11:11; Dan. 1:2) and it (the house) shall be established, and set there (fixed and settled) upon her own base (fixed resting place)."

The things symbolized are clear and must refer to the future time. They cannot refer to the destruction of Babylon for the whole thought is that of restoration. At the time of this prophecy, Babylon had been taken by the Medes but not destroyed. If it then refers to restoration, that must be yet future, for Babylon has never been restored from that day to this. The ephah speaks of commerce "going forth" throughout the earth as in verse 3; the lead symbolizes the heaviness of the traffic and the richness of the business. The woman is explained to be "wickedness" which is from a Hebrew word **rasha,** meaning the "wickedness of the restless fallen nature of man as manifest in all lawlessness and unrestraint," Job. 3:17; Isa. 57:20, 21. The house is representative of the restoration of Literal Babylon as the center of this lawless commerce and traffic of the nations in Shinar; and the wings of the stork and the wind in the wings speak of the speedy accomplishment by supernatural powers of the restoration of Babylon as a commercial center of the world.

This will be preparatory to the final and sudden judgment of Rev. 18 and other prophecies of the Bible. This then makes the two women to symbolize the infernal powers, thus causing a condition of wickedness in the lives of men. This corresponds with the supernatural power of Satan in the lives of the Antichrist and false prophet and other men at the end of the age, who will want a place where no restraint is possible to hinder them in their wickedness. We do know this much about this passage; i.e., that the theme is the rebuilding of Babylon in Shinar as the seat of the lawless activities of men in the last days. If this be true, then undoubtedly Babylon is the site Satan has chosen as the center of his activities in the last days that he may with advantage operate against Jerusalem and the Jews.

A brief history of Babylon will reveal that she has never been destroyed as stated in both Testaments and that her present state is the cause of continued neglect and decay throughout the centuries. Thus, it will be proved that she must be rebuilt and destroyed to fulfill these prophecies, which require a sudden destruction by God Himself, and that in the last days.

Old Babylon, the capital of Hammurabi and his successors, was partially destroyed by Sennacherib, the king of Assyria, who came against Jerusalem as in Isa. 37-39. Esarhaddon rebuilt it, but during his elder son's revolt in Babylon against Assyria, it was again captured by Assurbani-pal. It was under the Assyrian Empire until that kingdom fell. Babylon was freed at that time by Nabopolassar. Upon his death, Nebuchadnezzar rebuilt the city and made it the greatest of the east. It was then that Babylon attained its greatest fame.

The Medes and Persians took the city at the end of seventy years of its glory (Dan. 5) and made it their royal city. It went through many sieges from that time on because of its rebellion against the Persians, and suffered much until it was conquered by Alexander the Great, when it became a great city in his kingdom. Some historians claim that when Seleucia was built in Chaldea by Seleucid, the king of Syria and Babylon, after Alexander's empire was divided, he forced the people to leave Babylon and move to the new city. However, the history of Babylon did not end there, for cuneiform texts under the Seleucids show that it was still a great city. Where historians disagree among themselves and the source of information has faded, we can rely upon the Bible and Jewish history. In the time of the apostles, Babylon was a populous place as is plainly stated in 1 Peter 5:13. Five hundred years after Christ, there were Jewish academies there which produced the Babylonian Talmud. It is clear from the following passages that prophecy concerning the final and complete destruction of Babylon has not been fulfilled, Isa. 13:19-22; Jer. 50:3, 13, 39-46; 51:26, 29, 37, 43; Rev. 14:8; 16:19; 18:1-24.

Babylon was restored several times from the time of Nimrod to its last desolation, and each time in the same vicinity but not exactly on the same spot as in previous times. Why could this not be true in the future? There is now a city called Hillah built just south of the ruins of Babylon which have been looted to build it, and this in itself would be contrary to Scripture, if Babylon has been finally destroyed, Jer. 51:26. Hillah is in a wonderful agricultural belt which is becoming more productive every year through the restoration of the ancient system of irrigation that Babylon had. It has large bazaars and is a great grain market. It is built on both sides of the Hillah branch of the Euphrates and has a population of 263,837. Hillah could be extended north so as to take in the ancient site of Babylon; or, it is entirely possible that a new town site could be planned and Babylon fully restored on its own site. And the city could become large enough to take in Hillah and many miles of the surrounding country. This is just as easy to comprehend as to understand how any other city could be built, and this, and this alone, will meet the requirements of Scripture.

The Doom of Literal Babylon.

In Rev. 18 we have a more complete and detailed revelation of the destruction of Literal Babylon than in all previous prophecies. In the Old Testament we have the prophecies concerning Babylon in the future mixed with those of her ancient judgment by the Medes, while here we have only prophecy of the future in detail showing her doom, the cause, the time, and the rest. The following are the main points of this chapter:

1. The Indictment of Literal Babylon.

"And after these things I saw another angel come down from heaven, having great power; and the earth was lightened with his glory. And he cried mightily with a strong voice, saying, Babylon the great is fallen, is fallen, and is become the habitation of devils, and the hold of every foul spirit, and a cage of every unclean and hateful bird. For all nations have drunk of the wine of the wrath of her fornication, and the kings of the earth have committed fornication with her, and the merchants of the earth are waxed rich through the abundance of her delicacies," Rev. 18:1-3.

The chapter starts with "And after these things." After what things? Clearly, the things concerning the explanation of the whore (Mystery Babylon) and the beast of Rev. 17:1-18. Rev. 17 is a complete revelation in itself before Literal Babylon is dealt with in detail. It is merely mentioned as falling under the seventh vial, Rev. 14:8; 16:19. This is enough proof that this Babylon is different from that in Rev. 17 and that the revelation of the previous one is completed in Rev. 17:18. Rev. 18 is a continuation of the seventh vial (16:17-21) which was broken into by the parenthetical chapter on Mystical Babylon.

The **cause of the fall of Babylon** is here given. She will "become the habitation (only here and Eph. 2:22) of demons, and the hold (prison, Rev. 2:10; 20:7) of every foul (unclean) spirit, and a cage (same as "hold" above) of every unclean and hateful bird." This pictures Babylon as the headquarters of the demon world and the concentration of all wickedness. Besides this, she will play the whore and make all nations drunk on the wine wherewith she is drunk, so that they will partake of the wrath of the fornication wherewith she will partake. The kings of the earth will commit fornication with her and become partakers of her sins, and the merchants of the earth will wax rich through the abundance of her luxuries. Thus, we have Babylon as a literal city whose inhabitants in general will be spiritists, unclean and vile in their living, in the very depths of degradation, and subject to demon possession so that no true and righteous God can endure the sight of them.

Because this city will live luxuriously and commit fornication with kings and nations like the Babylon of Rev. 17 is no proof that one Babylon only is meant. Cannot two different institutions commit illicit intercourse with nations and kings, one religiously and the other commercially? Babylon will be the habitation of demons who will inspire men to live as stated in Rev. 9:20, 21; 13:4, 12-18; 14:8-11; 16:2, 9. Demon worship will be as common, no doubt, as in Africa, and image worship as in pagan Rome, for which apostasy men will partake of the judgments of God. That Literal Babylon can commit spiritual fornication is plainly taught in Jer. 51:7 which was given long before Mystery Babylon was ever mentioned. See also Rev. 14:8.

2. The Verdict on Literal Babylon.

"And I heard another voice from heaven, saying, Come out of her, my people, that ye be not partakers of her sins, and that ye receive not of her plagues. For her sins have reached unto heaven, and God hath remembered her iniquities. Reward her even as she rewarded you, and double unto her double according to her works: in the cup which she hath filled fill to her double. How much she hath glorified herself, and lived deliciously, so much torment and sorrow give her; for she saith in her heart, I sit a queen, and am no widow, and shall see no sorrow. Therefore shall her plagues come in one day, death, and mourning, and famine: and she shall be utterly burned with fire: for strong is the Lord God who judgeth her," Rev. 18:4-8.

This passage is spoken by a voice different from that in the first four verses. This is perhaps the voice of God, for it speaks of certain people in the city as "my people." The command for God's people to come out of Babylon is the same as that in Jer. 50:4-9; 51:5-8, 45. The purpose of their leaving the city is that they may not partake of her sins and plagues. The word for "sins" means falling aside from prescribed law, and always in a moral sense, showing the terrible corruption of the morals of Babylon.

The plagues will be sent on this account, for her sins will reach even up to God, who will remember her and give her double for her sins and her treatment of His people. Compare the phrases "reached unto heaven" and "hath remembered her" with Gen. 18:20, 21; Rev. 16:19. God states that she must be rewarded double according to what she has done to others. According to the Greek texts, the word "you" in Rev. 18:6 should be omitted and the word "others" supplied. This simply means full compensation according to her sins.

The cup of destruction of which she will make others drink, she will receive, and to the extent that she will have lived in luxury and glory she will receive torment and sorrow, Jer. 51:24; Isa. 47:8-11. Because of these things God enumerates plagues corresponding to her exaltations and luxuries. They will be death for her life; mourning for her exaltation as a queen, non-widowhood, and lack of sorrow; famine for her delicacies; and fire for her works.

This verdict will be a just one as can be plainly seen from her state of living and pride. These plagues are to "come in one day." The word for "come" is the same as in 2 Pet. 3:10 and means "suddenly," thus indicating the manner of her destruction. The suddenness and completeness of Babylon's destruction and disappearance from the face of the earth are the prominent features of this prophecy, proving that such a judgment has not yet come and that Isa. 13:19-22; Jer. 50:13, 39, 40; 51:29, 37, 43, etc., have not been fulfilled. This further proves that God is the one bringing the judgment and that it is entirely different from the judgment of the Babylon of Rev. 17:14-17, which is by the kings of the earth, as we have already seen.

3. Lamentation over the Destruction of Literal Babylon.

The lamentation over the destruction of Babylon is to be done by three worlds, showing the greatness and universality of her commerce, influence, and her luxurious centralization, Rev. 18: 9-19.

(1) By the Governmental World.

"And the kings of the earth, who have committed fornication and lived deliciously with her, shall bewail her, and lament for her, and they shall see the smoke of her burning, standing afar off for the fear of her torment saying, Alas, alas, that great city Babylon, that mighty city! for in one hour is thy judgment come," Rev. 18:9, 10.

What a contrast to the result and destruction of the Babylon in Rev. 17:16, 17! Such language is too literal for one to mistake the reference as being anything else than to a material city, for the inhabitants of it, as well as others, will lament over its destruction. The kings are to be the instruments of the destruction of Mystical Babylon and vent their wrath on her freely. If there were no other proof that the two Babylons will be different, this one would be sufficient. These kings will commit fornication, and live in luxury with Literal Babylon right up to the time of her destruction, while, as seen in the other chapter, they will tire of Mystical Babylon before her destruction and rejoice over her fall. This certainly is a literal city for its burning is an object of sight by the whole world in that vicinity, for they "see" her burning, Rev. 18:9-19. People are to stand afar "off." This word is from the Greek **apo** and denotes motion from the surface of an object, thus showing that they will flee from the city during the time of the great earthquake under the seventh vial, Rev. 16:17-21. The fear they will have will be because of their narrow escape from the destruction which the city will receive at the hands of God. Their loss will be so great that in their frenzied state they will cry, "Alas, alas that great city Babylon, that mighty city! for in one hour is thy judgment come." It will be such a supernatural judgment that they will recognize it as from God, thus further proving that this is not the same as the destruction of Mystical Babylon by the beast and ten kings, Rev. 17:14-17.

(2) By the Commercial World.

"And the merchants of the earth shall weep and mourn over her; for no man buyeth their merchandise any more: The merchandise of gold, and silver, and precious stones, and of pearls, and fine linen, and purple, and silk, and scarlet, and all thyine wood, and all manner vessels of ivory, and all manner vessels of most precious wood, and of brass, and iron, and marble, and cinnamon, and odours, and ointments, and frankincense, and wine, and oil, and fine flour, and wheat, and beasts, and sheep, and horses, and chariots, and slaves, and souls of men. And the fruits that thy soul lusteth after are departed from thee, and all things which were dainty and goodly are departed from thee, and thou shalt find them no more at all. The merchants of these things which were made rich by her, shall stand afar off for the fear of her torment, weeping and wailing, and saying, Alas, alas that great city, that was clothed in fine linen, and purple, and scarlet, and decked with gold, and precious stones and pearls! For in one hour so great riches is come to naught," Rev. 18:11-17a.

This passage shows the merchants of the earth weeping over her destruction, because they have been made rich by her commerce. They use practically the same statement at the destruction of Babylon that the kings do, only along a different line. A list is given of thirty different kinds of merchandise sold and bought in Babylon at this time. The list consists mainly of luxuries as in Rev. 18:3. The clothing is explained here as being the riches that are in the city. This further shows that this city is to be a great commercial center of the ten future kingdoms under Antichrist. It is very reasonable that such a center should be located in Shinar. It forms the crossroads of the world, and no doubt it will become a great trading point of the world where many nations can pool their resources and centralize their business. The "urge to merge" is very evident even now. Soon much of the commercial and financial world will be linked in some way so as to demand such a central place, and when this takes effect, the city will not be far off. The merchants will also realize that Babylon's judgment is from God. This can refer only to a literal city, for no religious system will control the markets of the old world as will the Antichrist and his kingdom in the last days, Rev. 18:11-18; Dan. 8:25; 11:38, 39, 43.

(3) By the Maritime World.

"And every shipmaster, and all the company in ships, and sailors, and as many as trade by sea, stood afar off, and cried when they saw the smoke of her burning, saying, What city is like unto this great city! And they cast dust on their heads and cried, weeping and wailing, saying, Alas, alas that great city, wherein were made rich all that had ships in the sea by reason of her costliness! for in one hour is she made desolate," Rev. 18:17b-19.

Thus, the three worlds will lament the destruction of Literal Babylon and cry, "Alas, alas that great city," realizing that her judgment is sudden and from heaven. They will all see her burning and weep and wail because her riches are come to naught in "one hour" as in Rev. 18:10, 17, 19; Isa. 47:11; Jer. 50:26; 51:8. These and all other passages indicate a literal city and its destruction. The language is so simple and literal that it could not apply to anything else. If this city were a system, then it would be hoarding in all the riches instead of placing others on a basis to wax rich through her. The cry of all will be the destruction of such riches and not of a few lives or of the destruction of a system.

4. Rejoicing over the Destruction of Literal Babylon.

"Rejoice over her, thou heaven, and ye holy apostles and prophets; for God hath avenged you on her," Rev. 18:20.

Here we have the command for the heavenly world to rejoice over the destruction of Babylon. The literal reading of this verse makes it more clear, "Rejoice over her, O heaven, and ye saints, and ye apostles, and ye the prophets; for God did judge your judgment upon her." Cf. Rev. 18:24. This means that the angels and redeemed mankind and all creatures in heaven will have passed or sanctioned this particular judgment of God upon Babylon and will rejoice because He has done it in His own justice. It does not mean that this Babylon has existed throughout all ages and has persecuted all the saints and that God is judging her for that, for there are other inhabitants of heaven who have not been redeemed who are avenged because of persecution by some Babylon on the earth.

5. The Cause and Utter Doom of Literal Babylon.

"And a mighty angel took up a stone like a great millstone, and cast it into the sea, saying, Thus with violence shall that great city Babylon be thrown down, and shall be found no more at all. And the voice of harpers, and musicians, and of pipers, and trumpeters, shall be heard no more at all in thee; and no craftsman, of whatever craft he be, shall be found any more in thee; and the sound of the millstone shall be heard no more at all in thee: and the light of the candle shall shine no more at all in thee, and the voice of the bridegroom and of the bride shall be heard no more at all in thee: for thy merchants were great men of the earth; for by thy sorceries were all nations deceived. And in her was found the blood of prophets, and of saints, and of all that were slain on the earth," Rev. 18:21-24.

The violence of the destruction of Babylon is first pictured. She is to be cast down in such violence that she will be no more at all. This is illustrated by an angel taking a great stone like a great millstone and casting it with furious rush into the sea so that it is seen no more at all. The phrase "no more at all" is used six times. It is an expression showing the absolute truthfulness of the statement as well as the utter destruction of the city. This corresponds with the many passages above in the Old Testament concerning the destruction of Babylon, thus showing that after it is rebuilt and destroyed under the seventh vial that it will be utterly ruined and made desolate forever.

The Different Causes of the Fall of Babylon:

(1) Her pride, Isa. 13:19; 14:4; Jer. 50:29-34; Rev. 18:7, 8.

(2) Her oppression of Israel, Isa. 13:1; 14:2-22; Jer. 51:24, 25.

(3) Her pleasures, sins, and luxuries, Isa. 47:8-11; Rev. 18:3-19.

(4) Her sorceries, Isa. 47:12, 13; Rev. 18:23.

(5) Her idol worship, Jer. 50:2; 51:47; Rev. 13:14; 16:2.

(6) Her fornication, Rev. 14:8; 18:3, 9.

(7) Her intercourse with demons, Rev. 18:2.

(8) Her persecution of saints, Rev. 18:6, 24.

Rev. 18:24 seems to indicate that Babylon has existed from the beginning of the human race, for in it is found all that were slain on the earth. This is not to be taken to mean that, however, for Babylon was not begun until over two thousand years after the death of Abel. We know that all people have not been slain in Babylon. This would not be so if Babylon were a religious or commercial system. Nor does it mean that the slain in Babylon are the same as the saints slain by Mystical Babylon, for both Babylons are guilty of slaying saints. This verse should be understood to involve the same principle as that in which Jesus pronounced His judgment upon the Pharisees, saying that they were worse than all preceding generations but prided themselves of being better, Matt. 23:29-36. This shows that Babylon will be the final concentration of martyrdoms and reigns of terror. Therefore, its destruction will culminate the wrath of God, under the seventh vial.

Chapter Thirty-eight

THE MARRIAGE OF THE LAMB

(Parenthetical, Rev. 19:1-10.)

"And after these things I heard a great voice of much people in heaven, saying, Alleluia; Salvation, and glory, and honor, and power, unto the Lord our God: for true and righteous are his judgments: for he hath judged the great whore, which did corrupt the earth with her fornication, and hath avenged the blood of his servants at her hand. And again they said, Alleluia. And her smoke rose up for ever and ever. And the four and twenty elders and the four beasts fell down and worshipped God that sat on the throne, saying, Amen; Alleluia. And a voice came out of the throne, saying, Praise our God all ye his servants, and ye that fear him, both small and great. And I heard as it were the voice of a great multitude, and as the voice of many waters, and as the voice of mighty thunderings, saying, Alleluia: for the Lord God omnipotent reigneth. Let us be glad and rejoice, and give honour to him: for the marriage of the Lamb is come, and his wife hath made herself ready. And to her was granted that she should be arrayed in fine linen, clean and white: for the fine linen is the righteousness of saints. And he saith unto me, Write, Blessed are they which are called unto the marriage supper of the Lamb. And he saith unto me, These are the true sayings of God. And I fell at his feet to worship him. And he said unto me, See thou do it not; I am thy fellowservant, and of thy brethren that have the testimony of Jesus: worship God: for the testimony of Jesus is the spirit of prophecy," Rev. 19:1-10.

This passage is generally taken to be parenthetical, and such is the case, for it is given after the vial judgments, but will be fulfilled in heaven when all the tribulation saints and the two witnesses are raptured at the end of the Week. The return of Christ will take place at the seventh vial or soon after, and the marriage supper will be before He comes, so the passage must be parenthetical, explaining what takes place in heaven just before Christ comes back to earth with the saints. It is clear that these multitudes in heaven will be giving glory to God because He has already judged the "great whore" and the smoke of the destruction of Literal Babylon is at that time ascending up.

This whore could not be the same as the whore in Rev. 17, for she will have been destroyed three and one-half years before this event and her smoke would not be ascending at this time. Then, too, this judgment will be from God Himself who will have avenged the blood of His servants at her hand. Hence, this rejoicing is to be in obedience to the command of Rev. 18:20, calling all of "heaven, and ye saints, and ye apostles, and ye prophets" to rejoice over her judgment. Her smoke is to ascend to God "for ever and ever" which term is used fourteen times in this book. This corresponds to the eternal desolations of Literal Babylon in Isa. 13:19-22; Jer. 50:13, 23, 39, 40; 51:26, 37, 62. This may be the one place where the eternal lake of fire will be visible to the earthdwellers in the New Earth after the Millennium, Isa. 66:22-24; Rev. 14:9-11.

Next, we have mention of the elders and living creatures worshipping God. This is the last time they are seen in Revelation. Then a voice from the throne says, "Praise our God, all ye his servants, and ye that fear him, both small and great." After this, is heard the voice of a great multitude with a voice as of many waters and powerful thunderings saying, "Alleluia: for the Lord God omnipotent reigneth." (See chapter two, point V.) Then, the angel shows John the marriage of the Lamb, while in Rev.

21:9 he shows him "the bride, the Lamb's wife."

"His wife hath made herself ready," shows that there are certain preparations to make in order to be ready. This seems clear from her white robe which is the righteous works of the saints. It is impossible to describe the wedding supper as we have no description given us of it.

The Greek word for "marriage" means "marriage feast" and proves that the supper will be just as literal and real as any we know of on the earth. Cf. Matt. 22:2; 25:10. The magnitude of such a wedding supper need not disturb the reader for "with God all things are possible" and if we can conceive of thousands eating here at some banquet we can understand on the same basis how innumerable companies will do so in heaven. (See chapter forty-five for a study of the bride of Christ.)

When John saw these things, he fell down to worship the angel as he would worship God, but was immediately restrained from doing so, and was told that he (the angel) also was a redeemed person and was a fellowservant, and of the brethren and of those who have the testimony of Jesus, which is the spirit of prophecy. The words "testimony" and "prophecy" are the same as in Rev. 1:2, 3, for which see chapter two, points 7-9.

No supper in the Air

The often repeated theory that the marriage supper will be in the air where Christ meets the saints at the rapture (1 Thess. 4:16-17), and not in heaven, and that He will remain in the air having his supper for three and one-half to seven years, is unscriptural. In the first place, there is no ground in the air to land upon and have such a banquet.

It is clear that the supper takes place in heaven (Rev. 19:1-11), and it is also clear that after Christ meets the saints in the air He will go immediately back to heaven, with them, to present them before the Father (John 14:1-3; 1 Thess. 3:13). The supper in heaven is further proved by the fact that, after the supper, Christ will start from heaven with His saints (Rev. 19:11), to carry out the second advent, as in Zech. 14:5; Jude 14-15; Rev. 19:11-21. As before at the rapture, they will not tarry in the air, and will continue to the earth to deliver Israel and set up a kingdom in the earth to remain for ever.

Chapter Thirty-nine

THE SECOND COMING OF CHRIST

"And I saw heaven opened, and behold a white horse; and he that sat upon him was called Faithful and True, and in righteousness he doth judge and make war. His eyes were as a flame of fire, and on his head were many crowns; and he had a name written, that no man knew, but he himself. And he was clothed with a vesture dipped in blood: and his name is called The Word of God. And the armies which were in heaven followed him upon white horses, clothed in fine linen, white and clean. And out of his mouth goeth a sharp sword, that with it he should smite the nations: and he shall rule them with a rod of iron: and he treadeth the winepress of the fierceness and wrath of Almighty God. And he hath on his vesture and on his thigh a name written, KING OF KINGS AND LORD OF LORDS," Rev. 19:11-16.

The second coming of Christ is the chief theme of Revelation. (See chapter two, point IV.) **We shall briefly state here the facts on the subject as found in this passage.**

1. He is coming from heaven, Rev. 19:11, 14. Cf. Matt. 24:29-31; 2 Thess. 1:7; Dan. 7:13, 14.

2. He is coming on a white horse, Rev. 19:11.

3. His appearance will be somewhat similar to that in the first vision, Rev. 1:12-18. Five of the eight characteristics of Christ dealt with in chapter three are enumerated here again, Rev. 19:12, 13.

4. His titles and names are "Faithful," "True," "The Word of God," and "KING OF KINGS AND LORD OF LORDS," besides a name that no man knows, but He Himself, Rev. 19:11-16.

5. He is coming with authority and for the purpose of judging and making war upon the nations (Isa. 11:4; 49:2), of treading them in the fierceness of the winepress of the wrath of Almighty God (Isa. 63:3; Rev. 14:17-20; 19:15), and of ruling (shepherding) them with a rod of iron, Ps. 2:9. Cf. Rev. 2:27; 12:5; Ps. 149:7-9.

6. He will command the armies of heaven who will follow Him on white horses, clothed in linen white and clean, which is the righteousness of the saints, Rev. 19:14.

These six points sum up the glorious coming of Christ with His saints and angels to defeat the dragon, the beast and the false prophet with their armies, and to deliver Israel and establish a reign of righteousness on earth. Never will there be a more glorious event or a more beautiful sight than this spectacle of all the hosts of heaven, clothed in spotless white and in perfect order and rank, following Christ on white horses, anxious for the fray, to take vengeance on the enemies of God. (For spirit horses in heaven, see "War in Heaven," chapter nineteen.)

On the following pages is a brief study of the second advent as found elsewhere in Scripture.

1. The Fact of the Second Coming of Christ.

(1) Testimony of the Old Testament prophets: Enoch (Gen. 5:21-24; Jude 14, 15); Jacob (Gen. 49:10); Balaam (Num. 24:7, 17-19); Isaiah (59:20; 63:1-5); Jeremiah (23:5, 6; 25:30-33); Ezekiel (34:23-29; 37:17-29; 43:7); Daniel (2:44, 45; 7:13, 14); Hosea (2:18-23; 3:4, 5); Joel (2:28-3:21); Amos (5:15-21); Micah

(1:3, 4; 2:12, 13; 4:1-5:7); Nahum (1:5, 6); Habakkuk (2:13, 14); Zephaniah (1:14-18; 3:8, 9); Haggai (2:6, 7, 21-23; Heb. 12:25-29); Zechariah (2:10-13; 3:8; 6:12, 13; 8:3-23; 12:4-14; 13:1-9; 14:1-21); Malachi (3:1-4:6); etc.

(2) Testimony of the New Testament prophets: Jesus (Matt. 16:27; 24:1-25:46; Luke 17:22-37; 21:1-33); Peter (Acts 3:21; 2 Pet. 1:16; 3:3-9); Paul (Rom. 11:26, 27; 2 Thess. 1:7-10; 2:1-8; Heb. 9:28); John (Rev. 1:7; 19:11-21); Jude (14, 15).

(3) The Lord's Supper declares it, Luke 22:19; 1 Cor. 11:26.

(4) Angels declare it, Acts 1:10, 11. Cf. Luke 1:26-35; 2:8-18.

(5) In the Old Testament there are many times as many references to the second coming as there are to the first coming of Christ. In the 260 chapters of the New Testament the subject is referred to about three hundred times. Every time one repeats the Lord's Prayer he is praying for the Lord's coming. Nearly every book in both Testaments directly or indirectly records His second coming.

2. Some Theories of His Second Coming.

(1) That He spiritually descended on the day of Pentecost. This theory does not hold true, for all the New Testament was written after that day and all the writers wrote of a **future** coming of Christ. Jesus, in speaking of the Holy Spirit, said He would be **another** Comforter and not a second coming of Himself, John 14:16, 17, 26; 15:26, 27; 16:7-16.

(2) That the Lord comes at the conversion of the sinner. This cannot be, for at conversion there is no literal coming of the sinner to Jesus nor the literal coming of Jesus to the sinner. It is a spiritual work in the heart of the sinner who merely repents.

(3) That death is the coming of the Lord. This would be absurd, for about three souls die every two seconds; ninety every minute; 5,400 hourly; 129,600 daily; 907,200 weekly; and 47,304,-000 annually.

(4) That His coming transpired at the destruction of Jerusalem in 70 A. D. This view is fallacious, for at His coming He is to restore Jerusalem, not destroy it, Zech. 14:1-15; Luke 21:24.

(5) That His coming is the preaching of the gospel. This is certainly not correct, for the preaching of the gospel has occupied centuries, while His coming is to take place suddenly, Matt. 24:27-51; 2 Thess. 1:7-10.

(6) That all the prophecies concerning His coming are to be spiritually interpreted and that there is no literal coming. This would practically destroy the veracity of God's Word and render it of none effect as did the belief of the Jews when they spiritualized the prophecies of the first coming which were literally fulfilled, Luke 1:31. If this verse was literally fulfilled in the first coming of Christ, so must Luke 1:32, 33, relative to the second coming, be literally fulfilled. It is a gross perversion of Scripture to make a literal meaning carry such an erroneous message as a purely spiritual coming. This will be readily seen by the reader upon perusal of such passages as given above on this subject.

3. The Time of His Second Coming.

Because some have vainly and foolishly endeavored, during the past years, to set a definite time for the second coming of Christ, and failed, it does not eliminate the fact of His coming or any part of this glorious subject, for we have been warned by Jesus Himself, against such date-setting hypotheses, Matt. 24:32-51; 25:13.

Although we cannot know the day nor the hour of His second coming, we can know and should realize that it is to be a pre-Millennial, and not a post-Millennial coming. That is, He is coming before and not after the one thousand years reign of Christ on earth, Rev. 20:1-7. The theory of post-Millennialism is dangerous because it would have us substitute man and his works for the work of God. The theory is that man ushers in the Millennium through his own efforts, and secures his own happiness without the grace of God. This school of interpreters believes that the organized church is to prosper and extend its scope until the whole world is converted, thus bringing in the Millennium, when in reality, the church is less near the accomplishment of this than in the time of the apostles. It further teaches that Christ could not, or would not come back to earth while the world is sinful and that, when it is converted, men will invite Christ back to the world to reign. This certainly is not the teaching of Scripture. The purpose of this dispensation is not the conversion of the world, for all will not believe. It is the calling out of a people to serve as kings and priests with Christ during the Millennium and forever, Rev. 1:5, 6; 5:9, 10; 20:4; 22:5. The above passages under point 1 certainly do not harmonize with the idea of a converted world or picture such at Christ's coming.

4. Reasons for a Pre-Millennial Second Coming.

(1) The Antichrist, who is confessed on all sides to be pre-Millennial, is destroyed with the brightness of Christ's coming (19:11-21; 2 Thess. 2:8). This fixes His coming as pre-Millennial.

(2) The coming of Christ is "immediately after the tribulation," Matt. 24:27-31. The tribulation is just before the Millennium, Matt. 24:15-31; Zech. 14.

(3) When Christ comes He will separate the tares from the wheat, but, as the Millennium is after this, He must come before the Millennium, Matt. 13:40-43.

(4) The same conditions existing in the days of Lot and Noah will be existent when Christ comes, Matt. 24:37-51; Luke 17:22-37; 2 Tim. 3; 4:1-3; 2 Pet. 3:2-5. These passages certainly are out of harmony with post-Millennialism.

(5) The Millennial kingdom will be a literal kingdom and not simply the exaltation of the Church, or the continuance of a converted world (Rev. 5:9, 10; 11:15; 20:1-10; Dan. 2:44, 45; 7:13, 14; Zech. 14).

(6) The resurrections prove a pre-Millennial coming, as only the righteous will be raised before the Millennium, for they are

to live and reign with Him during the Millennium. The wicked dead will not be raised until after the Millennium (Rev. 20:1-15).

(7)   When Christ comes, Satan is to be bound, and since he is to be bound during the Millennium, there can be no Millennium until Christ comes (Rev. 20:1-7).

(8)   The Jews will be restored and regathered when Christ comes (Matt. 24:31) and, as they are in a state of restoration during the Millennium, Christ must first come before the Millennium, Ezek. 36:24-28; Isa. 11:10-16.

The time of His second coming to earth, then, is immediately after Daniel's Seventieth Week and at the beginning of the Millennium (Rev. 19:11-21; Zech. 14; Matt. 24:27-31). It takes place at the beginning of "the day of the Lord" as is clear in all the passages in which this expression is found. The day of the Lord never refers to the rapture, for it does not begin until after that event. Paul does not correct the early Christians for expecting the rapture of the Church but he does for expecting "the day of the Lord," 1 Thess. 5:1-11; 2 Thess. 2:1-12.

5. Signs of the Second Coming of Christ.

There are many events as signs to come to pass and many prophecies to be fulfilled yet before Christ can come back to the earth. The following signs are not all, but are sufficient to cause one to know that we are even now only a few years from His coming to earth, and, if this is near, how much nearer is the rapture of the Church? **We are to expect in the future:**

(1)   The Revised Roman Empire and the Revived Grecian Empire, Dan. 2:38-44; 7:23, 24; 8:20-25; 11:35-45.

(2)   The revelation of the Antichrist after the Revised Roman Empire, and **after** the rapture of the Church, but **before** the revival of the Grecian Empire, which will be Antichrist's kingdom, Dan. 7:7, 8, 24; 8:20-25; 9:27; 11:35-45; 2 Thess. 2:3-9; Rev. 6:1, 2.

(3)   The Seventieth Week or the seven years covenant between Antichrist and the many" Jews (Dan. 9:27), during which time all of Rev. 6:1-19:21 will be fulfilled.

(4)   Partial regathering of Israel, Ezek. 37:12-21; 38:1-39:24.

(5)   Travel and increase in knowledge, Dan. 12:4.

(6)   All the signs of Matt. 24, 25; Luke 17:22-37; 21:1-33.

(7)   The rapture of the Church. (See chapter six.)

(8)   Cry of peace and safety by the unbelieving world, 1 Thess. 5:1-9. Cf. the wars of Antichrist, Dan. 7:24; 11:40-45; Ezek. 38, 39.

(9)   Great apostasy and terrible moral conditions, 2 Thess. 2:3; 1 Tim. 4:1-5; 2 Tim. 3:1-13; 4:1-4; 2 Pet. 3:3-5.

(10)   Increased operations of satanic powers, 2 Thess. 2:9-12; Rev. 13:1-18; 16:13-16; Matt. 24:15-26; Dan. 8:20-25.

(11)   Great deceptions and delusions, 2 Thess. 2:9-12; Rev. 13.

(12)   The outpouring of the Holy Spirit, Acts 2:14-21; James 5:7. (For other signs see chapter eight, point II.)

6. The Manner of His Second Coming.

There are four Greek words concerning the manner of His

coming which we will consider, together with the main passages in which each occurs.

(1) **Parousia** means "personal coming, immediate presence, arrival, advent or return." The word is used in this connection in Matt. 24:3, 27, 37, 39; 2 Thess. 2:8; 2 Pet. 3:4. It is translated "coming" in every one of these passages and refers to the personal appearance of Christ to the earth.

(2) **Phaneros** means "to shine, be apparent, to appear publicly, be manifest and be seen." It is only used in this connection in Matt. 24:30.

(3) **Erchomai** means "to go or come." It is used generally relative to the second coming of Christ as in Matt. 24:30, 42, 43, 48; 25:13, 19, 27, 31; John 21:23; Acts 1:11; 1 Thess. 5:2; Jude 14; Rev. 1:7; etc. The English translations in these passages are "come," "cometh," and "coming."

(4) **Epiphaneia** means "advent, appearing, brightness, to give light or become visible." It is used in 1 Tim. 6:14; 2 Tim. 4:1, 8; Titus 2:13; Heb. 9:28. The English translations are "appear" and "appearing."

The above passages bring out the following facts concerning the manner in which Christ will come back to the earth:

(1) He is coming "as the lightning cometh out of the east, and shineth even unto the west," Matt. 24:27. This has reference to the direction from which He is to come to Mount Olivet, Isa. 63: 1-5; Zech. 14:1-5. It also has reference to the local coming of Christ to one place in the world as He went away.

(2) He is coming as a destruction upon the ungodly as did the flood, Matt. 24:38-51; 25:31-46; 1 Thess. 5:2; 2 Thess. 1:7-10; 2:8; Jude 14, 15; Zech. 14.

(3) He is coming visibly as He went away, Acts 1:11; Rev. 1:7.

(4) He is coming in mighty brightness and fire, 2 Thess. 1:7-10; 2:8; Ezek. 38:17-21; Mal. 4:1-6.

(5) He is coming in vengeance and wrath to punish His enemies, Rev. 14:14-20; 19:11-21; Jude 14; 2 Thess. 1:7-10.

(6) He is coming with great glory and power, Matt. 24:27-31.

(7) He is coming with all His saints and angels, 19:11-21; Zech. 14:5; 2 Thess. 1:7-10; Jude 14, 15; Matt. 24:31.

(8) He is coming with the clouds, Rev. 1:7; Dan. 7:13, 14; Matt. 24:27-30; Rev. 19:11-21.

(9) He is coming as Judge and King, Rev. 19:11-21; Isa. 11; Zech. 14; Matt. 25:31-46.

(10) He is coming "as a thief," 1 Thess. 5:2-4; 2 Pet. 3:10; Rev. 16:15. These are the only places where this expression is used of the second advent and the day of the Lord. It is not used in reference to the rapture. It is used only one other time in the Bible and that is as a warning of judgment to the church at Sardis. This manner of Christ's coming is clearly pictured in Matt. 24:36, 39, 42-51; 25:13, as being sudden and unexpected as a thief.

Chapter Forty

THE BATTLE OF ARMAGEDDON OR
SUPPER OF THE GREAT GOD

The last part of Rev. 19 is devoted to the Battle of Armageddon or "the supper of the great God." The idea that Armageddon must be fought between nations as any common war is wrong. When the last two world wars broke out some of the dailies printed flaming headlines reading "Armageddon!" or "Is it Armageddon?"

I. The Place Where Armageddon Will Be Fought.

The word "Armageddon" occurs only once in Scripture. It is the name of a place where the greatest battle of all times will be fought. The battle itself is mentioned many times in Scripture. The place, as we have seen, is where the three unclean spirits will gather the nations together to battle, Rev. 16:13-16. Armageddon is called "the valley of Jehoshaphat" in other places, which identifies the location of the battle from Mount Carmel southeast to Jerusalem, Joel 3.

The word "Armageddon" is from two Hebrew words, **har,** meaning "a mountain or range of hills, hill country," and **Megiddo,** meaning "rendezvous." The two words put together (Har-Megiddon) refer to the Hill of Megiddo on the south side of the valley of Megiddo or Esdraelon (2 Chron. 35:22; Zech. 12:11) southeast of Mount Carmel. "Megiddo" was the capital of a portion of Canaan that fell to Joshua (Josh. 12:21; 17:11; Judg. 1:27). It is at the entrance to a pass across the Carmel mountain range, on the main highway between Asia and Africa, and the key position between Euphrates and the Nile. It was the battlefield of many ages and peoples. Thothmes III, the founder of the old Egyptian empire, said, "Megiddo is worth a thousand cities."

This place will no doubt be the headquarters of Antichrist when he comes down from the north, after having conquered Russia and the countries of the north and east of the old Roman Empire. Rev. 16:13-16 says, "And he gathered them together into a place called in the Hebrew tongue Armageddon." There he will await the return of Christ who is expected to come from heaven to set His feet on the mount of Olives and deliver Israel when half of the city of Jerusalem is taken, Zech. 14:1-5. The Devil "knoweth that he hath but a short time" (Rev. 12:12) and it will be common knowledge to the Antichrist and others that Christ is expected at the end of the 1,260 days of Rev. 12:6, 14; 13:5.

By some means, the Antichrist will have lost out in his control of Jerusalem toward the last part of the Week. He will have been personally directing his armies against the countries of the north and east and the Jews will get control of the city again and will be in possession by the time Antichrist comes down from the north to destroy them. The two witnesses will have a hand in helping the remnant of Israel get control of the city by the use of the miracles they will be able to perform. At any rate, it is clear from Zech. 14 that the Antichrist comes back from the north and gathers the nations against the Jews and Jerusalem by the time Christ comes back to earth.

Ezek. 38, 39 is also clear that after Antichrist conquers Russia, Germany, and the other countries of the north and east of his empire, that he comes back from the north with these newly conquered countries and the ten kingdoms and other nations that co-operate with him, to destroy Israel and stop Christ from setting up His kingdom. These chapters in Ezekiel are generally interpreted as proving that Antichrist will come from Russia because he is "the chief prince of Meshech and Tubal," leading Russia and Germany and others down from the north into Palestine, but Dan. 11:44 proves he first conquers these countries of the north and east before he can be their chief prince and lead them down against the Jews.

II. The Time Armageddon Will Be Fought.

1.   At the time Israel will be safe in the wilderness and "Sheba, and Dedan, and the merchants of Tarshish, with all the young lions thereof (called Edom, Moab, chief of the children of Ammon, including all the Arabian chiefs of the Arabian peninsula, Dan. 11:41; Rev. 12:6, 14-17), shall say to thee, Art thou come to take a spoil? . . . to carry away silver and gold, to take away cattle and goods, to take a great spoil?" Ezek. 38:1-16.

2.   At the time Antichrist has completed his conquest of Russia, Germany, and the other countries of the north and east of his ten-kingdom empire, Dan. 11:44; Ezek. 38:1-16.

3.   At the second coming of Christ to deliver the Jews and Jerusalem from the armies of the Antichrist, Joel 3; Zech. 14; Isa. 63:1-6; Jude 14; 2 Thess. 1:7-10.

4.   Immediately after the tribulation, Matt. 24:29-31; 25:31-46.

5.   After the marriage supper of the Lamb, Rev. 19:1-21.

6.   At the time Satan is bound for the one thousand years, Rev. 19:11-20:3.

7.   At the time Jerusalem is surrounded by the armies of the nations and half of the city is taken, Zech. 14:1-15; Rev. 14:14-21; 16:13-16.

8.   Just before the Millennium, Rev. 19:11-20:3.

9.   At the end of this age, Matt. 13:40-43; 25:31-46.

10. At the time God sets up His kingdom on earth, Dan. 2:44; 7:13, 14, 18-27.

11. When the first resurrection has been completed, Rev. 19:11-20:6.

12. At the end of Daniel's Seventieth Week, Dan. 9:27; Rev. 3:5; 19:11-21.

13. Forty-two months after Antichrist is given power over the ten kingdoms, Rev. 13:5; 19:11-21.

14. When men will think there will be universal peace because Antichrist will have conquered much of the world, 1 Thess. 5:1-3.

15. At the beginning of the day of the Lord, 2 Thess. 2:1-12; 1 Thess. 5:1-3; Rev. 19:11-21; 20:1-3.

III. The Combatants at Armageddon.

The battle of Armageddon will not be an ordinary battle between two sets of earthly nations, as some teach. It will be a battle between the armies of heaven under Christ and the armies of earth under the dragon, the beast and false prophet. **On the side of Christ** there will be earthly Israel (Zech. 14:1-15), the angels of God (Matt. 25:31-45; 2 Thess. 1:7-10), and the resurrected saints of all ages (Zech. 14:1-5; Jude 14; Rev. 19:11-21). **On the side of Antichrist** there will be the Devil and his angels and demons (Rev. 12:7-12; 16:13-16; Rev. 20:1-3), the ten kings (Rev. 17:14-17; Dan. 2:44; 7:19-27), the countries of the north and east of the ten kingdoms who will have been recently conquered by Antichrist (Dan. 11:44; Ezek. 38, 39; Rev. 16:12), and many other nations that will cooperate with the Antichrist through the ministry of the three unclean frogs (Rev. 16:13-16; Zech. 14:1-5, 16; Ezek. 38, 39.

IV. The Purpose of Armageddon.

The purpose of God will be to deliver Israel from total destruction by the Antichrist and the many nations under him (Zech. 14; Isa. 63:1-10), to punish the nations for their persecution of the Jews (Matt. 25:31-46), to set up a kingdom on earth with Christ as its head (Dan. 7:13, 14; Luke 1:32), to rid the earth of all rebellion and restore God's dominion on earth as before the fall (1 Cor. 15:24-29; Eph. 1:10), and to give man one more dispensational test before destroying every rebel on earth and establishing the eternal perfect state (Eph. 1:10; Rev. 20:1-10; 21:1-22:5; 2 Pet. 3:10-13). **The purpose of man and Satan** will be to stop God's plan in taking over the earthly governments, and to avert their own impending doom, should they be defeated (Rev. 12:12; 19:19-21; 20:1-10; Zech. 14:1-5).

V. The Length of Armageddon.

According to Zech. 14:1-14, the battle will only be one day long: "The Lord my God shall come, and ALL THE SAINTS WITH THEE. And it shall come to pass IN THAT DAY, that the light shall not be clear, nor dark: but it shall be ONE DAY which shall be known to the Lord, not day, nor night: but it shall come to pass, that at evening time it shall be light."

VI. The Results of Armageddon.

1. There will be total defeat to the armies of the earth and the spirit forces under Satan, Isa. 63:1-6; Rev. 19:19-20:3; Ezek. 38, 39.

2. All the vast armies of the nations will be destroyed but "the sixth part," Ezek. 39:2; Rev. 19:19-21; Zech. 14:1-15; Joel 3.

3. These armies will make carcases for the fowls of the heavens to eat for seven long months, Ezek. 39:4-24; Rev. 19:17-21; Matt. 24:27, 28, 40-42; Luke 17:34-37; Job 39:27-30.

4. The beast and false prophet will be consigned to the lake of fire, Rev. 19:20; Dan. 7:11; 8:25; 11:45; 2 Thess. 2:8, 9.

5. The Devil and angels will be consigned to the bottomless pit, Rev. 20:1-7.

6. Blood will flow up to the horses' bridles, Rev. 14:14-20; Ezek. 39:17-24.

7. Israel will be delivered and vindicated and God's eternal kingdom will be set up, Matt. 25:31-46; Dan. 2:44; 7:18, 23-27; Rev. 11:15; Rev. 20:1-10; 21:2-22:5.

Ways Antichrist's Armies Are Destroyed.

1. By the brightness of Christ's coming, 2 Thess. 2:8.
2. By the angels, Matt. 24:27-31; 2 Thess. 1:7-10.
3. By the saints, Zech. 14:5; Jude 14; Rev. 17:14; 19:11-21.
4. By hail and rain from heaven, Ezek. 38:22; Rev. 16:21.
5. By the Jews, Zech. 14:14.
6. By the beast's army slaying each other, Ezek. 38:21; Zech. 14:13.
7. By fire, brimstone, and pestilence falling from heaven, Ezek. 38:22; 2 Thess. 1:7-10.
8. By consumption of their own flesh, Zech. 14:12.
9. By the rod and sword of Christ's mouth, Isa. 11: 4; **Rev.** 19:15.

VII. The Supper of the Great God.

This title is found in Rev. 19:17. In Rev. 16:14 it is called "the battle of that great day of God Almighty." God is to make a great supper for certain created beings. The supper will be closely related to the second coming of Christ and will be necessary to cleanse the land of all refuse of the Battle of Armageddon.

1. The Invited Guests.

"And I saw an angel standing in the sun; and he cried with a loud voice, saying to all the fowls that fly in the midst of heaven, Come and gather yourselves together unto the supper of the great God," Rev. 19: 17; Ezek. 39:17-23; Matt. 24:28, 40-42; Luke 17:34-37.

2. The Supper Foretold.

"That ye may eat the flesh of kings, and the flesh of captains, and the flesh of mighty men, and the flesh of horses, and of them that sit on them, and the flesh of all men, both free and bond, both small and great," Rev. 19:18; Isa. 34:3; Ezek. 39:17-23; Matt. 24:28; Luke 17:37.

3. The Supper Gathered.

"And I saw the beast and the kings of the earth, and their armies, gathered together to make war against him that sat on the horse, and against his army," Rev. 19:19; 14:14-20; 16:13-16; 17:14; Ezek. 38, 39; Joel 3; Zech. 14; 2 Thess. 1:7-9; Jude 14; Isa. 63:1-5.

4. The Supper Slain and Prepared.

"And the beast was taken, and with him the false prophet that wrought miracles before him, with which he had deceived them that received the mark of the beast, and them that worshipped his image. These both were cast alive into a lake of fire burning with brimstone. And the remnant were slain with the sword of him that sat upon the horse, which sword proceeded out of his mouth," Rev. 19:20, 21a; Isa. 34; 63; Ezek. 38, 39; Joel 3; Zech. 14; Rev. 14:14-20.

5. The Supper Eaten.

"And all the fowls were filled with their flesh," Rev. 19:21b; Ezek. 39:4, 17-23; Matt. 24:28; Luke 17:37.

THE MILLENNIUM—THE THOUSAND YEARS AND AFTER

In Rev. 20:1-15 we have the expulsion of Satan from the earth, the Millennial Reign of Christ and His saints, Satan's post-Millennial career and doom, and the final judgment.

I. The Expulsion of Satan from the Earth.

"And I saw an angel come down from heaven, having the key of the bottomless pit and a great chain in his hand. And he laid hold on the dragon, that old serpent, which is the Devil, and Satan, and bound him a thousand years. And cast him into the bottomless pit, and shut him up, and set a seal upon him, that he should deceive the nations no more, till the thousand years should be fulfilled: and after that he must be loosed a little season," Rev. 20:1-3.

This passage is the continuation of the Scripture on the Battle of Armageddon of Rev. 19:11-21 and shows the confinement of the dragon in the abyss. After Armageddon an angel will come down from heaven having the key to the abyss. This angel is explained under the fifth trumpet in chapter twelve, and the abyss is explained in chapter thirty-one, for which see. Just as other spirits are there now, so will Satan be confined there for one thousand years. How an angel or a spirit can be bound by a literal chain and be cast into a material place is only understandable when we see that angels have bodies and can be localized and confined to material places. If this be not true, how are demons bound in this abyss now to be loosed under the fifth and sixth trumpets? How angels can be confined to tartarus in chains (2 Pet. 2:4; Jude 6, 7) and how all wicked men, demons, fallen angels, and rebellious creatures of all kinds can be confined in the lake of fire forever can be understood only on this basis. Matt. 25:41; Rev. 14:9-11; 19:20; 20:10-15.

This angel will "lay hold" on Satan, overpower him by actual combat, "bind him" with a great chain, cast him into the abyss where he is to be for a thousand years and "set a seal upon him," or literally, seal the abyss over him to keep him here so that he cannot deceive the nations until the Millennium is over. Thus we see that Satan is literal, his doom is literal, he is to be bound by a literal angel, with a literal chain, cast into a literal place, and sealed with a literal seal for the period of the Millennium.

In Rev. 12 we have seen that the dragon and his angels will be cast out of heaven to the earth in the middle of the Week, where they will remain until the Battle of Armageddon when they will fight against Christ and His angels and saints. It is not stated whether Satan's angels will be cast into the abyss with him or not. It may be that they will be confined there and loosed with him after the Millennium to help him deceive the nations again.

II. The Millennial Reign of Christ and His Saints.

"And I saw thrones and they sat upon them, and judgment was given unto them: and I saw the souls of them that were beheaded for the witness of Jesus, and for the word of God, and which had not worshipped the beast, neither his image, neither had received his mark upon their foreheads, or in their hands; and they lived and reigned with Christ a thousand years. But the rest of the dead lived not again until the thousand years were finished. This is the first resurrection. Blessed and holy is he that hath part in the first resurrection:

271

on such the second death hath no power, but they shall be priests of God and of Christ, and shall reign with him a thousand years," Rev. 20:4-6.

This passage shows that the tribulation martyrs will also have a part in the reign of Christ in the Millennium and forever. If there were no other passage in the Bible to teach the doctrine of the Millennium this one would be sufficient, for the word simply means "one thousand years," which term is repeated six times in the first seven verses of this chapter. **Before we take up this subject in the Scriptures, let us note what Rev. 20 says about the Millennium.**

1. **Satan must be bound before the Millennium can begin,** Rev. 20:1-10. This certainly implies the fulfillment of all the events of Rev. 4-19. Therefore, the thousand years cannot come until these things are fulfilled.

2. **Satan will be bound during the Millennium,** Rev. 20:3.

3. **After the binding of Satan, John saw "thrones" and their occupants,** Rev. 20:4. The occupants of the thrones will be the tribulation martyrs. They will reign as kings and priests with Christ as well as all other redeemed heavenly peoples. (See point 2, theory 1, chapter seventeen.)

4. **In Rev. 20:5 John shows that the tribulation martyrs have a part in the first resurrection,** which is before the thousand years and includes all the different companies of redeemed and every individual saved from Adam to the binding of Satan. This verse also implies that the tribulation saints will be the last redeemed company resurrected and translated. The first resurrection ends with the rapture of this company and the two witnesses. All other passages on the resurrections in Scripture, except a few on the rapture of the Church, speak of the first and second resurrections as being one, and occurring at the same time, but this passage and 1 Cor. 15:20-23, 51-58; Phil. 3:10-14; 1 Thess. 4:13-18; 2 Thess. 2:1, 6-8; 2 Cor. 5:1-6; Eph. 5:26, 27; Heb. 11:35; 1 John 3:1-3 speak of a resurrection from out of the dead, or the resurrection and translation of all dead and living saints before the thousand years. In Rev. 20:11-15 "the rest of the dead" of Rev. 20:4-6 or the wicked dead who have no part in the first resurrection and who will be resurrected after the thousand years, are pictured as standing before the white throne to be judged. This will be the second resurrection. It includes all the wicked dead from Adam to the end of the Millennium.

5. **Next, a blessing is pronounced upon all that have part in the first resurrection,** for "on such the second death (the lake of fire, Rev. 2:11; 19:20; 20:10-15; 21:8) hath no power, but they shall be priests of God and of Christ, and shall reign one thousand years."

6. **"When the thousand years are expired, Satan shall be loosed out of his prison.** And shall go out to deceive the nations which are in the four quarters of the earth, Gog and Magog, to gather them" against God. Then fire will come down out of

heaven to devour his armies, and he himself will be cast into the lake of fire, where the beast and false prophet are and have been for the one thousand years, Rev. 19:20; 20:7-10.

7. **Then, the wicked dead will be resurrected and there will be the final judgment,** after which the renovation of the earth and heavens will take place. The result will be a New Heaven, and a New Earth, as pictured in Rev. 21, 22.

Now with these facts as a basis, we can understand the many other Scriptures which speak of the reign of the Messiah without distinguishing between His reign during the first thousand years and His reign forever.

In addition to the thoughts above in Rev. 20 on the Millennium, the following is a brief study of the subject.

1. The Definition.

This dispensation is so-called because God Himself, along with the Son and Holy Spirit, will set up a divine government on earth over all nations forever. **It is called in Scripture:**

(1) "The thousand years" reign of Christ, Rev. 20:1-10.

(2) "The dispensation of the fulness of times," Eph. 1:10.

(3) "The day of the Lord," Isa. 2:12; 13:6, 9; 34:8; Ezek. 30:3; Amos 5:18; Joel 2:1; Zeph. 1:7, 8, 18; 2:2, 3; Zech. 14:1-21; Mal. 4; 1 Thess. 5:2; 2 Thess. 2:1-8; 2 Pet. 3:10.

(4) "That day," Isa. 2:11; 4:1-6; 19:21; 24:21; 26:1; Ezek. 39: 22; 48:35; Hos. 2:18; Joel 3:18; Zech. 12:8-11; 13:1; 14:1-9; Mal. 3:17.

(5) "The world (age) to come," Matt. 12:32; Mark 10:30; Luke 20:35; Eph. 1:21; 2:7; 3:21; Heb. 6:5.

(6) "The kingdom of Christ and of God," Eph. 5:5; Matt. 20: 21; Luke 1:32-35; 19:12-15; 22:29, 30; 23:42; 2 Tim. 4:1; John 18: 28-37; 1 Cor. 15:24-28; Dan. 7:13, 14.

(7) "The kingdom of God," Mark 14:25; Luke 19:11; 22:14-18.

(8) "The kingdom of heaven," Matt. 3:2; 4:17; 5:3, 10, 19, 20; 7:21; 8:11; 10:7; 13:43; 18:1-4; Luke 19:12-15.

(9) "The regeneration," Matt. 19:28; Eph. 1:10.

(10) "The times of the restitution (restoration) of all things," Acts 3:20, 21.

(11) "The consolation of Israel," Luke 2:25.

(12) "The redemption of Jerusalem," Luke 2:38.

2. The Length, Rev. 20:10.

This dispensation will last one thousand years, Rev. 20:1-10. The expression "thousand years" is mentioned six times in this one passage. Although the length is mentioned only in this passage, the age is referred to in all parts of Scripture, as we shall see. It will begin with the binding of Satan at the return of Christ to the earth to re-establish the throne of David and set up God's kingdom on the earth, Matt. 24:29-31; Rev. 19:11-20:7. It will last until the loosing of Satan, the last rebellion, the renovation of the earth by fire and the great white throne judgment,

Rev. 20:11-15; 2 Pet. 3:8-13.

3. The Favorable Beginning.

Man will have a beginning more favorable than in any other dispensation. Besides many of the wonderful conditions of other ages, man will have the God of heaven for a ruler and enjoy all the privileges that such rulership will bring. The following points concerning the divine government and the blessed conditions on the earth during the Millennium will clearly reveal the favorable conditions in this dispensation.

(1) The Kingdom Foretold.

God's earth-bound covenants to Abraham and David guaranteed to Israel an everlasting earthly kingdom and that they would be the channel of blessing to all the families of the earth. It seemed that these covenants and promises would fail when Israel was divided into two kingdoms about 1009 B.C. After this, God raised up many prophets who continued emphasizing to Israel that God would still bring to pass His promises to them, but would have to use different means of doing it than would be necessary if they would fulfill His righteous requirements. Sixteen of these prophets left writings concerning the coming king and kingdom. Note in the following passages that, because of the rebellion of Israel, they were to go into captivity and be scattered among the nations where they would be "many days" without a king, a sacrifice or a knowledge of the true God; and that after this they would be gathered back to their own land and be brought very low because of the oppression of the Gentiles. Then they would be delivered from the nations by the Messiah who would come from glory to set up the kingdom, Isa. 1:2-9, 25-28; 2:2-5; 9:6, 7; 11:2-16; 27:12, 13; 32:1-5, 15-19; 34:1-17; 63:1-6; Jer. 33: 17-26; Ezek. 24:11-30; 36:16-38; 37:1-28; Dan. 7:12-27; 8:16-27; 9:24-27; 11:36-12:13; Hos. 2:14-23; 3:4, 5; Joel 2:28; 3:21; Mic. 4; 1-13; 5:1-15; Zech. 8:1-14:21; Mal. 3:1-4:6; Luke 1:30-35; 21:20-24; Acts 15:13-17; Rom. 11:25-27; Rev. 1:5; 5:10; 11:15; 20:1-4. Men looked for it through the ages, Heb. 11; 2 Sam. 7; Isa. 9:6, 7; Mal. 4; Mark 15:43; Heb. 12:25-28; Acts 3:19-21.

(2) When Will the Kingdom Be Set Up?

A. At the return of the King from glory, Matt. 25:31-46; Isa. 9:6, 7; Dan. 2:44, 45; 7:13, 14; 8:18-22; Zech. 14; 2 Thess. 1:7; Jude 14; Rev. 17:14; 19:11-20:7.

B. After the Church is raptured (1 Cor. 15:51-58; 1 Thess. 4: 13-17), for the Church comes back with Christ to help Him set up the kingdom and reign over the nations, Zech. 14:1-5; Jude 14; Rev. 1:4, 5; 5:10; 17:14; 19:11-21. It is not until after the days of the Church that Christ comes to build again the house of David, Acts 15:13-18; Isa. 9:6, 7; 11:11; Hos. 3:4, 5; Luke 1:32-35. The Church is raptured before the revelation of the Antichrist (2 Thess. 2:7, 8), and Antichrist is revealed before Christ comes (2 Thess. 2:1-6. See chapter seven), so the kingdom cannot be set up until these events take place.

C. After the future tribulation, for Christ does not come to the earth with the saints until then, Matt. 24:15-31; Zech. 14: 1-21; Dan. 12:1-13; Rev. 19:11-21.

D. After the great apostasy and the revelation of the Antichrist, for Antichrist is destroyed at Christ's coming to earth, so he must be here when Christ comes, 2 Thess. 2:1-12; Rev. 19:11-21; Dan. 7:18-27; 8:16-27; 9:27; 11:36-12:13.

E. At the time the Antichrist is destroyed and Satan bound for a thousand years, Rev. 19:11-20:7. Christ reigns on earth during the thousand years that Satan is bound, Rev. 5:10; 20:1-7. During the church age and the future tribulation Satan is loose, 1 Pet. 5:8; Rev. 12:12-17; 13:1-8; 20:1-7. The Devil is still loose so we are still in the church age and will be until Christ comes to bind the Devil.

F. After the first resurrection, for the saints reign with Christ on earth for one thousand years, Rev. 5:9, 10; 20:1-6. Therefore, the saints must first be resurrected before they can reign with Him. This is the period of suffering for Christ, not the period of reigning with Him, Rom. 8:18; 1 Cor. 15:20-58; 2 Cor. 5:6; Phil. 1:23; 3:20, 21; Col. 1:24; 2 Tim. 2:12; 3:12. The thousand years are between the resurrection of the righteous and that of the wicked, Rev. 20:4-6, 11-15.

G. At the time Ezekiel's temple is built, Ezek. 40:1-43:7. The reign of Christ will be set up in Jerusalem in Ezekiel's temple (Ezek. 43:7); therefore, the kingdom cannot be set up in the temple until it is built, Isa. 9:6, 7; 52:1-8; 62:6-14; Ezek. 36:24-36; 41:1; 43:7; Zech. 6:12, 13; 14:1-21; Matt. 23:37-39; Luke 1:32-35; Acts 15:13-18.

H. After Israel is gathered back from all countries, Ezek. 20: 33-36; 36:17-38; 37:1-28; Hos. 3:4, 5; Dan. 9:27.

I. When the Jews are delivered from the armies of the nations and they become a blessing to all the families of the earth, Gen. 12:1-3; Psa. 2:6-8; Isa. 9:6, 7; 25:6-9; Zech. 9:9-11; 14:1-21; Acts 15:13-18; Luke 1:32-35.

J. In the days of the ten kings of Revised Rome and Revived Grecia, Dan. 2:40-45; 7:18-28; Rev. 17:8-18.

K. After all of Rev. 4-19 is fulfilled, for Christ comes in Rev. 19, 20 to set up the kingdom.

According to these facts, the kingdom is yet future—**after all the above events.** Christ Himself taught in the following passages that the kingdom would be yet future at His second advent, Matt. 16:21-27; 19:28; 20:23; 23:37-39; 24:3-31; 25:31-46; 26:29, 64; Acts 1:6, 7; 3:19-21; John 14:3; Luke 9:26; 19:11-27; Rev. 5:9, 10; 11:15; 20:1-7.

The apostles taught that the kingdom was yet future at the second coming of Christ, Acts 1:7-11; 1 Pet. 1:7; 5:4; 2 Pet. 1:16; 3:3, 4; Jas. 5:7; 1 John 2:28; Jude 14; 1 Tim. 6:14, 15.

(3) Will It Be a Literal Earthly Kingdom?

The kingdom will be as earthly and literal as any other one that has been on the earth. It will be the ninth kingdom mentioned in Daniel and Revelation—Egypt, Assyria, Babylon, Medo-Persia, Greece, Rome, Revised Rome, Revived Greece, and the Kingdom of Heaven, Isa. 9:6, 7; Dan. 2:44, 45; 7:13, 14, 17-27; Zech. 14; Rev. 17:8-18. As all the preceding kingdoms have been literal, so must this one be literal. The following studies will further prove that this kingdom will be a literal kingdom on earth.

The Seventh-Day Adventists and others teach that the earth will be desolate during the thousand years and that this earth is the bottomless pit where the Devil will be bound for that period. There is not one word of truth to this theory. The bottomless pit is a department in the underworld for the confinement of certain demon and angelic spirits. (See chapter thirty-one, point 4.) That the earth will not be desolate during this period is proved by the Scriptures in the following points.

(4) What Will Be the Form of Government?

It will not be monarchic, democratic, or autocratic, but a theocratic form of government, i.e., **God reigning through:**

A. **Jesus Christ,** His only begotten Son, 2 Sam. 7; Psa. 2; 89: 35-37; Isa. 2:2-4; 4:2, 3; 9:6, 7; 11:1-15; 16:5; 24:23; 32:1-4; 40: 9, 10; 42:1-4; 52:7; Jer. 23:5-8; Ezek. 43:7; Dan. 2:44, 45; 7:13, 14; Mic. 4; 5:1-7; Zech. 6:12, 13; 14:1-21; Matt. 25:31-46; Luke 1:32-35; Rev. 11:15; 20:1-10.

B. **David, the king of Israel,** Jer. 30:9; Ezek. 34:24; 37:24-28; Hos. 3:4, 5.

C. **The Apostles and ALL Saints from Adam to the Millennium,** or those who have part in the first resurrection, Psa. 149:5-9; Dan. 7:18-27; Matt. 19:28; 1 Cor. 4:8; 6:2; Eph. 2:7; 2 Tim. 2:12; Heb. 11; Rom. 8:17; 2 Thess. 1:4-7; Rev. 1:6; 2:26, 27; 5:9, 10; 11: 15; 12:5; 20:4-6; 22:5. All saints will be judged and rewarded according to the deeds done in the body and will be given places of rulership according to their rewards, not according to the company of redeemed of which they are a part, or the age in which they were redeemed. This is the only true and just basis for rewards. If some New Testament saint were rewarded and given a greater place in the kingdom than some Old Testament saint, on the mere grounds that he was redeemed in a different age, this would be unjust. But if all will be rewarded "according to their works" regardless of the age in which they are redeemed, then God cannot be accused of injustice or respect of persons. It is up to every man to make good in every age and prove true to his own particular test. From the above passages in point B, we learn that David will have a greater rulership than any one of the apostles. He is to be king over all Israel under Christ, while the apostles will have only one tribe each.

Some Old Testament saints did more for God and had more power than the average New Testament saint. Take an ordinary professed follower of the Christ today and compare his life and works with Enoch, Abraham, Moses, Elijah, etc. Shall the New Testament person be given a greater degree of reward and responsibility in the eternal kingdom than these men just because he was saved in a different age? See Prov. 24:12; Psa. 62:12; Jer. 31:16; Rom. 14:12; 2 Cor. 5:10, 11; 1 Cor. 3:11-15; Jas. 2:21-25; Rev. 14:12; 20:12-15; 22:12. Certain classes will not have part in reigning with Christ, Matt. 18:1-13; Luke 9:62; 14:27; John 3:3-5; Rom. 8:9; 1 Cor. 6:9, 10; Gal. 5:19-21; Eph. 5:5; 2 Tim. 2:12; Heb. 12:14; 1 John 3:10; Rev. 20:15.

(5) Where Will the Seat of Government Be?

Jerusalem, rebuilt and restored to a greater glory than ever before, will be the seat of the government, the world capital, and center of worship forever, 1 Chron. 23:25; 2 Chron. 33:4-7; Psa. 48:8; Isa. 2:2-4; 11:11-12:6; Jer. 17:25; Ezek. 34:1-31; 43:7; Joel 3:17, 20; Micah 4:7; Zech. 8:3-23; 14:1-21; Acts 15:1-18.

(6) What Will Be the Extent of the Kingdom?

It will be world-wide and will forever "increase" in every respect that every other kingdom does, except in sin and rebellion, Isa. 9:6, 7; 11:9; Psa. 72:8; 97:9; Dan. 7:13, 14; Mic. 4:1-3; Zech. 9:10; 14:1-21; Rev. 11:15.

(7) Who Will and Will Not Be the Subjects of the Kingdom?

Various classes will be excluded from the kingdom, Matt. 5:20; 13:49, 50; 24:45-51; 25:25-28, 31-46; Rev. 14:9-12. All nations now in existence on the earth and who will be living when Christ comes will continue as such in the kingdom forever and ever. "All people, nations, and languages should serve him: his dominion is an everlasting dominion, which shall not pass away, and his kingdom that which shall not be destroyed," Dan. 7:13, 14, 18, 22-27; Isa. 9:6, 7; Zech. 14:1-21; Luke 1:32-35; Rev. 11:15.

After the Battle of Armageddon and the judgment of the nations at the return of Christ, there will be many of all nations left who will go up from year to year to worship the Lord of hosts and keep the feast of tabernacles. It is these people that will populate the earth during the Millennium and forever, Isa. 2:1, 2; Zech. 14:16-21; Matt. 25:31-46; Rev. 11:15; 20:1-10.

The Russellists teach that the atonement of Christ was for Adam only; that one man could only atone for one man; that all the sons of Adam must remain dead until the Millennium, when they will be resurrected and given a second chance; and that all who will not accept God during this second probation will be annihilated.

This is one of the most erroneous and unscriptural teachings in the country. It denies the very heart of the gospel. Jesus died for every man, as proved in Matt. 1:21; 26:29; Luke 24:47; John 1:12-16; 3:5, 16-19; 6:37-40; 14:6; Acts 2:38; 4:12; Rom. 1:16; 5:6-11, 15-21; 6:23; 8:1-4, 32; 2 Cor. 5:14-21; Eph. 1:7; Col. 1:14, 20-22; Heb. 1:3; 2:9, 10; 9:11-28; 10:4-22, 29; 1 Pet. 1:18-23; 1 John 1:7.

What is it in all these passages that makes God just in forgiving every man today who repents and believes the gospel? It is the one sacrifice of Christ for all men of all times, not only for Adam. If one man could only atone for the sins of one man, then to be redeemed, every man that has ever been born must have God die in his stead separately. God would then have to do what He did in Christ numberless times. Such a thing is absurd. If men are going to have another chance in the Millennium, the basis of their reconciliation must be the same as it is now. Thus, their teaching of Christ being able to die for one man only is contradicted by their teaching that men will have a second chance during the Millennium, else how are they to be saved then unless Christ dies separately for each individual as they teach must be the case in the doctrine of the atonement?

The Bible teaches that all the righteous dead will be resurrected **before** and the wicked dead **after** the Millennium, Rev. 20:4-15. How could the wicked be resurrected and be given a second chance during the Millennium, if they are not to rise until after the Millennium? In no place does the Bible teach a second chance. On the contrary, "it is appointed unto men once to die, but **after this** the judgment" (Heb. 9:27), not "after this" a second chance and then annihilation, if they fail again. The Bible does not teach annihilation for any man. Men during their natural lifetime have hundreds of chances to get right with God, and if they fail to do so they will be cut off and "that without remedy," Prov. 29:1.

So it is clear that the subjects of the millennial kingdom will not be the wicked dead who will be raised to life again, but the natural living nations who will be on the earth at the coming of Christ with the saints to set up the kingdom, Isa. 2:1-4; 11:11; 66:17-21; Zech. 14:16.

(8) Will There Be Laws for the Subjects of the Kingdom?

There will be laws in this kingdom for the same purpose as in any other kingdom. There are laws even in heaven and in all the universe. Adam was given laws to keep before he fell. Men will have laws to keep in all eternity after mankind has been redeemed from the fall, so why not during the Millennium? Even if there were no sinners during the Millennium, God would of necessity have laws to make known His will to His subjects. It is necessary to have certain laws to govern free wills, else there would be no need of a free will to choose between right and wrong. The very nature of a free will demands law and revelation in order to be enlightened as to the specific will of the Creator and give him something to cause the will to be exercised.

This kingdom will be a literal earthly one with earthly subjects, many of whom will be rebels in heart against the rule of Christ and will openly rebel at the first chance they get when the Devil is loosed out of the pit at the end of the thousand years, Rev. 20:1-10. Anyone who has really been "born again" and baptized in the Holy Spirit and has fellowship with God during the thousand years certainly will not rebel with Satan at that time. That there will be sinners here during the Millennium is clear from Isa. 2:2-4; 9:6,7; 11:3-5; 16:5; 65:20; Psa. 2:6-9; Mic. 4:3; Zech. 14:16-21; 1 Cor. 15:24-28; Rev. 20:7-10.

Many unsaved people will be permitted to live and go through the Millennium because of keeping the outward laws of the government, but in their hearts they will be rebellious against the government. On the other hand, many will be executed during the Millennium because of committing sins worthy of death, Isa. 11:3-5; 16:5; 65:20. It will be these rebels in heart who will openly rebel against God at their first chance when the Devil is loosed. There will have to be laws to govern such people during this time, else there would be no basis of judgment and there could be no transgression of the law to bring judgment.

(9) What Laws Will There Be?

The laws of God revealing His will in detail as given by Moses and Jesus Christ will be the laws of the kingdom. This includes the laws of both the Old and New Testaments. The outward laws, of course, will be the only ones enforced upon man. Outward laws could never govern the desires of a free will. It is clear from Isa. 2:2-4; Mic. 4:2; Ezek. 40:1-48:35, and the books of the law themselves, that the law of Moses will again become effective during the Millennium and forever.

The writers of these passages knew only of the law of Moses when they wrote, so when they mentioned "the law," they could have had in mind only the law of Moses. The law revealed the governmental plan and laws of God in detail which were sufficient to govern **natural man** regardless of his attitude to spiritual things. Will God govern man in the future by anything short of His revealed will as written in the law? When God gave the law to Moses He gave it in eternal terms, thus emphasizing the truth that the law was eternal and should be observed by Israel and all nations forever. Israel or no other nation ever kept the law, yet the law was given for them to keep forever. If they ever keep it as God intended it will yet be future. This will be proved in the following studies.

Besides these natural outward laws for the **natural man** in the kingdom, there will be laws governing the **spiritual man**; i. e., the man who will desire spiritual things and live in the Spirit. This kind of man will have to keep the outward laws just as much as the man who rejects spiritual things, and as long as he obeys the outward laws he will not be punished because he has broken no law. The same thing is true in any government today. A man does not have to accept spiritual things to escape the clutches of the law. He may be ever so rebellious as far as spiritual things are concerned, but as long as he keeps the outward laws he is not apprehended by the law. On the other hand, the man who accepts Christ as his Savior and walks in the Spirit must also keep the outward laws. Besides being under the laws of the government, he is under the laws of Christ, Matt. 5-7; etc.

In these laws of Christ governing the spiritual man there are laws which the natural man will not be required to keep. For example, the law concerning adultery affects all men, but the one, "whosoever looketh on a woman to lust after her hath committed adultery with her already in his heart," Matt. 5:27-30, would kill the spiritual man in that he would be cut off from God in sin and become spiritually dead, but it would not affect the rebel against spiritual things because he is already dead spiritually.

(10) Who Will Execute These Laws?

Christ and the glorified saints who have been made kings and priests will execute these laws forever. (See Scriptures under point (4) above.)

(11) Where Will the Different Nations Be Located?

The Gentile nations will perhaps live in the same places they do today, with the exception of those who live in the lands promised to Abraham and his seed for an everlasting possession. This promised land is from the Mediterranean Sea on the west to the River Euphrates on the east, taking in all the Arabian Peninsula and the wilderness countries south and east of Palestine, Gen. 15:14-18; 17:6-19; Exod. 32:13; Lev. 25:23-34; Deut. 4:40; Josh. 14:9; 2 Chron. 20:7; Isa. 60:21; Jer. 25:5; Ezek. 47:13-23.

(12) How Will This "Everlasting Possession" Be Divided?

This promised land will be divided in wide strips running east and west. There will be twelve great strips, one for each of the twelve tribes. The portion for Dan will be on the extreme north and that for Gad on the extreme south and the other tribes between. Judah and Benjamin will have their two portions joining the "holy oblation," a portion of land sixty miles square and divided into three parts: 24x60 on the north for the Levites, 24x60 in the middle for the priests, and 12x60 on the south for the city of Jerusalem and its suburbs and gardens. (See our chart, "the Bible on Canvas.") The city itself will be twelve miles square and will be a miniature of the New Jerusalem, Ezek. 48:1-35.

(13) Will the Jews Have a Temple During the Millennium?

Yes. It will be located in the priest's portion. The temple and its enclosure called "the sanctuary" (Ezek. 45:1-4) will be one mile square (Ezek. 40:1-45:14). It will not be the one that will be built in the last days before the second coming of Christ and in which the Antichrist will sit during the last three and one-half years of the age of Grace, Matt. 24:15-22; 2 Thess. 2:4; Rev. 11:1, 2. This one will be destroyed at the second coming of Christ. The millennial temple will be built by Christ Himself when He comes to the earth to set up the kingdom, Zech. 6:12, 13. It will be the place for Christ's earthly throne forever, Ezek. 43:7.

(14) The River of the Millennial Temple.

There is to be a literal river flowing out from this temple east-

ward and from the south side of the altar. It will then turn and
run southward through Jerusalem and immediately south of
Jerusalem will be divided, with half flowing westward into the
Mediterranean Sea and half flowing eastward into the Dead Sea.
The Dead Sea is to be healed so that multitudes of fish will be
found in it, Ezek. 47:1-12; Zech. 14:8. When Christ sets His feet
on the mount of Olives there is to be a great earthquake and
the whole country will be changed, Zech. 14:4, 5. The Dead
Sea will be raised so that it will have an outlet to purify the
stagnant waters which have been shut up for all these centuries.
There will be marshes left to provide salt. There will also be
trees on both sides of the river whose leaf shall not fade, neither
shall the fruit be consumed. The trees shall bring forth new fruit
according to their months, which shall be for meat and preservation of natural life for the nations. This river is not the same
as the one in the New Jerusalem, for that does not come down
to the earth until the New Earth after the Millennium (Rev.
22:1-5), as we shall see in chapter forty-five.

(15) Will There Be Priests in the Millennial Temple?

There will be earthly priests in the future temple just as there
were in the first temple, Ezek. 43:19-27; 44:9-31. The Levites
who went astray with the northern kingdom of the ten tribes
will not be permitted to do the most holy work, but shall serve in
other parts of the temple; i.e., their descendants will serve in the
future temple worship. The sons of Zadok who stayed true to the
house of David will do the most holy work, Ezek. 43:19-27; 44:9-31.
See 1 Kings 1:39; 2 Sam. 8:17; 15:24; 20:25.

The priesthood of the law of Moses was an eternal one, Exod.
29:9; 40:15; Num. 25:11-13; 1 Chron. 23:13. This would seem to
conflict with Heb. 7:11-28 where the writer speaks of a change
in the law and priesthood of old. There is really no conflict. As
far as the means of approach and the way of salvation and
mediation to God are concerned, there has been a change. Men
under the law had to come through the priests and offer certain
sacrifices as a token of their faith, but today Christ our passover
has been sacrificed once and forever for us by the which we
can individually draw nigh to God any time we desire. But there
will be the earthly priesthood and offerings in the future ages for
earthly peoples; not for salvation, for the blood of bulls and
goats did not take away sins even when they were offered; but
for a memorial or object lesson to demontrate that the people
believe in what has been done for them through Christ.

There is no question but what God intends to have a temple,
an earthly priesthood, sacrifices, and feasts in the future, for that
is what He revealed to Ezekiel (chapters 40-48) and promised
Israel when He gave them ordinances to be observed throughout
all their generations forever, as we shall see below. These outward observances will not supercede the present individual salvation, or the means of approach to God, but will be added for
earthly peoples to satisfy the natural instinct in man for some-

thing outward in religion.

(16) Will There Be Offerings in the Future Temple?

Every offering mentioned in the law was to be observed by Israel forever as proved by the following statements in the law, which are found from two to eight times in a single chapter.

"It is a statute for ever."

"By a statute forever throughout their generations."

"This shall be an everlasting statute unto you."

"By a perpetual statute."

"By an ordinance forever."

There are many other such statements in connection with the offerings and feasts of the law which can only be taken in a literal sense. These offerings are definitely mentioned as being in the future temple described by Ezekiel to be the place where Christ would reign in the midst of the children of Israel forever, Ezek. 43:7. **The offerings found in the Millennial chapters of Ezekiel are:**

A. Burnt offerings, Ezek. 43:24-27; 45:17-25; 46:1-24. Cf. Lev. 7:16.

B. Sin offering, Ezek. 43:19-23; 45:17-25; 46:1-24. **Cf. Lev.** 4:14-21.

C. Meat offering, Ezek. 45:17-25; 46:1-24. Cf. Lev. 6:14-23.

D. Trespass offering, Ezek. 46:20. Cf. Lev. 7:1-10; 14:12.

E. Peace offering, Ezek. 43:27; 45:17; 46:1-24. Cf. Lev. 7:11-38.

To some, it seems unreasonable that the old sacrifices and ceremonial law will be established in the Millennium and forever, but when we consider that neither Jews nor Gentiles have ever kept the law in its true sense, with the heart as well as externally, it does not seem unreasonable. These ordinances will not be the means of salvation then any more than they were in Old Testament times, Heb. 9:12-15; 11:4. They will serve as memorials in a deeper significance than they ever served as types of old. We observe today the Lord's Supper and water baptism in a deep spiritual way, and yet they are mere outward observances of what has actually been done. Neither one saves a soul from sin, but both are acts of obedience and have a true significance if observed in the right way. One is an outward symbol of what has been wrought in the heart and the other is a memorial of what has been done on Calvary for us. Christ is to observe the Lord's Supper when He comes, Luke 22:16. Ezekiel describes these things as "A PERPETUAL ORDINANCE UNTO THE LORD" (46:14). See also Exod. 12:14, 24; 27:21; 28:43; 30:21; Lev. 6:13, 18, 22; 7: 34-36; 10:9-15; 16:29-31; 17:1-7; 23:14, 21, 31, 41; 24:3; Num. 10: 8; 18:8; 25:13; 28:3, 6, 10, 15, 23, 24, 31; 29:11, 16, 19, 22, 25, 28, 31, 34, 38; etc.

(17) Will the Feasts of Jehovah Be Observed in the Millennium?

The feasts are nearly all mentioned in Ezekiel and Zechariah as being kept in the time of the reign of the Messiah. **They are:**

A.   Passover, Ezek. 45:21. Cf. Lev. 23; Exod. 12; 1 Cor. 5:7.

B.   Unleavened Bread, Ezek. 45:21. Cf. Lev. 23; 1 Cor. 5:8.

C.   Firstfruits, Ezek. 44:30. Cf. Lev. 23; 1 Cor. 15:23.

D.   Pentecost, or Weeks, Ezek. 46:9. Cf. Lev. 23; Acts 2:1.

E.   Trumpets, Ezek. 44:5; 45:17. Cf. Lev. 23; 1 Cor. 15:52; 1 Thess. 4:16; Matt. 24:31.

F.   Day of Atonement, Ezek. 45, 46. Cf. Lev. 23; Heb. 8-10.

G.   Tabernacles, Ezek. 45:25; Zech. 14:16-21. Cf. Lev. 23.

Besides these offerings and feasts, the new moons, the sabbaths and "all the ordinances of the house of the Lord, and all the laws thereof" and "all solemnities of the house of Israel" will be observed during the Millennium, and even in the new earth, forever, Ezek. 44:5; 45:17; 46:1-3; Isa. 66:22-24.

(18) **What Will Be the Spiritual Conditions in the Millennium?**
A.   **The outpoured Spirit,** Joel 2:28-32; Isa.32:15; Ezek. 36:25-27. Although the prophecies of Joel and others of the outpouring of the Spirit (called the baptism in the Spirit in Acts 1:4, 5; 2:1-16; etc.) were fulfilled in a partial way on the day of Pentecost and in the early Church (Acts 2:1-16; 2:38, 39; 9:17; 10:44-48; 11:14-18; 19:1-6), and are now being fulfilled in these last days (Acts 2:38, 39), yet they will not be completely fulfilled until the Millennium and forever. In other words, what was received by the early Church is being received today and will be received in a greater way throughout all eternity from the time the Messiah comes to bring universal religion, peace, and prosperity to all nations forever, Dan. 7:13, 14, 18-27; Rev. 11:15; 20:1-21:13.
B.   **Universal knowledge,** Isa. 11:9; Hab. 2:14; Zech. 8:22, 23. There will be universal knowledge so that all will know the ways of the Lord, whether they want to walk in them or not. Many will not walk in the ways of God spiritually as is clear from points 8, 9, and 10 above. Everyone can see what a great change there must be in order for this to be realized. There are only about 682,400,000 professed Christians of nearly 2,000,000,000 people in the world today.

How many real "born again" Christians are there of these professed followers of Christ? If true facts were known, the percentage would be small, for "not every one that saith unto me, Lord, Lord, shall enter into the kingdom of heaven; but he that doeth the will of my Father which is in heaven," Matt. 7:21. One must be "born again" and made a "new creature" in Christ and live a consistent life of holiness before he can call himself a true follower of Christ, or a "Christian," John 3:1-8; 2 Cor. 5:17; Rom. 12:1; Heb. 12:14; Jas. 4:4; 1 John 2:15-17; 3:8-10.
C.   **Jewish missionaries,** Isa. 2:2-4; 40:9; 52:7; 61:6; 66:18-21; Zech. 8:23. The Jewish people will become the missionaries of the gospel and priests of the law during this age and forever. They will, for the first time, really carry out God's plan when He called out Abraham and promised to make his seed a blessing to all nations. The missionary program will be carried on then

by the same means it is being carried on today, with the exception that it will be a governmental enterprise and not merely the enterprise of some small societies.

Such a universal missionary program will necessitate the co-operation of all the governmental and news agencies, the various organizations and the establishment of churches and schools in every locality and many other things too numerous to mention in this present work.

D. **Universal religion,** Mal. 1:11; Zech. 14:16-21; Isa. 2:2-4; Joel 2:28-31; Jer. 31:31-36. This will be the result of the preaching of the gospel and the publishing of salvation unto the ends of the earth. It will become popular then to serve God and the Lord Jesus Christ, so it will not take long for this universal religion to be realized. Everybody will go to church and have a Bible in his own language. Every community will be as the days of heaven on earth.

E. **The Glory of God will be continually manifest,** Isa. 4:4-6; Ezek. 43:1-5. This glory cloud will be seen forever over the millennial temple when the Messiah reigns. It left the temple just before the captivities (Ezek. 11:22-25) and will not come back until the nation is fully restored under the Messiah, who will build the future temple for the restored glory, Zech. 6:11, 12.

F. **Salvation for all,** Joel 2:32; Acts 2:16-21; Isa. 2:2-4; 11:9; 52:7; Heb. 8-10. However, it will benefit only those who repent and accept as it is today.

G. **Divine Healing for all,** Isa. 32:1-5; 33:24; 35:3-6; 53:5; Matt. 8:17. God will start the race out as He did Israel in coming out of Egypt. He healed them all and there was not a feeble person in their tribes, Psa. 105:37; 107:20.

(19) **What Will Be the Living Conditions During the Millennium?**

A. **Satan will be bound** so there will be no tempter, Rev. 20: 1-10; Isa. 24:21; 25:7.

B. **Universal peace,** Isa. 2:4; 9:6, 7; Mic. 4:3, 4. This means that there will be no taxations to keep up large armies and navies. "They shall beat their swords into plowshares, and their spears into pruninghooks; nation shall not lift up sword against nation, neither shall they learn war any more." Class prejudices and national ills will be forgotten because of the great turning to God by all nations after hearing the gospel. Spiritual revivals will break out in every land and many people will become one in serving the great King. The universal conversation will not be about wars, treaties, armaments, depressions, varied religions, forms of government, or anything that makes the common talk of today, but all peoples will be fully satisfied in peace and prosperity and will have no excuse to talk about anything but the goodness of God and the wonderfulness of His reign, Mal. 1:11.

C. **Universal prosperity,** Isa. 65:24; Mic. 4:4, 5. There will be no charity fund raised every year, no unemployment, and no poverty. The billions now spent on tobacco, drinks, sickness, hospitals, cosmetics, crime, worldly amusements and many other things, will supply everybody with plenty. All investments will be safe and there will be no financial crashes to retard business throughout eternity. The God of all will prosper all in any legitimate business, and all will be capable of succeeding in life in all its varied aspects.

D. **Financial system,** Mal. 3:7-12. Tithing was the system before the law (Gen. 14:20; 28:22), under the law (Lev. 27:30-33; Num. 18:21; Neh. 10:37; 13:10-12; Prov. 3:9,10) as well as since (Matt. 23:23; Rom. 2:22; 1 Cor. 9:7-18; 16:1-3; Heb. 7), so no doubt the same system will be used by the government of Christ in the coming ages. There will be plenty of money from such a system to balance the budget and have plenty to spare. There will be no corrupt politics or graft, as Christ and the glorified saints will reign in righteousness and true holiness, Isa. 32:1-5. They will need no salaries, as they will own the universe and all things will be theirs. All the money that anyone will get for personal use will be that given to the earthly missionaries and servants of the government. There will be no need of special taxes on automobiles, gasoline, food products or any other thing. This financial system, if practiced by governments today, would solve all financial problems. Especially so, if the governments would take up the program of evangelizing the world, for God would so bless such an undertaking and make them to prosper beyond human conception. Christ's government will be the first to set the example along this line as we shall see in the ages to come.

E. **Full justice for all,** Isa. 9:6,7; 11:3-5; 65:20; 57:15; 66:1,2; Matt. 5-7. Crime waves will be a thing of the past. There will be no political, lodge, personal or church pull in that day. The Lord and His glorified saints will try and judge all men, thus assuring justice to all alike. If a man commits a sin worthy of death, he will be immediately tried and executed. There will not be a thousand ways of staying execution or prolonging trial. The law will be enforced to the letter, as it should be under man today.

F. **Human life will be prolonged,** Isa. 65:20; Zech. 8:4; Luke 1:33. Human life will be prolonged to a thousand years and then those who do not rebel against God with Satan at the end of the Millennium will be permitted to live on forever and ever, as we shall see in the next chapter.

G. **Increase of light,** Isa. 30:26; 60:18-22. The light of the sun will be increased seven times and the light of the moon will be as the light of the sun today.

H. **Changes in the animal kingdom,** Isa. 11:6-8; 65:17-25; Rom. 8:18-23. All animals will have their natures changed. There will be no more fierce or poisonous creatures. Things will be as they were in the garden of Eden before the curse, with the exception of the serpent, who will still be cursed, Gen. 3:14; Isa. 65:25.

I. **Land restored,** Isa. 35:1-10; 55:12,13; Ezek. 36:8-12; Joel 2:18-27; 3:17-21; Amos 9:13-15. All lands will be restored to a wonderful beauty and fruitfulness, with the exception of the site of Babylon and perhaps a few more centers of great rebellion against God, which will be used as object lessons to coming generations of God's wrath on sin, Isa. 34; 13:17-22; Jer. 50, 51. The earth will not be fully restored to the original condition until after the Millennium, Rom. 8:18-23; Rev. 21:22; 2 Pet. 3.

J. **Love and righteousness will prevail,** Isa. 9:6, 7; 11:5; 32:1-5; 65:17-25. The Gentiles will love the Jews, who will then be the head of the nations, Deut. 28:1-14.

These facts go far to prove that the seventh and last dispensation is to have a most favorable beginning and will be a better age throughout than any other age we have ever had. These days will, indeed, be the days of heaven on earth, Deut. 11:21.

4. The Test, Psa. 2; Rev. 5:10; 11:15; 20:1-10.

The test of man in this dispensation will be to obey the laws of the divine government, obey Christ and the glorified saints, and to mould one's character in harmony with God by the Holy Spirit and the power of the gospel.

5. The Purpose of God in This Dispensation.

(1) To put down all rebellion and all enemies under the feet of Christ, so that God may be all and all as before rebellion, 1 Cor. 15:24-28; Heb. 2:7-9; Eph. 1:10.

(2) To fulfill the everlasting covenants made with Abraham (Gen. 12; 13; 15; 17); Isaac (Gen. 26); Jacob (Gen. 28:13); David (2 Sam. 7); and others.

(3) To vindicate and avenge Christ and His saints, Matt. 26: 63-66; Rom. 12:19; Psa. 2; Isa. 63; Rev. 1:7; 6:9-11; 19:1-10; 1 Pet. 1:10, 11; 2 Tim. 4:7, 8; Rom. 8:17-21.

(4) To restore Israel and deliver them from the nations and make them the head of all nations forever, Acts 15:13-17; Matt. 24:31; Isa. 11:11; Ezek. 20:33-44; 38, 39; Deut. 28.

(5) To exalt the saints of all ages in some kingly or priestly capacity according to the promises and according to their works, Rom. 8:17-21; 14:10, 11; 2 Cor. 5:10; Phil. 3:20, 21; Col. 3:4; 1 Pet. 1:10-13; 5:1, 4; Rev. 1:5; 2:26; 5:10; 11:18; 12:5; 20:4-6; 1 Cor. 6.

(6) To gather together in "one" all things in Christ which are in heaven and in earth (Eph. 1:10), and restore all things as before rebellion, Acts 3:20, 21; 1 Cor. 15:24-28.

(7) To judge the nations in righteousness and restore the earth to its rightful owners, Isa. 2:2-4; 11:1-11; Matt. 25:31-46; Dan. 7:9-27; 1 Cor. 6.

(8) To restore a righteous and eternal government on earth as originally planned, Isa. 9:6, 7; 11:1-9; 42:1-5; Dan. 2:44, 45; 7:13-27; Luke 1:32-35; Rev. 11:15; 19:11-16; 20:4-6.

(9) To fulfill the scores of prophecies concerning the reign of the Messiah, Dan. 9:24; Acts 3:20, 21; 1 Pet. 1:10-13.

6. The Means of Accomplishing This Purpose.

God will send His Son Jesus Christ with the mighty angels and all the resurrected and glorified saints from heaven to put down all rebellion on the earth, bring all rebels into judgment and complete the dispensational dealings of God with men, so that all the curse may be removed and the kingdom of God become established permanently over the earth as in the beginning, Matt. 24: 29-31; 25:31-46; 2 Thess. 1:7-10; Rev. 19:11-21; 20:1-10.

III. Satan's Post-Millennial Career and Doom.

"And when the thousand years are expired, Satan shall be loosed out of his prison, and shall go out to deceive the nations which are in the four quarters of the earth, Gog and Magog, to gather them together to battle, the number of whom is as the sand of the sea. And they went up on the breadth of the earth, and compassed the camp of the saints about, and the beloved city: and fire came down from God out of heaven, and devoured them. And the devil that deceived them was cast into the lake of fire and brimstone, where the beast and the false prophet are, and shall be tormented day and night for ever and ever," Rev. 20:7-10.

This passage has already been dealt with to some extent. It needs no explanation. This, with the above passages on the Millennium, shows that Christ is to reign on the earth and that Satan is to be cast from the earth into the abyss.

After Satan is loosed, he will go out to all the nations of the world and deceive them by leading them into the error of believing that they can dethrone Christ and overthrow His kingdom. The word for deceive is **planao,** meaning to cause to wander or go astray. It is used of doctrinal error and religious deceit. This explains how Satan will deceive men and for what purpose. Millions of these natural men on earth at that time will have had about one thousand years to accept Christ as a Savior and God as a Father, and to partake of salvation and have the Holy Spirit in their lives as men receive today. But they will have put this off and remained at enmity against God, still retaining their fallen Adamic nature, which is naturally corrupt and subject to Satan, so that when they see the opportunity presented to overthrow Christ and His kingdom, with the possibility of living in liberty and sin without restraint, they will seize it and make the best of it for this short time.

Satan can and will find a multitude of men who are ready to help him overthrow the kingdom, so he will lead them up against the saints at Jerusalem to battle. These nations will be as the number of the sand of the sea. The expression "Gog and Magog" refers to the Gentiles who will rebel at this time. The destruction of Gog and Magog in Ezek. 38, 39 is pre-Millennial, but the destruction of this host from the east and west is post-Millennial.

In their march on the city and against the kingdom to battle, fire will come down from God and devour them, and the Devil that deceived them will be cast into the lake of fire where the beast and the false prophet have been imprisoned since the battle of Armageddon, before the Millennium. This is an unanswerable argument for the eternity of hell. The beast and false prophet will have been there a thousand years without being burned up and with no prospects of such, for they are to be tormented day and night forever and ever. This will finish the history of Satan, the beast, and the false prophet and all wicked rebels on earth.

Chapter Forty-two

THE GREAT WHITE THRONE JUDGMENT

"And I saw a great white throne, and him that sat on it, from whose face the earth and the heaven fled away; and there was found no place for them. And I saw the dead, small and great, stand before God; and the books were opened: and another book was opened, which is the book of life: and the dead were judged out of those things which were written in the books, according to their works. And the sea gave up the dead which were in it; and death and hell delivered up the dead which were in them: and they were judged every man according to their works. And death and hell were cast into the lake of fire. This is the second death. And whosoever was not found written in the book of life was cast into the lake of fire," Rev. 20:11-15.

This passage will be fulfilled after the Millennium and the revolt of Satan. Immediately after the above events, John saw a great white throne occupied by God, from whose face the earth and heaven fled away. This is no doubt the same throne seen throughout the book. Here is the only place that a description of the throne is given. God, the occupant of the throne, is described before, but not the throne itself.

The Greek for "face" is **prosopon**, meaning the countenance, aspect, appearance, surface, front view, outward appearance, face, and person. It is used nine times in Revelation and is the only word translated "face," singular and plural. It shows that God has a real body and an outward appearance, as proved in the passages in which it is used, Rev. 4:7; 6:16; 7:11; 9:7; 10:1; 11:16; 12:14; 22:4. This is further proved by its usage in the rest of the New Testament where it appears forty-eight times, and always of bodily presence, actual faces, or external appearance of the subject in question. The earth and heaven fleeing away will be dealt with in the next chapter.

The fact that Christ and His throne are not mentioned here does not necessarily imply that they are absent. Both Christ and the Father will be present and have a part in the final judgment. **In its varied aspects, this judgment may be understood from the following facts in Scripture:**

I. The Judges.

1. God the Father is spoken of as the judge, Heb. 12:23, 24; 13:4; Rev. 6:10; Acts 17:30, 31.

2. God the Son is spoken of as the judge, John 5:19-27; Acts 10:42; 17:30, 31; 2 Tim. 4:8; Rev. 19:11.

3. Both the Father and Son will judge, 2 Tim. 4:1.

4. God the Father is to judge by His Son, Acts 17:31; Rom. 2:16.

5. God the Father will decree, the Son will execute, John 5:22-27; Rom. 1:32-2:5.

II. The Subjects Judged.

1. Wicked men of the whole human race, except the beast, false prophet, the goat nations, tares, etc., will be the subjects judged, Acts 17:31; Rom. 3:6; Rev. 20:11-15. That those judged at the judgment of the nations will not be judged at the final judgment seems clear from Matt. 13:30, 39-43, 49, 50; 24:51; 25:30, 41, 46; Rev. 14:9-11; 19:20, 21; 20:10. These already will have had sentence pronounced upon them a thousand years before the

final judgment, so they will not need to be judged again. These are the dead judged, but at the judgment of the nations there are no dead.

2. The angels "that sinned" and "are now bound" in tartarus will also be loosed from their long confinement and be judged at this judgment, 2 Pet. 2:4; Jude 6, 7.

III. The Time of the Judgment.

The time of this judgment will be after the Millennium and after the doom of Satan in the lake of fire is realized, Rev. 20:7-15. It is called "the day of judgment" and so there must be a definite time set for it, Matt. 10:15; 11:24; 12:36; Acts 17:31; 2 Pet. 2:4; Jude 6, 7.

IV. The Place of the Judgment.

The judgment is to be before the great white throne of God, which will still be in heaven, for it is not to come down to the earth until after the renovation of the earth by fire and after the New Heaven and the New Earth are completed, Rev. 21:1-5. This seems to be proved further by 2 Pet. 3:7 where the renovation of the earth takes place at the final judgment. It seems to be pictured also in Rev. 20:11 at the same time of the final judgment.

V. The Purpose of the Judgment.

1. To give every man a trial before his condemnation, and punishment, especially so in this case which involves the eternal destiny of immortal souls.

2. To judge the "secrets of men," Rom. 2:16.

3. To judge all idle words, Matt. 12:36.

4. To judge all the works, thoughts, actions and sins of man, 1 Tim. 5:24; 1 Pet. 1:17; Rev. 20:12, 13.

VI. The Basis of Judgment.

1. The conscience, Rom. 2:12-16.

2. The law, Rom. 2:12-16; Rev. 20:11-15.

3. The gospel, Rom. 2:12-16; John 12:47, 48; Rev. 20:11-15.

4. The book of life, Rev. 20:11-15.

A man who passes through such a judgment will have no excuse or criticism of the sentence passed regardless of what the decision will be, for in a sense he will be his own judge. The actual manifestation of his failure to live up to his conscience, the law or the gospel, the fact that his sins and misdeeds are like mountains before him, and the absence of his name in the book of life, will automatically condemn him.

The "books" mentioned in Rev. 20:12 do not refer to the records of men written in books and kept by a recording angel, for we have no knowledge of such in Scripture, but they refer to the Word of God which is to judge man in that day. The book of life is mentioned in Exod. 32:32, 33; Dan. 12:1; Luke 10:20; Phil. 4:3; Rev. 3:5; 13:8; 17:8; 20:12, 15; 21:27; 22:19, and has reference to the book in which the name of every man who is to enter into life, is recorded. It alone will be sufficient to condemn a man.

These dead dealt with here could not include the angels, for the former are the occupants of "death and hell." This proves that hades, the present and temporary hell, is different from the lake of fire or eternal hell. The sinner is placed in hades to await his committal to the lake of fire, even as the criminal is placed in jail before his trial and consignment to the penitentiary. The sinner is guilty while in hades, although he is not formally condemned before the final judgment. Therefore, he suffers fire in hades as well as in the lake of fire, Luke 16:19-31.

VII. The Nature of the Judgment.

It will be one of justice and righteousness to every man, Psa. 9:8; Matt. 7:2; 2 Tim. 4:8; 1 Pet. 2:23.

VIII. The Result of the Judgment.

1. If anyone is not found to be written in the book of life, he will be cast into the lake of fire. Hades is the present place of the souls of the wicked dead. It never means the grave where the body of man goes. It is a place of consciousness, where men are in torment until the resurrection, Gen. 42:38; Num. 16:30-33; Deut. 32:22; 2 Sam. 22:6; Psa. 55:15; 116:3; Isa. 14:9; Luke 16:19-31; Eph. 4:7-11; etc. The word is never in the plural, bodies never go there, it is never located on the surface of the earth, man never digs or makes one, man never touches one and never sees one. The Hebrew **queber** and its New Testament Greek equivalent **mnaymion,** are the words for "grave" and "sepulchre," and is the place where the body goes at death.

2. The degrees of punishment will be the result of this judgment as degrees of reward will be the result of the judgment of the saints at the judgment seat of Christ, Matt. 7:2; 10:15; 11:22-24; 12:41-45; 23:12-14; Mark 6:11; Luke 10:14; 11:31,32; Rev. 20:11-15. Hell, as far as the torment of fire is concerned, will be alike for all the lost, as much as heaven, as far as bliss and comfort are concerned, will be alike for all the redeemed. The degrees of punishment will come through the torment of the conscience and the inward self over the deeds committed, which will eat more deeply into the innermost being as the eternities come and go. This is just the opposite of the rewards for the saints, which will be ever increasing in glory and splendor as the ages come and go.

IX. The Length of the Judgment.

The judgment passed upon each individual will be eternal. The same terms that are used in describing the eternity of God are used in describing the eternity of hell, so if one is eternal, the other one must be, Isa. 66:22-24; Matt. 5:22,29,30; 10:28; 13:42, 50; 18:9; 23:15,33; 24:51; 25:30,41-46; Mark 9:43-47; Luke 12:5; Heb. 6:2; 10:26-31; Rev. 14:9-11; 19:20; 20:10-15; 21:8. It is noticeable that in Matt. 25:41,46, the words "everlasting" and "eternal," showing the eternity of bliss and torment, are taken from one Greek word, **aionion,** which never means anything but "forever." Therefore, since the life is to be eternal, the punishment must also be, for the same Greek word is used.

THE RENOVATION OF THE EARTH BY FIRE

The subject of the renovation of the earth is as much misunderstood as any other in the Bible. The ideas prevailing in general, that the world is coming to an end; that the coming of Christ ends all things on the earth; that this present heaven and earth are to be annihilated and cease to exist; that the New Heavens and New Earth never existed before; that all men are to be glorified and that none will exist in a natural state after the Millennium; that we are to spend eternity in heaven; that men and animals will not multiply and continue on earth forever, are all unscriptural, as we shall see in our future studies. Now, before we study the New Heavens and the New Earth, eternal conditions and peoples on the earth, we shall determine how the present heavens and earth are purified by fire, with the result of new or renewed ones, as pictured in Rev. 21, 22; Isa. 65:17; 66:22-24; 2 Pet. 3:10-13.

The only consistent way to get at an understanding of this subject, or any other in the Bible, is to collate all Scriptures on the subject and harmonize the seemingly difficult passages, regardless of how inconsistent they may seem to our finite minds. Until we have done this with any subject, it is evidently unwise to speak with authority or judge another's research. Having done this with this subject, we advance the following:

1. **The time of the renovation of the earth** and the elements will be after the Millennium, the battle of Gog and Magog, and the casting of Satan into the lake of fire, and during the great white throne judgment, 2 Pet. 3:7. This passage in Peter further indicates that the final judgment will take place in heaven where God's throne is and will be until after the renovation. Then the throne will come down to the New Earth, with the Holy City, to be forever with men.

2. **The present heaven and earth will not pass out of existence.** This idea is the result of a superficial reading of 2 Pet. 3:10-13; Rev. 20:11; 21:1. That this is not taught in these passages is clear from a study of the words and expressions in them in conjunction with other passages on the subject that are more clear.

(1) 2 Pet. 3:10-13, as it reads, does not convey the idea that the present heaven and earth will be annihilated. In fact, fire does not cause anything to cease to exist. Fire can merely change something from one condition to another or renovate and cleanse, as the case may be. Peter shows that there will be a renovation of the earth by fire and that the future renovation will not blot out the earth any more than did the destruction of the world by water in the beginning.

He further reveals three definite periods of the earth: first, the world (kosmos) "that then was," before Adam (see our book God's Plan for Man, Lesson 7)   which was destroyed and which destruction affected the heavens and earth; secondly, the restoration of **kosmos** and the heavens and the earth **"which are now,"** since the six days of Gen. 1:3-2:25; thirdly, the renovation of this present heaven and earth, with the result of New Heavens and a New Earth, or the Eternal Perfect State and the continuation of all life in them forever. The **kosmos** that is, will never be destroyed by the future fire, as was the **kosmos** (social system) by water in the beginning.

These facts alone prove that the heavens and the earth, "which are now," will never cease to exist, but will merely be renovated by fire and exist in a renewed state, wherein dwelleth righteousness. This is proved by a study of the different words found in this passage. It does not state that the present **kosmos** is reserved unto renovation, but the earth and the elements only, or just the parts that require it, as made clear by other passages which we shall consider below.

This renovation will end the day of the Lord and begin the day of God, 2 Pet. 3:10-13. "In which (day of the Lord) the heavens shall pass away." The word for "pass away" is from the Greek **parerchomai** and means "to go by or away from in the sense **of from one condition to another."** It never means cessation of existence. It is used over seventy-five times as follows: for the passing of time (Matt. 7:28; 9:10; 11:1; 13:53; 19:1; etc.); of events coming to pass (Matt. 24:6; Luke 21:7; John 14:29); of the infallibility of the Word of God, showing that it would be easier for heaven and earth to be changed than for the Word of God to fail (Matt. 5:18; 24:34, 35; Mark 13:31; Luke 16:17; 21:32, 33); of people passing by certain places (Mark 6:48; Luke 18:37); to denote passing over or neglect (Luke 11:42; 15:29); and of the coming of an individual (Luke 12:37; 17:7). Thus, we see from the various uses that it never conveys the idea of passing out of existence. As used in 2 Pet. 3:10, it means passing from one condition to another, as clearly expressed in Heb. 1:12; 12:27, 28. This "change" is to take place with "a great noise."

"And the elements shall melt with fervent heat," 2 Pet. 3:10, 12. The word for "elements" in these two verses is **stoicheion,** meaning "something orderly in arrangement, element, principle, or rudiment" and refers to the foundation principles of the question involved. It is used in Gal. 4:3, 9; Col. 2:8, 20; 2 Pet. 3:10, 12 in reference to the principle of sin and of the present world system, such as the sinful nature, disease germs, and spirits that cause men to corrupt themselves. The meaning also includes the things which man has made that must be destroyed before the earth can be purified and loosed from its present state of bondage and corruption, Rom. 8:18-25.

The word for "melt" is **luo,** meaning "to loose, put off, unbind, untie or set free," and is so translated in Matt. 21:2; Luke 19:30, 33; John 1:27; 11:44; Acts 7:33. It is translated "dissolve" in 2 Pet. 3:11 and 12. These passages show that all that is to happen to this present heaven and earth in this renovation is the loosing of them from the present bondage into a new state, as in Rom.

8:21-23. This loosing will be done by fervent heat, which is the best method of renovation and cleansing known to man. If the English word "dissolve" in this passage means "cessation of existence," as is generally held concerning this passage, why not give it the same meaning in Psa. 75:3; Isa. 14:31; 24:19; 34:4; 2 Cor. 5:1? It can be seen from these passages that this is not the idea. This word further expresses the idea of a "change" in the present heaven and earth into a new and better state wherein everything is good and worthy of the presence of God among men forever.

"The earth (ground) also and the works that are therein shall be burned up," 2 Pet. 3:10. The word for "works" is **ergon**, meaning "work, toil, deed, labour, and the acts of men." It is used of religious works as well as of other works. The word for "burned up" is **katakaio**, meaning "to burn down to the ground and wholly consume by fire." It has reference to the things of man on earth, which he has made, that will not be permitted in the New Earth and the Eternal Perfect State. They will be burned entirely up.

These facts are made clear from the next verses, "Seeing then that all these things shall be dissolved (loosed) . . . the heavens being on fire shall be dissolved (loosed), and the elements (sinful things of this world system) shall melt (Greek **teko**, meaning "to liquify or melt." It is not the same Greek word translated "melt" (above) with fervent heat." This passage is simple when we consider that it merely records the act of loosing the heaven and the earth from all effects of the curse and corruption and making everything clean and pure for man forever. The result of all this will be the fulfillment of the promises to man of a "new heaven and a new earth, wherein dwelleth righteousness."

(2)   Rev. 20:11 is often misconstrued to mean that the earth and the heavens we now have will cease to exist, but it does not teach this. The meaning of **pheugo**, translated "fled," is "to flee away, to shun, or to vanish." It is used both in a figurative and literal way. That its usage here is figurative is clear from its usage in Rev. 6:14 and 16:20 where, if taken literally as some would do in Rev. 20:11, we should have the passing out of existence of the heavens and every island and mountain under the sixth seal and again under the seventh vial. This could not be the case, for they are all eternal, as proved by the following: **Islands** (Ps. 72:8-10, 17; 97:1-6; Isa. 42:1-4, 8-12; 51:5; 60:9; 66: 18-24); **mountains** (Gen. 49:26; Ps. 125:1; Isa. 42:10-12; 52:7; Nah. 1:15; Hab. 3:6); **earth** (Ps. 78:69; 104:5; Eccl. 1:4); **heaven** (Ps. 89: 29; 119:89).

Examples of figurative language concerning these things may be seen in Ps. 18:7; 60:2; 68:8; Isa. 44:23; 54:10; 55:12; 64:1-3. The language of things passing away in Rev. 6:14; 16:20; 20:11, is all figurative of the shaking of the heavens and earth at the time of God's wrath before and after the Millennium. This passage, Rev. 20:11, pictures the same renovation of the earth as 2 Pet. 3. The actual heaven and earth are pictured as if they had passed away and no place was found for them, but the language being figurative merely pictures the renovation of them and taking away the things which God is to destroy in them before they can be made new in character.

(3) Rev. 21:1 is also misconstrued to teach that the present heaven and earth will cease to be. The correct understanding hinges upon the right understanding of the word "new." The Greek for this is **kainos,** meaning "renewed or new," especially in freshness and character, but never new in existence. It is in direct contrast to the Greek **neos,** meaning "new in existence." A contrast between the two words is found in Matt. 9:16, "men put new wine (**neos,** newly made wine) into new bottles (**kainos,** freshened or renewed wineskins), and both are preserved." This same contrast can be seen wherever the two words are used. Compare Matt. 13:52; 26:28, 29; 27:60; Mark 1:27; 14:25; 16:17; 2 Cor. 3:6; 5:17; Gal. 6:15; Eph. 2:15; 4:24; Heb. 8:8, 13; 2 Pet. 3:13; Rev. 2:17; 3:12; 5:9; 14:3; 21:1, 2, 5, where **kainos** (renewed or new in character or freshness) is used, with 1 Cor. 5:7; Col. 3:10; Heb. 12:24, where **neos** (new in age) is used. Thus the expression, "new heaven and new earth," in 2 Pet. 3:13; Rev. 21:1, has reference to this present heavens and earth being made new in character, renewed and loosed from the old curse. The Old Testament word **khaw-dawsh,** used in Isa. 65:17, 66:22, of the same New Heavens and New Earth, means the same as the Greek **kainos.** This simplifies the meaning of Peter's doctrine of renovation.

3. **The Scriptures further reveal the extent of this renovation** and show that many things will not be burned by fire. Only those things that are not made new at the beginning of the Millennium will be renovated by fire at the end of that time. In the next chapter, we shall list the eternal things which will remain on the earth forever after this renovation. There is not one passage in the Bible which shows the extinction of any species of living creatures that God has created.

On the other hand, there are scores of passages teaching that they will go on eternally. This is required in order to have an everlasting covenant with all flesh as in Gen. 9. Did God just intend to make man and animals on earth for a few thousand years and then destroy them altogether? This idea would destroy the very eternal plan of God and the purpose of His dispensational dealings, which is to rid the earth of all rebellion and to place man on the earth that he may replenish it forever as Adam was to have done before he fell. The "whole creation" that was created by God at the time of Adam will remain forever, and all that will be done is the deliverance of that creation from the present bondage of corruption into the glorious liberty and manifestation of the sons of God, Rom. 8:18-25.

The millennial kingdom, with its every phase of activity except the curse and its effects, will go on forever, and not be burned up by this fire of renovation. See the many Scriptures on the Millennium above which prove that the literal city of Jerusalem, the temple, etc., are all eternal. In Heb. 12:26-28, we have a definite Scripture stating that some things are to be destroyed and removed, while others are to "remain." It further states that we shall receive a "kingdom which **cannot** be moved." These verses do not only refer to things after the renovation of the earth as being immovable, but also to things before the renovation, for we shall receive the kingdom at the beginning of the thousand years, and reign throughout eternity. Even through the renovation will the kingdom continue with its peoples, rulers, system of government and material equipment, Isa. 9:6,7; Dan. 7:18-27; Luke 1:32,33; Rev. 11:15.

In Heb. 1:10-12, we have another statement to the effect that all that is to happen to the earth and heavens is a "change," not an annihilation of them. Can we conceive of God sending His Son to this earth to put down all rebellion, and then, after His accomplishment of this in the thousand years, destroying the earth and all things therein? Just what is to be destroyed is in God's own hands, and the how of it can certainly be left in the hands of Him who never fails, or makes a mistake, and who has the best interest of His creatures at heart. Are not the natures of animals changed and many other things fully restored at the beginning of the Millennium? Cannot God destroy some things with fire and not touch other things in the earth?

The God that did this with the three Hebrew children, and the burning bush, can certainly do it with the whole creation and the things that are left can come out without even the smell of fire upon them. "Our God is a consuming fire" and can do all things, whether we can fully understand them or not. We can rest assured that the judge of the whole earth shall do right, and not one of his humblest servants need fear in His august presence. In the rebellion of Satan and all mankind on the earth (20:7-10), fire will consume the wicked rebels, but the camp of the saints, which will be earthly Jerusalem, will remain forever without being touched, and the natural people who do not rebel will be privileged to continue on earth and have dominion over it, as did Adam before he fell.

Chapter Forty-four

THE ETERNAL PERFECT STATE

Under this heading we shall consider the last two chapters of Revelation, and deal with the New Heavens, New Earth, New Jerusalem, New Peoples, New Conditions, New Temple, New Light, New Paradise, and the Conclusion of the Book. We advance the following to be the teachings of Scripture concerning things in the ages of the ages to come.

The New Heaven and the New Earth, Rev. 21:1-22:5.

"And I saw a new heaven and a new earth: for the first heaven and the first earth were passed away; and there was no more sea," Rev. 21:1.

This New Heaven and New Earth are the result of the renovation by fire. The complete destruction of all wickedness and the old order of things under the curse will make them new in freshness and character. This destruction will terminate the last time in all eternity that they will be marred by sin and rebellion of the creatures therein. The old order of things will pass away in the same sense that all old things pass away and all things become new at regeneration, 2 Cor. 5:17. The same Greek word **kainos,** meaning "renew," as explained in the previous chapter, is used in both passages. From this point onward, John was shown only those things which belong to the new order of things after the curse is removed. All the following studies must be understood in this light. **Before we take up a study of the things in these chapters concerning the New Heaven and New Earth, let us note the statements of the other three passages where they are mentioned.**

1. The "new heavens and the new earth," Isa. 65:17-19.

(1) They are to be created or brought into existence in the new state.

(2) The New People will be called upon to rejoice "for ever," or as the Chaldee Targum renders it, "in the world of worlds"; i.e., the most glorious world.

(3) Jerusalem is to be created "a rejoicing, and her people a joy." This shows that the same people who were given Jerusalem as an eternal possession will still be there in the New Earth, else they could not be made a joy forever. It also shows that earthly Jerusalem itself is to be in the New Earth. It is clearly stated to exist forever in 2 Chron. 33:4; Jer. 17:25; Ezek. 43:7.

(4) God is to rejoice in the eternal city of Jerusalem and in His people, and the voice of weeping and crying will no more be heard in the city. This is additional proof of the eternity of earthly Jerusalem and the people on earth, for it is not until God Himself comes to earth in the New Jerusalem that the weeping and crying of earthly peoples will be wiped away, Rev. 21:1-5.

2. In Isa. 66:22-24 God again assures Israel that they shall be an eternal earthly people and as long as "the new heavens and

new earth" remain the following will also remain:

(1) "So shall your (Israel's) seed and your name remain." The Hebrew word for "seed" is **zera,** meaning "seed, fruit, plant, or posterity." It is the only word translated "seed" in the Old Testament, except in the case of Joel 1:17. It is used 273 times in the Old Testament and in every case of natural seed, whether seed sown in the ground or the natural offspring of natural man, Isa. 59:21. This means that Israel, as a natural, imperishable people, will go on forever, even as Adam was to have done. If true of Israel, it is also true of all other peoples, as we shall see. Not only is Israel's seed to remain forever but Israel's name also, which is always used in an earthly connection.

(2) There will be new moons and sabbaths in the worship of "all flesh" before God forever. The only new moons and sabbaths we know of in worship are revealed in the law of Moses, thus showing the eternal observance of that law, as seen under the Millennium above. The Hebrew word for "flesh" is **basar,** meaning flesh, skin, nakedness, body. It is used 252 times. It always means the natural flesh of animal life. This proves that the people mentioned here will be natural people as men are today.

(3) They (all flesh, peoples) will go forth and look upon the men that have transgressed against God, who will abide in the lake of fire where "their worm shall not die, neither shall their fire be quenched; and they shall be an abhorring unto all flesh." This is a picture of the people in eternal torment and shows that part of the lake of fire will be visible to the natural people on earth at that time as an everlasting monument of God's wrath on sin. This scene will be an object lesson to the natural men on earth forever that their wills may run in the right channel and that they may live true to God. (See Rev. 14:9-11.)

3. The third passage mentioning the New Heavens and New Earth is 2 Pet. 3:10-13. In this passage we learn that only "righteousness" will dwell in the new state forever. This refers to the right doings of the new peoples of the future ages.

The only other passage mentioning the New Heaven and the New Earth are these chapters under consideration. The only thought we have not mentioned before is the sentence "There was no more sea." This is often taken to mean that there will be no water left on the earth, but this is not the thought, as is clear from many other passages in the Bible. The thought is that l a r g e o c e a n s covering about three-fourths of the earth will be no more. There will be an abundance of rivers, lakes, and small seas on earth forever. That there will be waters on the earth is clear from the following passages where there are islands and waters mentioned on the earth as making the border of the eternal allotment of the land to Israel in this time, Ps. 72:8-10, 17; 97:1-6; Isa. 42:1-4, 8-18; 5:5; 60:21; 66:18-24; Ezek. 47:8-48:38; Zech. 9:10; 14:8. There could not be islands nor seas for borders if they were not to exist after the Millennium. Another reason why some seas will be eternal is that they were created by

God in the beginning for His pleasure and are stated to be eternal, Jer. 5:22; 31:35, 36; Ps. 146:6; Prov. 8:29; Acts 4:24; 14:15; Rev. 10:6; 14:7. Water will be necessary to fulfill Gen. 8:22; Isa. 35; Amos 5:8; 9:6. See also Job 38:4-16, 22-30; Ps. 104:5-11, 25-28.

The New Peoples and New Conditions.

"And I heard a great voice out of heaven saying, Behold, the tabernacle of God is with men, and he will dwell with them, and they shall be his people, and God himself shall be with them, and be their God. And God shall wipe away all tears from their eyes; and there shall be no more death, neither sorrow, nor crying, neither shall there be any more pain: for the former things are passed away. And he that sat upon the throne said, Behold, I make all things new. And he said unto me, Write: for these words are true and faithful. And he said unto me, It is done. I am Alpha and Omega, the beginning and the end. I will give unto him that is athirst of the fountain of the water of life freely. He that overcometh shall inherit all things; and I will be his God, and he shall be my son. But the fearful and unbelieving, and abominable, and murderers, and whoremongers, and sorcerers, and idolaters, and all liars shall have their part in the lake which burneth with fire and brimstone: which is the second death," Rev. 21:3-8.

In connection with this passage, **the following points prove that the new peoples and conditions will be as natural and as earthly as they are today,** with the difference that all things will be made imperishable and new in character, righteousness, and holiness forever, instead of being under the present curse and sinful state.

1. **The above quotations are the statements of two persons;** one speaks "out of heaven," while the other speaks "from the throne." One seems to be the voice of Christ; the other is the voice of God who sits on the throne. **The statements of the two voices are:**

(1) **The voice from out of the throne, Rev. 21:3, 4.**

A. "Behold, the tabernacle of God is with men." This tabernacle will be a literal material one, as is proved in chapter twenty-four. It will come down from God out of heaven with the New Jerusalem. It is in the New Jerusalem, as we shall later see. The preposition "with" is from Greek **meta** and denotes amid, among (Matt. 26:58; Mark 1:13), or in company with (Matt. 9:15; 2 Thess. 1:7; Rev. 14:13), thus further proving that natural men on the earth are the reference, for glorified men will have already been with God for one thousand years.

This shows that God will come down to earthly men, not that men will go up to God, as will the glorified peoples. These men will be the ones who will have lived through the Millennium without rebellion against the kingdom at the revolt of natural men at Gog and Magog, led by Satan. These men, instead of becoming a glorified people, will simply remain in a natural imperishable state as God intended man to do when He created him.

The fall of man did not cause God to change His eternal purpose for man, for He who cannot ultimately suffer a defeat, turned it into a blessing by His plan to gather heavenly people out of the human race to reign over the natural peoples who will be redeemed from the fall and all its effects after the Millennium. The fall of man simply delayed the purpose of God and by the delay God has gained more than He would have done otherwise.

B. "And he will dwell with them, and they shall be his people, and God himself shall be with them, and be their God." The word "dwell" indicates that God is to tabernacle among men, in their midst as in John 1:14; Rev. 7:15; 12:12; 13:6. The thought is that God the Father, Himself, will be in visible form before men and thus be the final fulfillment of "Immanuel, God with us," Ps. 68:16-18; Isa. 7:14; Zech. 2:10, 11; 8:3; Matt. 1:23; Rev. 22:5. These passages will not permit an interpretation of invisible dwelling as can be readily seen, especially in this latter passage. The men whom God will dwell with, will be His people and He will be in their midst and be their God. The word for people is in the plural and means all peoples and all nations as in Rev. 21:24.

C. God Himself, the Father, who dwells among all peoples "shall wipe away all tears from out of their eyes." This is quoted from Isa. 25:8 where the word for "wipe" means to stroke, rub, erase, touch, abolish, and utterly wipe away. The Greek word in this passage means "to smear out, obliterate, or wipe away." This will be done by the removing of those things which cause tears of sorrow and regret, Rev. 7:17; 21:4. Nothing indicates here that there will not be tears of joy, for God will not destroy the created faculty to shed tears, any more than He will destroy other created faculties of the human body.

D. "There shall be no more death, neither sorrow, nor crying, neither shall there be any more pain: for the former things are passed away." These former things will have caused the sorrow, and when they are no more, tears of sorrow will also be no more. These things are the effects of sin and its penalties and when the curse and sin are removed from the human race they will be no longer in the perpetual race. They will still be in existence, but only in the lake of fire, which is the second death, where pain, sorrow, tears of remorse, weeping and wailing and gnashing of teeth will go on through the ages.

Natural men will inherit the earth in fulfillment of Exod. 32:13; Ps. 25:13; 37:9-11, 22, 29, 34; 69:36; 82:8; Isa. 60:21; Matt. 5:5; 25:34. Death is the fruit and penalty of sin and the Devil has used both to rule the human race, but both the law of sin and of death will be destroyed and made ineffective after the Millennium by the doom of the executor of these laws in the lake of fire, Gen. 2:17; Rom. 5:12-14; 8:2; 1 Cor. 15:24-28; Heb. 2:14; Rev. 1:18; 20:10-15. Thus, the conditions of the New Earth will be adjusted to perfection for the good and perpetuity of the race of Adam. Although human beings will not die in the New Earth the animals will continue to die and be sacrificed as under the law of Moses, as seen above in the Millennium, and as we shall see below.

(2) **The voice from God who sits upon the throne,** Rev. 21:5-8.

A. "Behold, I make all things new." The word for "new" is the same as in Rev. 21:1 and further proves that all things are not to be done away with but merely renewed, for they cannot cease to exist and also be made new.

B. To emphasize the truth and literalness of these things, God tells John to "Write (see point 5, chapter twenty-three): for these words are true (from the Greek **alethinos,** meaning "genuine, real, and substantial" as contrasted with that which is fictitious, unreal, shadowy, or symbolical, John 6:32; 15:1) and faithful (from the Greek **pistos,** meaning "something to be believed, faithful, something reliable and trustworthy," 2 Cor. 1:18)."

C. "It is done. I am Alpha and Omega, the beginning and the end. (See chapter two, point V.) I will give unto him that is athirst of the fountain of life freely. He that overcometh shall inherit all things; and I will be his God and he shall be my son. But the fearful (Matt. 8:26; Mark 4:40) and unbelieving (faithless), and the abominable (Rom. 2:22), and murderers, and whoremongers, and sorcerers (users of drugs and commerce with evil spirits, Gal. 5:20; Rev. 9:21; 18:23; 21:8; 21:15), and idolaters, and all liars, shall have their part in the lake which burneth with fire and brimstone; which is the second death." These statements are exhortations that may apply throughout the life of any individual in this dispensation as well as Rev. 21:27 and 22:6-21, which we shall consider later. Compare the list of evils under the sixth trumpet, chapter twelve.

2. **There will be eternal generations of natural peoples,** Gen. 9:12; 13:15; 17:7, 19; Exod. 3:15; 12:14, 42; 27:21; 30:8, 21; 31:16; 40:15; Lev. 3:17; 6:18; 10:9; 17:7; 23:14, 21, 31, 41; 24:3; 25:30; Num. 10:8; 15:15; 18:23; Deut. 5:29; 12:28; 28:46; 29:29; 2 Sam. 7:24-26; 1 Chron. 23:25; Ps. 12:7; 45:17; 72:5; 79:13; 89:4; 100:5; 102:12, 24; 106:31; 119:90; 135:13; 145:13; 146:10; Isa. 51:8; 59:21; Jer. 31:35, 36; 32:38-40; Ezek. 37:24-28; Luke 1:55; Lam. 5:19; Dan. 4:3, 34; Joel 3:20. Besides all these, which are just as plain as they read, and mean just what they say, **there are three passages speaking of a "thousand generations"** (Deut. 7:9; 1 Chron. 16:15; Ps. 105:8), which is a Hebraism for "perpetual generations," as is plainly stated in Gen. 9:12. In Ps. 90:10 we have the allotted life of man to be seventy to eighty years. If the "thousand generations" were to be figured on this basis we should have the continuance of the human race for 70,000 to 80,000 years. This would be just as hard to conceive of as eternal generations, and where do we get any information that they are to cease even after this long period? The word "generation" (singular and plural) is used 213 times in the Bible and in every case except in Gen. 2:4, it is used of natural generations of men and their multiplying posterity in the earth. The references in the following points are just as clear as the above and need no interpretation. Although many of them have been postponed until the time of the repentance and restoration of the persons who failed after the promises were made, yet none of them have been or ever will be annulled.

3. **Eternal natural priesthood of Aaron's seed,** Exod. 29:9; 40:15; Num. 25:11-13; 1 Chron. 23:13. Such would not be possible if his seed were not natural and eternal.

4. **Eternal incense burning on the altar,** Exod. 30:8; 2 Chron. 2:4.

5. **Eternal covenants,** Gen. 9:16; 17:7, 19; Exod. 31:16; Lev. 24:8; Num. 18:19; 2 Sam. 23:5; 1 Chron. 16:17; Ps. 105:10; 111:5, 9; Isa. 55:3; 61:8; Jer. 32:40; Jer. 50:4, 5; Ezek. 16:60; 37:26. Such could not possibly be if the parties of the covenants were not eternal.

6. **Eternal sacrifices and offerings,** Exod. 30:8-18; Lev. 3:17; 6:18-23; 7:34-38; 10:15; 16:29-34; 24:5-9; Num. 18:8-11, 19-23; 19:10; 2 Chron. 2:4; Ezek. 46:14.

7. **Eternal land of promise to Abraham and his eternal posterity,** Gen. 13:15; 17:6-8; 48:4; Exod. 32:13; Lev. 25:23, 30, 34; Deut. 4:40; Josh. 14: 9; 2 Chron. 20:7; Isa. 60:21; Jer. 25:5. Such could not be true of heavenly saints, for they will inherit all things and reign over these peoples.

8. **Eternal feasts,** Exod. 12:14, 17, 24; Lev. 23:14, 21; 2 Chron. 2:4; Zech. 14:16-21.

9. **Eternal light in the sanctuary,** Exod. 27:20, 21; Lev. 24:2-4. This, as well as other ceremonial parts of worship, will be carried on in the eternal temple, as seen in chapter forty-one.

10. **Eternal priestly garments upon the natural priests,** Exod. 28:43.

11. **Eternal ceremonial cleansings,** Exod. 30:17-21; Num. 19:21.

12. **New moons and sabbaths,** Exod. 31:16, 17; Lev. 16:31; 2 Chron. 2:4; Isa. 66:22-24.

13. **Planting and harvesting, cold and heat, summer and winter while the earth remains,** Gen. 8:22; Psa. 104:5; Eccl. 1:4. Certainly glorified saints will not be the ones to plow, sow, reap, and enjoy the fruits of such labors.

14. **Eternal natural life of men and multiplication of beasts,** Gen. 9:9-17. Beasts will be used in the sacrifices and offerings as stated before. God would not make such a covenant with men and living creatures if they were not eternal.

15. **David's natural seed, throne, and kingdom are all eternal and will be ruled by Christ, the Son of God, forever,** 2 Sam. 7:11-17, 24-29; 22:51; 23:5; 1 Kings 2:45; 9:3-5; 1 Chron. 17:7-15, 22-27; 22:10; 28:4-9; 2 Chron. 13:5; 21:7; Ps. 89:3, 4, 35-37; 145:13; Isa. 9:6, 7; Ezek. 43:7-9; Dan. 2:44, 45; 7:13, 14, 18-27; Mic. 4:7; Luke 1:32-35; Heb. 1:8; 12:28; Rev. 11:15; 22:5.

See also Gen. 17:13; Lev. 6:12, 13; 10:9; 17:7; 24:5-9; Num. 10:8; 15:15; 18:20-24; 1 Chron. 15:2; Josh. 4:7, 19-24; 2 Kings 17:37; Ps. 125:1; Isa. 45:17; 51:6-11; 54:8; 55:13; 56:5; 60:15, 19, 20 **for other eternal things.**

In all these passages the English words "everlasting," "forever," "perpetual," etc., are used. The same words are used for eternity of God, so if one is eternal the others must be. We have no right to take them to mean anything but what they say, unless such is clearly implied in the passages where they are found, or some statement is found elsewhere to the contrary. Any other usage of the words than in an eternal sense is always clear in the passages themselves. When used dispensationally they mean eternal and everlasting in every case.

God recognized the possibility of the perpetuity of the race in sin when He drove Adam from the tree of life lest he should eat of it and live forever in the natural sinful state. What is the purpose of the tree of life in the New Earth if it be not for the preservation of natural life? Rev. 22:1, 2. Eternal bodily life of the heavenly saints will not depend upon such trees for they will have immortal bodies.

Some may object to our taking the Scripture so literally, but we find no authority for doing otherwise. Others may object because of the seeming impossibility of the earth to hold so many multiplying generations to come, and refuse to believe. But is the God who created all things now limited in power that He cannot do what He has foretold? God could easily take care of future generations, when necessary, by populating other planets or enlarging this one. From Ps. 8 we understand that man was supposed to have dominion over all the works of God's hands. This would include the planets. It seems, therefore, logical to believe that in the future restoration, when man comes into full possession of his rights, that he will have access to these planets which are a part of God's handiwork.

On the earth itself, after the restoration, it will be possible for vast multitudes of people to live. Even now, in Japan about three-fifths of the arable land is owned by small peasant proprietors who provide for their families on holdings of one acre, more or less. How much greater will be the possibilities when the ground is freed from the curse so that it will yield more abundantly?

Possibly a few figures in connection with the area of the earth and the many people it might be capable of holding will be interesting here. It is said that the total area of the earth is 196,950,000 square miles. There are now 1,000,000 square miles of lake and river surface, not counting, of course, the area of the oceans. Granting that there will be no oceans in the New Earth, let us suppose that 4,650,000 square miles will be necessary for seas, rivers, and lakes and that 2,250,000 square miles will be necessary for the site of the New Jerusalem. That will leave 190,000,-000 square miles for man and his activities. If one acre were given to one person there would be room for about 121,600,000,000 people on this earth, or about 119 billions of people more than what is on the earth now. At the present time we number only some over two billion people.

It may be stated further in connection with this subject that men will not multiply on the earth as fast after the restoration as before. It is clear from Gen. 3:16 that with the curse came the multiplication of conception. When the earth and all therein are loosed from the present bondage, this part of the curse will go with the rest, and a normal condition will be restored.

Chapter Forty-five

THE BRIDE OF CHRIST

We shall study the different phases of truth throughout Scripture concerning the New City, its names, source, preparation, location, outward appearance, walls, measurements, materials, streets, buildings, lighting and water system, inhabitants, traffic, food, foundations, restrictions, and rulers. **All these prove it to be a literal city and not a symbol of a company of people.**

1. The Names of the City.

"And I John saw the holy city, new Jerusalem, coming down from God out of heaven, prepared as a bride adorned for her husband . . . And there came unto me one of the seven angels which had the seven vials full of the seven last plagues, and talked with me, saying, Come hither, I will shew thee the bride, the Lamb's wife. And he carried me away in the spirit to a great and high mountain, and shewed me that great city, the holy Jerusalem, descending out of heaven from God," Rev. 21:2, 9, 10.

(1) **New Jerusalem**, Rev. 3:12; 21:2. The Greek word for "new" is the same as in Rev. 21:1. The idea here, however, could not be that this city has been sinful and corrupt and needs a regeneration or renovation by fire like the earth and the immediate heavens. The meaning of the word being "freshness or new in character" applies to eternal things that need no renovation, as well as to those which need it. Everything in the eternal presence of God is kept new and fresh by that very presence. God can keep anything new as well as make it new. This word does not show that the city is new in age and time, but new in freshness. It has been that way ever since it was made.

The actual age of the city is unknown, but possibly it was created with the heavens and the earth in the beginning, because it is now the location of the throne of God, which has been established there ever since the heavens were created, Ps. 11:4; 93:2; 103:19; Isa. 6:1; 66:1; Rev. 4:2-10; 5:1-13; 7:9-17; 8:3; 22:1-3. It was in existence in Abraham's day, for God promised him and all Old Testament saints the city, Heb. 11:9-11, 14-16.

The word "Jerusalem" is used about 810 times in the Bible and always as the name of a literal city, as is clear in every passage where it is used. It is never used as a symbol or in a figurative way. God never uses something that does not exist to picture any phase of truth. If such a city in heaven does not exist, then God used an unreal city to picture truth, but we are confident that He did not do that. Why would the word "new" be used with the city, and why should not there be some explanation or even implication that this was a symbol if we are not to believe in a literal heavenly city?

(2) **The Holy City**, Rev. 21:2; 22:19. Here it is called a "city with the qualifying word "holy." This adjective "holy" is used hundreds of times in the Bible to show the character of certain things that are actual, but it is never used to portray the character of a symbol. Several times it is used with the earthly

Jerusalem, so why not understand this vision to be of the literal heavenly city? In Rev. 22:19, God has promised to take out of this city the portion of every man who has not lived true to God in this life, and according to this book. The term, "holy city," in this latter passage, is used not with other symbols, but with other literal things as this prophecy and the book of life. If the city is symbolical, then these other things are also, for the same things are spoken of all of tnem.

It should not be hard to conceive of a literal city in heaven when we know that heaven itself is a literal place and contains real inhabitants, and living conditions necessary to such inhabitants. The words "city" and "cities" occur over thirteen hundred times in Scripture and are never used symbolically. In Rev. 17:18, we have seen that the great whore is called a city, and we have further seen that this city will be a literal one—the headquarters of the whore which will dominate the nations of the world up to the middle of the Week. See chapter twenty-nine, point 6.

(3) **The Bride, the Lamb's Wife, Rev. 21:2, 9.** This is the expression which has caused interpreters to symbolize the city as the Church. But why such an expression should be misleading, in view of such a plain literal description of a real heavenly city, is not clear to us. There is not one indication that this city is a symbol. Should there not be something definite to show the city to be a symbol besides a mere expression like this? That a literal heavenly city and redeemed peoples are both seen in this description is clearly implied, if not stated. There can be no city with just material buildings, and there can be no city with just a company of people without material buildings in which to live. It takes both to make a city. John, having been previously shown the redeemed saints of all ages, was here shown the material city where those saints will dwell forever. Hence, the city is inseparable from its inhabitants and can be called "the bride, the Lamb's wife," as is seen in the case of earthly Jerusalem and Israel many times in the Old Testament, where God often speaks of Jerusalem with the same terms as He does His chosen family Israel.

The whore is called "that great city, which reigneth over the kings of the earth," Rev. 17:18. It has been proved that the whore is false religion and the city its headquarters, and that both are inseparable and are seen in the vision. She is called "that great city" for the purpose of fully explaining her identity. So likewise here the revelation of "things shortly to come to pass" would not be complete without showing the descension to earth of the literal city, Jerusalem, which is the abode of all saints of all ages, thus lowering the tabernacle of God with men to be with them forever. See Matt. 12:25; Mark 3:25; Luke 11:17 where the words "city" and "house" are used for the inhabitants of the city and house.

Is the Bride of Christ Only the New Testament Church?

It is believed by many that the bride of Christ is to be made up of only the New Testament saints, but this cannot be true as we shall see below and as is clear from Heb. 11:8-16, 40. In this passage all Old Testament saints from Abel on were promised the same city as New Testament saints are, so all saints of all ages must be the bride of Christ, Rev. 21:9.

It is therefore unscriptural to call any one group of redeemed, the bride of Christ. The Church will be a part of the bride, as every other redeemed company will be a part, but to call the Church or any one company of redeemed the bride, is like calling a local church, or any one person, or any single part of a city by the name of the city of which they are only a part. Any one who lives in New York City is only a part of that city, so it is with the Holy Jerusalem. Any person or group of persons who go to live in that city are as much a part of the bride as any one else who lives in that city. Since all saints of all ages go to live in the New Jerusalem, all saints make the bride and not just a select few as taught by some. See chapter seven, point 9, for proof the Church is a "man" and not a woman, a bride, a lady, etc. Hence, it is not proper to call the Church the bride of Christ. The bride is a city and not a church as is clear in Rev. 21:9.

Is the New Testament Church Now Married to Christ?

The common belief is that Israel was married to God all through the Old Testament days, but that the Church is not now married to God and will not be until the future marriage of the Lamb, Rev. 19:1-10. This is inconsistent, for if Israel was married to God in the Old Testament days because of the covenant God made with them, on the same basis the New Testament Church is also married to God at the present time. In fact, anyone whom God made a covenant with in any age could be considered married to God by covenant relation. It is definitely stated in the New Testament that the present Church is married or united to God now in the sense that Israel was in Old Testament times. **Note the following New Testament proofs:**

A. Jesus called Himself "the bridegroom" of the disciples that were with Him during His earthly ministry, Matt. 9:15; Mark 2:19, 20. These disciples were the first ones in the present Church. What did Jesus mean if He was not then the bridegroom? Certainly He knew what to call Himself. If He was the bridegroom of the first members of the "called-out" body of people in this age, then He is also the bridegroom of the last members of this body of people. The Greek word for "bridegroom" is **numphios,** which means "a young married man, or a newly married man." Every passage where this word is used proves this. (Matt. 9:15; 25:1-10; Mark 2:19, 20; Luke 5:34, 35; John 2:9; 3:29; Rev. 18:23.)

B. John called Christ the bridegroom, John 3:29. The bride of Christ is going to be composed of people in the new creation in Christ. The Old Testament saints were not made a part of the new creation until after Christ for He is the head of the new creation and the "firstborn" of every creature, Rom. 8:28,29; Col. 1:15-18; Heb. 12:23. Their sins were not atoned for and could not have been legally blotted out until the New Testament was made, Rom. 3:25; Heb. 9:15. John belonged to the old order of things and was merely a forerunner and herald of the head of the new creation and his salvation was upon the same basis as that of the Old Testament saints, and that was on a credit basis. God blessed them by faith in what was to be done on the cross. Their new birth was on this basis of Christ finally paying the debt for them. All Old Testament saints were made a part of the new creation after Christ had made atonement for them. Therefore, as members of the new creation after Christ, the Old Testament saints will become members of the future bride of Christ as much as the New Testament saints, Heb. 11:8-16,40.

It is generally believed that John was not to be a member of the bride of Christ because he claimed to be a "friend" of the bridegroom. There is no statement in John 3:29 that says that he could not become a member of the bride of Christ after the Old Testament saints were a part of the new creation. John merely recognizes that he belonged to the old order of things and at the time he made this statement he was not legally a part of the new creation. He was only a part by faith and it became legally so when Christ died. If John was not to become a member of the future bride of Christ because he considered himself a "friend" of the bridegroom, on the same basis it can be proved that the New Testament saints are not to be members of the final bride of Christ, for they are also called "friends" of the bridegroom in the same sense that John was, Luke 12:4; John 11:11; John 15:13-15. Abraham is called a "friend" of God (2 Chron. 20:7; Isa. 41:8; Jas. 2:23) and "the father of all them that believe" (Rom. 4:11-16; Gal. 3:7-9), and therefore, must be a member of the final bride of Christ if his children in faith are, Heb. 11:8-16, 40.

C. It is definitely stated in Heb. 11:40 that the Old Testament saints will not be made perfect without the New Testament saints, implying that they would both be made perfect together. This certainly teaches that both classes of people will finally be united in one great heavenly family and be members together of the bride of Christ.

D. The Old Testament saints were all united to God by the terms of the new covenant (Rom. 3:25; Heb. 9:15) and saved by the same blood of the New Testament by which Church saints were saved. What would make the difference between them and the New Testament saints? Certainly just living in a different age would not make a difference. If Israel was married to God because God made a covenant with her, then why would not the Church be now married to God because of the covenant Christ made with believers in this age? Are we not now in covenant relationship to God just as Israel was in the Old Testament? If we are, then we are married to God just as much as Israel was. That we are in such covenant relationship now is clear from Matt. 26:28; Luke 22:20; 1 Cor. 11:17-30; 2 Cor. 3:1-18; Heb. 7:22; 8:1-10:38; 12:24.

E. Paul tells the Roman Jews that if they would become dead to the law by the body of Christ and be made alive under the terms of the New Testament, they would be married to Jesus Christ, Rom. 7:1-6. This was to be a present union with Christ, not future.

F. Jesus, in Rev. 22:16, 17, after His ascension into heaven, recognized that believers in the earth were already His bride. If this be not true, how could "the bride" say, "Come . . . take of the water of life freely"? This "bride" was in the earth inviting anyone to come and be saved. If this does not refer to believers now and in every generation, to whom does it refer? The Greek word for "bride" here is **numphe,** which means "a young married woman, or a newly married woman." Thus, it is established beyond doubt that the present believers are already married to God under the terms of the new covenant just as Israel was under the old covenant.

G. Paul in 1 Cor. 11:2; 12:12-28; Eph. 4:12-16; 5:21-33, uses the marriage relationship of a man and a woman to teach the relationship between Christ and His Church. Paul evidently knew what he was doing.

H. The New Testament speaks of believers now being "joined" to the Lord, 1 Cor. 6:16, 17. Men in Old Testament times are spoken of as being "joined" to God, so if they were married to God, why are not the New Testament saints married to God, as Israel was in Isa. 56:6; Jer. 50:5?

Other plain scriptural arguments could be multiplied, but these are sufficient to prove that New Testament saints are now married to God. **Now let us examine the few passages which are used to teach that they are not now married to God but will be in the future at the marriage of the Lamb in heaven.**

A. The first passage is 2 Cor. 11:1, 2. The apostle tells the Corinthians that he had espoused them to one husband, that he might present them a chaste virgin to Christ. This, instead of referring to the whole bride of Christ, refers to Paul's own converts. He was jealous over his converts and was desirous of their remaining true to Christ so that he could present them without fault before God. This is the same desire as in 1 Thess. 2:19, "What is our hope, or joy, or crown of rejoicing? Are not even ye (Paul's own converts) in the presence of our Lord Jesus Christ at his coming?" Paul did not intend to teach in 2 Cor. 11 that he was the one entrusted with the whole body of Christ to present it to the Lord. On the contrary, he taught in Eph. 5 that Christ was the one to present the Church to Himself.

The Greek word for "espoused" here is **harmodzo,** meaning "to join in actual marriage relationship." Instead of teaching that the believer is not yet married to Christ and God, it teaches that he is joined to Christ in marriage relationship.

B.   The second Scripture that is used to teach that the Church is not yet married to Christ is Rev. 19:1-10. In this passage we have the future "marriage of the Lamb" in heaven, after the rapture of the Church. It is argued that if the Lamb is to be married in the future, that He is not married now. It is very evident that if the Church is now married to Christ, and John pictures a future marriage, that there is something wrong. Some have tried to explain this marriage in connection with Israel, but this is wrong, as we have seen. We do not have to believe this in order to have harmony between the facts that the believer is now married to Christ and will also be in the future. It seems from this passage that whoever is referred to is called "his wife," and that she is already His before the marriage supper of the Lamb. This is in perfect harmony with what has been stated before concerning the relationship of Christ and all believers in all ages who are to be glorified and made heavenly people. We will now quote from "The International Standard Bible Encyclopedia" to illustrate how the believer could be spoken of as being married to God now, and still to be united to Him in final ceremonies in the future at the marriage supper of the Lamb.

"Betrothal with the ancient Hebrews was of a more formal and far more binding nature than the engagement with us. Indeed, it was esteemed a part of the transaction of marriage, and that the most binding part. Among the Arabs today it is the only legal ceremony connected with marriage. Gen. 24:58-60 seems to preserve for us an example of an ancient formula and blessing for such an occasion. Its central feature was the dowry (mohar), which was paid to the parents, not to the bride. It may take the form of service (Gen. 29; 1 Sam. 18:25). It is customary in Syria today, when the projected marriage is approved by both families, and all financial preliminaries have been settled, to have this ceremony of betrothal. It consists in the acceptance before witnesses of the terms of the marriage contracted for. Then God's blessing is solemnly asked on the union thus provided for, but to take place probably only after some months, or perhaps some years.

"A similar custom prevails in China and Japan, and in cases becomes very oppressive. The marriage may have been intended by the parents from the infancy of the parties, but this formality of betrothal is not entered on till the marriage is considered reasonably certain and measurably near. A prolonged interval between the betrothal and marriage was deemed undesirable on many accounts, though often an interval was needed that the groom might render the stipulated service or pay the price—say a year or two, or, as in the case of Jacob, it might be seven years. The betrothed parties were legally in the position of a married couple, and unfaithfulness was 'adultery,' Deut. 22:23; Matt. 1:19."

For the marriage ceremony, see chapter eight. After this ceremony, which had no formal religious ceremony connected with it, as with us, the marriage supper followed. The marriage was consummated by the entrance into the "chamber" which was followed by the above-mentioned supper. The marriage supper of the Lamb is merely the consummation of the union between God and all heavenly and gloriifed saints of all ages. It could never refer to the first and final union of the believer to Christ.

The above passages are the only ones which could be taken to teach such a theory except a few historical events in the Old Testament which are not worthy of consideration here in view of the many plain passages on the subject.

We conclude, therefore, that the Old and New Testament saints and all who have part in the first resurrection will dwell in the New Jerusalem, which city and its glorified inhabitants are called "the bride, the Lamb's wife," as in Rev. 21:2, 9. It may be proper then to call each individual in any company of redeemed a member of the final bride of Christ, John 14:1-3; Heb. 11:8-16, 40; 13: 14; Rev. 3:12. It is not proper to refer to any individual or company of people in any particular age as the sole bride of Christ. Although there are different companies saved in different ages, yet in the final end all will become one as the final bride of Christ, Rev. 21:9. Just like each local church or individual could not be called the city of which they are a part, the New Testament Church can never be called the bride of Christ. It is just a part of the bride. As we have seen in chapter seven, point 9, the Church is compared to a man and not a woman, masculine pronouns are used of the Church, and the Church is not the city, but will be a part of the city, which is the bride, the Lamb's wife.

(4) **The Tabernacle of God, Rev. 13:6; 15:5; 21:3.** This has been considered under point 1, (1), A, on page 298 and in chapters nine and twenty-four, for which review.

(5) **The Great City, the Holy Jerusalem, Rev. 21:10.** After the angel told John that he was to show him "the bride, the Lamb's wife," he carried him away in the spirit (see chapter two, point VI, for "in the spirit"), to a great and high mountain, and showed him "that great city, the holy Jerusalem, descending out of heaven from God." He then explained the details of the literal city which could not possibly be a symbol of redeemed peoples. Who can explain all of these details in connection with a company of people? If this cannot be done, then it follows that the passage is a detailed description of a literal city, as is evident. In this description, the word "city" is used several times, as we shall see in the detailed study below.

(6) **The Heavenly Jerusalem, Heb. 12:22.** The Greek word **epouranies** simply means "heavenly, that which is above the sky, celestial, in heaven, or on high," Matt. 18:25; John 3:12; Eph. 1:3, 20; etc. It certainly cannot be said that Paul, in this passage, was symbolizing the Church when he spoke of a heavenly Jerusa-

lem. The word "heavenly" in the following passages shows the contrast between earthly and heavenly things, 1 Cor. 15:48, 49; Eph. 1:3, 20; 2:6; 3:10; Heb. 3:1; 6:4; 8:5; 9:23; 11:16; Gal. 4:25, 26. In every one of these passages the heavenly things are just as actual and real as the earthly things. In Heb. 11:16; 13:14; Gal. 4: 25, 26, we have the heavenly country and heavenly city mentioned and they are just as material as the earthly countries and cities. In Heb. 12:22, Paul speaks of believers as coming not unto the earthly mount that was burned with fire, etc., but to the heavenly Mount Zion, and unto the city of the living God, the heavenly Jerusalem. This is certainly most peculiar language if the believers are the heavenly Jerusalem.

Gal. 4:25, 26 mentions a Jerusalem that is "above" in contrast with the Jerusalem which is "below" on earth. Paul here speaks of the Jerusalem as already being above when he writes. This could never be said of the Church, for it is not yet above. This passage declares that the Jerusalem which is above is free, which is the **mother** of us all. If this were a reference to the Church, then it would plainly mean that the Church was at that time in heaven, and that the Church was the mother of all the saints. Therefore, it follows that this city above does not refer to the Church, but to a literal city, whose God and ruler is the source of all saints.

2. **The source and origin of the New Jerusalem,** Rev. 3:12; 21:2, 10; John 14:1-3; Gal. 4:26; Heb. 9:11; 11:10-16; 12:22. These passages show that the New Jerusalem was prepared by God and is coming from the heaven to the earth to be the eternal city and dwelling place for God and His heavenly people.

3. **The preparation of the New Jerusalem,** Rev. 21:2; John 14: 1-3; Heb. 11:10-16; 13:14. Let us study these passages in their order.

(1) In Rev. 21:2 we have the declaration that the city was prepared and built. There has always been a purpose for the preparation of everything God has ever made. The word "prepared" means to make ready, prepare, or provide. The meaning in Rev. 21:2 is that the New Jerusalem is made ready just as a bride is made ready for her husband. What is it made ready for if not for the abode of heavenly saints and in order that the tabernacle of God may be located among earthly men throughout all ages, Rev. 21:3?

(2) In John 14:1-3 we have the definite promise of Jesus to go to heaven to prepare for the saints a place composed of "many mansions." If the saints were the New Jerusalem, then Christ would be going to prepare the saints for themselves. The Greek word for "mansions" is **mone,** meaning "a residence, abode, or mansion" and plainly shows the thought of Christ. These mansions are in "my Father's house." The Father then has a house. The word "house" is used 1,650 times in the Bible. The Hebrew and Greek words mean "a house" in the greatest variety of applications and meanings. When a family or household is the

reference, the literal dwelling of that family or household is always understood, and when the literal dwelling place is the reference the family or household is always understood. The same is true of any city or country. There cannot be a household without a place to dwell.

So with the New Jerusalem, both the city and its inhabitants are seen, the city being the main thought of the vision, while the inhabitants are understood. The word "house" is used 197 times in the New Testament and only twenty-seven times of a family, and then it is always clearly distinguished from a building. Even in these twenty-seven references the building is understood. All other times the building itself is the foremost thought. Jesus indicated that the Father had a house and why could it not be literal? If God has a throne, there must be some location of it, as we have seen before. If Jesus is to sit on an earthly throne in the earthly Jerusalem and that throne is to be in the millennial and eternal temple (Ezek. 43:7), and if the glorified saints are to sit on thrones judging the natural people on earth, their thrones must be located some place in some building on earth in order for natural people to come before them to be judged. If such is conceivable during the Millennium and on earth with Christ and glorified saints, why cannot we conceive of these mansions as material buildings in heaven which are to come down to the New Earth? Jesus, for fear some would misunderstand such a plain statement, said, "If it were not so, I would have told you. I go to prepare a place for you. And if I go and prepare a place for you I will come again and receive you unto myself; that where I am there you may be also." Surely Christ did not designate the saints as the place and mansions He was going to prepare for them.

The word "prepare" does not imply that Christ is now building a place for the saints as they send up material, or that the size of the different mansions depends upon how much and what kind of material we send up during this life. All the mansions are already created. This was done long before Christ talked to the disciples on this occasion. The idea is that He is to make a place for them in the mansions that are already in the Father's house. See the usage of the word "prepare" in Matt. 20:23; 22:4; 25:34; 26:17; 1 Cor. 2:9; 2 Tim. 2:21; Rev. 8:6; 9:7, 15; 12:6; 16:12.

It does not have the idea of creation or beginning of existence, but arrangement or making ready something that already is in existence. The mansions might have been occupied by the fallen angels. Whatever may be the case, we know that they are there, if we believe the Bible to mean just what it says. The differences in rewards of saints will not be in connection with mansions, which they will have, but they will have to do with responsibilities and positions in the eternal reign of Christ on the earth and throughout the universe.

(3) In Heb. 11:10-16; 13:14 we have other passages speaking of the preparation of the city and also mentioning for whom

it is being prepared. In Heb. 13:14 we have the idea that it is a "continuing" or eternal city and that it is yet to come as far as saints are concerned. Paul here classes himself in the number who do not have a continuing city here on earth, but who are seeking one to come. This plainly shows that the apostle and the early saints looked for a city to come and left no doubt in any passage where it is spoken of as to whether it was a literal one or not. They believed it was a material city as much as any down here, as is clear in the statements made concerning it. Did Paul try to express in this passage the idea that here we have no continuing Church, but seek one to come? That is what he meant if the city is the Church.

In Heb. 11:10-16 we learn that Abraham sojourned in a strange country, and had the promise of a city and country to come. Just when God gave him the revelation of this city is not known, but we do know that he believed the things God had told him, and so by faith "looked for a city which hath foundations (Rev. 21:14-20), whose builder and maker is God."

The word for builder is **technites,** meaning "architect, designer, or craftsman," Acts 19:24, 38; Rev. 18:22. This word is from the root word **tekton,** rendered "carpenter," and means "a builder or constructor," Matt. 13:55; Mark 6:3. The word for maker is **demiourgos,** used only here, but it was used by the Gnostics, Plato, and others, for the Creator of the world. All this goes far to prove that the city is literal and has been planned and constructed by God and that it has foundations as all other cities have.

Paul continues by saying that "These all (including all previous faith-worthies of the Old Testament) died in faith not having received the promises (of the seed, city, etc.), but having seen them afar off, and were persuaded of them, and embraced them, and confessed that they were strangers and pilgrims on the earth. For they (anyone) that say such things declare plainly that they seek a country. And truly if they (who seek a better and true home) had been mindful (exercised memory or desire) of that country from whence they came out, they might have had opportunity to return. But now (having no desire to go back) they desire a better country, that is, an heavenly (a country in heaven): wherefore (because they desire the country of God and heaven in preference to the earthly) God is not ashamed to be called their God: for he hath prepared for them a city."

In the Greek the definite article is before "city" in both Heb. 11:10 and 16 and shows a definite city which God has prepared for those on earth who forsake this land and seek a better country; that is, an heavenly one. What could be more plain than such language concerning a city to come? Not one passage concerning the city could possibly be understood as a symbol of redeemed people. In every case it is the saints who are looking for the city. How could they look for a city and be that city, or be symbolized by that city? We have further evidence that this city was probably prepared before the time of Abel in that he also looked for it as well as all saints of all ages. Could it be possible that all these saints were looking for themselves to come? No.

4. **The eternal location of the New Jerusalem,** Rev. 3:12; 21:2, 10. The present location, according to these passages, is in heaven. It has been there ever since it was created by God for the abode of eternal beings. These passages also picture the city as "coming down from God out of heaven." Its eternal location will be on earth and not in mid-air, as some believe. What would be the use of foundations to a city suspended in mid-air? The natural meaning of the descent of anything out of heaven is that it comes on down to earth, unless otherwise stated. The fact that the nations of men on the earth will bring their glory and honor into it, shows that it will be located on the earth, Rev. 21:24-26; 22:1-5. It will come down to the earth after the Millennium, immediately after the renovation of the earth and the beginning of the Eternal Perfect State, for the earth will be made new before it comes down from God out of heaven. Another reason for the city's being literal is that Rev. 3:12 speaks of the saints as having the name of the city put upon them, and such would be impossible if they were the city.

5. **The Outward Appearance of the New Jerusalem.**

"Having the glory of God: and her light was like unto a stone most precious, even like a jasper stone, clear as crystal," Rev. 21:11.

God, who sits upon the throne, as seen throughout the book, is pictured in Rev. 4:3 as looking like a jasper stone, for which see chapter nine, point 2. This helps us to understand the light of the city and its outward appearance which radiates the glory of God. Cf. 1 Tim. 6:16; 1 John 1:5-7.

6. **The Wall, Gates, and Foundations of the New Jerusalem.**

"And had a wall great and high, and had twelve gates, and at the gates twelve angels, and names written thereon, which are the names of the twelve tribes of the children of Israel: On the east three gates; on the north three gates; on the south three gates; and on the west three gates. And the wall of the city had twelve foundations, and in them the names of the twelve apostles of the Lamb. And he that talked with me had a golden reed to measure the city, and the gates thereof, and the wall thereof. And the city lieth foursquare, and the length is as large as the breadth: and he measured the city with the reed, twelve thousand furlongs. The length and the breadth and the height of it are equal. And he measured the wall thereof, an hundred and forty and four cubits, according to the measure of a man, that is, of the angel. And the building of the wall of it was of jasper: and the city was pure gold, like unto clear glass," Rev. 21:12-18.

The wall of the city is great and high and has three gates on each of the four sides. This is the same construction which is to be used in the eternal earthly city Jerusalem, built at the beginning of the Millennium, Ezek. 48:30-35. Both John and Ezekiel wrote as they were moved by the Holy Spirit, and their descriptions refer to two different cities. Both of them will be material eternal cities. That the earthly city is eternal has already been proved in chapter forty-one under "The seat of government." That this heavenly city is eternal there is no question. The distance between the locations of the two is not revealed, but they may be in the same part of the earth. There will be no great oceans as there are now, so there will be sufficient room.

The glorified saints will have been occupying the New Jerusalem from the time of their rapture before the Millennium. On the other hand, the earthly Jerusalem will have been the capital of the kingdom of Christ and the city of earthly Israel throughout that period, and will continue as such throughout eternity. The earthly city will be a miniature of the heavenly city. Christ and the glorified saints who rule the earthly peoples during the Millennium will have their thrones in their respective places on the earth during the Millennium and will never remove them after the New Jerusalem comes down to earth. The New Jerusalem will serve as the abode of saints, but their thrones will be in different parts of the earth. Christ will have an eternal earthly throne in the Millennial and eternal temple (Ezek. 43:7). He will also have another throne, a heavenly one, in the New Jerusalem in company with God, the Father.

The twelve gates in the wall will have the names of the twelve tribes of the children of Israel. In Ezek. 48:30-35, we read whose names are in the gates of the earthly Jerusalem. No doubt the same names are to be in the gates in the New Jerusalem. At the gates there will stand twelve angels. This is certainly different from the common idea that Peter is a gatekeeper in the New Jerusalem.

The wall has twelve foundations and in them the names of the twelve apostles of the Lamb. The presence of the names of the twelve tribes and the twelve apostles in the gates and foundations of the city further shows that in this city the saints of all ages will dwell. It is not only for the New Testament Church saints. The twelfth apostle will be Matthias, who was chosen in the place of Judas and upon whom God set His seal, Acts 1:15-26. The inspired writer of Acts states by the Holy Spirit long after this decision that "he was numbered with the eleven apostles." Paul also speaks of the twelve as being witnesses of the resurrection, and affirms definitely that he, himself was not one of the twelve, 1 Cor. 15:1-9.

7. The Measurement of the New Jerusalem.

"And he (angel of Rev. 1:1; 19:10; 17:1; 21:9; 22:8-10) that talked with me had a golden reed to measure the city, and the gates thereof, and the wall thereof. And the city lieth foursquare, and the length is as large as the breadth: and he measured the city with the reed, twelve thousand furlongs. The length and the breadth and the height of it are equal. And he measured the wall thereof, an hundred and forty and four cubits, according to the measure of a man, that is of the angel," Rev. 21:15-17.

The angel had a "golden reed" with which to measure the city, the gates and the wall. A measuring reed is about twelve and one-half feet long, Ezek. 40:5; 41:8; 43:13. Of all cities, this one is the most important and greatest in size. It lies foursquare. The length, breadth, and height of it are equal, being twelve thousand furlongs or fifteen hundred miles. To conceive of it as a cube, we must understand the city to be either hollow inside as an empty box of about 3,375,000,000 cubic miles with the mansions built on the bottom and top of the cube, or else we must conceive of it as having numbers of layers, or stories, such as we see in our modern skyscrapers, with mansions on each story and some means of ascent from story to story. Of the two, the latter would seem more probable, if the city were a cube. However, it is more probable that the city is not a cube or a solid body with six square and equal sides. There is no statement in this passage that would teach such.

The expressions "the length and breadth and the height of it are equal" and "the city lieth foursquare" are best understood to mean that the base of the city lies on the earth, with all four sides equal, and that from the base it towers as a mountain peak to the same height as the measure of the length of the base of the city. The city, as a mountain peak, would have about 4,054,000 square miles. If we conceive of the mansions as having several stories, it is clearly evident that billions of persons could live in this one city.

There are sufficient reasons in this passage itself to show that the city is not a cube, but like a mountain peak, with mansions throughout the city.

(1)   Such is the most reasonable and logical idea of the city and is in perfect harmony with plain statements of the description.

(2)   The wall of the city is 144 cubits. If a cubit is considered eighteen inches, the wall is only about 216 feet high. This wall up the sides of a cube would seem entirely out of place. What would be the advantage of such a low wall if the outside of the city were a cube fifteen hundred miles high? If it be a cube, it is sure to have an outer wall as a part of the cube, hence, no need of a wall. But if it be admitted that the city towers from the base to a peak fifteen hundred miles high, it can be seen that such a wall around the city would be useful. Other reasons will be given below.

8.   The Materials in the New Jerusalem.

"And the building (material) of the wall of it was of jasper: and the city was pure gold, like unto clear glass. And the foundations of the wall of the city were garnished with all manner of precious stones. The first foundation was jasper; the second, sapphire; the third, a chalcedony; the fourth, an emerald; the fifth, sardonyx; the sixth, sardius; the seventh, chrysolyte; the eighth, beryl; the ninth, a topaz; the tenth, a chrysoprasus; the eleventh, a jacinth; the twelfth, an amethyst. And the twelve gates were twelve pearls; every several gate was of one pearl: and the street of the city was pure gold, as it were transparent glass," Rev. 21:18-21.

9.   The Streets of the New Jerusalem.

The Greek word **plateia** means "a broadway or street." The singular number here does not indicate that there is only one street in the city any more than it does in Rev. 11:8. The same word is translated "streets" in Matt. 6:5; 12:19; Luke 10:10; 13:26; 14:21; Acts 5:15. There are streets and mansions in the city, and other buildings as well. There are at least twelve great broadways in the city, leading to the city and into it through the twelve gates, as is clear from Rev. 21:12, 13, 21, 24-26. The streets of the city are paved with transparent gold, a material foreign to us. This is the same material of which the buildings of the city are made.

10. The Temple of the New Jerusalem.

"And I saw no temple therein: for the Lord God Almighty and the Lamb are the temple of it," Rev. 21:22.

See the meaning and usage of the word **noas** for "temple," and other words under "The Heavenly Tabernacle," chapter twenty-four, which prove that there is a literal temple in the New Jerusalem. The idea here is that God and the Lamb will be the sanctuary for all peoples in the eternal state instead of a sanctuary without the personal presence of God and the Lamb as the objects of worship, as has always been the case with worship on earth. In Rev. 3:12 the promise to the overcomer is that he shall have authority in the temple of God and shall no more go out, thus proving that there will still be a temple in the city when it comes to the earth. See also Rev. 7:15; 11:19; 14:15, 17; 15:5, 8; 16:1, 17, where the same literal temple of the city is seen as an eternal temple.

11. The Light of the New Jerusalem.

"And the city had no need of the sun, neither of the moon, to shine in it: for the glory of God did lighten it, and the Lamb is the light thereof . . . And there shall be no night there; and they need no candle, neither the light of the sun; for the Lord God giveth them light," Rev. 21:23, 25; 22:5.

The light of the city will surpass the light of the sun, moon, and stars. We have seen that the light of the sun will be increased sevenfold and that the light of the moon will be as the light of the sun during the Millennium (Isa. 30:26), so if the glory of God outshines this new light of the sun and moon it will be wonderful beyond words. These passages do not teach that the sun and moon will cease to shine, but that in this particular city there will be no need for them, for there will be a greater light. Neither do these passages teach that there will be no more night in the rest of the earth, for all through eternity the sun and moon and day and night will not cease, Gen. 8:22; Ps. 89:2, 3, 29, 35-37.

In other parts of the earth there will be need for the light of the sun and moon as ever before. This light will probably radiate from the throne of God and the Lamb which are upon the pinnacle of this city, giving light to the whole city below. This further seems to show that the city is not a cube, else this could not be possible, for if the light were to be located on the top story it would be shut off from many stories by the intervening ones. It is beyond man to picture how marvelous the dazzling light from the glory of God shining on this city of transparent gold decked with all manner of precious stones and pearls, will be. This is merely one of the many things which God has prepared for them that love Him, 1 Cor. 2:9-13.

12. The Traffic of the New Jerusalem.

"And the nations of them which are saved shall walk in the light of it: and the kings of the earth do bring their glory and honor into it. And the gates shall not be shut at all by day: for there shall be no night there. And they shall bring the glory and honour of the nations into it. And there shall in no wise enter into it any thing that defileth, neither whatsoever worketh abomination, or maketh a lie: but they which are written in the Lamb's book of life," Rev. 21:24-27.

The nations of natural men on earth who will still be divided into nations and peoples and live throughout the New Earth to plant, harvest, build, multiply, and replenish it, will traffic in the light of the New Jerusalem and pass in and out of its gates, which will not be shut at all in the eternal day of the city. This further proves that men will still be in a natural state and constitute the subjects in the eternal kingdom ruled by God and the saints forever. These are to be the sheep nations which enter the Millennium as well as the New Earth, having been purged from the sinful and rebellious nature. See Matt. 25:31-46. They will have natural kings over them, known as "the kings of the earth," as well as glorified saints. These kings and peoples will bring their glory and honor into the city regularly. This will perhaps consist of the fruit of the earth and the wonderful glory man came short of when Adam fell. While these nations will traffic in the New City, there will never enter into it anything that is sinful. Only they whose names are written in the Lamb's book of life may enter.

13. The Water of the New Jerusalem.

"And he showed me a pure river of the water of life, clear as crystal, proceeding out of the throne of God and of the Lamb . . . and the Lamb shall lead them into living fountains of waters," Rev. 7:17; 22:1.

There will be an abundance of water in the city, twelve rivers, as proved in point 14 below, and living fountains of waters. These waters are as clear as crystal and are called living rivers and living fountains. If the city is to be like a mountain peak with the thrones at the top, the rivers will have a gradual flow for fifteen hundred miles from the top to the base of the city, where they will flow on down into some part of the earth. The expression "waters of life" does not imply that they will be the medium of eternal life. They are simply living waters in the same sense that the river which flows out from under the earthly sanctuary is, Ezek. 47:1-12; Zech. 14:8.

14. The Food of the New Jerusalem.

"In the midst of the street of it, and on either side of the river, was there the tree of life, which bare twelve manner of fruits and yielded her fruit every month: and the leaves of the tree were for the healing of the nations," Rev. 22:2.

This passage seems to teach that in the middle of each of the twelve streets and on either side of the rivers there are trees of life. From a picture of this one street we conclude that in every one of the twelve great broadways leading from the throne to the twelve great gates at the base of the city there will be a river of living water flowing down the middle of it, with trees of life on each side. This is entirely consistent with the greatness of the city. Could it be that there will be only one street, one river, and one tree of life on only one side of the city, running through only one of the gates, with no streets, rivers, or trees of life on the other three sides or to the other gates?

Will all nations be able to eat of one tree? It must be kept in mind that John is not giving us a detailed description of everything in the city, but just sufficient details to give us an under-standing of the city and to show the greatness and beauty of it. The same language concerning the "street" (singular) is used concerning the "river." If there are twelve streets, then it is possible that there are twelve rivers, and surely it is logical, for whether the city is a cube or a mountain peak, only one river would not harmonize with the rest of the description. The other three sides have gates and streets, and since this "river" is in-separable from the "street" and since there are twelve streets, there must be twelve rivers. The word for "river" is translated in the plural in Rev. 8:10; 16:4. Cf. plural of "fountain" in 7:17; 14:7; 16:4. There will, no doubt, be many other streets in such a large city.

The trees of life will bear twelve manner of fruits according to the months; i. e., each month they will bear a different kind of fruit. There is not to be a mixture of twelve kinds of fruits twelve times a year. The leaves of the trees will be for the preservation of the natural life of the coming generations and not for the healing of sickness, for there will be no more sin, pain or any part of the curse at that time. Thus, we have in these trees and rivers the divine provision for the pleasures and life of all peoples. The fruit of the trees will be for the pleasure of the inhabitants of the New Jerusalem as promised the overcomer (2:7; 22:14) as well as for the pleasure of the nations. The leaves are God's provision for preserving natural life and eternal health. Besides this fruit, "hidden manna" will be given to the in-habitants of that city (2:17), as well as other food, Luke 22:16, 18, 30; Rev. 19:1-10; Ps. 78:25; etc.

15. The Rulers of the New Jerusalem.

"And there shall be no more curse: but the throne of God and of the Lamb shall be in it; and his servants shall serve him. And they shall see his face: and his name shall be in their foreheads, and they shall reign for ever and ever," Rev. 22:3-5.

This passage is the conclusion of the vision of the New Heaven, the New Earth, the heavenly Jerusalem and the Eternal Perfect State. Here we have the statement that God's servants shall reign for ever and ever in the New State. This city will be the center of the universe from which God will reign. This passage at least is clear that the servants of God shall see His face and His name shall be in their foreheads. This is in fulfillment of the promise to the overcomer, Rev. 3:12. Glorified saints are to be the servants mentioned here who will reign for ever and ever with God and Christ after all enemies have been put down.

Eternity Is Merely the Continuation of Time.

The common conception is that, at a certain point, time ceases to be and eternity begins. But the fact is that we are now in eternity, for eternity is the extension of time forever. There never will be a time when there will be no time. The word "time" means "infinite duration, or its measure. A definite portion of duration." The word "eternity" means "infinite duration, or time." Time is commonly contrasted with eternity. This is true as far as things which have a beginning are concerned, but such could not be true of things that have no ending. The heavens and earth and all things therein as originally created are eternal. Since the creation of these things, eternity has been broken up into times and seasons, days and nights, months and years, and ages and periods, and God always recognizes this in His Word. Men generally think of eternity as beginning with the next life, or with the New Heavens and New Earth, but this is not true. When men enter the next life and the heavens and the earth are made new, there is no change made in time or eternity. They remain the same. The change is made in men and in the heavens and earth, in that they enter into a new state which is eternal and unchangeable. The Bible teaches that times and seasons, day and night, and summer and winter, shall not cease, for these things are regulated by the sun, moon, and stars, which are eternal, Gen. 1:14-18; 8:22; Ps. 89:29, 35-37; Rev. 4:8; 7:15; 14:11; 20:10.

The Bible never teaches that time will cease to be. This error has been brought about through the mistranslation and misinterpretation of two passages of Scripture. The first, Rev. 10:6, instead of reading "time should be no longer," should read "delay should be no longer." It could not mean that time will be no longer, for after this the tribulation runs its course for three and one-half years and Christ comes to the earth to reign a thousand years before the supposed eternity begins. The second, Rev. 21:21, is misinterpreted to mean that there will be no night in the new earth, but the passage really refers to the Holy City itself and not the earth. There will be no night in the Holy City, but there will be in the rest of the earth, as is proved by the above passages.

No Perfect Age Before the New Earth.

Some Bible students teach that before the New Earth there will be another dispensational age called "The Perfect Age," which will be 33,000 years long. This theory is based upon the expression "thousand generations." According to them a generation is thirty-three years, or the average length of life today. Naturally, if the phrase "thousand generations" teaches another future age, and a generation is thirty-three years, the age would be 33,000 years long.

This phrase does not teach another future dispensational age of 33,000 years, but is a Hebraism of eternal generations as seen in chapter forty-four, under "New Peoples." If it did teach another probationary period for man, it could not be proved that it would be 33,000 years long. It would be a much longer period than this, for the average life in Bible days was much longer than thirty-three years, depending upon the particular period. Before the flood, the average life was over nine hundred years. If we interpreted the "thousand generations" in this light, we would have the so-called future age over 900,000 years long. Since the flood to our day, the length of a generation has varied from six hundred to thirty-three years, Gen. 11:10-32. Just which generation have we authority to choose to prove the length of such an age as mentioned by these students?

This theory is not the teaching of the Bible as can be readily seen by the studies of the last three chapters. The Bible teaches that the perfect age is the one beginning with the New Heavens and New Earth, after the Millennium, and it is eternal, as has been abundantly proved. There is no mention of any other age between the Millennium and the New Earth in any passage of the Bible. The last chapters of Revelation give the future ages that will be. They are the Millennium (Rev. 20) and the new eternal perfect age (Rev. 21, 22).

The Conclusion of Revelation.

In Rev. 22:6-21 we have the conclusion of the book, including the confirmation of its truths, an example of a common mistake in worship, the last instructions and the last promise and prayer.

1.　The Confirmation of Revelation.

"And he said unto me, These sayings are faithful and true: and the Lord God of the holy prophets sent his angel to shew unto his servants the things which must shortly be done. Behold I come quickly: blessed is he that keepeth the sayings of the prophecy of this book," Rev. 22:6, 7.

2.　A Common Mistake in Worship.

"And I, John saw these things, and heard them. And when I had heard and seen, I fell down to worship before the feet of the angel which shewed me these things. Then saith he unto me, See thou do it not: for I am thy fellowservant, and of thy brethren the prophets, and of them which keep the sayings of this book: worship God," Rev. 22:8, 9.

3.　The Last Instructions to "His Servants."

"And he saith unto me, Seal not the sayings of the prophecy of this book; for the time is at hand. He that is unjust, let him be unjust still; and he which is filthy, let him be filthy still: and he that is righteous, let him be righteous still: and he that is holy, let him be holy still. And, behold, I come quickly; and my reward is with me, to give every man according as his work shall be. I am Alpha and Omega, the beginning and the end, the first and the last. Blessed are they that do his commandments, that they may have right to the tree of life, and may enter in through the gates into the city. For without are dogs, and sorcerers, and whoremongers, and murderers, and idolaters, and whosoever loveth and maketh a lie. I, Jesus have sent mine angel to testify unto you these things in the churches. I am the root and the offspring of David, and the bright and morning star. And the Spirit and the bride say, Come. And let him that heareth say, Come. And let him that is athirst come. And whosoever will, let him take the waters of life freely. For I testify unto every man that heareth the words of the prophecy of this book. If any man shall add unto these things, God shall add unto him the plagues that are written in this book: And if any man shall take away from the words of the book of this prophecy, God shall take away his part out of the book of life, and out of the holy city, and from the things which are written in this book," Rev. 22:10-19.

4.　The Last Promise and Prayer in the Book and in the Bible.

"He which testifieth these things saith, Surely I come quickly. Amen. Even so, come, Lord Jesus. The grace of our Lord Jesus Christ be with you all. Amen," Rev. 22:20, 21.

FINIS